AF810809

Postdisciplinary Studies in Discourse

Series Editor
Johannes Angermuller
Centre for Applied Linguistics
University of Warwick
Coventry, UK

Postdisciplinary Studies in Discourse engages in the exchange between discourse theory and analysis while putting emphasis on the intellectual challenges in discourse research. Moving beyond disciplinary divisions in today's social sciences, the contributions deal with critical issues at the intersections between language and society. Edited by Johannes Angermuller together with members of DiscourseNet, the series welcomes high-quality manuscripts in discourse research from all disciplinary and geographical backgrounds. DiscourseNet is an international and interdisciplinary network of researchers which is open to discourse analysts and theorists from all backgrounds.

Editorial Board
Cristina Arancibia
Aurora Fragonara
Péter Furkó
Tian Hailong
Jens Maesse
Eduardo Chávez Herrera
Michael Kranert
Jan Krasni
María Laura Pardo
Yannik Porsché
Kaushalya Perera
Luciana Radut-Gaghi
Marco Antonio Ruiz
Jan Zienkowski

More information about this series at
http://www.palgrave.com/gp/series/14534

Markus Rheindorf

Revisiting the Toolbox of Discourse Studies

New Trajectories in Methodology, Open Data, and Visualization

palgrave
macmillan

Markus Rheindorf
Department of Linguistics
University of Vienna
Vienna, Austria

Postdisciplinary Studies in Discourse
ISBN 978-3-030-19368-3 ISBN 978-3-030-19369-0 (eBook)
https://doi.org/10.1007/978-3-030-19369-0

© The Editor(s) (if applicable) and The Author(s) 2019
This work is subject to copyright. All rights are solely and exclusively licensed by the Publisher, whether the whole or part of the material is concerned, specifically the rights of translation, reprinting, reuse of illustrations, recitation, broadcasting, reproduction on microfilms or in any other physical way, and transmission or information storage and retrieval, electronic adaptation, computer software, or by similar or dissimilar methodology now known or hereafter developed.
The use of general descriptive names, registered names, trademarks, service marks, etc. in this publication does not imply, even in the absence of a specific statement, that such names are exempt from the relevant protective laws and regulations and therefore free for general use.
The publisher, the authors and the editors are safe to assume that the advice and information in this book are believed to be true and accurate at the date of publication. Neither the publisher nor the authors or the editors give a warranty, expressed or implied, with respect to the material contained herein or for any errors or omissions that may have been made. The publisher remains neutral with regard to jurisdictional claims in published maps and institutional affiliations.

Cover design by Akihiro Nakayama

This Palgrave Macmillan imprint is published by the registered company Springer Nature Switzerland AG
The registered company address is: Gewerbestrasse 11, 6330 Cham, Switzerland

Preface

For someone who enjoys co-authorship as thoroughly as I, writing this book on my own was an unusual experience. There are many ways, nevertheless, in which this book has profited from the collaboration, discussion, and advice of others. I would like to thank Ruth Wodak and Rudolf de Cillia for their continual readiness to join methodological discussions of the most abstract sort at a moment's notice. For comments and lively discussions over coffee, I want to thank Susanne Kopf and Sabine Lehner. I also owe a debt of gratitude to Helmut Gruber, Martin Reisigl, Benedikt Lutz, Ernst Berger, Karin Wetschanow, and Birgit Huemer for their encouragement, feedback, and understanding patience. Many of you have also contributed in various ways to the foundations of the case studies I have revisited in this book, and I greatly appreciate your input and confidence in those collaborations.

Thank you, Ana, for supporting me through the long hours and weekends.

This book's companion website, Revisiting the Toolbox, offers additional figures, tables, and interactive visualizations detailing the results of the case studies in Part II. These can be found here: https://homepage.univie.ac.at/markus.rheindorf/revisitingthetoolbox/.

Vienna, Austria Markus Rheindorf

Contents

List of Figures

List of Tables

1

Introduction

The idea that Discourse Studies has access to, provides or even constitutes a 'toolbox' or 'toolkit' of methods à la Foucault (1994 [1974]), rather than a consistent, singular methodology, has been around for several decades and is used in many publications to explain or justify the authors' methodological choices (for a critique of specific instances, see, e.g., Forchtner and Tominc 2012). Indeed, the notion has inspired interdisciplinary work and provided an impetus to methodological plurality, albeit not usually as an 'anything goes' but—to borrow from Lawrence Grossberg (1997)—a 'you go where you need to', i.e. in order to pursue a particular research interest. However, the precise nature of that toolbox has remained largely un-theorized, indeed unattended. Indeed, from a typological perspective, it can be argued that we are dealing with many different toolboxes insofar as there are many distinct schools within Discourse Studies, each setting different theoretical and conceptual frameworks for the respective toolbox and its contents.[1]

[1] My reference to Discourse *Studies* rather than *Analysis* indicates a broad view of the field, with a correspondingly broad view of its methodologies (on this recent shift in major publications, see

© The Author(s) 2019

M. Rheindorf, *Revisiting the Toolbox of Discourse Studies*,
Postdisciplinary Studies in Discourse,
https://doi.org/10.1007/978-3-030-19369-0_1

This book argues that such a pertinent methodological issue should not be simplified to 'What do we discourse analysts want – or need – this toolbox to be?' Instead, we should look back on discourse analytic practice and ask along the following lines: Are there sets of tools within that box? Can and should we combine tools at will? What advantages can such combinations offer, especially if they cut across traditional divides such as those between disciplinary traditions or between qualitative and quantitative methods? Can we (and how can we) be accountable for methodological choices, given the nature of such a toolbox? For the purpose of this book, mainly linguistically informed approaches to Critical Discourse Studies (henceforth CDS) will be considered.

My reason for focusing on CDS here and, more specifically, for using the Discourse-Historical Approach for the case studies in Chapters 7–10 is two-fold: First, it is the approach that I have worked with and worked to develop for the past 20 years; and I agree with Gerlinde Mautner (2016, 24) that acknowledging one's academic socialization should be standard practice in academic publishing. Second, approaches in CDS have been heavily criticized for limitations such as cherry-picking and its proponents have been highly active in expanding their toolbox, experimenting with and integrating new methods, at least partly in response to such criticism. Critical Discourse Studies thus make an excellent case for discussing methodological experimentation and innovation.

The theoretical and methodological discussion of these questions in Part I draws on existing notions of 'mixed methods', 'triangulation', 'multivariate data', 'sequential/multi-stage research design', etc. but emphasize the potential of integrating methods beyond a simply additive or sequential approach. I further argue that current trends in the (Digital) Humanities and Social Sciences and beyond, in particular Information Visualization (InfoVis) and Visual Analytics as well as Open Data/Open Science initiatives, also require researchers in CDS to re-examine the 'toolbox' conception of their methodological choices, and consequently move beyond one-dimensional notions of 'mixing' or 'triangulating' methods. These initiatives also bring an explicitness and transparency to method-

Macgilchrist 2016; Richardson et al. 2014; Wodak and Meyer 2016; Krzyżanowski and Forchtner 2016).

ological concerns that CDS would do well to embrace. They also require us to develop new ways of providing access to analyses-in-process or to data in various states of processing that make use of visual, online, and interactive formats that allow readers/researchers to engage with our work. Unfortunately, even if for good reasons, such approaches are currently rare in CDS. Part I thus contributes to several salient debates in and beyond CDS, providing both a succinct overview and new impulses that address the needs of researchers as well as educational settings.

The chapters of Part I, then, address the need of researchers in CDS to choose tools from the 'box' that fit the changing nature of their work and meet one or several of the following challenges: working with large data sets (corpora) that need to be carefully compiled, prepared, processed, and interpreted in a way that can meaningfully integrate with qualitative analyses (Chapter 2); working with different types of data, including the non-linguistic (Chapter 3); relating and integrating analyses at different levels of discourse (e.g. official, frontstage and backstage politics, media, semi-private) (Chapter 4); mapping the complexity of discursive configurations and change from diachronic perspectives (Chapter 5); visualizing both data and results to provide fresh insights and, through interactivity, increase accessibility (Chapter 6).

Through four case studies, the chapters of Part II apply and develop these ideas, not to provide definite answers but to indicate possible trajectories for CDS. The approach of 'showcasing' methodology through critically discussing case studies and then revising them aims to stimulate cutting-edge methodological discussion on a level of detail and openness that is rarely achieved in research articles, if only due to word limits. The chapters of Part II thus aim to address the conceptual and methodological needs of researchers in CDS by providing integrated and purpose-built methods that hope to both inspire and spark discussion. Each of the case studies in Part II exemplify several, if not always all, of the challenges discussed in the chapters of Part I, including the use of data repositories and visualization. The companion website REVISITING THE TOOLBOX provides supplementary material such as tables, results, and interactive visualizations as indicated in the respective case study.

1.1 Eclecticism, Mixed Methods, and Triangulation in the Toolbox

In discussions of integrating new methods or non-linguistic data into CDS, e.g. via corpus linguistics (CL) or multimodal analysis, appeals are frequently made to "triangulation" or "mixed methods" in the basic meaning of using of several methods to study the same phenomenon (Creswell and Miller 2000). These are often blanket statements that do not detail how exactly the use of multiple methods is supposed to improve, verify or check *research results*—this, at the very least, is the requirement spelled out by Cicourel (1969) for research triangulation. Sometimes, these statements also misrepresent the actual work being done, underselling the degree of methodological integration—consider, for instance, Baker (2006, 16) labelling his own approach as "eclectic", when the research design in that publication was, in fact, cyclic and systematic.

Conceptually, the term "triangulation" is derived from land-surveying techniques that use "the convergence of measurements taken from two other distinct points" to determine a specific point in space, where multiple reference points beyond that can further improve reliability, especially if there is any noise in the individual data or results (Rothbauer 2008, 892). By analogy, research in the social sciences can involve the use of multiple datasets, entirely different types of data, multiple investigators, theories or models as well as multiple categorization schemes or analytical methods (Denzin 2009). Especially in predominantly qualitative research, triangulation helps researchers overcome the limitations of a specific method or their own bias, thus offering an alternative to quantitative measures of reliability and validity. Thus, "triangulation" in CDS has meant the combination of very broad theoretical frameworks (e.g. van Dijk's 2006 multi-disciplinary framework for triangulating discourse, cognition, and society), multiple datasets (e.g. Wodak et al. 2009) and specific, elaborate methodological combinations (e.g. Baker et al. 2008). These different dimensions of triangulation are, of course, interrelated as a particular theoretical perspective may be associated with a set of methodological tools and analytical practices; similarly, particular types of data may be associated with specific theories, models or analytical approaches (Hocking 2015, 193).

The freedom of borrowing, combining, and adapting methods associated with the term 'eclecticism' is welcomed by most researchers in CDS, often explicitly so. There are, of course, good reasons for doing so, such as avoiding methodological fragmentation by disciplinary boundaries. Discourse, being a social practice, should arguably be studied not only through varied linguistic or semiotic methods but an even broader array of social science methodology: "My inclination is towards trying to draw together the diverse methodological approaches that currently make up social research, in the belief that fragmentation – especially when 'paradigmized' – is a barrier against progress towards more effective scientific study of social life" (Hammersley 2003, 772). Overcoming CDS's own growing orthodoxy is another reason that is often cited for methodological eclecticism: "If we want to meaningfully advance a critical discursive agenda we need to be less orthodox [...] and embrace the potential for undertaking CDA in combination with other research methods" (see the vignette by Cliff Oswick in Mautner 2016, 228).

Although most would characterize CDS as highly heterogeneous (Wodak and Meyer 2009, 5), one can discern a stable 'core' (Mautner 2011, 85–86) of what I would describe as theoretical assumptions or principles: CDS proceed from social issues or problems that manifest, among other things, in language; CDS proceed from the constructivist assumption that language and social reality are dialectically related, and that discourse is thus both mirror and driver of social change; this constructivist-dialectical framework also informs the emancipatory aim to not only analyze discursively constructed reality but to intervene. There are also broad methodological common denominators in CDS, such as studying only authentic language data or including analyses of potentially all levels of linguistic realization from macrostructures to lexicogrammar and phonology. Significantly, Mautner (2011) also includes in this 'core' a view of texts as whole, as entities embedded in socio-political, cultural or historical contexts in which they are produced, distributed, and received. This particular tenet places certain constraints, for example, on how CL methods can be used in CDS. In exploring such contexts, CDS often draw on related fields of research, including sociology, history, and political science—making it an interdisciplinary field. While this can be limited to findings from other disciplines, it can also extend to their methodology, raising the stakes of eclecticism due to different epistemologies.

This state of flux can therefore also be reason for concern and has, indeed, been read as a sign that "the methodology of discourse analysis is [...] always on the verge of crisis" (Lynch 2007, 512). Others have warned that there are tensions between methodological innovation and theoretical foundations/assumptions (Gabrielatos and Duguid 2014). Reexamining the toolbox of discourse analysis, while primarily a methodological project, thus also has a strong theoretical and conceptual dimension. It is a key proposition of this book that such concerns are best addressed by focusing on the aims and effects of methodological triangulation rather than flouting eclecticism. Triangulation has been given some consideration within CDS, particularly in approaches that emphasize methodology (such as CL-based and multimodal CDS, e.g. Marchi and Taylor 2009, 6; Hocking 2015; Baker 2014, 2015; Baker and Levon 2015) or interdisciplinarity and mixed methods (such as the DHA, e.g. Wodak et al. 2009). With few notable exceptions, however, the benefits of triangulation are alluded to in rather general terms as 'complementing', 'verifying' or 'supporting' results, achieving a 'multiperspectival' study or 'increasing reliability'.

A fundamental distinction that needs to be made in CDS is between triangulation through *multiple sets of data* (which may implicate multiple methods of data collection) and triangulation through *multiple methods of analysis* (Hocking 2015, 192; Candlin and Crichton 2013). Another fundamental distinction concerns how the methods are interrelated during the research process, i.e. through 'synthesizing' methods into a new form of analysis (e.g. Wodak and Rheindorf 2017), through 'integration' into a staged research design (e.g. Baker et al. 2008), or as separate components carried out sequentially or simultaneously with the initially separate results brought together in a comparison and consolidation of findings (e.g. Baker and Levon 2015, 234).

The general literature on triangulation is extensive (e.g. Cicourel 1969; Creswell 2014; Flick 2017) and contains several taxonomies for distinguishing possible aims/effects of combining methods. Among these, Bryman (2006, 105–7) provides an excellent overview that, given the 'core' of CDS's principles, can be condensed as follows. Triangulation through multiple methods or datasets may aim for

a. corroboration or confirmation (through convergence or correspondence of results),
b. diversity of views (including methods informed by different theories or models),
c. offset or contrast (including contrastive or comparative selection of data),
d. complementary results (data or methods are combined to gain a fuller picture),
e. enhancement of results (through expanding, detailing or deepening analysis),
f. explanation or clarification (usually of quantitative results by qualitative analysis),
g. exploration/initiation (seeking new perspectives, discoveries or contradictions),
h. instrument development (results from one method helping to develop another),
i. sampling or downsampling (by using or enabling the combination of methods),
j. contextualization (studying attendant social practices or the historical dimension),
k. illustration (where one method provides the overall results and another identifies and demonstrates analysis through illustrative examples),
l. increased credibility (as an interpersonal goal, this stands apart).

A particular research design or specific combination of data or methods may aim for, and achieve, one or several of these effects, as they are not mutually exclusive. For instance, a combination of CL methods that focus on lexical patterns and detailed qualitative analysis of argumentative patterns, applied to a large corpus and a subset of that corpus, respectively, may aim for diversity of views, complementary results, and enhancing results—the research design may also include an approach to downsampling that combines methods. Such potential depends, of course, on the specific theoretical-conceptual framework and research interest pursued. In the context of this book, this larger issue unfolds, first, through the five methodological chapters of Part I and, second, through the case studies of Part II.

1.2 Part I: Key Issues in Methodology

Comprising a total of five chapters, Part I provides an overview of key methodological and conceptual issues in CDS, related debates, and previous research pertaining to them. Each chapter thus contributes to the overall discussion of the Foucauldian 'toolbox' in the context of contemporary Digital Humanities and Open Science initiatives.

Chapter 2, *Working with Corpora Small and Large*, outlines the use of text corpora in CDS, in particular as compiled, processed and analyzed in the emergent field of corpus-based CDS. The chapter begins by relating the methodological foundations of CL, most prominently the concept and implementation of 'corpus', to 'discourse'. In this context, the so-called 'quantitative-qualitative divide' is critically discussed as the reification of an unnecessary, and often impractical, separation. Chapter 2 then gives a brief overview of the history of attempts to integrate CL into CDS, arguing that these are informed by commonalities between the two as well as critiques of CDS methodology. The main body of the chapter then lays out the methodological arguments for and against using CL methods in CDS, highlighting the advantages and challenges of such an integration. On the one hand, this refers to key criticisms of CDS, such as researcher bias or cherry-picking, and how CL methods can help to address any such limitations; on the other hand, this refers to the risks of using CL methods in CDS, such as shallow integration, data gluttony or decontextualization, and how balanced research designs can avoid or counteract these risks. Finally, the chapter offers some conclusions on research practice when using CL methods in CDS.

Chapter 3, *Working with Different Types of Data*, focuses on the analysis of multiple, distinct types of data. The chapter covers broad arguments for analyzing varied data from object- or problem-centered perspective, before focusing on the approach known as Multimodal (Critical) Discourse Analysis. On the one hand, this concerns different types of data within the linguistic domain, such as different genres and text types, or spoken and written text. Since such data cannot simply be analyzed without addressing the specifics of each type, the combined results of such analyses offer potential benefits in terms of triangulation; but they also carry risks, as findings from different types of data cannot simply be added up. On the other hand, this chapter pertains to multimodal data that, unlike text corpora, cannot be processed with the help of CL methods or, in many cases, any linguistic methods at all.

Much work in CDS, even in linguistically grounded approaches such as the DHA, has conceived of discourse as social meaning-making practice including—even privileging—the linguistic but not limited to it. Even if the primacy of language in the social construction of meaning is assumed (e.g. Koselleck 2007), researchers have found it useful and, indeed, necessary to include or even focus on non-linguistic data. This has included images (e.g. charts, photography, illustrations or paintings), video (e.g. documenting group discussions, documentaries, TV dramas, news or feature films), musical scores and soundscapes, architecture, monuments, spatial configurations, toys and material objects and practices of various kinds. It is tempting to recognize the various 'turns' that have swept through the Humanities and Social Sciences in these forays into non-linguistic data. Even more urgently than with CL, criticism of such work has argued that discourse analysts' work on different types of data requires (a) a discussion and acknowledgment of possible incompatibilities between methods, and (b) either an interdisciplinary team to carry out the analysis or an earnest engagement with other disciplines (and their methodologies), be it musicology, visual design, ethnography etc. Failing that, CDS risks the analysis becoming highly subjective, reinventing the wheel, practicing linguistic imperialism, becoming inconsistent with core methodologies of CDS, or ceasing to be CDS altogether. After engaging with these arguments, Chapter 3 offers some recommendations for research practice when analyzing different types of data in CDS.

Chapter 4, *Combining Analyses at Different Levels of Discourse*, addresses an integral issue in research design for CDS: conceptualizing the structuredness of discourse and operationalizing the analysis at a particular level of discourse. While this is not immediately a methodological issue, it has clear implications for methodological choices and triangulation. For if discourse is structured—e.g. into levels, layers, a center and periphery, etc.—then analyzing data from different loci within that structure offers several of the potential benefits of triangulation outlined above. This chapter discusses prevalent conceptions of discourse with respect to their assumptions about the structuredness of discourse, including discourse as *social superstructure* and as structured into different *levels of linguistic realization*. Levels of discourse in this sense are, inter alia, discourse macro-structures or macro-topics, discursive (macro-)strategies, argumentation patterns, representation, attribution, social actors, transitivity patterns, modality, and metaphor. Chapter 4 then contrasts different approaches to connecting the micro- and macro-level(s) of discourse, specifically as they relate to conceptualizations of agency, context, and social action. In research practical terms, perhaps the most consequential conceptions of discourse structure view discourse as structured by social hierarchies (e.g. state representation, institutions, distinct publics) or as situated in and interlinked with social fields of action (e.g. media, politics, jurisprudence). Other structural concepts that have been applied in CDS, such as notions of a discursive core/periphery, sedimentation, strands, and knots, are discussed before concluding comments on research practice.

Chapter 5, *From Synchronic to Diachronic Perspectives*, tackles another question to which CDS has developed numerous conceptual and methodological responses: the nature of discursive change and its relation to social change. Although already present in Foucault's notion of an 'archaeology of knowledge', CDS has developed specific approaches to the diachronic study of discourse. This chapter engages with methodological answers to the Escheresque conundrum present in the assumption that discourse is 'always already there', indicating that discourse as an object of research always already has a history. While none of the established approaches in CDS preclude a diachronic perspective, some suggest or even require engaging with the history of the discourses to be studied as part of a standardized research program. Whether and how to study the diachronic dimension of discourse in a specific research effort is the central issue of this chapter. More specifically, Chapter 5 outlines the conceptual and methodological implications of working with notions that denote specific forms or mechanisms of discursive change, such as *recontextualization*, *normalization*, and *colonization*, or relate to a specific level of discursive change, such as *discursive strategies* or *legitimization*. Beyond approaches that primarily engage in diachrony through the historical context of current discourses, the chapter also details the methodological options for operationalizing diachrony empirically, e.g. through strategies of periodization and segmentation of the timeframe covered. As in all chapters of Part I, comments on research design and practice conclude the discussion.

Chapter 6, *Opening Up Critical Discourse Studies*, covers the potential of using visualization techniques and online, interactive visualization to complement traditional publication forms. Although there is a long tradition of visualization in the Humanities and Social Sciences, recent technological advances and the emergence of specialized fields such DataVis, InfoVis, and Visual Analytics have opened up new possibilities for visualizing discourse-related data and findings in addition to models or concepts. So far, little work in CDS has explicitly attempted or discussed visualization techniques for its specific aims and purposes. Especially with large-scale quantitative results and complex interrelationships, visualization offers a means to increase accessibility and comprehensibility, but qualitative results may be just as suitable for visualization.

Chapter 6 covers some basic theory on visualization as external cognition and its potential benefits in relation to previous chapters, e.g. the combined presentation of data/results on different levels of discourse or the visualization of diachronic change. Established forms of visualization such as bar charts and scatter plots are a solid starting point for those in CDS seeking to visualize their work. However, choosing the right visualization should follow criteria for effectiveness, expressiveness, appropriateness that relate to the data at hand, the readers/users to be reached, and the tasks the readers/users are expected to perform on the visualization, such as *explore* or *compare.*

After establishing this framework, Chapter 6 focuses on the specific challenges of visualizing language- and discourse-related data. The possibilities of interactive visualization, using online platforms that integrate multiple interrelated views, increase the potential of opening up CDS to readers as fellow researchers. While visualization can condense and relate complexity, interactivity can make that complexity explorable for readers/users. In doing so, it can also deliver on key objectives of Open Science by opening up research on different levels of data processing and analysis (raw data, processed data, categorization, lexical analysis, argumentation analysis, etc.). In particular, Chapter 6 develops the notion of *dashboards* that offer a partly visualized, interactive space for exploring an emergent analysis. For researchers working in CDS, the advantage of utilizing such approaches is that they are relatively easy to implement and to adapt to one's specific research agenda and/or publication requirements. Ideally, they facilitate more inclusive publications that allow readers an in-depth and multi-perspectival engagement with our research. Criteria for integrating (interactive) visualization into research design and practice conclude this final chapter of Part I.

1.3 Part II: Case Studies

Each of the four case studies in Part II engages with a particular research project conducted in the past, often in collaboration with other researchers, whose contributions have been invaluable. Each chapter begins with the brief presentation of *the original study* in terms of its theoretical-conceptual frame, research questions, methodology, and results. This is followed by a critical discussion of the limitations and weaknesses of the original study, suggesting changes such as expanding the dataset, including new methods of analysis or including other levels of discourse and/or linguistic realization. Sometimes, this involves shifting or adding to the conceptual framework of the study as well, such as including argumentation theory or the notion of chronotopes. The analytic implementation of these concepts draws on established operationalizations and, where promising, proposes a new method of analysis, a new combination of methods, or new visualization strategies to leverage the concept's potential.

Chapter 7, *Retold Narratives of Holocaust Survivors and Their Children*, revisits research on the narratives of Holocaust survivors as passed on and told by their children (Wodak and Rheindorf 2017). The original study conducted biographical interviews with 29 children of Viennese 'returnees' who were persecuted by the Nazis for, among other reasons, being Jewish or political dissidents. The interviews focused on the stories told to these children, now aged between 60 and 75 themselves, by their parents as well as on the circumstances of their telling. The original study pursued three interrelated research interests: (1) the marginality of the group as reflected in their discourse about the war, persecution, and the Holocaust—in relation to Austria's mainstream, hegemonic discourses; (2) how the interviewees' deal with and position themselves in relation to their parents' narratives in their retellings; and (3) evidence of intergenerational traumata in these retold stories. Methodologically, the original study combined quantitative and qualitative methods: First, CL methods (frequency, keyword, and semantic field analyses) were used to identify the main topics in the interview corpus and contrast it to a reference corpus of biographical interviews. Topically, the former differed from the latter significantly with respect to politicization, engagement in civil society, and historical events. Second, qualitative analyses operationalized the narratological concepts of 'positioning', 'story ownership', and 'narrative affectivity' in linguistic terms. The study found that, unlike Holocaust narratives told by survivors, the stories retold by the returnees' children are not framed by ownership and authenticity but by disclaimers and uncertainty. Third, the original study operationalized Bakhtin's notion of 'chronotope', i.e. specific space-time configurations that characterize the stories shared by a particular social group and, through their stories, also the group itself. The original study found that the interviewees' narratives about the war, persecution, and the Holocaust were devoid of specific time references (dates) and emphasized spatial references, often metonymically or euphemistically. This pattern was not found in their narratives about events before 1939 or after 1945.

The revisited study addresses (1) the weak conceptual link between narrative and discourse; and (2) the limited focus on positioning of the interviewees' narrative 'I'. Methodologically, it develops a new approach to mapping and visualizing narrative structures (key roles and their actions/relations) on the discourse level by integrating qualitative and quantitative methods from CL and Systemic Functional Linguistics. The revised study thus adds a discourse-level view of the narrative patterns present in the interviews, categorized by key actors and entities as well as verb processes. The results reveal a strong relation between the interviewees and their parents in terms of passing on stories or withholding them, of knowing or not knowing what happened; but they also show that, across the interview corpus, the interviewees' parents are set in relation to places rather than events, and as *doing* rather than *being done to*. Aggregating results on the discourse level furthermore allows visualizing the overall pattern of narrative roles and interrelations as a network graph, inspired by sociological Social Network Analysis, providing an intuitive and explorable overview.

Chapter 8, *Normalization of Populist Terms in Political Discourse and Beyond*, revisits work done in an extensive research project on the discursive construction of national identities in Austria (Rheindorf 2017, 2018). The original study focused on a discursive shift that occurred in January 2015, during a highly mediatized political debate over demands for 'punitive' laws against migrants who were 'unwilling to integrate' (Resolution 3237/6). The original study found that this term, while present on the World Wide Web, had not been used in Austrian newspapers before the debate but became normalized through it. The study pursued the following research interests: (1) the relation between the 'scandal' triggering the debate and the news reporting in terms of mediatized politics; and (2) the representation of migrants and other social actors in the media reporting. Methodologically, the original study analyzed the argumentative structure of Resolution 3237/6, which sparked the debate, and used CL methods to analyze a corpus of 280 texts representing the mediatized debate itself. Based on the quantitative results, qualitative analyses were then used to identify the social actors represented in that corpus as well as the manner of their representation (nomination and predication).

The revised study addresses three key limitations of the original study: (1) the narrow empirical focus on a four-week period as a short-term discursive shift; (2) the narrow empirical focus on media as a single social field of action; and (3) the lack of qualitative results on how the media related to the populist arguments of Resolution 3237/6: (a) an alleged link between terrorism and migrants' unwillingness to integrate, (b) the usefulness of criminal law to enforce integration and thereby prevent terrorism, and (c) politicians' responsibility to change current laws on integration to prevent terrorism. The revised study thus develops both the short- and long term perspective on discursive change. First, it analyzes additional corpora of parliamentary debates, court rulings related to integration, and legal texts, to extend the analysis to the social fields of politics, legislation, and jurisprudence. In doing so, it also extends the diachronic perspective from 4 weeks to 20 years (1998–2018), finding prior usage of the term 'unwillingness to integrate' that complicates the account of its normalization. Second, it qualitatively analyzes all 280 media texts in the original corpus for their relation to the three populist arguments above, then quantifies and visualizes the results for the four-week timeframe to track the discursive shift in more detail, showing that normalization did not apply to all arguments equally.

Chapter 9, *Media Representations of Refugees, Asylum Seekers, Immigrants, and Migrants*, revisits research on media discourse during the so-called refugee crisis of 2015/2016 (Rheindorf and Wodak 2018). The original study was interested in (1) how the media represented refugees and related groups of people; (2) the extent to which this representation distinguished or conflated these groups; and (3) how these patterns changed in the course of a 14-month period. The study collected a corpus of nearly 6000 newspaper articles, used CL methods to identify patterns of nomination and predication with respect to each group, and evaluated the intercollocational overlap between them. The qualitative analysis and categorization of collocations into semantic fields was integral to this predominantly quantitative approach. The original study found that the intensity of media reporting correspond to national and international events related to the construction of the so-called crisis; it also found a gradual shift in the media's attention from refugees to the broader category of migrants. In terms of broad collocational patterns, results showed that both refugees and migrants were closely linked to being a burden on the Austrian state and Austrian people, but that migrants were more often seen as abusing the Austrian welfare system. The analysis also found a clear conflation between refugees and asylum seekers as well as a strong collocational overlap between refugees and migrants.

The revised study addresses the following issues: (1) the inconsistency of the original study in focusing on data that covers a 'crisis', i.e. short-term discursive change, but only linking publication intensity and nomination frequencies to social context; and (2) treating the newspaper texts simply as newspaper reporting, without conceptualizing and empirically addressing that the data includes a substantial extent of mediatized politics. Methodologically, the revised study introduces a way to track short-term collocational shifts for key terms like 'refugee'. It also extends the original study conceptually by studying the legitimation strategies used by political actors in terms of argumentation, mapping the results for both argumentation and legitimation diachronically across the 14-month period. Since the sheer amount of data makes a complete qualitative analysis impossible, the revised study also introduces an innovative form of downsampling which uses previously obtained quantitative results in an iterative process defined by saturation criteria for the qualitative analysis.

Chapter 10, *A Diachronic View of Register and Argumentation in Early Film Theory*, revisits work on canonical film theoretical writings before the 1960s (Rheindorf 2005a, b, 2006, 2007). The original study used a purely qualitative approach to trace the terminological and argumentative development of film theory across a multilingual and transnational body of texts, including genres such as film reviews, pamphlets, and academic papers. The terminological analysis indicated the predominance of terms conceptually related to three versions of the 'film as language' analogy: (a) film as a visual Esperanto, (b) film as a symptom-like language of the collective unconscious, and (c) film as medium for the language of things. While these conceptions were found throughout the material, the original study found that each was foregrounded in the context of a particular period and socio-political context: from 1910 to the onset of World War II, during the war, and after the war until Christian Metz's thorough critique of the 'film as language' analogy. Using argumentation theory, the original study identified 49 thematic topoi throughout the material and visually mapped their characteristic interrelations with each of the three conceptions of 'film language'. It concluded that early film theoretical discourse showed three characteristic configurations of the argumentative field, each related to a particular understanding of 'film language'.

The revised study addresses key limitations linked to the purely qualitative nature of the original study as well as its neglect of genre as mediating construct. First, the revised study acknowledges the potential bias of the original corpus due to an unequal distribution of genres across rime and expands the corpus by balancing for genre, doubling its size to nearly 2 million words. Second, for the terminological aspect of the research design, it uses translations of all non-English texts in the material (French, German, Hungarian, Italian, and Russian). CL methods are then used to gain a more accurate, quantified picture of the terminological diversity and development of early film theory, specifically its figurative use of language-related terminology. Third, the 49 previously defined topoi and their interrelations are qualitatively identified across the entire corpus and then quantified. Fourth—pertaining to terminology, argumentation, and genre—the revised study tests different periodization strategies to ascertain the validity of results. Finally, an interactive dashboard accessible online presents the argumentative field of early film theory as a manipulable network graph, interlinked with supplementary information on topoi definitions, respective source texts, exemplary text extracts, and frequency information for topoi and their interrelations.

Chapter 11, *Concluding Remarks*, returns to the toolbox analogy for methods in CDS and draws conclusions for triangulation from the methodological chapters and cases studies. It also reflects on the neglected twin-effect of methodological plurality and triangulation, i.e. the decentering of the research account and deferral of closure. If there is always a next method, another aspect of discourse, and another perspective to contribute, we do not simply expand or support our results by combining methods, we also open up the research process in a way that invites critique and participation—two Open Science goals that CDS should find easy to embrace.

References

Baker, Paul. 2006. *Using Corpora in Discourse Analysis*. Continuum Discourse Series. London and New York: Continuum.

———. 2014. *Using Corpora to Analyze Gender*. London: Bloomsbury.

———. 2015. "Chapter 12. Does Britain Need Any More Foreign Doctors? Inter-Analyst Consistency and Corpus-Assisted (Critical) Discourse Analysis." In *Studies in Corpus Linguistics*, edited by Nicholas Groom, Maggie Charles, and Suganthi John, vol. 73, 283–300. Amsterdam: John Benjamins Publishing Company. https://doi.org/10.1075/scl.73.13bak.

Baker, Paul, and Erez Levon. 2015. "Picking the Right Cherries? A Comparison of Corpus-Based and Qualitative Analyses of News Articles About Masculinity." *Discourse & Communication* 9 (2): 221–36. https://doi.org/10.1177/1750481314568542.

Baker, Paul, Costas Gabrielatos, Majid KhosraviNik, Michał Krzyżanowski, Tony McEnery, and Ruth Wodak. 2008. "A Useful Methodological Synergy? Combining Critical Discourse Analysis and Corpus Linguistics to Examine

Discourses of Refugees and Asylum Seekers in the UK Press." *Discourse & Society* 19 (3): 273–306. https://doi.org/10.1177/0957926508088962.

Bryman, Alan. 2006. "Integrating Quantitative and Qualitative Research: How Is It Done?" *Qualitative Research* 6 (1): 97–113. https://doi.org/10.1177/1468794106058877.

Candlin, Christopher, and Jonathan Crichton (eds.). 2013. *Discourses of Trust: Palgrave Studies in Professional and Organizational Discourse.* Houndmills, Basingstoke, Hampshire and New York, NY: Palgrave Macmillan.

Cicourel, Aaron V. 1969. *Method and Measurement in Sociology.* New York: The Free Press.

Creswell, John W. 2014. *Research Design: Qualitative, Quantitative, and Mixed Methods Approaches*, 4th ed. Thousand Oaks: Sage.

Creswell, John W., and Dana L. Miller. 2000. "Determining Validity in Qualitative Inquiry." *Theory into Practice* 39 (3): 124–30. https://doi.org/10.1207/s15430421tip3903_2.

Denzin, Norman K. 2009. *The Research Act: A Theoretical Introduction to Sociological Methods.* New Brunswick, NJ: Aldine Transaction.

Flick, Uwe. 2017. *Doing Triangulation and Mixed Methods*, 1st ed., The Sage Qualitative Research Kit. Thousand Oaks, CA: Sage.

Forchtner, Bernhard, and Ana Tominc. 2012. "Critique and Argumentation: On the Relation Between the Discourse-Historical Approach and Pragma-Dialectics." *Journal of Language and Politics* 11 (1): 31–50.

Foucault, Michel. (1994 [1974]). "Prisons et asiles dans le mécanisme du pouvoir". In *Dits et Ecrits, t. II*, 523–4. Paris: Gallimard.

Gabrielatos, Costas, and Alison Duguid. 2014. "Corpus Linguistics and CDA: A Critical Look at Synergy." Presented at the CDA20+ Symposium. September 9, 2014, University of Amsterdam.

Grossberg, Lawrence. 1997. *Bringing It All Back Home: Essays on Cultural Studies.* Durham, NC: Duke University Press.

Hammersley, Martyn. 2003. "Conversation Analysis and Discourse Analysis: Methods or Paradigms?." *Discourse & Society* 14 (6): 751–81. https://doi.org/10.1177/09579265030146004

Hocking, Darryl. 2015. "Health Communication and Corpus Linguistics: Using Corpus Tools to Analyse Eating Disorder Discourse Online." In *Corpora and Discourse Studies: Integrating Discourse and Corpora*, edited by Tony McEnery and Paul Baker, 192–219. London: Palgrave Macmillan.

Koselleck, Reinhart. 2007. *The Practice of Conceptual History: Timing History, Spacing Concepts*, Reprint, Cultural Memory in the Present. Stanford, CA: Stanford University Press.

Lynch, Michael. 2007. "Discourse Analysis." In *The Sage Handbook of Social Science Methodology*, edited by William Outhwaite and Stephen Turner, 499–515. London: Sage.

Marchi, Anna, and Charlotte Taylor. 2009. "If on a Winter's Night Two Researchers…: A Challenge to Assumptions of Soundness of Interpretation." *Critical Approaches to Discourse Analysis Across Disciplines: CADAAD* 3 (1): 1–20.

Mautner, Gerlinde. 2011. "Die Kritische Masse. Korpuslinguistik Und Kritische Diskursanalyse." In *Korpuspragmatik. Thematische Korpora Als Basis Diskurslinguistischer Analysen*, edited by Ekkehard Felder, Marcus Müller, and Friedemann Vogel, 83–114. Berlin and Boston: de Gruyter.

———. 2016. *Discourse and Management: Critical Perspectives Through the Language Lens.* Basingstoke, UK: Palgrave.

Rheindorf, Markus. 2005a. "Die Ausdruckskraft Der Körper: Natürlichkeit Und Physiognomie in Der Filmtheorie Der Zwischenkriegszeit." In *Leibhaftige Moderne: Körper in Kunst Und Massenmedien 1918 Bis 1938*, edited by Michael Cowan and Kai M. Sicks, 217–30. Bielefeld: Transcript.

———. 2005b. "Film as Language: The Politics of Early Film Theory (1920–1960)." *Journal of Language and Politics* 4 (1): 143–59.

———. 2006. "The Languages That Films Speak—Discourse-Historical Perspectives on Film Theory: Dis/Continuities and Contexts." PhD thesis, University of Vienna, Vienna.

———. 2007. "Die Sprachen, Die Filme Sprechen: Die Geschichte Der Deutschsprachigen Filmtheorie Als Diskursgeschichte." *Zeitschrift Für Kulturwissenschaften. Themenheft Filmwissenschaft Als Kulturwissenschaft* 2: 11–24.

———. 2017. "Integration Durch Strafe? Dic Normalisierung Paternalistischer Diskursfiguren Zur „Integrationsunwilligkeit"." *Zeitschrift Für Diskursforschung* 5 (2): 182–206.

———. 2018. "Disciplining the Unwilling. Normalisation of (Demands for) Punitive Measures Against Immigrants in Austrian Populist Discourse." In *Doing Politics: Discursivity, Performativity and Mediation in Political Discourse*, edited by Michael Kranert and Geraldine Horan, 179–208. Amsterdam: John Benjamins.

Rheindorf, Markus, and Ruth Wodak. 2018. "Borders, Fences, and Limits—Protecting Austria from Refugees: Metadiscursive Negotiation of Meaning in the Current Refugee Crisis." *Journal of Immigrant & Refugee Studies* 16 (1–2): 15–38. https://doi.org/10.1080/15562948.2017.1302032.

Rothbauer, Paulette. 2008. "Triangulation." In *The Sage Encyclopedia of Qualitative Research Methods*, edited by Lisa M. Given, 892–94. Los Angeles, CA: Sage.
van Dijk, Teun. A. 2006. "Discourse, Context and Cognition." *Discourse Studies* 8 (1): 159–77. https://doi.org/10.1177/1461445606059565.
Wodak, Ruth, and Markus Rheindorf. 2017. "'Whose Story?'—Narratives of Persecution, Flight and Survival Told by the Children of Austrian Holocaust Survivors." In *Linguistic Diversity and Superdiversity: Sociocultural Linguistic Perspectives*, edited by Anna de Fina, Didem Ikizoglu, and Jeremy Wegner, 17–36. Washington, DC: Georgetown University Press.
Wodak, Ruth, and Michael Meyer. 2009. "Critical Discourse Analysis: History, Agenda, Theory and Methodology." In *Methods of Critical Discourse Analysis*, edited by R. Wodak, & M. Meyer, 1–33. London: Sage.
Wodak, Ruth, Rudolf de Cillia, Martin Reisigl, and Karin Liebhart. 2009. *The Discursive Construction of National Identity*, 2nd ed., Critical Discourse Analysis. Edinburgh: Edinburgh University Press.

2

Working with Corpora Small and Large: Qualitative and Quantitative Methods

2.1 Introduction

This chapter discusses the use of text corpora in Critical Discourse Studies (CDS), in particular as compiled, processed, and analyzed with corpus linguistic methods within CDS (most prominently, the approaches elaborated by Paul Baker and Gerlinde Mautner). Within the general framework of this book, I regard such combinations as instances of methodological plurality and as the key area for integrating quantitative and qualitative methods in CDS.[1] In the specific context of the current chapter, triangulation relates to the combination of qualitative and quantitative methods (Baker and Levon 2015, 223).

The combination of CL and CDS has many advocates and some opponents. Ken Hyland's enthused "[c]orpora and discourse approaches are perfect bedfellows" (Hyland 2009, 110) is indicative of the former, but

[1] Methods and concepts explicitly considered include corpus compilation; frequency; keywords, key keywords, reference corpora; collocation, concordance and cluster analysis; semantic tagging and semantic fields (or key categories), and cumulative keyness; lexical priming, semantic preference, discourse prosody.

© The Author(s) 2019

M. Rheindorf, *Revisiting the Toolbox of Discourse Studies*,
Postdisciplinary Studies in Discourse,
https://doi.org/10.1007/978-3-030-19369-0_2

the relationship between the two fields is not as easy as the metaphor implies. Having said that, recent assessments of the current spread and acceptance of such combinations vary widely, ranging from "corpus investigation [having] become commonplace as a research tool in Critical Discourse Studies" (Caldas-Coulthard and Moon 2010, 100) to the assertion that "that corpus linguistic techniques are not yet generally regarded as being at the core of CDA's methodological canon" (Mautner 2016a, 155). Indeed, Mautner (2016c) still asks how we can overcome the quantitative-qualitative divide, marking the continued relevance of addressing this issue.

This chapter takes an earnest look at CL methods as potentially valuable methodological options in carrying out CDS. It seeks to address the specific value of integrating CL methods into such research and avoid vague declarations of "synergy" or "building bridges" as well as blanket appeals to "triangulation" or "mixed methods". By itself, the fact that adding CL methods to an otherwise qualitative study makes it, by definition, a case of triangulation/mixed methods, allowing "different perspectives on the data" (McEnery and Hardie 2012, 233), offers little insight. More than two decades after the first attempts to integrate CL into CDS, we need to be articulate and specific in assessing the potential contributions of this particular "move towards methodological pluralism" (McEnery and Hardie 2012, 233). Back then, Hardt-Mautner rightly linked this potential to the prime goal of CDS to "unravel how particular discourses, rooted in particular socio-cultural contexts, construct reality, social identities and social relationships" (Hardt-Mautner 1995, 1). In other words, the standard we should hold ourselves to today is being able to say precisely what the value of integrating CL methods into CDS is, in a particular case, with respect to what kind of data studied and which questions asked, as well as acknowledging their limitations (Mautner 2011, 84). Although equidistance is difficult to achieve, this chapter is meant for discourse analysts who use corpora and corpus linguists who do discourse analysis.

The chapter begins with some conceptual remarks on CL as a potential source of methods to integrate into CDS frameworks. Specifically, the notions of 'discourse' and 'corpus' as well as the so-called qualitative-quantitative divide are addressed. This is followed by a brief look at the history of CL methods in CDS and the two fields' commonalities. The chapter then sets out in the form of arguments the *advantages* and *challenges* of using CL methods within CDS. This discussion takes into account arguments on the level of methodology, research design, and research practice. In particular, it addresses criticisms of discourse analysts' work that have been cited as reasons for using CL methods in CDS (e.g. small text samples as unrepresentative and researcher bias), the potential solutions offered by CL methods (e.g. downsampling rather than cherry-picking) as well as subsequent criticisms of incorporating CL methods into CDS (e.g. as abandoning the terrain of discourse analysis). In discussing these arguments on the methodological level, previous work is reviewed as examples of using CL methods in CDS; in this, criteria for triangulation and mixed methods are applied where appropriate. By way of conclusion, key benefits and pitfalls of using CL methods in CDS are identified regarding research design and practice.

2.2 Methodological Remarks on Corpus Linguistics

I want to begin by acknowledging CL as a field, and as one that I came to relatively late in my own academic socialization, even if for the remainder of this chapter I will be mainly interested in what CL has to offer to CDS (much like CL looks to mathematical statistics for workable solutions). This is not meant to denigrate CL approaches or CL studies in their own right, but it does raise the question of CL's theoretical foundations and the epistemological status of its methods. While both aspects will surface time and again in the following subchapters, some preliminary remarks are in order.

Even if CL is relatively 'poor' in theory, it is neither free of conceptual assumptions nor purely objective—irrespective of the question whether its methods are entirely ore mainly quantitative (see below). Ironically, both misconceptions are sometimes voiced by those who embrace the empiricist notion of an objective science as well as by those who argue CL is merely a collection of more or less handy tools. Speaking of tools: Much like discourse analysts, corpus linguists also use the 'tool' metaphor to refer to various things: "Corpora", as Anthony (2013, 141) observes, "are often referred to as the 'tools' of corpus linguistics". It seems conceptually sound to distinguish, with Anthony, between the linguistic data compiled, prepared and organized into corpora on the one hand, and the (partly automated, algorithm-driven) methods typically used in CL, which does include procedures for compiling corpora. In analogy with the methodological discourse of CDS, the latter would be considered 'tools'—not only but also when reified in specialized software used to view and analyze corpora (Anthony 2013, 141).

In contrast to CDS, however, CL methods and its technologies are conceptually very close and at times seem to blend into one another. Indeed, the concrete functions available in software tools largely equate with corpus linguistic methods and thus effectively limit the conceptual frame of CL research (Anthony 2013, 141). However, there is at least one principal theoretical controversy beyond this, and it pertains directly to integrating CL methods into CDS: One school of thought in CL, usually termed the "corpus-driven approach" (Tognini-Bonelli 2001), argues that the starting point of all analyses should be direct observations of the corpus without any prior linguistic theorization or categorization (Anthony 2013, 142). The other large school of thought, commonly referred to as the "corpus-based approach" (McEnery and Hardie 2012), holds not only that prior theorization or categorization is useful, but that it is in fact "impossible to completely remove all pre-existing ideas about language before observing corpora" (Anthony 2013, 142). The corpus-based approach is seen as giving the researcher more control, using the corpus as "a way of testing out existing hypothesis", while the corpus-driven approach provides better replicability and limits bias (Baker et al. 2013, 26). Following this distinction, studies conducted in the spirit of the former can be characterized as inductive, i.e. regarding the corpus itself as the data to be studied and treating the patterns to be found in it as "expressing regularities (and exceptions) in language", while research in the latter category would use corpora to look for examples, "to check researcher intuition or to examine the frequency and/or plausibility of the language contained within a smaller data set" (Baker 2006, 16). While this distinction is certainly not absolute and practice often blurs the boundaries between categories, the two opposite orientations affect the use of corpora in CDS in general and the building of corpora for such studies in particular.

While a strictly corpus-driven approach favors large general corpora and would seem to conflict with pre-selecting data on grounds of genre or content, i.e. pertaining to specific fields or discourses, a corpus-based approach seems more in line with the theoretical frameworks of CDS and pre-existing categorizations such as those of SFL. In practice, however, a specialized corpus may be assembled (based on certain pre-existing categories of genre, social field or even topic) and then analyzed inductively. Clearly, such a study would not be able make claims about general language use. Another compromise can be attempted through corpus annotation: While initially rejected for corpus-driven work for its interference with "pristine" data, modern corpus tools are fully capable of selectively showing/hiding different layers of annotation or markup of texts (Anthony 2013, 149), thus voiding the dichotomy. Regardless of the approach, the value of any corpus clearly depends "not on its size but on what kind of information we can extract from it" (Anthony 2013, 146). After all, "the corpus can only ever reveal its own contents" (Baker et al. 2013, 30).

To return to the CL understanding of 'tools', we need to acknowledge that these are of a different kind than most qualitative methods, precisely because they are technologically implemented and largely automated. Related to the criticism that CDS implements CL methods not well understood (see below), we should not downplay the time and effort involved in learning how to use these methods. This is not simply about learning how to use the software so that some results can be generated; it is largely about "develop[ing] the type of mindset that can appreciate the potential of the method, recognize its limitations, hone [our] analytical skills and refine [our] discovery procedures, so that ultimately [we] are able to fashion your research designs accordingly" (Mautner 2016a, 171). Mautner's point is well taken inasmuch as the challenge is not simply to apply the methods but to know them well enough to develop meaningful research designs in the first place—needless to say, that is exactly the point at which methodological issues arise with integrating CL methods into CDS.

Taking the argument even further, Anthony suggests that critical discourse analysts should not "neglect the intricacies of programming", because when it comes to powerful software "even basic choices will have effects" (Anthony 2013, 149). This includes essential differences between available tools (or settings to be chosen), such as the respective tool's operationalization of 'word'. However, Anthony's solution, i.e. that analysts should program corpus tools themselves (Anthony 2013, 154–55), may be overstated and impracticable—after all, this might easily lead to an even greater heterogeneity of settings, and likely less transparency, than we already have (Mautner 2016a, 171).

2.2.1 Corpus and Discourse

Corpus Linguistics has been described as a methodology so flexible and broadly compatible (Mautner 2011, 103) that it "can be aligned to any theoretical approach to language" (Thompson and Hunston 2006b, 8). However, given its emphasis on "comparing differences through counting, and creating rather than deconstructing categories", corpus linguistic research can also be seen as "incompatible" with the kind of post-structuralist theorizing that informs CDS (Baker 2006, 9). Although several theoretical aspects have been indicated as potential sites of conflict between theory-heavy CDS and theory-light CL, none are more pertinent than the conceptualization of 'discourse' and its relationship to the notion of 'corpora'. Since both have immediate methodological as well as practical consequences—i.e. they are by necessity if not always explicitly operationalized in empirical studies—corpus-based CDS need to address this issue.

Corpora are often defined in relation to 'text' or even as 'text collections'. To conceptualize their relationship, Sinclair (2004, 189) defines 'text' not in terms of semiotics or pragmatics but how texts are recontextualized in research practice: Researchers can know texts in their entirety, can locate all the phenomena in a given text accurately and have it at their fingertips. In contrast, he defines corpora as qualitatively distinct from having *n texts* in a collection of texts, because it entails a change of methodology: "a corpus in its characteristic mode is almost by definition outside this level of close reading and control". Unlike texts, corpora do not have a semiotically or pragmatically significant or intended beginning, middle or end. Indeed, the order of texts in a corpus may well be deliberately arbitrary unless tagged for date of production/publication. As Sinclair (2004, 189) puts it, "the whole point of making something a corpus rather than a collection of texts is in order to observe things which cannot be directly observed because they are too far apart, they are too frequent or infrequent, or they are only observable after some kind of numerical or statistical process". The key point of taking a corpus approach, and by implication of creating a corpus, is not the amount of language contained or the criteria of selection, but the mode of engagement with linguistic data: The corpus approach does not engage with the texts directly, as individual texts, but uses methods of indirect observation (frequency lists, collocators, concordancers, etc.). It is this shift in perspective that allows certain patterns to show through the specifics of texts and their variations (Sinclair 2004, 189). Remarkably, this definition holds several similarities to the notion of discourse, such as a focus on patterns above-the-text and regularities in language use among a speech community or in a field.

In contrast to Sinclair's data- and method-oriented conceptualization of corpora, discourse is generally defined in more abstract, theoretical terms in CDS: While corpus is clearly understood as an artefact (or tool) of linguistic research, discourse is theorized as socio-linguistic practice irrespective and outside of linguists' research activities. The most straightforward way to relate discourse to corpora is to take a view of 'discourse as corpus', i.e. seeing corpora as *representing* discourse/s to a certain extent. Clearly, this view does not match conceptions of 'discourse as the totality of regularities' (Faulstich 2007, 484).

At this point, it is helpful to recall Foucault's characterization of discourses as practices which systematically form the objects of which they speak (Foucault 1972/1989, 49). The analytical level at which discursive regularities can be studied is thus social practice: perceptual codes and structures, ways of ordering things, conscious and unconscious conceptual grids, categorizations and classifications. The anonymity of this conception can be daunting: Discourse in this sense is governed by rules that no one knows or is responsible for. In Michael Stubbs' (1996, 193) words: "We reproduce it, but piecemeal, and unintentionally. No one has designed the whole." In Stubbs' view, corpora are the ideal tool for analyzing discourse in this sense precisely because they are also situated at that level. Hence, corpora are seen as instrumental to empirically linking micro-level linguistic patterns (e.g. lexical choices) and macro-level social phenomena (e.g. racism), a relationship conceptualized as the former providing traces of the latter (Koller and Mautner 2004). In addition to leveraging the analysis to above-the-text level, corpus size is seen as particularly important to this end, as "recurrent discursive phenomena revealed through large corpora offer something of 'an observable record' of unconscious behaviors through which dominant meanings are discursively reproduced" (D. Hunt and Harvey 2015, 135).

Indeed, using corpora in Sinclair's sense has struck a chord with many in CDS who, like Koteyko (2006), feel that if we really want to study the archive in the Foucauldian sense, we need much larger text samples than critical discourse analysts have traditionally studied (using qualitative methods). The argument is that in order to study "the rules (practices, technologies) which make a certain statement possible to occur and others not at particular times, places and institutional locations" (Foucault 1972/1989, 21), we need corpora that represent language use in a particular time, place and social context. Clearly, this requires either specialized, purpose-built corpora or general corpora that are tagged so as to facilitate contextualized analysis (see below).

As a consequence, the principled compilation of texts in the form of corpora should thus follow a number of criteria that make a corpus not merely a tool or a different way of saying 'data', but a concept in CDS. There have, of course, already been considerations along those lines: According to Busse and Teubert (1994, 14) corpora represent a particular discourse (i.e. are a 'segment' of that discourse) if they deal with a particular theme, object, knowledge complex or concept; are socially interconnected (specifically through the purpose of communication or field of social action); are defined by parameters such as time period, geographical area or text type; and are characterized by implicit or explicit intertextual or contextual relationships. If we accept the latter point as integral, tagging a corpus' texts in terms of chronology or other documentation pertinent to the research interest becomes an essential characteristic of discourse as corpora (Koteyko 2006, 149).

To return once more to Foucault's characterization of discourses as practices which systematically form the objects of which they speak (Foucault 1972/1989, 49): This broadly inclusive view has been read in various ways, with conceptualizations of discourse centring on different topics (e.g. unemployment, war), types of language use (e.g. genres), social groups (e.g. presidents, judges, students), social settings (e.g. the workplace, education), media (e.g. newspapers) and contexts of production/reception (e.g. online); in contrast, they have also been defined as specific ways of speaking about the world (e.g. the discourse of *refugees as a burden*) or serving a particular function (e.g. *medicalizing* discourse) (D. Hunt and Harvey 2015, 135). Significantly, all of these conceptualizations but the final two are open to being operationalized on the assumption that corpora can be built to represent discourses.[2] This does not do away with the need to define 'discourse' in advance of studying discourse, as the different conceptions outlined above translate into different approaches to compiling and sampling texts for corpus-building, nor does it mean that any collection of texts will represent the discourse we want to study. Thus, the fundamental conceptualization of the relationship between 'discourse' and 'corpus' requires reflection and explication beyond the fact that CL has developed rigorous approaches to compiling corpora and beyond the fact that the use of larger corpora was one of the key impulses driving the integration of CL methods into CDS in the 1990s.

Indeed, all the conceptualizations of 'discourse' listed above can be found in corpus-based CDS. For instance, D. Hunt and Harvey (2015, 134) define discourses in relation to corpora as representing "the situated linguistic behavior of a socio-cultural group or groups". They go on to indicate that, accordingly, corpora are compiled *from* the discourses of individuals and organizations whose "ideological inclinations [and] agendas for reproducing forms of social dominance" we want to study (D. Hunt and Harvey 2015, 135). Significantly, this approach requires the use of specialized, even purpose-built corpora for CDS (Bednarek and Caple 2014, 136), as has been demonstrated in numerous studies combining topic/medium/genre/social setting as criteria (e.g. *Europe* in Mautner

[2]The different approaches to 'discourse' carry great implications for combining methodologies. For instance, Baker (2006, 86) refers to concordance lines as "demonstrat[ing] the discourses of refugees described above [...]" or showing "a range of discourses: refugees as victims, as the recipients of official attempts to help, as a natural disaster and as a criminal nuisance". This implies a view of discourse as a specific way of talking about a subject matter, here refugees, rather than discourse as all language use on a given topic, in a specific medium, genre, context etc.

2000; *refugees*, *asylum seekers*, *immigrants*, and *migrants* in Baker et al. 2008; *Islam* and *Muslims* in Baker et al. 2013).

In such cases, the sampling procedure by which texts are chosen from a whole population of texts, e.g. newspaper articles from *The Guardian*, and the linguistic operationalization of the topic of interest are crucial. The work of Costas Gabrielatos has dealt extensively with this methodological issue and I can only summarize some key concerns here: Conceptually, such corpus compilation requires the selection of a *query term* or *query terms*, which may be used individually or in combination, e.g. to select texts that contain either *Islam* or *Muslim* as opposed to texts that contain both *Islam* and *Muslim*. As both Chowdhury (2010, 170) and Gabrielatos (2007) indicate, there is a trade-off between 'precision' and 'recall' or rather a tension between 'incompleteness' and 'noise'. On the one hand, corpora in which all included texts are relevant to the topic of interest may not contain all relevant texts within the population; on the other hand, corpora that contain all relevant texts available may also overreach and include irrelevant texts. In practice (e.g. Gabrielatos and Baker 2006), mention of the word "Islam" may be irrelevant to the study if it occurs as part of a name; and we might miss texts that do refer to Islam but only through the label "believer" or "Muhamad". Variant spellings, in particular, can present a problem here. In order to tackle such issues, researchers compiling a specialized corpus must initially define what their corpus would ideally contain and only then set their parameters, considering what is feasible in the circumstances (Sinclair 2004, 81).

2.2.2 The Quantitative-Qualitative Divide

In a controversial argument, Fairclough (2015, 20) asserts that "[c]orpus linguistics simply counts words and co-occurrences between words in a corpus", which is a gross simplification of the variety of statistical procedures applied and developed in CL, some of which are straightforward and some of which are highly complex. In and of itself, however, this does not automatically void Fairclough's (2015, 20) conclusion that the "widely-used term 'corpus linguistic analysis' is a misnomer: corpus linguistics is not analysis, it is a tool which can serve analysis." Without commenting on Fairclough's demotion of the entire field of CL (note his reference to corpus linguistics as such, not its methods) to a potential tool of discourse analysists, I would argue that this seemingly damning statement could be applied to any method, procedure or categorization scheme. They are all 'tools' in the sense that analysis is never in the means but in the using of those tools, the interpretation of their results. By that measure, corpus linguistic methods are as much (or as little) analysis as any other methods in the toolkit of CDS. It seems likely, however, that the actual distinction on Fairclough's mind here is that between qualitative and quantitative methods.

Contributions to the debate on using CL methods in CDS almost always include an appeal to the *quantitative* nature of the former as well as to the benefits of combining quantitative with *qualitative* methods. In this dichotomous opposition, quantitative approaches are frequently linked to objectivity, researcher control, experimental and reliable results, offering hard, replicable data and thus generalizable analyses; in contrast, qualitative methods are seen as more naturalistic, descriptive, process-oriented, valid, holistic and deep in terms of data, but also subjective and restricted to ungeneralizable single case analyses (Lazarton 2002, 33). Arguments for using CL methods in CDS sometimes seem to be premised on the assumption that Corpus Linguistics is a purely quantitative approach. Such a portrayal may well be more rhetoric than substance (e.g. the phrasing in Freake et al. 2011, 27); after all, it does raise the stakes and highlights the accomplishment of integrating CL methods into CDS. Nevertheless, this dichotomy is a misrepresentation: CL was never purely quantitative, even if the most prominent results produced by CL methods are quantified (e.g. frequencies or statistical relations); nor did CDS abstain from stating frequencies or quantities. As Paul Baker (2006, 175) points out, any corpus linguistic study "involves a great deal of human choice at every stage: forming research questions, designing and building corpora, deciding which techniques to use, interpreting the results and framing explanations for them." The remainder of this section discusses the arguably substantive (and perhaps growing) qualitative aspects of CL methods as used in CDS.

Given the breadth of Baker's position quoted above, one might insist that even though the overall research design involves subjective and qualitative elements, CL methods if considered in isolation are still purely quantitative. While this is true of the computations performed by the software after pushing certain buttons, this would reduce CL methodology to entirely automatic procedures in which the researcher becomes superfluous. Moreover, a number of CL methods explicitly integrate qualitative elements, such as the grouping of lexical items into semantic categories (e.g. for collocates of "refugee" into *quantification, movement, attempts to help, tragic circumstances, criminals* and *nuisance*, see Baker 2006, 79–85). Similarly, the concepts of "key categories" (rather than "keywords") and "cumulative keyness" (Baker 2004, 353)—which seek to address the problem that lower frequency synonyms tend to be overlooked in a keyword analysis (Baker 2006, 143)—rely on semantic groupings based on qualitative analyses that can account for homonymy, contextualized meaning etc. In this approach, the frequencies of related words increase their cumulative keyness as a category: Cumulative keyness is calculated after adding the grouped items' separate frequencies using, as for regular keywords, log-likelihood or chi-square calculations (Baker 2004, 355).

Another qualitative aspect in CL are decisions on cut-off points in, e.g., frequency lists or concordance lines to be investigated more closely (Baker 2006, 179). The apparent arbitrariness of selecting, say, the 10 or 20 most frequent items may obscure decisions based on convenience—in which case an explicit qualitative approach would be preferable. A related issue is the choice from the wide variety of available statistical measures, algorithms, and related software settings. Such decisions, if not explicated, "might mean that data can be subtly 'massaged' in order to reveal results that are interesting, controversial or simply confirm our suspicions" (Baker 2006, 179). While Baker himself argues above all for consistency in using, e.g., a log-likelihood test with a range of −4 to +4 for collocational analysis, an alternative approach is to integrate and explicate qualitative perspectives on the resulting choices. Thus, using the mutual information measure for collocations could be based on its tendency to foreground low frequency lexical words that reveal a wider range of prosodies (Baker 2006, 179), *if and only if* a wider range of items are examined.

Arguably the most obviously qualitative aspects in CL methodology relate to the actual analysis (rather than selection) of concordance lines (e.g. Baker et al. 2008; Baker et al. 2013). Again, this can be downplayed or acknowledged: Numerous articles, in describing this stage of analysis, simply refer to a "close reading" or "close look" at concordances without explicating the qualitative method involved, if any. How a qualitative method can be meaningfully integrated here, then, is much more significant than whether we should "switch hats", as Fairclough (2015) puts is, between quantitative and qualitative methods. If, for instance, the overall framework of a corpus-based study is the Discourse-Historical Approach, the qualitative analysis should not simply take place within that framework but use an identifiable and accountable method, procedure, categorization etc.[3] Otherwise, 'analyzing concordance lines' becomes a readily available but unspecific token statement, inviting criticism from all sides.

Indeed, I would argue that the way in which we approach co-text (concordance lines, extended concordances or entire texts retrieved by CL tools) around specific lexical patterns identified by CL tools should be a key point of interest in the debate on 'combining' or 'integrating' quantitative and qualitative methods in CDS. Strategies for doing so should therefore be developed and existing practices at this intersection should be scrutinized. Even if it remains a contested space in research design and practice, it should not be targeted for polemic.

2.3 A Brief History of Corpus Linguistics in Critical Discourse Studies

The integration of CL methods into CDS can be traced back to the 1990s, with publications by Caldas-Coulthard (1995), Hardt-Mautner (1995), Krishnamurthy (1996), and Stubbs (1996, 2001) taking initial steps to demonstrate the usefulness of corpus approaches for the field. Amidst the many publications that followed, three strands of pioneering work on integrating CL into CDS stand out (Baker and McEnery 2015, 7): firstly, work conducted at the University of Birmingham by Stubbs, Hunston, Louw, Krishnamurthy, Teubert, and Caldas-Coulthard; a second strand of work, perhaps more closely connected to schools of critical discourse analysis, is linked to Lancaster University and the collaboration between

[3] One frequently used qualitative approach at this level is Systemic Functional Grammar (e.g. Goatly 2004; Thompson and Hunston 2006b; Coffin et al. 2004; Hunston 2013).

Baker, McEnery, Gabrielatos, and Wodak; the third strand is linked to the University of Bologna and Corpus Assisted Discourse Studies developed by Partington, Taylor, and Marchi, among others (e.g. Partington, Duguid, and Taylor 2013).

Looking back recently, Partington asserted that "the alliance of corpus techniques to traditional close readings" constitutes nothing less than a "revolution" (Partington 2015, 242). Indeed, advances in home computing power, software technology, and the increase of readily available digital text as well as methodological development, often by trial and error, have led to strongly integrated approaches. Baker et al. (2013, 27), for instance, advocate beginning with context-based analysis of a topic via history, politics, culture or etymology before establishing research questions and building specialized corpora, then moving from broad quantitative analyses to more fine-grained qualitative analyses and back again. Indeed, most methodologically pronounced work in CDS that integrates CL methods today uses some form of cyclical process that involves multiple qualitative and quantitative steps ("shunting" back and forth, as it were, see Morley 2010, 10).

2.3.1 Linked by Commonalities and Shared Goals

While the differences between discourse analysis and corpus linguistics are sometimes emphasized—e.g. in highlighting either the synergies to be gained from combining them (triangulation) or in discussing the potential inconsistencies which an eclectic combination of methods might cause—and sometimes backgrounded—e.g. by assuming they are a 'natural fit' or 'perfect bedfellows'—several remarkable commonalities should be acknowledged in any such discussion (for a similar argument, see Mautner 2011, 90).

First, neither discourse studies nor corpus linguistics today are monolithic. Both fields comprise multiple theoretical models and methods of analysis. As Charles et al. (2009b, 1) put it: "Within both traditions there is diversity". Both fields are frequently, even routinely combined with other strands of linguistic theory and research, most prominently Systemic Functional Linguistics—so much so that one might consider SFL a connecting bridge in some research settings (see, e.g., Thompson and Hunston 2006b; Charles et al. 2009a). The crucial commonality here is that corpus linguistics is based on the assumption "that language variation is both systematic and functional" (Gray and Biber 2011, 141).

Second, discourse analysis and corpus linguistics can be said to share a 'common ancestry'. Mautner (2016b) recognizes such a shared point of origin in Firth's (1935, 13) conception of a "contextual and sociological technique" for studying focal words or "keywords", a term similarly used by one cultural studies' founding figures, Raymond Williams (Williams 2000). Indeed, the work of both Stubbs and Sinclair links to Williams in seeking to "make ideological structures tangible" (Stubbs 1996, 21; see also 166–72). Following from this goal, both approaches are concerned with authentic language use, i.e. language in use, and are interested in patterns and regularities, e.g. the traces of social norms and conventions, rather than rules. Specifically, Firth saw language as a 'social reflector', regarding the semantic phenomena on which CL was to focus as sociologically symptomatic. The corresponding research program, so Firth, would study "the detailed contextual distribution of sociologically important words" (Firth 1935, 10, see also Mautner 2011, 90).

Decades later, the work of Michael Stubbs explicated the potential of CL in this respect, convinced that it was to provide an empirical counterpart to theories of social constructivism: CL would allow us to observe, with the help of computational technologies, those "areas of meaning" in which "recurrent phrasings" are used "to express cultural knowledge and where it has significant resources for categorising things" (Stubbs 2006, 32). The aim of studying the lexicogrammatical and phraseological patterns of language in use as an approach to studying social patterns at large is not only similar to approaches in CDS, it also assumes (but does not theorize) a similar link between the micro-level of linguistic analysis and the interpretation of such results on the macro-level of social reality. Stubbs' basic conception of this link—"No terms are neutral. Choice of words expresses an ideological position." (Stubbs 1996, 107)—will seem at once familiar to discourse analysts and too narrowly focused on lexical phenomena:

> Native speakers of a language have thousands of collocates stored in their memories and hearing or reading one word may often prime another, due to all of our previous experiences of hearing that word in a particular context. From an ideological point of view, collocates are extremely interesting, as if two words are repetitiously associated with each other, then their relationship can become reified and unquestioned. (Stubbs 1996, 195)

This particular issue will be discussed below (Sects. 2.4.11 and 2.4.12), but it is worth noting that Stubbs' elaboration of this link beyond the simple observation of collocations, i.e. in terms of 'priming' or 'discourse prosody', remains one of the key elements in integrating CL in DS. For instance, Mautner (2005) holds that the semantic associations revealed via the analysis of concordances can be used "to establish lexical or discursive profiles of culturally and sociologically important words".

Significantly, this conceptualization was also cause for Stubbs' own warning of the "dangers" inherent in relying exclusively on large corpora. While they do offer "vast new resources for studying vocabulary", he argued, great care is "required in interpreting data which can be collected with such ease". In particular, he stressed that the "kinds of semantic development and cultural influence studied by Williams" would be invisible to computational methods alone (Stubbs 1998, 10).

2.3.2 Linked by a Response to Criticism

Many of the methodological arguments for integrating CL methods in CDS (then CDA) were informed and motivated by critique of the latter's empirical approach (Mautner 2011, 88). The developments covered in this section were thus driven, not only but prominently, by a number of criticisms leveled sometimes at CDS in general and sometimes at specific methods of data collection, analysis or interpretation. This is the second broad narrative about how and why CDS and CL might work well together: Unlike the "commonalities" frame summarized above, this one begins with CDS as deficient or limited in some respects—the tone of criticism varies—and posits CL methods as a way address these limitations. Although this frame first emerged in the 1990s, it remains the dominant narrative on why to integrate CL methods in CDS today. This is often phrased as a way not only of improving the approach but of countering criticism or improving credibility: The use of corpus linguistic methods, writes Prentice (2010, 406), "allows the criticisms levelled at particular methods of CDA to be addressed"; more specifically, Baker et al. (2013, 25) extol the advantages of studying larger amounts of data as making findings "more credible", and Baker and McEnery (2015, 5) seem acutely aware of the need to "reassure readers that our analysists are actually presenting a systematic analysis, rather than writing a covert polemic".

The initial debate informing this frame took place in the mid-1990s, arguably led by Henry Widdowson (e.g. 1995a, b, 1996) and Roger Fowler (1996), drawing responses from Fairclough (1996) and Stubbs (1997, 2001b), among others. Roughly at the same time, Stubbs and Gerbig (1993), Caldas-Coulthard (1993), Hardt-Mautner (1995), Krishnamurthy (1996), and Stubbs (1998) were already working towards a practicable integration of CL methods into CDS to solve many of the problems identified. The controversy flared up again some ten years later with Widdowson (2004), to whom Wodak (2006d) and others responded. Most of the points raised then have remained relevant and are also addressed in recent publications, specifically the qualitative approach to linguistic analysis and its limited data samples, presumably resulting in "fragmentary [and] exemplificatory" analyses (Fowler 1996, 8), and a more general lack of 'academic rigor' that manifests in 'cherry-picking' in data selection and analysis. These limitations are seen as confirming researcher bias, meaning that the analysis is influenced by the researcher's own agenda and ultimately shaped by the desired result (Widdowson 1996, 2000a, b).

Stubbs (1997) too criticized CDA for their lack of representativeness in using short or fragmentary texts and selecting data without clear, reproducible criteria as well as for interpreting results without comparing them to larger norms or patterns in language use. Koller and Mautner (2004, 216), in recalling their own motivations in the 1990s, argue that it was the decision to analyze larger bodies of texts that ultimately made the qualitative methodology used in CDA less suitable and "called for an alternative analytical procedure, combining the use of concordance programs with CDAs traditional qualitative analysis". In a review of three edited collections of CDA studies, Widdowson (1998) had strongly condemned CDA analyses for being "resolutely uncritical of [their] own discursive practices" (151) and thus little more than "the record of whatever partial interpretation suits your own agenda" (148); yet he had exempted studies which used CL in their discourse analysis, arguing that their interpretations were "grounded in systematic language description" (148). In perhaps more generous terms, Partington (2015, 223) has recently affirmed that "[u]sing corpus techniques in discourse analysis can obviate the Observer effect".

As is readily discernable from this brief glimpse of the debate, much of the immediate criticism was geared specifically towards—or at least invited—quantitative methods as a solution to the issues identified. This has given rise to views of CL as a fix-all for CDS, often without attending to the problems potentially caused by combining the two approaches or CL's own limitations. The former was over-shadowed by enthusiasm for the 'synergies' to be gained and a pragmatic attitude focused on combining only methods. This is exemplified by Cheng's (2012) concern with "marrying the qualitative methods of CDA [...] and the quantitative CL methodology" or Orpin's (2005, 39) focus on deciding "which aspects of the CDA approach can be best served by corpus analysis". Rarely has this pragmatic view been complemented with considerations of the theoretical and conceptual compatibility of the two approaches. The latter, i.e. CL's own limitations, is addressed by those researchers who accept that quantitative methods per se do not guarantee or even increase objectivity vis-à-vis qualitative methods (Mautner 2011, 105), and that researcher reflexivity remains a strong necessity despite the integration of quantitative methods (e.g. Baker et al. 2013, 24–25).

2.4 The Methodological Argument

Despite two strong narratives supporting the integration of CL methods into CDS, the current status of such integration remains disputed. Mautner (2011, 83) sees a growing conviction that CL methods can make a valuable contribution to studies principally grounded in CDS but warns of hastily claiming that CL has already become a fixed part of the "methodological canon" of CDS. In the following, I engage with arguments on

Table 2.1 Benefits, risks, and general limitations of CL methods in CDS

Benefits	Risks of integration	General limitations
Mitigating research bias	Lack of understanding	Decontextualizing data
Increasing representativeness	Shallow integration	Semiotic impoverishment
Preventing cherry-picking	Potential incompatibilities	Bias toward lexical phenomena
Increasing reproducibility	Data gluttony	Failure to address higher levels of linguistic practice
		Over-emphasis on statistics
		Revealing the obvious
		Sham-objectivity

the level of methodology and research design in three broad groups: (1) benefits, i.e. arguments that support the integration of CL in CDS insofar as they identify a weakness in qualitative CDS that can be addressed by CL methods, (2) risks, i.e. arguments that have been raised specifically against the integration of CL into CDS, and (3) general limitations, i.e. arguments that address general weaknesses of CL methods that would, if left unattended, also affect corpus-based CDS. Within these three groups, the arguments can be identified as in Table 2.1.

2.4.1 Mitigating Researcher Bias

Perhaps the most fundamental critique voiced against traditional, qualitative CDS is that they simply confirm the researcher's preconceptions and can only produce ideologically desirable results, partly because of the openly political stance taken by critical discourse analysts (see van Dijk 1998, 11 on the discourse analyst as an "activist" of "applied ethics") and partly because of its lack of methodological rigor in data selection and analysis. Indeed, Widdowson (1995a, b) has linked the two, arguing that strong political commitment aimed at unveiling the role of language in maintaining existing power relations to the advantage of dominant groups negatively influences methodological rigorousness.

While objectivity remains a practical impossibility due to the subjective nature of all human decision-making (Burr 1995), this does not mean we should abandon our efforts to reach what is better described as intersubjective plausibility: to avoid bias or, where impossible or in conflict with CDS's critical agenda, to achieve a high degree of transparency and reflectivity. However, as Mautner (2011, 88) duly notes, CDS in particular seem to be vulnerable to this form of critique precisely because they so actively and clearly declare their political position where other forms of analysis tend to obfuscate.

The resulting argument is that, even if bias is not entirely avoidable when conducting social research, CDS must strive to be credible and convincing, separating themselves from polemic, not despite but precisely because they have a political agenda and want to make a difference. In the words of Paul Baker,

> any analytical tools and methods that are rigorous and grounded in scientific principles such as representativeness, falsification, data-driven approaches, using statistical approaches to test hypotheses and a desire to provide a full picture of representation (not just the negative cases) can only serve to help to improve CDA's standing, ultimately making its findings more influential. (Baker 2012, 255)

From a methodological point of view, the lack of rigor in CDS is seen as a failure to provide the necessary checks and balances on unavoidable subjectivity, leading critics and practitioners alike to suggest that fixing such methodological limitations should be possible without abandoning the critical stance informing CDS (e.g. Baker and McEnery 2015, 8). In short, corpus linguistic approaches have been discussed as an effective way to facilitate higher levels of intersubjectivity and systematicity as well as consistency in the use of tools, resulting in more robust and valid findings (Lukac 2011, 191). This relates particularly to interpretation in qualitative analyses itself, on which CDS traditionally depend heavily but not always systematically (Lin 2014, 226).

The effects of researcher bias in CDS are sometimes visible in "under-analysis through summary", attributing beliefs or policies to the speaker prior to analysis and thereby "changing the object of analysis even before the analysis starts in earnest" (Antaki et al. 2003). It is similarly present in "underanalysis by taking sides", when analysts offer their own political stance towards the quoted text in lieu of analysis, whether they align themselves with or critically distance themselves from it. In addition, such practices are likely to flatten discursive complexity if the analyst selects illustrative quotations merely "for the rhetorical effect of appealing to the readers as co-sympathisers or co-scolders" (Antaki et al. 2003). Researcher bias may also manifest cognitive biases in the scope of the study or the sampling process. These related phenomena are sometimes labelled as "cherry picking" (see below) to indicate that more emphasis is given to data and/or results that confirm initial assumptions than to those that contradict them (Gabrielatos and Duguid 2014; McEnery and Gabrielatos 2006). Stubbs makes a similar argument about using computers "as instruments of observation and memory", helping considerably not only with representativeness or coverage, but also making it "more difficult to overlook inconvenient instances, and are to that extent a move towards descriptive neutrality" (Stubbs 1996, 154).

In looking toward corpus linguistic methodology as providing "checks and balances", as Mautner (2016a) puts it, on our own biases as researchers, we need to avoid the naïve view that these are entirely objective or even more objective simply because they are (largely) quantitative (see below); we also need to be specific as to which effects a particular method is supposed to counter or mitigate. Baker (2006, 11) concretely identifies cognitive biases related to political positions, including so-called confirmation bias, the primacy effect or the hostile media effect (by which media coverage may be consistently perceived as being biased against one's own side of a controversial issue). By engaging with corpora, Baker (2006, 12) argues, we can "place a number of restrictions on our cognitive biases", making it "less easy to be selective about a single newspaper article when we are looking at hundreds of articles." His hope (sic) is that overall patterns and trends will show through, thanks to larger data samples and quantification of linguistic phenomena (Baker 2006, 12). Indeed, this advantage has been linked to Firth's and Williams' "intuitive" approach (see above), which it would replace with a means to more or less objectively identify "widespread patterns of naturally occurring language and rare instances, both of which may be overlooked in a small-scale analysis" (Baker 2004, 346).

Specifically, it may be possible to avoid confirmation bias (e.g. finding racist discourse in likely places) through increased corpus reach and/or consulting a reference corpus (Baker 2006, 17). However, as Baker (2012) is ready to admit, this potential solution faces several challenges, among them finding an adequate reference corpus that is not itself biased towards the topic, genre or period it is to be compared against. Moreover, it begs the question of how to operationalize value judgements or critique in term of quantitative methods. In short, this solution makes it necessary to quantify the thing potentially criticized, e.g. newspaper reporting bias or racism in reporting. Baker has approached this conundrum in terms of "acceptable bias", and his methodological experiments[4] conclude that even a purely quantitative answer would rely heavily on subjective decisions of the researcher, e.g. selecting a particular newspaper as a benchmark for "responsible" reporting on Islam, then judging other newspapers according to how strongly they deviate. This comparison would include more decisions on criteria, using either overall frequency of negative representation, proportional frequency, relative size of the social group being represented, the strength of negativity or the context of representation (Baker 2012, 254).

Other methodological innovations have targeted particular aspects of researcher bias, including computing "key keywords" to avoid focusing on salient items at the cost of representativeness (Baker 2004, 350). A key keywords list reveals how many texts a keyword appears in as key. Appropriate reference corpora may also help avoid bias and/or confirm critique in terms of comparing the collocational strength of lexical items. A general language corpus can allow us to establish the associations that are generally embedded in words due to their continual pairing with other words and thus show that a certain word or phrase contains bias ('exposing' its hidden collocations) and explain why (Baker and McEnery 2005, 223).

Discourse prosody, as a corpus linguistics inspired concept attended by specific methodology, may nonetheless provide a way to test and limit subjectivity. In essence, the notion captures the observation that the fre-

[4]Baker (2012) reports on a methodological experiment testing the reliability of qualitative/quantitative methods by using a "recursive model", moving "back and forth between quantitative and qualitative forms of analysis, with each stage informing the subsequent stage" (Baker 2012, 247).

quent collocates of a word effectively become part of its meaning. As Mautner (2016a, 171) puts it, focusing on discourse prosody can open "a window on values and attitudes present throughout a discourse community rather than held only by individual researchers." Rather than our intuitive judgement of evaluative meanings associated with a particular choice of words, corpus-based collocational information can provide evidence of evaluative meanings widely shared in a discourse community (Stubbs 2001b, 2). Indeed, much of the appeal of CL in CDS hinges on the notion of prosody (e.g. Jaworska and Krishnamurthy 2012) as it is a concept uniquely suited to the interests of CDS, linking directly to the assumption (shared by CDS and CL) that no choice of words is innocent: "The semantic prosodies express attitudinal and pragmatic meaning; they are the junction of form and function. The reason why we choose to express ourselves in one way rather than another is coded in the prosody, which is an obligatory element of a lexical item" (Sinclair 2004, 174). However, this solution may be complicated by domain- or genre-specific patterns, as suggested by O'Halloran (2007) in developed the notion of "register prosody". According to this argument, a word like 'erupt' may be neutralized in a specific social setting, e.g. newspaper reporting, despite its general association with natural catastrophe.

While some researchers continue to appeal to true objectivity through quantification and computer-aided analysis (e.g. O'Halloran 2017), others such as Baker and McEnery (2015, 8) acknowledge that CL studies suffer from "less conspicuous" forms of bias. For one, many of its methods such as frequency lists, keywords, collocates, and concordances focus on *difference* and therefore tend to ignore *continuity* or *stability*. For another, the analytical process itself allows—even requires—researcher decisions (and thus invites interference and bias). This pertains to software settings, search parameters to be selected, choices about which keywords or concordance lines to focus on, etc. The latter can be particularly subjective, as Baker and McEnery (2015, 9) point out, and highlight the qualitative element in corpus-based analysis.

In summary, CL methods can be integrated into CDS to mitigate aspects of researcher bias, in particular the effects of confirmation bias in data selection and the interpretation of results, but they can also serve to test and verify researcher intuition. Part of this benefit comes from being able to consider larger amounts of data in the shape of corpora, enabling the researcher to identify patterns across a larger stretch of discourse (see the following section). Significantly, this benefit will depend, first and foremost, on the quality of corpus building and selection criteria. However, quantified patterns are simply transformed data and still need to be interpreted and evaluated, making any such conclusions potentially subject to human bias. In Paul Baker's words, this "does not mean we should throw out the baby with the bath water and abandon CL processes within CDA research, but we ought to be careful in overstating the ability of CL to reduce researcher bias" (Baker 2012, 255). Indeed, we would be doing CDS a disservice to trust solely in the 'objectifying power' of the quantitative, computer-assisted analyses offered by CL, neglecting our commitment to researcher reflexivity (Watt 2007; Attia and Edge 2017).

2.4.2 Increasing Representativeness

Many of the calls to integrate CL methods into CDS relate—directly or indirectly—to increasing the amount of data that can be covered in the analysis and the representativeness of results thus obtained. Both are straightforward and admirable goals in their own right and were embraced by critical discourse analysts seeking to extend the scope of their analyses. Beginning in the 1990s, researchers thus turned to corpus linguistics not only in response to criticism but from the need to tackle larger data sets. As Hardt-Mautner (1995, 1) recalls, it was the "mismatch" between the analytical frame of CDA and the quantity of the data to be analysed that "led to the development of an alternative analytical procedure, combining the use of concordance programmes with CDA's traditional qualitative analysis". The previously only qualitative methodology of CDS had effectively limited analyses to small amounts of text, making them "theory-rich" but "data-poor". Enabling CDS to significantly broaden its empirical base thus remains a key argument for integrating CL methods (Mautner 2011, 89–90; 2016b, 157).

Here, too, the dominant narrative became "how corpus linguistics could help to overcome the limits of CDA" (Degano 2007, 362). The underlying criticism is that researchers in CDS, especially in its early stages, often selected a small number of texts or text fragments that could not be expected to reveal the "big picture" (Gabrielatos and Baker 2006), i.e. discourse patterns rather than a very limited number of specific instances (Koller and Mautner 2004). In a more critical tone, others have suggested that these texts might in fact be selected for their suitability in demonstrating a point; that, in other words, pre-existing assumptions about discourse pre-determine the choice of a small number of example texts, thus biasing the analysis to the point where it becomes a self-serving affirmation of beliefs. The criticism of "false survey" (Antaki et al. 2003) draws attention to criteria for selecting material for analysis, a challenge that also needs to be addressed in large-scale studies that include qualitative analyses of samples (Mautner 2011, 88; see "cherry picking" below). Although sometimes seen as a trade-off in which qualitative methods provide depth but lose breadth, while quantitative methods provide breadth but not detail (Hardt-Mautner 1995, 3), meaningful integration of both types of method in a single study should aim to provide balance.

With respect to increasing sample size and thereby also increasing representativity (even to the point of analyzing a complete dataset), findings will likely be more reliable and valid if shown across a larger dataset (Baker and Levon 2015, 222). In turn, this has led to questions if CL methods are useful for CDS analyzing relatively small corpora due to the effort involved in corpus building as well as insufficient data to show precisely those regularities that CL methods would be able to reveal (Mautner 2011, 107–8). It is also important to keep in mind that the size and composition of the corpus studied dictates the quality of all results that can be obtained, including their level of generality; although homogeneous, specialized corpora need not be as large as general language or reference corpora (Hardt-Mautner 1995, 23).

A further issue has been raised in connection with qualitative CDS focusing on a small number of texts: If those are all present-day texts (and this is more likely if the number of texts we can analyze is strongly limited by our methodology), then it may render CDS a-historical (Blommaert 2005, 137). Indeed, quantitative methods can make it easier to expand our perspective into the past, if data are available. And while the Discourse-Historical Approach (Reisigl and Wodak 2015), for instance, includes provisions for qualitative analyses to ensure that no discourse is analyzed outside its history, this aspect is worth considering in greater detail (see Chapter 5).

The benefits of using large data sets, however, go well beyond identifying patterns of language use and providing evidence for the extent of their spread. In combination with keyword methods, silences or especially rare language use in a particular discourse may also be identified in relation to an appropriate reference corpus (Baker and McEnery 2005, 198). In other words, systematically applied CL methods can guard against a focus that follows saliency (e.g. shocking or extreme positions, scandal, the breaking of taboos) at the cost of ignoring normalcy and normalization (Baker 2006, 88).

A pertinent example of how CL methodology and the critical interests of CDS come together in the analysis of large, representative data samples is the notion of discourse prosody and its operationalization. While the notions of 'lexical priming' and 'semantic prosody' relate to individual word choice, discourse prosody is built up through larger stretches of text (Stubbs 2001b; Baker 2006a; Jaworska and Krishnamurthy 2012). While the former can thus be studied through frequency or collocation calculations, i.e. on a purely lexical level, the latter requires the researcher to study concordance lines (S. Hunt 2015, 271) or expand the analysis to the text level—essentially a move from lexical to textual analysis (see below on lexical bias).

The prevalence of certain patterns in discourse prosody, when viewed as 'habituation' or the 'incremental effect of discourse', does not simply indicate the spread of a particular use of language. As Fairclough (2015, 45) argues with respect to the effects of media power: "[They] are cumulative, working through the repetition of particular ways of handling causality and agency, particular ways of positioning the reader, and so forth". More generally, repeated patterns (frequency and spread) are considered a shared reality of the respective discourse community (Stubbs 2001a, 215). Because a particular word or phrase can "trigger a cultural stereotype" (Baker et al. 2013, 26), such patterns can indicate the subtle ideological foundations of habitual ways of thinking and writing that only emerge across large data sets (Baker and Levon 2015, 230). From a methodological perspective, it is highly significant that such prosodies are built up incrementally, i.e. through a multitude of cases of association which are beyond the scope of any single text (Baker 2006, 13) but also beyond any one moment. As Gerbner et al. (1986) have shown, media reporting has a long-term effect that compounds over time as a result of repetition. On a conceptual level, this meshes well with the CDS view of discourse constituting and constituted by social reality. Inasmuch as this concerns the issue of addressing higher levels of linguistic practice than the lexical, a neglect of which CL is sometimes accused of, the potential link between discourse prosody and *topoi* is also addressed below.

2.4.3 Preventing Cherry-Picking by Downsampling

Critical Discourse Studies have often been criticized on grounds of "arbitrary text selection", especially as this seems to reinforce its alleged subjectivity (Widdowson 1995a, b, 1996, 2004; for responses see Koller and Mautner 2004, 225; Orpin 2005, 38; Partington 2004, 13; Baker 2012, 247). Some points of clarification are in order before proceeding: The phenomenon also known as "cherry-picking" does relate to subjectivity, e.g. picking highly salient texts that are likely to confirm views held by the researcher while also overlooking other, inconvenient evidence (on conformation bias, see Baker et al. 2013, 22), but that is exactly why it is *not arbitrary*. While it is certainly a weakness of any study to select texts without explicating criteria for doing so, this is a separate issue: One could, for instance, select data from a tabloid that has previously been shown to propagate racist views either to investigate its handling of a particular issue or its general outlook under new management, while openly acknowledging these criteria. To specify: The actual issues to avoid are a lack of transparency regarding selection criteria, a lack of explicating assumptions, and the narrow scope of research investigating only very few texts. While the first two aspects can be addressed well within qualitative CDS, the integration of CL methods may reinforce awareness of the need to specify selection criteria and hypotheses; but it is the final limitation that can be most clearly addressed by corpus-based methods.

In this respect, CL methods may offer studies that retain a strong qualitative aspect a distinct advantage by guiding qualitative analyses through *downsampling* of large corpora. As Baker and Levon (2015, 222) aptly put it, they can help analysts "pick the right cherries" by indicating "areas of interest" for further analysis (Gabrielatos and Baker 2006, 2008, 6; Baker et al. 2008, 284–85). Although downsampling might be regarded as a form of cherry-picking as well, that metaphor is usually used pejoratively and would not suit a transparent, informed selection procedure. Conventional wisdom is that there is a trade-off between the quantity of data and the level of detail in any analysis, but downsampling procedures that combine quantitative and qualitative methods can balance the stakes (regardless of whether CL methods are used in any other way to generate results; see Mautner 2011, 105 on this point).

Given CDS's qualitative roots, the strategy of "drilling down" (S. Hunt 2015, 283) at interesting points to analyze the text at micro-level, while it clearly requires time and effort, offers a good compromise for expanding the data analyzed on the quantitative level. It is also preferable to purely random selection and can be used in combination with other sampling methods. Regarding such methods, Potts (2015, 285) emphasizes the need for flexibility and a "keen understanding of the content of the corpus (including how it might help to address various hypotheses)". In brief, there is no singular CDS way of gathering, sampling, or downsampling data, "because choices have to be made in the light of the investigator's goals" (Wodak and Meyer 2009, 27; Mautner 167). This discussion can, however, benefit greatly from a general consideration of sampling methods:

(1) Random sampling, in which accident or a random number generator can be used, is popular in CL studies dealing with numerous concordance lines obtained from large corpora (e.g. Caldas-Coulthard and Moon 2010, 103).

(2) Probabilistic sampling may be unfeasible in CDS because the total of texts is unknowable, precluding a point of reference for choosing every n-th element for analysis.

(3) Saturation sampling, while suffering from a similar caveat, works well in combination with other forms of sampling to increase content validity (Phillips and Hardy 2002, 74; Francis et al. 2010, 1230). Sinclair (1999), for instance, recommends a combination of random and saturation sampling, i.e. selecting 30 concordance lines at random, analyzing their patterns, then moving on to another set of 30 randomly selected lines, then another and another, until the point of saturation is reached.

Hunston (2002, 52) and Baker (2006, 90) have adapted this approach for hypothesis testing: When a new pattern has been identified, more data is analyzed to determine whether the pattern occurs on a wider scale.

(4) Some work in CDS has also used theoretical sampling, originally developed for Grounded Theory, in first analyzing a small data set and then, in an iterative process, adding more data on the basis of insights gained from the previous set (Bauer and Aarts 2000, 31); this approach, like (5) snowball sampling and (6) convenience sampling, faces criticism for cherry-picking and does not address the issue of initial selection criteria.

Finally, (7) purposive sampling has often been used in CDS, e.g. in Wodak et al. (2009), to focus on specific texts, high-profile speakers, moments of acute crisis or prominent genres, e.g. because the socio-political or historical context indicates that they are especially pertinent to the research question (see also Abulof 2015, 83). This sampling method can either be followed by probabilistic downsampling once a finite corpus of texts has been established or by downsampling based on quantitative results obtained by CL methods.

Since such downsampling would be based on patterns identified by CL methods, this raises the question what kind of patterns and which methods could be used. The options range from the number of data points per period (e.g. newspaper articles per month), lemma frequency, collocational strength, and keywords to complex procedures to select a subset of data such as key keywords, semantic groups or consistent collocates (e.g. Gabrielatos and Baker 2008, 7). Even relatively simple statistical calculations can—through transforming the data and generating preliminary insight (Stubbs 1996, 232)—indicate complex patterns to investigate (Mautner 2011, 105; Baker 2004, 348). Each of these options has its uses and limitations: downsampling by frequency may invite criticism, especially if frequency is equated with saliency (Cheng and Ho 2017), while more complex or custom-built options require substantial effort (e.g. Baker et al. 2008; Gabrielatos and Baker 2008).

In considering these options, it is imperative that we keep in mind that a corpus approach does not automatically guard against the risks of cherry-picking or intentionally selecting data for analysis. First and foremost, we should elaborate the specific aims of downsampling in the context of our research and adopt, combine or modify existing methodology accordingly.

Clearly, qualitative approaches require critical reflection and explicit criteria, but so do corpus-based approaches. Perhaps the greater danger lies in blindly trusting in the overstated objectivity of numbers.

Pertinent cases in which CL methods can help operationalize selection criteria for CDS are the notions of *salience* and *typicality*. Care must be taken that features are not simply declared to be typical based on impressions, instead the typicality of a particular linguistic feature of interest can be determined in relation to a reference corpus. Although not popular in corpus-based CDS, the resource-intensive method of probabilistic topic modelling has been suggested to help downsample for qualitative analysis by ranking texts according to the extent to which they refer to the topics typical of the corpus (e.g. Abulof 2015, 83). In contrast, texts might be "singled out for analysis" precisely because they are *not* typical (Hardt-Mautner 1995, 3). Salience can thus be operationalized as atypicality (e.g. of register), emphasis or lexical innovation (Baker and McEnery 2005, 223; 2015, 2) to address criticism that CDS often focus on glaring examples but ignore counter-examples. However, after testing for precisely this effect in their corpus-based study of argumentative patterns, Freake et al. (2011) conclude that frequency-based downsampling did not reveal minority counter-discourses that were spotted only through qualitative analysis. In fact, the text containing the counter-discourse showed typical properties, highlighting the limitations of quantitative procedures in this context (Freake et al. 2011, 38).

Another limitation becomes evident in this context: limits on publication space, i.e. word or character limits, are a driving force behind random sampling in the form of cut-off points for word or collocation lists. Baker (2006, 178–79) takes this as a cue to suggest that transparency in reporting research outcomes, e.g. in the form of including full word lists or keyword lists as appendices to research, should allow the reader to "challenge or fine-tune the researcher's findings". Chapter 6 will take this line of argument further and argue that Open Science and interactive dashboards offer solutions to this particular impasse.

2.4.4 Increasing Replicability

With transparency and explicitness in corpus compilation, data selection, downsampling, and analytical procedure comes increased replicability, i.e. the possibility to not only retrace, appreciate, and question the steps taken by the analyst, but also to conduct similar if not identical studies. Some work in CDS, however, has been criticized for a lack of consistency and transparency in choosing analytical categories and methods. In a particularly scathing review, Widdowson (2004, 107) argued that "[a]nalysts simply take their pick of whatever grammatical and lexical features suit their pretextual purpose." While it is controversial whether research should be corpus-driven or not (see above), it is certainly true that CDS is methodologically open, to use a neutral phrase, which is variously seen as a strength or weakness (Mautner 2011, 89). This openness reinforces the need for explicit, accountable selection of categories and methods: The less transparent the analysis and the wider the space of interpretation without explicit criteria, the higher the risk of partiality (Widdowson 2004, 109).

As in other contexts, corpus linguistic methods have been suggested as a solution to these issues, largely because they are seen as (more) standardized and able to generate clear, comparable measurements through quantification. Corpus linguistic analyses, in other words, are easier to replicate (given transparency of the research design and access to the same data and tools; see Baker et al. 2013, 26) and can thus allow validating claims made by previous studies (Widdowson 2004; Abulof, 80). In particular, the corpus-driven (as opposed to corpus-based) approach has been posited as free from researchers' preconceived notions: In its pure form, this 2015is corpus linguistics without theory, previously established categories or models, "allow[ing] the research to be driven by whatever is found to be salient or frequent in the corpus" (Tognini-Bonelli 2001).

Some have rightly questioned the dichotomy of corpus-based versus corpus-driven approaches in CL, arguing that these are opposite points on a gradual distinction rather than absolutes. Indeed, a weak version of corpus-driven approach (e.g. accepting some social theory but limiting prior linguistic categorization) is not only compatible with but close to what some CDS embrace in the sense of abductive approaches, developing categories from the material (e.g. Wodak et al. 2009). Irrespective of whether and which CL methods are integrated into a particular study, CDS need not abandon their political position to increase replicability. But they do need to emphasize transparency in their methodological choices, the distinction between empirical findings, interpretation, and critique, as called for in a programmatic statement by Wodak as early as 1989 (Wodak 1989, xiv; on critique in discourse analysis, see Forchtner 2011; Herzog 2016).

2.4.5 The Risks of Using CL Methods not Well Understood

Given the range of arguments for using CL methods in CDS, it is little wonder that many researchers have eagerly taken up one or the other method. Regrettably, this has not always been done with in-depth knowledge of the respective method and associated software tools, the attendant methodological reflection, and the required transparency in presenting the study. Increasingly, therefore, critics have called attention to the fact that corpus linguistic principles and methods—in particular statistical, mathematical, and software-related operations—are often not fully understood or even misapplied by researchers in CDS; clearly, critical discourse analysts who use CL methods need to learn how to do so.

Many of these concerns relate to using software competently, choosing statistical settings on an informed basis or actually programming one's own software. At the most basic level, we should be aware that the "key limiting fact are capabilities of the software, as well as the features – mainly in terms of composition and annotation – of the electronically held corpora" (Mautner 2016a, 158). For an untagged corpus, for instance, that means that the program will count the occurrences of all strings with a space on either side as 'words', conflating homographs representing different word classes and different meanings, while also separating the elements of open-form compounds (in English) as well as phrasal verbs, idiomatic expressions, and other phrasal constructions. In any corpus, it means that frequency counts are directly and inevitably affected by the software's working definition of what constitutes a word (e.g. including or excluding numerals and symbols). "Frequency", as Hardt-Mautner (1995, 11) explains, thus "is a relative notion." In fact, since there is no universal standard of comparison, we risk a similar lack of transparency and eclecticism as decried in CDS.

Anthony (2013) has also pointed to the often unnoticed differences in the underlying mathematical models and assumptions that influence CL results, advocating against dabbling in CL without robust knowledge of the software and the algorithms it implements. In short, including CL methods in CDS should not be seen as a quick and easy fix; when it is, the complexity of the methods (and software tools) is regularly underestimated. Given the effort needed to collect and prepare texts into a corpus as well as learning to use the software, doing CL well is just as time consuming as qualitative analyses; doing both in an integrated fashion most definitely requires a greater commitment of resources and time (Baker 2006, 10).

These arguments can be taken as either a call for interdisciplinary cooperation within research teams (as embodied, e.g., by the collaborative work of Paul Baker, Costas Gabrielatos, Majid KhosraviNik, Michal Krzyzanowski, Tony McEnery, and Ruth Wodak, published in Baker et al. 2008) or for individual researchers to develop strong, hybrid competences (as embodied, e.g., in the work of Gerlinde Mautner, published in Mautner 2016a). Either way, this issue will certainly have substantial impact on the future of CDS.

2.4.6 Shallow Integration of CL Methods

A related argument, albeit from a different angle, is that CL methods are often not well integrated into CDS, i.e. that quantitative results are not meaningfully related to the aims or questions pursued by the respective research, or to results of qualitative analyses in the same study. In part, this criticism correctly targets the sometimes careless and overly enthused ways in which the relation between CL methods and CDS is superficially described or labelled rather than conceptualized. There is no shortage of studies that claim to 'combine' or 'integrate', 'blend' or 'mesh' qualitative and quantitative analyses, but often the nature and purpose of that relation for the overall research design remains unclear.

To be clear, this should not deter anyone from integrating CL methods into their CDS framework but encourage deliberate design and methodological reflection. As Stubbs (2001a, 142) reminds us, "[n]o single method can do everything", but any "method assemblage" (Law 2004, 41–42) should follow a clear goal and blueprint. After all, it is partly in order to increase transparency and replicability, and to reduce eclecticism that we turn to CL. The question of integration should thus be met with an explicit engagement with the principles and criteria of triangulation rather than a blanket appeal. The responses to this challenge have been myriad and range from the simple co-use of methods without indicating the type of integration or even sequence, the complementary use of methods on the same, partial or separate data sets, combinations to off-set respective limitations, the sequential use of methods in which one method's results inform another's implementation, to elaborate designs of multiple back-and-forth between qualitative ("close-up") and quantitative ("wide-angle") stages informing each other (Hardt-Mautner 1995, 15, 24).

Shallowness of integration can thus mean the unconnected co-use of qualitative and quantitative methods, but it can also mean interpretative positivism: direct connection is assumed between patterns identified in a corpus and the world-views in the discourse(s) it represents. Fowler and Kress's warnings from 1979 still ring true today: "there is no analytic routine through which a text can be run, with a critical description issuing automatically at the end" (Fowler and Kress 1979, 197). Without interpretation, statistics are just numbers. More recently, Fowler also argued that "[c]ritical interpretation requires historical knowledge and sensitivity, which can be possessed by human beings but not by machines" (Fowler 2005, 68). Ultimately, no machine-run procedure can be sufficient for the purposes of CDS, not just because of the endless permutations of historical and social contexts as well as research questions, but because "there is no constant relationship between linguistic structure and its semiotic significance" (Fowler 2005, 90). Failure to acknowledge this limitation leads to misinterpretations of data, e.g. taking at face value subversive or cynical language use, parody, and satire. Clearly, this risk is related to CL methods' bias toward lexical-phenomena and potential failure to address higher levels of linguistic practice (see below). As Hardt-Mautner (1995, 9) points out, the complete text in which a particular lexical phenomenon is identified must be accessed "to gauge the full ideological significance" of the phenomenon. She continues: "It is at this stage that the critical discourse analyst's traditional toolkit will once more come into its own."

2.4.7 Potential Incompatibilities Between CDS and CL

In a related argument, it has sometimes been asserted that the kind of questions CDS ask (and the methods they use to answer them) are not compatible with the kind of questions CL asks (and the methods it uses to answer them). The implication is that researchers who use CL methods are no longer doing 'proper' CDS and vice versa (see Fairclough 2015, 20–21). This argument, while clearly not applicable to all discourse analytical practice, points to relevant methodological concerns that need to be addressed. CL, as I have argued above, is not a quick and easy fix for the criticisms directed against CDS in the past.

It is true that, all too often, the two approaches' compatibility is simply asserted based on assumed utility, i.e. compatibility and utility are conflated (e.g. Abulof 2015, 80), without addressing questions of a specific combination's methodological implications. In general terms, corpus linguistics' quantitative dissection of texts-as-corpus, i.e. an amalgamation that is built on—indeed requires—the capacity to blend out textual boundaries, seems to conflict with CDS's aim of studying discourse at all levels of linguistic practice (Hardt-Mautner 1995, 3). While the former tend to isolate components of language use in the process of analysis, the latter emphasize context and the relation between linguistic forms or levels of linguistic practice.

A common response to this concern has been that CL can, after all, include the analysis of concordance lines, bridging the divide: "Corpus linguistics software offers both quantitative and qualitative perspectives on textual data, computing frequencies and measures of statistical significance, as well as presenting data extracts in such a way that the researcher can assess individual occurrences of search words, qualitatively examine their collocational environments, describe salient semantic patterns and identify discourse functions" (Mautner 2016a, 157). While Mautner's statement is entirely correct, it is worth taking a closer look at her wording here: She is describing *perspectives* on data *offered* by *software*, not research practice or CL methodology as such; she is describing what researchers *can* do with *data extracts presented* by the software. CL software does exactly that, and no more than that, with respect to qualitative analysis. In other words, CL software does not prevent qualitative analysis of concordance lines (older software may constrain it in terms of length), and it helps retrieve such data, but it contributes nothing to the actual qualitative analysis beyond that. Researchers still have to choose a separate approach, method or categories for doing said qualitative analysis, and until they do, very little can be said about the methodological compatibility or benefit of the specific combination of methods.

At this juncture, arguments regarding the weaknesses of CL methods and how to balance them come to the fore. With Partington (1998, 144), we could argue that corpus-based approaches are akin to a telescope, which allows one to zoom in on far-removed phenomena but loses the view of the entire night sky, or a microscope, which shows us individual cells but not the living organism in its habitat. With Baker (2006, 7), I would agree that Kenny's (2001) metaphor of the kaleidoscope is more convincing: The corpus-based approach can be both fascinating and disorienting as it allows us "to see textual patterns come into focus and recede again as others take their place."

With respect to methodological (in)compatibility, Mautner (2011, 109) provides a refreshingly distanced perspective, arguing that a comparative evaluation of methods should not play off the respective advantages and deficits but discuss each method's "enactment", i.e. the way in which it provides access to reality or, in deconstructivist terms, how each method constructs reality. Mautner mentions "decontextualization" and "recontextualization" of data in the course of analysis as examples of such processes (see below). The fact that different methods *deform the object of research* in different ways can thus be seen as the very foundation of any benefit to be gained from combining methods. From this perspective, I would argue, notions of compatibility or incompatibility have to be reframed as relative and highly specific to the research context.

2.4.8 The Temptations of Data Gluttony

Although associated mainly with statistics in general and, more recently, with big data, the notion of "data gluttony" has been linked to corpus-based approaches as well (Mautner 2016a, 172), specifically in data collection and corpus-building (text selection), but it might also apply to the already 'transformed data' that CL software offers in the form of frequency lists etc. Data gluttony describes tendencies to gather and/or include too much data in a study or to do so indiscriminately. But what is too much data? With so many of the arguments raised by the proponents of integrating CL methods into CDS hinging on studying more data, is there even such a thing as too much data? In part, the assumptions that 'more is always better', i.e. more data is always better data, and that 'the software can cope with more data just as well', i.e. there are no methodological disadvantages to more data, may stem from the enthusiasm of the newly converted. To critical discourse analysts with no or little formal training in CL, statistics or programming, the promises of fixing many of the problems of CDS by using CL methods on large corpora can, indeed, be tempting. The most obvious problem resulting from data gluttony is the amount of time and resources spent on collecting, preparing, and compiling the data into a corpus, realistically limiting how much time we can actually spend on analyzing it all. Other pitfalls are connected to having little or no criteria for selecting data—or neglecting them to increase corpus size (but see above on corpus-building). Because of these important consequences, even the best down-sampling strategy (see above) is not an adequate counter to data gluttony.

Many publications over-emphasize and, indeed, attach conceptual rather than practical significance to the amount of data: McEnery and Hardie (2012), for instance, assert that corpus methods are "a means to operationalizing two core notions of CDS: first, the idea that a discourse is not just a way of using language but *also a way of thinking* – patterns of usage on a large scale are in principle revealing of *patterns of thinking* that (a) are *widespread* and that (b) speakers are *not consciously* aware of" (emphasis added). This statement—in particular the claim about operationalizing—is misleading in that corpus methods cannot operationalize the theoretical assumption that discourse is "also a way of thinking", no matter how representative the data, because it is still language use. What they can operationalize is the aspect of *spread*, although a given discourse need not be *widespread* to be discourse. To operationalize any of the other claims included here, i.e. that discourse is a way of thinking and that speakers are not consciously aware of these ways of thinking, would require different methods.

However, as I hope to have clarified above, the advantages of large data sets come with strings attached. With respect to data gluttony, these include a potential 'embarras de richesses': In providing the researcher with a staggering amount of frequency-based information, CL methods can make it difficult "to separate the wheat from the chaff" (Baker and Levon 2015, 231); worse, they may even obscure the fact that the wheat needs to be separated from the chaff; or that there is chaff to separate in the first place. In short, the positivist emphasis on the presence of quantified reality may cause the researcher to lose sight of the need for critical reflexivity (Mautner 2016a, 172).

One consequence of this can be "under-analysis through description" (Antaki et al. 2003): As Baker and Levon (2015, 231) acknowledge, corpus approaches may lead to the fallacy that because there is so much data, we merely need to present the data either in its transformed form of frequencies or as examples, leading to purely descriptive analysis that "does not attempt to provide interpretation, critique or explanation for the patterns found". Disciplined, i.e. planned and systematic, qualitative analysis can counter-act this potential weakness. Baker and McEnery (2015a, 1–3) lay out a three-phase program to avoid under-analysis through corpus-based description: a first quantitative stage might focus on frequencies, keywords and collocates; a second stage might be qualitative and context-sensitive; a third stage would seek to provide explanation, "positioning our descriptive and interpretative findings within a wider social context".

While this is conceptually sound advice, in many cases simply adding more stages may be impractical; what is needed is a counter-strategy to stem overly expansive quantitative analyses in the first place. As Amanda

Potts points out in her aptly titled paper "Filtering the Flood", CL can "present the same researcher with a Pandora's Box of results to contend with" (Potts 2015, 285). With respect to the lexical focus of CL, a possible solution has been suggested in the form of semantic 'grouping' or 'filtering', not only to make lexical results more manageable but also to identify discourse prosody. Clearly, such categorization should not simply replace the lexical items with categories but offer these as an additional layer of abstraction; moreover, it adds a subjective element to the analysis even when the categorization is not "ad hoc" as decried by Potts (2015, 301; see also Bednarek 2008, 122). To reduce this subjective element (and therefore potential researcher bias, while increasing replicability) as well as greatly speeding up the process of grouping, automatic semantic tagging systems such as UCREL Semantic Annotation System (USAS) have been developed.[5] It must, however, be noted that such tagging systems suffer from similar caveats as all automated CL methods, including the inability to distinguish homonyms etc. In addition, they are language-specific and may be too general to reveal much in analyzing very content-specific discourses.

2.4.9 The Risks of Decontextualizing Data

Regarding CL methods used in CDS, the notion of decontextualization is used to refer to three related but distinct issues, depending on what we mean by 'context': (1) When preparing instances of language use for inclusion in a machine-readable corpus, said instances are reduced to electronically represented written linguistic signs. This causes typography, layout, accompanying pictures, etc. to be lost but also removes the selected texts from their (multimodal) co-text. While this issue is more appropriately termed *semiotic impoverishment* (see below), it is often discussed in conjunction with decontextualization because it happens at the same stage in corpus-building. Since this is, in fact, a prerequisite of corpus linguistic processing of text, "dematerializing texts and approaching them as a pack-

[5]The USAS framework was developed at Lancaster University. Its tagset consists of 21 major fields and 232 subdivisions arranged in loose correspondence to the Longman Lexicon of Contemporary English (Archer, Wilson, and Rayson 2002).

age of specific linguistic features" (Hyland 2009, 110) can also be seen as a positive and enabling transformation in corpus linguistic studies. In Ken Hyland's (2009, 110) words, however, it may be necessary to "rematerialize" features lost during corpus-building at a larger stage in order to understand how and why writers choose one linguistic feature over others.

(2) More fundamentally, corpus building involves decisions about what is to be considered the highest-level textual unit of the corpus, e.g. segments from newspaper articles, entire newspaper articles, a whole newspaper page or the entire newspaper (Hardt-Mautner 1995, 7). On the practical level, CL software is inevitably biased towards the discrete lexical unit (see below), although up-to-date concordancers allow immediate access to wider co-texts or even the full texts that a given concordance line is taken from. Especially with large general corpora, such co-text may not be known or retrievable to the researcher (Mautner 2011, 106). While Baker (2006, 175) acknowledges that "discourse analysis in particular benefits from the inclusion of full texts in corpora (rather than samples)", he links this preference only to semiotic impoverishment and the possibility of doing dispersion analyses, i.e. showing how the presence of a particular linguistic feature develops across a single text or set of texts. While both types of dispersion may offer insights (the latter in particular gains great significance for diachronic CDS, see Chapter 5), the ability to qualitatively analyze the entire text is indispensable if we take seriously notions of textuality and genre (see below).

(3) On their own, CL methods do not engage with what Baker and Levon (2015, 231) have termed "the wider social and historical context beyond the corpus" in any systematic way. This caveat is both conceptual (there is no consistent CL theory as such that explicitly theorizes the relations between language use and context) and methodological (corpus-building requires decontextualization of linguistic data): While the former can be addressed through meaningfully integrating CL methods with a specific theory in CDS—a move that seems more than warranted by Firth's or Stubb's keen interest in the social (see above on commonalities)—, the latter is integral to CL methods and therefore not easily amended.

While all three issues deserve elaboration, they require separate responses. In this context, Gerlinde Mautner has written of "a need to guard against" corpus linguistic "myopia", i.e. becoming so engrossed in studying individual words or associated patterns that one loses sight of the bigger picture (Mautner 2016a, 173). In this sense, CL methods used in CDS also run the risk of fostering "under-analysis through description" or "spotting features" (Antaki et al. 2003). Such studies, by failing to address context in any of the senses mentioned here, can only spot or contrast features without explaining the patterns observed (e.g. Cheng and Ho 2017). While this is not a requirement for corpus linguistics, it is vital to analysis in CDS (Baker et al. 2008, 279). In the terms proposed by Borsley and Ingham (2002), the social meaning of language use cannot be derived from a corpus, because a corpus abstracts language use from its context and thus treats language as a "self-contained object" (Baldry 2000, 36; see responses in Stubbs 2001b, 2002).

Given the importance that most definitions of discourse used in CDS attach to 'context' *and* to the relationship between discourse and context—consider, for instance, the DHA's definition of discourse and context being mutually constitutive—the disconnect that CL methodology forces between instances of language use and their wider context may well be the most significant caveat of CL methods from the perspective of CDS. Even a basic definition of context as "the social conditions of production and interpretation of texts" implies that the researcher must engage with them to interpret and explain language use (Fairclough 1989, 25). In Baker's (2006, 18) words, traditional CL methods not only do not achieve this but fail to accommodate what is, after all, a principle aim and premise of CDS: to analyze how a particular use of language exists within its context, i.e. outside the corpus.

Context in this sense can be differentiated into *context of production*, i.e. the identity and power of text producers, their agency and constraints, and *context of reception*, i.e. the number and identity of people who have access to a text and actually access it (Baker and McEnery 2005, 223). Corpus-based CDS have related frequency to context by, e.g., reading heightened frequency of a term as an indication of news value (Baker et al. 2013, 2), and hypothesizing that quantitative "spikes"—either in the number of newspaper articles using a particular linguistic feature (texts), the total frequency of that feature or an aggregated group of features—are connected to salient events or features of the context (Baker et al. 2013, 20). This perspective is arguably most useful in diachronic investigations in which such "spikes" are temporal artefacts on a timeline—although we cannot assume that each spike is caused by a single identifiable event (Baker et al. 2013, 97).

Beyond the situational context lies the larger social and historical context, including genre conventions, political affiliations, and institutional constraints, itself informing and construed by existing discourses (Reisigl and Wodak 2015). Although corpus mark-up or tagging for, e.g., genre, date or venue of publication, can help compensate the decontextualization of CL methods up to a point, situating patterns of socially meaningful language use within a broader context can only be done by qualitative analysis (see, e.g., Baker and Levon 2015, 232).

In discussions of decontextualization, a fourth understanding of context sometimes appears: context as general language use or other types of language use. Indeed, this is the definition of context most readily operationalized through CL methods: by relating the quantitative results for a specialized corpus to those for a reference corpus. Frequency counts may thus indicate the preference of a specific lexical choice over others in one corpus in contrast to a different pattern in another corpus, "which could relate to the presentation of a particular discourse or attempt to construct identity in some way" (Baker 2006, 68). To interpret or explain this difference, however, context is "paramount" (Baker and McEnery 2005, 223).

2.4.10 Implications of Semiotic Impoverishment

In most corpus-based studies, so-called semiotic impoverishment or the "loss of semantic richness" (Mautner 2016a, 167) is the result of preparing originally multimodal texts for machine-processing in a corpus. Since this process dictates stripping the text of most of its non-verbal properties, including layout, typography, photographs, graphs, and other visual elements, all common CL software effectively enforces semiotic impoverishment. In research practice, this may well be seen as an acceptable price to pay for studying representative amounts of linguistic data. Beyond that, it also connects to issues of efficiency or data gluttony, depending on one's perspective, as can be seen in the following rationale: To study nearly every newspaper article published in the UK that referred to Islam between 1998 and 2009, Baker et al. 2013, 13) gladly accept the data's semiotic impoverishment: "This gave us a much larger dataset to analyse than what we could have gathered if we had engaged in the expensive and time-consuming transcription of television or radio news".

While CL software requires this stripping, this fact need not dictate research design; there are, after all, other methods that can be used alongside or in combination with CL methods to analyze non-linguistic modes of semiosis (see Chapter 3). Depending on the research interest, corpus-based CDS may find it helpful or even necessary to refer to the original format of the data (Hardt-Mautner 1995, 7), whether these are newspaper articles, interviews or group discussions. This could be done with audio or video recordings, scans or the original material—the materiality of, e.g., the paper, may be significant too—and relates equally to co-text and multimodality. A similar argument for retaining original material and going back to it for "making sense of individual texts" is made by Baker (2006a, 178)—note, however, that such attention to multimodality seems to be founded on a more or less explicit understanding that 'text' and 'textuality' should matter in the analysis.

In contrast, it should be noted that applied linguistics—in Borsley and Ingham's (2002) view, that would include both CDS and CL—is still occasionally criticized for overstepping the boundaries of linguistics proper by taking an interest in non-linguistic aspects of language use, whether that concerns legal, economic or material aspects. Indeed, Borsley and Ingham's provocative article argues for a "pure" linguistics that would be antithetical to problem-centered, interdisciplinary research as advocated by most approaches in CDS. Consider, for instance, the DHA's explicit call to engage with historiographical, sociological or legal literature—but to also engage with the respective research community—to the extent it pertains to the object of research (Reisigl and Wodak 2015). If discourse is not purely linguistic, if neither its conditions nor its effects are entirely linguistic, studying discourse requires methodological *and* disciplinary openness.

2.4.11 Mitigating Lexical Bias: Addressing Higher Levels of Linguistic Practice

While CL methods are not limited to studying lexis (Stubbs 2001b)—both collocation and colligation are syntactic relations (see also Thompson and Hunston's 2006b and Hunston's [2013] insightful discussions of the relationship between CL and SFL)—it has often been noted that they are strongly focused on lexical units, i.e. show a strong lexical bias (Mautner 2016a, 158), and may thus neglect higher levels of linguistic practice, leading to under-analysis by "spotting features" (Antaki et al. 2003).

The analysis of concordance lines is often cited as evidence against CL's bias toward lexical phenomena. We see this view in Mautner (1995, 19), who argues that concordancing moves the perspective beyond below-sentence-level linguistic description and "can in fact open a window into larger-scale discoursal processes". She is quick to admit that "a word-based 'peg' to hang the analysis on" is still needed, i.e. a discrete and searchable item "around which the higher-level phenomenon that we are after is expected to cluster". Mautner's metaphors strike me as accurate: The extended concordance line can open a window, but it does not do it automatically—opening it and, more importantly, moving past it, requires additional methodology. As regards the "peg", Mautner's pragmatic 1995 response unfortunately returns us to the liabilities of subjectivity, cherry-picking, and researcher bias: "In issue-centred studies, as many CDA projects indeed are, a close reading of a small but reasonably representative sample of texts will usually reveal key terms that are central to the issue concerned" (Hardt-Mautner 1995, 19). Today, manual or automatic semantic grouping of keywords may be combined with such an initial reading. Beyond keywords, analytical methods rather than a 'close reading' are required. Nevertheless, vague appeals to 'concordancing tools' as 'adding a qualitative aspect' (e.g. Lukac 2011, 192; Salama 2011, 318), without specifying the analytical approach, are still common.

A fundamental criticism leveled against CL methods is that they tend to ignore texts as units (or variously textual unity). As Baker (2006, 49) has pointed out, dispersion analyses are one major way that CL can "take into account the fact that texts are discrete entities within themselves". O'Halloran and Coffin (2004, 194) similarly seek to "show that corpus technologies do not have to obscure the individual character and context of specific texts." However, the route they take to do so—foregrounding the qualitative analysis of a single text—only highlights the fact that staying within the narrow confines of quantitative analysis will lead exactly to that outcome. To be clear, there are some methodological constraints on CL methods which *might* prevent us from analyzing higher levels of linguistic practice in context, but these can be avoided. We should not hedge the issue: This requires not just additional methods, but a research design that acknowledges the methodological limitations of CL methods as well as their advantages.

Although it has been claimed that CL methods and CDS "overlap" in the analysis of concordance lines (Gabrielatos and Baker 2008, 15) or that concordancing effectively breaks down the quantitative/qualitative distinction (Hardt-Mautner 1995, 24), more ambitious attempts to integrate CL methods with CDS have moved "beyond the conventional concordance line's nine-word window" (D. Hunt and Harvey 2015, 113) (e.g. Partington, Duguid, and Taylor 2013; Baker 2006; Baker et al. 2008; Thompson and Hunston 2006a; Bevitori 2015). This complementary combination has been described in terms CL working "bottom-up", inferring discourse patterns from lexicogrammatical patterns in collocates and concordance lines, and qualitative methods working "top-down" (Freake et al. 2011, 29). While this complementary approach has certainly proved fruitful in many studies of specialized corpora, a number of issues have also been raised regarding its limitations (e.g. Miller et al. 2014).

Higher levels of linguistic practice that relate to patterns of production and reception (e.g. in relation to genres or media) thus represent potential blind spots resulting from a narrow focus on corpus linguistic methodology, particularly for general corpora. Although tagging corpus data can off-set this issue somewhat, a more practicable approach would be to use general corpora "sparingly, instead carrying out the analysis of discourses on more specialized corpora, where issues of production and reception can be more easily articulated" (Baker 2006, 180). Baker does offer some counter-arguments in favor of general corpora—i.e. that "society is inter-connected and all texts influence each other"; that if discourses are so "powerful, we would expect them to occur across a range of text types and genres"; and that "[t]herefore discourses encountered in private conversations are likely to be fuelled by discourses in newspapers or religious speeches" (Baker 2006, 180). However, these arguments are relevant to CDS only under the provision that such a general corpus is tagged for context, genre, etc., giving us the option to select and analyze texts individually or as subcorpora. Under these conditions, Baker's arguments relate to interdiscursivity and would allow us to observe any 'trickling down' or 'trickling up' from public to (quasi)private discourses—a key interest to recent CDS, e.g. in discussing the normalization of fringe discourses.

Several researchers have raised the concern that the social and political meaning and relevance of texts cannot be directly 'read off' the linguistic choices evident from language use, whether by qualitative or quantitative methods. This requires a theoretical framework (as provided by CDS) and consideration of the context of such language use. This caveat is arguably more severe for CL methods due to their lexical bias and must be balanced—within corpus-based CDS—either by existing qualitative methods or developing new methods. Mautner, for instance, asserts that the researcher's knowledge beyond the corpus, e.g. about genre conventions and the topic concerned, plays an important role (Hardt-Mautner 1995, 8). Baker and Levon (2015, 231) are keenly aware that, if analysis does not move beyond concordance lines, it will not be "effective at identifying nonpatterned uses of language such as legitimation strategies, topoi or intertextuality." This points to a pivotal question for CL efforts to link lexical-level analyses to higher levels of linguistics practice: To what degree are such practices patterned on the lexical level?

Although realized in part lexically, large-scale discursive phenomena are rarely bound to discrete lexical units. This pertains to argumentation, legitimation, discursive strategies, narrative patterns, metaphorical chains, and a host of other rhetorical devices such as parody or hyperbole (D. Hunt and Harvey 2015, 113). Even at the simplest level, we often deal with propositions that are realized in numerous different lexical units (Mautner 2011, 106).[6] Thus, neither frequency lists, collocations, nor keywords will sufficiently or reliably reveal what CDS is ultimately inter-

[6]On a related note, users of CL methods should be aware that figures generated for lexical items may only be approximate, as Caldas-Coulthard and Moon (2010, 101–12) point out, unless one manually excludes tokens which occur in names or are incorrectly tagged for word type and (also manually) disambiguates polysemous words and homographic terms.

ested in: the discursive construction of social reality (Baker 2004, 347). With anything more complex, the limits to what CL methods can reveal are apparent in the methodological experiments that seek to expand those limits (e.g. metaphors in O'Halloran 2007; Cheng and Ho 2017; Berber-Sardinha 2002; Charteris-Black 2004; or argumentation in Degano 2007; O'Halloran 2015; Sahlane 2012).

A significant number of such innovations have been attempted over the last two decades, seeking to explore more complex linguistic phenomena through CL tools. Baker (2006, 183) makes the general point that these efforts require us to "engage with the corpus" by "less mechanistic procedures", often combined with qualitative methods. Regarding the basic problem of the varying lexical realization of propositions, direct references (e.g. the word *asylum seekers*) are easily spotted, while anaphorical references to the same group or social actor are difficult to identify using only CL methods. Moreover, explicit representation is easier to spot than implicit representations (Baker and Levon 2015, 232) or the absence of a social actor (e.g. through agens-deletion in passives, which is traceable, if not by CL methods, or through complete suppression of the actor). Inasmuch as the identification of 'dominant discourses' in a corpus "is often premised on those lexical and discursive patterns that are numerically frequent" (Baker 2010, 125), this bias must be taken seriously. This particular methodological issue has been tackled in several corpus-based studies by integrating qualitative analyses based on SFL, in particular 'social actors analysis' (van Leeuwen 1996). As Baker (2006, 183) insists, the key danger related to lexical bias "is that some forms of analysis appear to be more 'convenient' than others" (on "counting only what is easy to count", see also Stubbs and Gerbig 1993, 78; Koller and Mautner 2004, 224). Therefore, methodological deliberation on combining or developing CL methods should be a priority for CDS.

The underlying issue is that the precise nature of the relationship between micro- and macro-level phenomena remains a black box—one that needs to be theorized at least. For instance, one might hypothesize that discourse prosody plays an important role in implicit, inferable argumentation, if and when it is tied to specific lexical patterns. Under these provisions, CL methods can reveal how prosodies help to "create, reinforce, or exploit a topos without the need for any explicit argumentation, in that the reader is more likely to attend to the connotational rather than the denotational level of particular frequent collocations (e.g. swarms of refugees)" (Gabrielatos and Baker 2008, 22; see also van Dijk 1991, 228). To operationalize this conception within CDS, discourse prosodies must be defined across individual lexical items, i.e. semantic groups identified manually or automatically. Care must be taken, however, not to equate such patterns with topoi—the link may be there in the sense that "the collective use of quantity/mass/group collocates (e.g. flood/river/tide/wave of refugees)" (Gabrielatos and Baker 2008, 22) serve to *support* the topoi of burdening (Reisigl and Wodak 2005, 76–78), but we cannot directly infer topoi from lexical patterns. On the one hand, this makes qualitative verification necessary; on the other hand, an unknown number of topoi may be overlooked by this approach.

Contributions advocating the integration of CL into CDS to counteract the weaknesses of qualitative analyses, in particular rigor, representativeness, and replicability, often fall short of providing adequate accounts of the qualitative methods used. Nowhere is this more evident than discourse studies that aim to analyze argumentation by CL methods, e.g. "reading concordance lines" to "build a picture of the argumentation scheme" (Prentice 2010, 418). Prentice goes on to take negative adjectives to indicate the *argumentum ad hominem* strategy, leading her to quantify any and all such instances as *argumentum ad hominem*. This is a remarkable leap of faith, given that the study offers no indication that the actual presence of *argumentation* was confirmed through additional analytical steps, thus assuming a reliable 1:1 relation between the use of negative adjectives and argumentation, specifically *ad hominem*.

Other attempts to operationalize argumentation with CL methods are beset by similar problems. For instance, in studying "arguments against the veil", Baker et al. (2013, 211) focus on lexical items and concordance lines to identify "reasons", i.e. warrants. However, the concept of argumentation is not theorized in the paper and no account is given of the means by which the "arguments" were identified in the corpus: No distinction is made between formal and content-related topoi, between explicit or implicit argumentation; nor does their work identify or mention argumentation as a logical and textual structure with warrants, conclusion rules, and conclusions. Indeed, different conclusions drawn in their data are not distinguished in the analysis. Degano's (2007, 361) corpus-linguistic operationalization of argumentation, too, is limited by lexical bias: Conceding that "argumentative structures stretch out through longer units of text", she simply proceeds to study only "those aspects of argumentation which are signalled by indicators, and are therefore electronically retrievable". In essence, this methodological limitation constrains her work to studying only those rare types of argumentation that are reliably indicated by lexical markers.

Other work has attempted to use CL methods to identify 'narrative patterns' on the textual level, linking the patterned sequence of linguistic means of expression to established narratives. This fledgling 'corpus pragmatics' thus posits a link between lexicogrammatical patterns, accessible to CL, and narrative (Bubenhofer et al. 2014, 2). Significantly, substantial qualitative analysis and coding efforts beyond standard CL methods are used in this work.

2.4.12 Avoiding Over-Emphasis on Statistical Results

Critics and proponents of CL in CDS have both warned of placing too much confidence in quantitative results in and of themselves. This has sometimes been linked, first, to a "childish fascination with computers, numbers, and statistics" that can lead to "the computer's tail [...] wagging the analyst's dog" (Hardt-Mautner 1995, 22). This also pertains to the somewhat controversial question of what constitutes *analysis* and what is the *epistemological status* of frequency, keyword or collocation lists obtained through CL software. As Mautner put it more than two decades after her above-quoted warning: "There is always a danger that the use of computers alone lulls us into feeling too confident about our findings, and into forgetting that no matter what method is involved, fundamental epistemological issues must be addressed" (Mautner 2016a, 174). Arguably the most fundamental of these issues is that the software accomplishes *data processing* rather than analysis. In other words, a CL method on its own never generates insight and critique, "and to claim that it does so would be seriously misguided or, at the very least, naive" (Mautner 2016a, 169).

Second, warnings against over-interpretation of statistics relate to the twin temptations to think that very large corpora cover "every potential discursive construction" and that CL methods can reveal everything, yielding exhaustive analyses (Baker 2006, 178). This second epistemological issue is related to the theoretical tension between *discourse* and *corpus*: Corpora are built (in specific ways) to allow us to observe language use, i.e. discourses, but corpora are not discourse (Mautner 2016a, 174). This issue extends to all results generated by CL, e.g. frequency lists, which may be taken to reveal hegemonic discourses on grounds of lexical frequencies. The view that "uses which can be identified as recurring are considered as more relevant than isolated examples" (Degano 2007, 363) cannot be upheld irrespective of contextual information. Thus, relying on frequency as a constant indicator is problematic in light of CL's tendency to not consider the context and genre of individual texts, as the discursive power of individual texts or speakers in a corpus is hardly evenly distributed (e.g. a presidential address vs. a news report in a local paper).

Depending on the corpus makeup, the relatively rare use of one linguistic form thus cannot be taken to indicate its marginality (Baker 2006, 19). How we interpret, say, the discrepancy between a prime minister's speech and hundreds of social media postings by 'ordinary people' and their respective positions in discourse is a complex issue not to be resolved by a simple frequency count. Ultimately, frequency should not "be divorced from the significance that the item in question has in a particular semantic and social context. Certain collocates or semantic prosodies may be very infrequent, in fact, and represent all the more marked choices in a given text precisely because of their rarity" (Koller and Mautner 2004, 224).

The notion of 'weight' and its operationalization through annotating texts for aspects of production and reception, author or readership has been suggested to address this problem. On a practical level, there is a need to guard against over-interpretation, specifically in news or media corpora, by identifying the effect of repeated stories (e.g. press agency reports). The frequency of some constructions may be linked to a single quote or report that was reproduced in multiple texts (Baker and Levon 2015, 230). However, only in-depth contextual knowledge and qualitative analysis may be able to trace what is left unsaid in hegemonic discourses: "A hegemonic discourse can be at its most powerful when it does not even have to be invoked, because it is just taken for granted" (Baker 2006, 19). Clearly, specific approaches in CDS will likely want to go into greater detail on this issue, as lexico-grammatical choices pertain to the tension between views of 'language as a set of rules' and 'language as free choice' (Gür-Şeker 2014) as well as to discourse as a set of constraining and enabling forces, defining at their extreme the sayable and the unsayable (Baker 2006, 48).

2.4.13 The Value of Revealing the Obvious

While under-analysis through description can be seen as a risk of using CL methods in CDS, the obvious counter is to delve deeper with qualitative analyses. As to the risk of "uncovering the obvious" (Baker et al. 2013, 30) in studies that cover much-studied types of data (e.g. tabloid newspapers) in conjunction with often-answered questions (e.g. regarding racism), these can be made more specific and contextually relevant. This is a question of overall research design rather than of CL methodology. In addition, arguments can made for 'uncovering the obvious' as part if not the whole of an empirical study in that it "at least gives more credibility to other non-obvious findings", providing "exact quantifications of vaguer suspicions", and documenting results "for future researchers, even future generations" (Baker et al. 2013, 30). Baker and McEnery (2015, 10) have referred to such findings as "so what"-results and argued that they should not be automatically dismissed: After all, what may seem obvious to one discourse analyst may not be obvious to another, and even that which is obvious to all discourse analysts may not be obvious to researchers in other fields or, indeed, the general public. Ultimately, we need to critically interrogate the notion of 'obvious' before dismissing any results on that basis and should certainly connect any such discussion to our considerations of cherry-picking and researcher bias (see above).

2.4.14 Avoiding Sham-Objectivity

A final criticism often raised in conjunction with over-emphasis of quantitative results is that of 'sham-objectivity' or conveying a sense of absolute objectivity with such results. Part of the issue here is a glorified or simplistic understanding of objectivity, as if the nature of numbers necessarily precluded all subjectivity; another part is the persistent denial of subjective elements in corpus-analytical procedures; and a final part is the understandable but misguided aim to make one's study immune to criticisms of researcher bias by equating 'quantitative' with 'objective'.

The first issue is theoretical and largely beyond the scope of this volume (but see Watt 2007; Attia and Edge 2017). The second issue has been answered in full in the methodological reflections of Paul Baker, Gerlinde Mautner, and others: Corpus-based studies cannot be understood as simply applying objective quantitative procedures. Corpus-based research, including but not limited to its integration into CDS, "involves a great deal of human choice at every stage" (Baker 2006, 175), *inter alia* forming research questions, designing and building corpora, potentially also eliciting data, choosing software, deciding which techniques to use, deciding parameters/settings for the software tools to apply, interpreting the results and relating them to context, even explaining or evaluating the findings in terms of critique. Inasmuch as CL methods transform or process data, "the interpretative skills of the researcher are still required" to relate it to higher-level concepts such as 'context' or 'discourse' as well as to one's research questions (Baker et al. 2013, 30). One might even go as far as to say that, in relation to the points made above, the achievements of 'analysis' and 'critique' come with a price in subjectivity.

2.5 Research Practice: Benefits and Pitfalls

Given the great appeal of CL methods, it is not surprising that a staggering number of papers have claimed to combine or integrate CL and CDS, and thereby to have gained advantages, benefits or synergies. What is surprising, then, is that despite the broad methodological arguments summarized above, general practice involves little explicit discussion on what exactly these benefits are or should be in the specific research design pursued. Given the complexity of the arguments, it is evident that the focus should be less on whether CL methods can or should be used in CDS at all, but about what can be gained and how. Since combining methods does not by default guarantee any benefit (and sometimes involves a disproportionate effort for little benefit), criteria such as those laid out in Chapter 1 should be used to develop and conduct research that integrates CL methods into CDS. While the previous sections have included brief commentaries on research practice in the spirit of Bryman's (2006, 2007) contrastive study of 'what researchers say they do' and 'what they are really doing', this section points out key benefits and pitfalls of integrating CL methods into CDS.

Corpus-based analyses of discourse can help identify and trace patterns and trends in language use, within and across texts, genres, social fields, and other contexts. CL methods can help extend the reach, representativeness, and precision of our conclusions, while also providing a check on potential researcher bias. They can also provide efficient approaches to downsampling large data sets for qualitative analysis. As Baker (2006, 183) points out, corpus linguistic methods can thus complement and support qualitative analyses in CDS but never replace them. In his words, CL is "an extremely useful instrument to add to the *workbox of techniques* available to discourse analysts" (emphasis added). Qualitative methods, in contrast, will always be more attentive to subtle social and linguistic patterns, more capable of linking discourse and context—but corpora may well be instrumental to that process. Although neither is inherently superior, qualitative analysis is essential to the critical project. Ultimately, qualitative and quantitative perspectives yield different and, ideally, complementary insights (Mautner 2016a, 175). We should frame our methodological discussion and research designs accordingly.

Since there is no standard procedure for a problem-centered field such as CDS, research designs must be specifically developed within approaches or schools such as the DHA. The methodological flexibility of CDS has allowed CL methods to be considered as a potential but not essential component in the particular combination of theory, research question, data, and method (Mautner 2011, 84). When integrating CL methods into CDS, we should

- not reduce CL to purely quantitative methods, denying their qualitative components,
- not exaggerate the measure of inter-subjectivity (or objectivity) of CL methods and related effects to be gained for CDS,

- not overstate the divide between CL and CDS in terms of their strict qualitative-quantitative orientation or the related objective-subjective divide,
- not use software, settings and statistical measures without at least a basic understanding of how these will affect results,
- not add CL methods mainly to ward off accusations of bias, cherry-picking etc.,
- in terms of research design, have a clear sense of how the CL methods used contribute to the overall quality of the study (see Bryman 2006),
- address corpus-building and its criteria as an integral element of research design,
- provide a methodological specification of the qualitative/quantitative methods to be used in analyzing concordance lines (or, beyond that, texts),
- address whether and how higher levels of linguistic practice will be investigated, specifically the relationship between micro-linguistic and macro-linguistic phenomena such as argumentation by including pertinent theories/models,
- conceptualize the relationship between essential concepts in one's CDS approach and CL notions and tools, such as 'discourse' and 'corpus',
- conceptualize the 'black box' of the relationship between linguistic practice (at any level) and social practice or context,
- address issues such as decontextualization and semiotic impoverishment of data,
- using a reference corpus, e.g. to generate keywords, make sure it relates meaningfully to our corpus in terms of, e.g., general language use, a contrasting genre, a more general thematic discourse or social context, media or period (on the use of reference corpora in CDS, see Mautner 2011, 96),
- let neither impressive numbers nor illustrative examples 'speak for themselves',
- be mindful not only of countable presences but absences, i.e. backgrounding, suppression or exclusion,
- find a meaningful way in which, under the specific circumstances of our research, CL and qualitative methods can be combined for down-sampling,

- bear in mind that, in today's publication practice, much depends on presentation: if our texts do not explicate and demonstrate our research designs, they will not be appreciated,
- take adequate steps to disambiguate language use identified and quantified through CL methods, e.g. ironic language use, negation, polysemy, because neither individual intent nor hegemony can be read off the numbers,
- acknowledge and integrate into our analysis relevant aspects of context, e.g. agency, access, distribution, and reception,
- ensure that we verify interpretations only indicated by CL methods, e.g. topoi, metaphors or ideological position, by using appropriate qualitative methods,
- quantify only that which can be quantified.

Finally, we should take to heart John Sinclair's (2004, 186) warning: "But make no mistake - just having a corpus isn't going to save anyone; more likely it will eventually expose poor research."

References

Abulof, Uriel. 2015. "Normative Concepts Analysis: Unpacking the Language of Legitimation." *International Journal of Social Research Methodology* 18 (1): 73–89. https://doi.org/10.1080/13645579.2013.861656.

Antaki, Charles, Michael Billig, Derek Edwards, and Jonathan Potter. 2003. "Discourse Analysis Means Doing Analysis: A Critique of Six Analytic Shortcomings." *Discourse Analysis Online* 1. http://extra.shu.ac.uk/daol/articles/v1/n1/a1/antaki2002002-t.html.

Anthony, Laurence. 2013. "A Critical Look at Software Tools in Corpus Linguistics." *Linguistic Research* 30 (2): 141–61.

Archer, Dawn, Andrew Wilson, and Paul Rayson. 2002. "Introduction to the USAS Category System." ucrel.lancs.ac.uk/usas/usasguide.pdf.

Attia, Mariam, and Julian Edge. 2017. "Be(Com)Ing a Reflexive Researcher: A Developmental Approach to Research Methodology." *Open Review of Educational Research* 4 (1): 33–45. https://doi.org/10.1080/23265507.2017.1300068.

Baker, Paul. 2004. "Querying Keywords: Questions of Difference, Frequency, and Sense in Keywords Analysis." *Journal of English Linguistics* 32 (4): 346–59. https://doi.org/10.1177/0075424204269894.
———. 2006. *Using Corpora in Discourse Analysis.* Continuum Discourse Series. London and New York: Continuum.
———. 2010. *Sociolinguistics and Corpus Linguistics.* Edinburgh Sociolinguistics. Edinburgh: Edinburgh University Press.
———. 2012. "Acceptable Bias? Using Corpus Linguistics Methods with Critical Discourse Analysis." *Critical Discourse Studies* 9 (3): 247–56. https://doi.org/10.1080/17405904.2012.688297.
Baker, Paul, Costas Gabrielatos, and Tony McEnery. 2013. *Discourse Analysis and Media Attitudes: The Representation of Islam in the British Press.* Cambridge and New York: Cambridge University Press.
Baker, Paul, and Erez Levon. 2015. "Picking the Right Cherries? A Comparison of Corpus-Based and Qualitative Analyses of News Articles about Masculinity." *Discourse & Communication* 9 (2): 221–36. https://doi.org/10.1177/1750481314568542.
Baker, Paul, and Tony McEnery. 2005. "A Corpus-Based Approach to Discourses of Refugees and Asylum Seekers in UN and Newspaper Texts." *Journal of Language and Politics* 4 (2): 197–226. https://doi.org/10.1075/jlp.4.2.04bak.
———. 2015. "Introduction." In *Corpora and Discourse Studies: Integrating Discourse and Corpora,* edited by Paul Baker and Tony McEnery, 1–19. London: Palgrave MacMillan.
Baker, Paul, Costas Gabrielatos, Majid KhosraviNik, Michał Krzyzanowski, Tony McEnery, and Ruth Wodak. 2008. "A Useful Methodological Synergy? Combining Critical Discourse Analysis and Corpus Linguistics to Examine Discourses of Refugees and Asylum Seekers in the UK Press." *Discourse & Society* 19 (3): 273–306. https://doi.org/10.1177/0957926508088962.
Baldry, Anthony, ed. 2000. *Multimodality and Multimediality in the Distance Learning Age: Papers in English Linguistics.* Campobasso: Palladino.
Bauer, Martin W, and Aarts, Bas. 2000. "Corpus Construction: A Principle for Qualitative Data Collection." In *Qualitative Researching with Text, Image and Sound,* edited by Martin W. Bauer and George Gaskell, 19–37. London: Sage.
Bednarek, Monika. 2008. "Semantic Preference and Semantic Prosody Re-Examined." *Corpus Linguistics and Linguistic Theory* 4 (2). https://doi.org/10.1515/CLLT.2008.006.
Bednarek, Monika, and Helen Caple. 2014. "Why Do News Values Matter? Towards a New Methodological Framework for Analysing News Discourse in Critical Discourse Analysis and Beyond." *Discourse & Society* 25 (2): 135–58. https://doi.org/10.1177/0957926513516041.

Berber-Sardinha, Tony. 2002. "Metaphor in corpora: A Corpus-Driven Analysis of Applied Linguistics Dissertations." *I Conference on Metaphor in Language and Thought*. Brazil: Catholic University of São Paulo.

Bevitori, Cinzia. 2015. "Discursive Constructions of the Environment in American Presidential Speeches 1960–2013: A Diachronic Corpus-Assisted Study." In *Corpora and Discourse Studies: Integrating Discourse and Corpora*, edited by Paul Baker and Tony McEnery, 110–33. London: Palgrave MacMillan.

Blommaert, Jan. 2005. *Discourse: A Critical Introduction*. Key Topics in Sociolinguistics. New York: Cambridge University Press.

Borsley, Robert D., and Richard Ingham. 2002. "Grow Your Own Linguistics? On Some Applied Linguists' Views of the Subject." *Lingua* 112 (1): 1–6. https://doi.org/10.1016/S0024-3841(01)00034-1.

Bryman, Alan. 2006. "Integrating Quantitative and Qualitative Research: How Is It Done?" *Qualitative Research* 6 (1): 97–113. https://doi.org/10.1177/1468794106058877.

———. 2007. "Barriers to Integrating Quantitative and Qualitative Research." *Journal of Mixed Methods Research* 1 (1): 8–22. https://doi.org/10.1177/2345678906290531.

Bubenhofer, Noah, Nicole Müller, and Joachim Scharloth. 2014. "Narrative Muster Und Diskursanalyse: Ein Datengeleiteter Ansatz." *Zeitschrift Für Semiotik* 35 (3–4): 419–44.

Burr, Vivien. 1995. *An Introduction to Social Constructionism*. London and New York: Routledge.

Busse, Dietrich, and Wolfgang Teubert. 1994. "Ist Diskurs Ein Sprachwissenschaftliches Objekt? Zur Methodenfrage Der Historischen Semantik." In *Begriffsgeschichte Und Diskursgeschichte: Methodenfragen Und Forschungsergebnisse Der Historischen Semantik*, edited by Dietrich Busse, Fritz Hermanns, and Wolfgang Teubert, 10–28. Opladen: Westdeustcher Verlag.

Caldas-Coulthard, Carmen Rosa. 1993. "From Discourse Analysis to Critical Discourse Analysis: The Differential Representation of Women and Men Speaking in Written News." In *Techniques of Description: Spoken and Written Discourse*, edited by John Sinclair, Michael Hoey, and Gwyneth Fox, 196–298. London: Routledge.

Caldas-Coulthard, Carmen Rosa. 1995. "Man in the News: The Misrepresentation of Women Speaking in News-as-Narrative-Discourse". In *Language and Gender: Interdisciplinary Perspectives*, edited by S. Mills, 226–39. Harlow: Longman.

Caldas-Coulthard, Carmen Rosa, and Rosamund Moon. 2010. "'Curvy, Hunky, Kinky': Using Corpora as Tools for Critical Analysis." *Discourse & Society* 21 (2): 99–133. https://doi.org/10.1177/0957926509353843.

Charles, Maggie, Diane Pecorari, and Susan Hunston, eds. 2009a. *Academic Writing: At the Interface of Corpus and Discourse.* London and New York: Continuum.

———. 2009b. "Exploring the Interface between Corpus Linguistics and Discourse Analysis." In *Academic Writing: At the Interface of Corpus and Discourse,* edited by Maggie Charles, Diane Pecorari, and Susan Hunston, 1–10. London and New York: Continuum.

Charteris-Black, Jonathan. 2004. *Corpus Approaches to Critical Metaphor Analysis.* Houndmills: Palgrave Macmillan.

Cheng, Winnie. 2012. "Corpus-Based Linguistic Approaches to Critical Discourse Analysis." In *The Encyclopedia of Applied Linguistics,* edited by Carol A. Chapelle. Oxford, UK: Blackwell. https://doi.org/10.1002/9781405198431.wbeal0262.

Cheng, Winnie, and Janet Ho. 2017. "A Corpus Study of Bank Financial Analyst Reports: Semantic Fields and Metaphors." *International Journal of Business Communication* 54 (3): 258–82. https://doi.org/10.1177/2329488415572790.

Chowdhury, G. G. 2010. *Introduction to Modern Information Retrieval.* 3rd ed. London: Facet.

Coffin, Caroline, Ann Hewings, Kieran O'Halloran, and Open University, eds. 2004. *Applying English Grammar: Functional and Corpus Approaches.* London: Arnold.

Degano, Chiara. 2007. "Dissociation and Presupposition in Discourse: A Corpus Study." *Argumentation* 21 (4): 361–78. https://doi.org/10.1007/s10503-007-9058-7.

Fairclough, Norman. 1996. "A Reply to Henry Widdowson's 'Discourse Analysis: A Critical View.'" *Language & Literature* 5 (1): 49–56.

———. 2015. *Language and Power.* 3rd ed. London and New York: Routledge, Taylor & Francis Group.

Faulstich, Katja. 2007. "Diskurslinguistik in Theorie Und Praxis." *Zeitschrift Für Germanistische Linguistik* 35 (3). https://doi.org/10.1515/zgl.2007.032.

Firth, John Rupert. 1935. *Papers in Linguistics: 1934–1951.* 1. ed., 4. reprinted. London: Oxford University Press.

Forchtner, B. 2011. "Critique, the Discourse-Historical Approach and the Frankfurt School." *Critical Discourse Studies* 8 (1): 1–14.

Foucault, Michel. 1989. *Archaeology of Knowledge.* London: Tavistock Publications.

Fowler, Roger. 1996. "On Critical Linguistic." In *Texts and Practices: Readings in Critical Discourse Analysis*, edited by Carmen Rosa Caldas-Coulthard and Malcolm Coulthard, 3–14. London: Routledge.

———. 2005. *Language in the News: Discourse and Ideology in the Press*. London and New York: Routledge.

Fowler, Roger, and Gunther Kress. 1979. "Critical Linguistics." In *Language and Control*, edited by Roger Fowler, Robert Hodge, Gunther Kress, and Tony Trew, 185–213. London and Boston: Routledge & Kegan Paul.

Francis, Jill J, Marie Johnston, Clare Robertson, Liz Glidewell, Vikki Entwistle, Martin P. Eccles, and Jeremy M. Grimshaw. 2010. "What is an adequate sample size? Operationalising data saturation for theory-based interview studies." *Psychology & Health* 25 (10): 1229–1245.

Freake, Rachelle, Guillaume Gentil, and Jaffer Sheyholislami. 2011. "A Bilingual Corpus-Assisted Discourse Study of the Construction of Nationhood and Belonging in Quebec." *Discourse & Society* 22 (1): 21–47. https://doi.org/10.1177/0957926510382842.

Gabrielatos, Costas. 2007. "Selecting Query Terms to Build a Specialised Corpus from a Restricted-Access Database." *ICAME Journal* 31: 5–44.

Gabrielatos, Costas, and Paul Baker. 2006. "Representation of Refugees and Asylum Seekers in UK Newspapers. Towards a Corpus-Based Analysis." BAAL/IRAAL 2006.

———. 2008. "Fleeing, Sneaking, Flooding: A Corpus Analysis of Discursive Constructions of Refugees and Asylum Seekers in the UK Press, 1996–2005." *Journal of English Linguistics* 36 (1): 5–38. https://doi.org/10.1177/0075424207311247.

Gabrielatos, Costas, and Alison Duguid. 2014. "Corpus Linguistics and CDA: A Critical Look at Synergy." Presented at the CDA20+ Symposium, University of Amsterdam, September 9.

Gerbner, George, Larry Gross, Michael Morgan, and Nancy Signorielli. 1986. "Living with Television: The Dynamics of the Cultivation Process." In *Perspectives on Media Effects*, edited by Bryant Jennings and Dolf Zillmann. Hillsdale, NJ: Lawrence Erlbaum Associates.

Goatly, Andrew. 2004. "Corpus Linguistics, Systemic Functional Grammar and Literary Meaning: A Critical Analysis of Harry Potter and the Philosopher's Stone." *Ilha Do Desterro. A Journal of English Language, Literature in English and Cultural Studies* 46: 115–54.

Gray, Bethany, and Douglas Biber. 2011. "Corpus Approaches to the Study of Discourse." In *The Continuum Companion to Discourse Analysis*, edited by Ken Hyland and Brian Paltridge, 138–54. London: Continuum.

Gür-Şeker, Derya. 2014. "Zur Verwendung von Korpora in Der Diskurslinguistik." In *Diskursforschung: Ein Interdisziplinäres Handbuch: Theorien, Methodologien Und Kontroversen*, edited by Johannes Angermuller, Martin Nonhoff, Eva Herschinger, Felicitas Macgilchrist, Martin Reisigl, Juliette Wedl, Daniel Wrana, and Alexander Ziem, 1, 583–603. Bielefeld: Transcript.

Hardt-Mautner, Gerlinde. 1995. *"Only Connect." Critical Discourse Analysis and Corpus Linguistics.* Lancaster, UK: UCREL Technical Paper 6. http://www.comp.lancs.ac.uk/ucrel/tech_papers.html.

Herzog, Benno. 2016. "Discourse Analysis as Immanent Critique: Possibilities and Limits of Normative Critique in Empirical Discourse Studies." *Discourse & Society* 27 (3): 278–92. https://doi.org/10.1177/0957926516630897.

Hunston, Susan. 2002. *Corpora in Applied Linguistics.* Cambridge: Cambridge University Press.

Hunston, Susan. 2013. "Systemic Functional Linguistics, Corpus Linguistics, and the Ideology of Science." *Text & Talk* 33 (4–5). https://doi.org/10.1515/text-2013-0028.

Hunt, Sally. 2015. "Representations of Gender and Agency in the Harry Potter Series." In *Corpora and Discourse Studies: Integrating Discourse and Corpora*, edited by Tony McEnery and Paul Baker, 266–84. London: Palgrave MacMillan.

Hunt, Daniel, and Kevin Harvey. 2015. "Health Communication and Corpus Linguistics. Using Corpus Tools to Analyse Eating Disorder Discourse Online." In *Corpora and Discourse Studies: Integrating Discourse and Corpora*, edited by Tony McEnery and Paul Baker, 134–54. London: Palgrave MacMillan.

Hyland, Ken. 2009. "Corpus Informed Discourse Analysis: The Case of Academic Engagement." In *Academic Writing: At the Interface between Corpus Linguistics and Discourse Analysis*, 110–28. London and New York: Continuum.

Jaworska, Sylvia, and Ramesh Krishnamurthy. 2012. "On the F Word: A Corpus-Based Analysis of the Media Representation of Feminism in British and German Press Discourse, 1990–2009." *Discourse & Society* 23 (4): 401–31. https://doi.org/10.1177/0957926512441113.

Kenny, Dorothy. 2001. *Lexis and Creativity in Translation: A Corpus-Based Study.* Manchester, UK and Northampton, MA: St. Jerome Pub.

Koller, Veronika, and Gerlinde Mautner. 2004. "Computer Applications in Critical Discourse Analysis." In *Applying English Grammar: Functional and Corpus Approaches*, edited by Caroline Coffin, Ann Hewings, and Kieran O'Halloran, 216–28. London: Arnold.

Koteyko, Nelya. 2006. "Corpus Linguistics and the Study of Meaning in Discourse." *The Linguistics Journal* 1 (2): 131–55.
Krishnamurthy, Ramesh. 1996. "Ethnic, Racial and Tribal: The Language of Racism?" In *Texts and Practices: Readings in Critical Discourse Analysis*, edited by Carmen Rosa Caldas-Coulthard and Malcolm Coulthard, 129–49. London: Routledge.
Law, John. 2004. *After Method: Mess in Social Science Research*. International Library of Sociology. London and New York: Routledge.
Lazarton, Anne. 2002. "Quantitative and Qualitative Approaches to Discourse Analysis." *Annual Review of Applied Linguistics* 22: 32–51.
Lin, Angel. 2014. "Critical Discourse Analysis in Applied Linguistics: A Methodological Review." *Annual Review of Applied Linguistics* 34 (March): 213–32. https://doi.org/10.1017/S0267190514000087.
Lukac, Morana. 2011. "Down to the Bone: A Corpus-Based Critical Discourse Analysis of Pro-Eating Disorder Blogs." *Jezikoslovje* 12 (2): 187–209.
Mautner, Gerlinde. 2000. *Der Britische Europa-Diskurs: Methodenreflexion Und Fallstudien Zur Berichterstattung in Der Tagespresse*. Deutsche Erstausg. Passagen Diskursforschung. Wien: Passagen.
———. 2005. "The Entrepreneurial University: A Discursive Profile of a Higher Education Buzzword." *Critical Discourse Studies* 2 (2): 95–120. https://doi.org/10.1080/17405900500283540.
———. 2011. "Die Kritische Masse. Korpuslinguistik Und Kritische Diskursanalyse." In *Korpuspragmatik. Thematische Korpora Als Basis Diskurslinguistischer Analysen*, edited by Ekkehard Felder, Marcus Müller, and Friedemann Vogel, 83–114. Berlin, Boston: de Gruyter.
———. 2016a. "Checks and Balances: How Corpus Linguistics Can Contribute to CDA." In *Methods of Critical Discourse Studies*, edited by Ruth Wodak and Michael Meyer, 3rd ed., 154–79. London: Sage.
———. 2016b. *Discourse and Management: Critical Perspectives through the Language Lens*. London: Palgrave Macmillan.
———. 2016c. "Mad about Method." presented at the Wiener Sprachgesellschaft, Wien.
McEnery, Tony, and Costas Gabrielatos. 2006. "English Corpus Linguistics." In *The Handbook of English Linguistics*, 33–71. London: Blackwell.
McEnery, Tony, and Andrew Hardie. 2012. "Corpus Linguistics: Methods, Theory and Practice." Cambridge University Press. https://corpora.lancs.ac.uk/clmtp/answers.php?chapter=7&type=questions.
Miller, Donna Rose, Paul Bayley, Cinzia Bevitori, Sabrina Fusari, and Antonella Luporini. 2014. "Ticklish Trawling: The Limits of Corpus Assisted Meaning

Analysis." In *Proceedings from the 24th European Systemic Functional Linguistics Conference and Workshop, Coventry, Department of English and Languages (DEL)*, edited by Siân Alsop and Sheena Gardner, 100–111. Coventry: Coventry University.

Morley, John. 2010. "Introduction: A Description of CorDis." In *Corpus-Assisted Discourse Studies on the Iraq Conflict—Wording the War*, edited by Paul Bayley and John Morley, 1–11. New York: Routledge.

O'Halloran, Kieran. 2007. "Critical Discourse Analysis and the Corpus-Informed Interpretation of Metaphor at the Register Level." *Applied Linguistics* 28 (1): 1–24. https://doi.org/10.1093/applin/aml046.

———. 2015. Counter-Discourse Corpora, Ethical Subjectivity and Critique of Argument: An Alternative Critical Discourse Analysis Pedagogy. *Journal of Language and Politics* 13 (4): 781–813.

———. 2017. *Posthumanism and Deconstructing Arguments: Corpora and Digitally-Driven Critical Analysis.* Milton Park, Abingdon, Oxon and New York, NY: Routledge.

O'Halloran, Kieran, and Caroline Coffin. 2004. "Checking Overinterpretation and Underinterpretation: Help from Corpora in Critical Linguistics." In *Applying English Grammar: Functional and Corpus Approaches*, edited by Caroline Coffin, Ann Hewings, and Kieran O'Halloran, 275–98. London: Arnold.

Orpin, Debbie. 2005. "Corpus Linguistics and Critical Discourse Analysis. Examining the Ideology of Sleaze." *International Journal of Corpus Linguistics* 10 (1): 37–61.

Partington, Alan. 1998. *Patterns and Meanings: Using Corpora for English Language Research and Teaching.* Studies in Corpus Linguistics 2. Amsterdam: John Benjamins.

———. 2004. "Corpora and discourse, a most congruous beast." In *Corpora and Discourse*, edited by Partington, Alan, John Morley and Louann Haarman, 11–20. Bern: Peter Lang.

———. 2015. "Corpus-Assisted Comparative Case Studies of Representations of the Arab World." In *Corpora and Discourse Studies: Integrating Discourse and Corpora*, edited by Tony McEnery and Paul Baker, 220–43. London: Palgrave Macmillan.

Partington, Alan, Alison Duguid, and Charlotte Taylor. 2013. *Patterns and Meanings in Discourse: Theory and Practice in Corpus-Assisted Discourse Studies (CADS).* Vol. 55. Studies in Corpus Linguistics. Amsterdam: John Benjamins. https://doi.org/10.1075/scl.55.

Phillips, Nelson, and Cynthia Hardy. 2002. *Discourse Analysis: Investigating Processes of Social Construction*. London: Sage.

Potts, Amanda. 2015. "Filtering the Flood: Sematic Tagging as a Method of Identifying Salient Discourse Topics in a Large Corpus of Hurricane Katrina Reportage." In *Corpora and Discourse Studies: Integrating Discourse and Corpora*, edited by Tony McEnery and Paul Baker, 285–305. London: Palgrave Macmillan.

Prentice, Sheryl. 2010. "Using Automated Semantic Tagging in Critical Discourse Analysis: A Case Study on Scottish Independence from a Scottish Nationalist Perspective." *Discourse & Society* 21 (4): 405–37. https://doi.org/10.1177/0957926510366198.

Reisigl, Martin, and Ruth Wodak. 2005. *Discourse and Discrimination. Rhetorics of Racism and Antisemitism*. London: Routledge.

———. 2015. "The Discourse-Historical Approach (DHA)." In *Methods of Critical Discourse Studies*, edited by Ruth Wodak and Michael Meyer, 23–61. London: Sage.

Sahlane, Ahmed. 2012. "Argumentation and Fallacy in the Justification of the 2003 War on Iraq." *Argumentation* 26 (4): 459–88.

Salama, Amir H.Y. 2011. "Ideological Collocation and the Recontexualization of Wahhabi-Saudi Islam Post-9/11: A Synergy of Corpus Linguistics and Critical Discourse Analysis." *Discourse & Society* 22 (3): 315–42. https://doi.org/10.1177/0957926510395445.

Sinclair, John M. 1999. "A way with common words." In *Out of Corpora*, edited by H. Hasselgard and S. Oksefjell, 157–79. Amsterdam: Rodopi.

Sinclair, John. 2004. *Trust the Text: Language, Corpus and Discourse*. London: Routledge.

Stubbs, Michael. 1996. *Text and Corpus Analysis: Computer-Assisted Studies of Language and Culture*. Language in Society 23. Oxford, OX, UK and Cambridge, MA: Blackwell.

———. 1997. "Whorf's Children: Critical Comments on Critical Discourse Analysis (CDA)." In *Evolving Models of Language*, edited by Ann Ryan and Alison Wray, 100–16. Clevedon: Multilingual Matters.

———. 1998. "From Angst to Zeitgeist: On German Loan Words and Cultural Stereotypes." *English Today* 53 (14): 19–26.

———. 2001a. *Words and Phrases: Corpus Studies of Lexical Semantics*. Oxford, UK and Malden, MA: Blackwell.

———. 2002. "On Text and Corpus Analysis: A Reply to Borsley and Ingham." *Lingua* 112 (1): 7–11. https://doi.org/10.1016/S0024-3841(01)00035-3.

———. 2006. "Corpus Analysis: The State of the Art and Three Types of Unanswered Questions." In *System and Corpus: Exploring Connections*, edited by Geoff Thompson and Susan Hunston, 15–36. London and Oakville, CT: Equinox Pub.

———. 2001b. "Texts, Corpora, and Problems of Interpretation: A Response to Widdowson." *Applied Linguistics* 22 (2): 149–72. https://doi.org/10.1093/applin/22.2.149.

Stubbs, Michael, and Andrea Gerbig. 1993. "Human and Inhuman Geography: On the Computerassisted Analysis of Long Texts." In *Data, Description, Discourse*, edited by Michael Hoey, 64–85. London: HarperCollins.

———. 2006b. "System and Corpus: Two Traditions with a Common Ground." In *System and Corpus: Exploring Connections*, edited by Geoff Thompson and Susan Hunston, 1–14. London and Oakville, CT: Equinox Pub.

Thompson, Geoff, and Susan Hunston, eds. 2006a. *System and Corpus: Exploring Connections*. London and Oakville, CT: Equinox Pub.

Tognini-Bonelli, Elena. 2001. *Corpus Linguistics at Work*. Studies in Corpus Linguistics 6. Amsterdam: John Benjamins.

van Dijk, Teun A. 1991. *Racism and the Press*. Critical Studies in Racism and Migration. London and New York: Routledge.

———. 1998. *Ideology a Multidisciplinary Approach*. London and Thousand Oaks, CA: Sage. http://site.ebrary.com/id/10567111.

van Leeuwen, Theo. 1996. "The Representation of Social Actors." In *Text and Practices: Readings in Critical Discourse Analysis*, edited by Carmen Rosa Caldas-Coulthard and Malcolm Coulthard, 32–70. London: Routledge.

Watt, Diane. 2007. "On Becoming a Qualitative Researcher: The Value of Reflexivity." *The Qualitative Report* 12 (1): 82–101.

Widdowson, Henry. 1995a. "Discourse Analysis: A Critical View." *Language and Literature* 4 (3): 157–72.

———. 1995b. "Review of Fairclough: Discourse and Social Change." *Applied Linguistics* 16 (4): 510–16.

———. 1996. "Discourse and Interpretation: Conjectures and Refutations [Reply to Fairclough, 1996]." *Language and Literature* 5 (1): 57–69.

———. 1998. "Review Article: The Theory and Practice of Critical Discourse Analysis." *Applied Linguistics* 19 (1): 136–51. https://doi.org/10.1093/applin/19.1.136.

———. 2000a. "Object Language and the Language Subject: On the Mediating Role of Applied Linguistics." *Annual Review of Applied Linguistics* 20 (January): 21–33. https://doi.org/10.1017/S0267190500200020.

———. 2000b. "On the Limitations of Linguistics Applied." *Applied Linguistics* 21 (1): 3–25. https://doi.org/10.1093/applin/21.1.3.

———. 2004. *Text, Context, Pretext: Critical Issues in Discourse Analysis.* Language in Society 35. Malden, MA: Blackwell.

Williams, Raymond. 2000. *Keywords: A Vocabulary of Culture and Society.* Nachdr. London: Fontana Press.

Wodak, Ruth. 1989. *Language, Power, and Ideology Studies in Political Discourse.* Amsterdam and Philadelphia: John Benjamins. http://public.eblib.com/choice/publicfullrecord.aspx?p=673092.

———. 2006. "Review Focus: Boundaries in Discourse Analysis." *Language in Society* 35 (4). https://doi.org/10.1017/S004740450606026X.

Wodak, Ruth, and Michael Meyer. 2009. "Critical Discourse Analysis: History, Agenda, Theory, and Methodology." In *Methods for Critical Discourse Analysis,* edited by R. Wodak, & M. Meyer, 1–33. London: Sage.

Wodak, Ruth, Rudolf de Cillia, Martin Reisigl, and Karin Liebhart. 2009. *The Discursive Construction of National Identity.* 2nd ed. Critical Discourse Analysis. Edinburgh: Edinburgh University Press.

[illegible]

3

Working with Different Types of Data: Methodological Plurality Within and Beyond the Linguistic

3.1 Introduction

While the previous chapter focused on the so-called qualitative-quantitative divide, data size, and related issues of data sampling—and thus related to triangulation in terms of analytical methods—the current chapter foregrounds triangulation through different types of data and the related methods of data collection, which may entail triangulation in terms of corresponding methods of analysis. Many publications have indicated a recent trend towards integrating more varied, even non-linguistic data into critical discourse studies (e.g. Bednarek and Caple 2014, 135; Machin and Mayr 2012) for reasons outlined briefly below.

Many of the arguments covered here are based on a—more or less justified—critique of CDS as focused on a narrow range of data or even one-dimensional data: written, monological language use. To some extent, this bias is even reinforced by introducing corpus linguistic methods to CDS (see Chapter 2, specifically on the "decontextualization" of data). Gerlinde Mautner's summary of the issue indexes two major perspectives in this debate: "many discourse analyses privilege written over spoken data,

© The Author(s) 2019
M. Rheindorf, *Revisiting the Toolbox of Discourse Studies*,
Postdisciplinary Studies in Discourse,
https://doi.org/10.1007/978-3-030-19369-0_3

and primarily textual over richly multimodal discourse (such as film)" (Mautner 2016, 214–15). In addition to this two-fold bias—firstly of written over spoken language and secondly of the linguistic over other modes—I discuss two related arguments, i.e. that discourse per se must be approached holistically and that a truly problem-centered approach to discourse cannot be limited to a particular type of data. These four interrelated perspectives all pertain to triangulation but inspire different approaches to the issue. In turn, each of them engenders specific challenges and can be met with more or less specific counter-arguments. Multimodality as the most articulate and developed of these approaches, specifically its prominent integration into Discourse Studies, are discussed at some length.

Clearly, attention to non-linguistic data raises the issue of intra- and interdisciplinary methodological plurality. In the literature, the discussion of this issue is often framed in the familiar terms of "tools" and providing a "set of tools" or "toolkit" (e.g. Machin and Mayr 2012, 1, 30). With Machin (2016, 332), I want to emphasize that the potentially interdisciplinary nature of collecting and analyzing very different types of data only raises the stakes with respect to methodological compatibility and consistency: "it is vital that more care is given to the kinds of tools and approaches that are required for different purposes – and tools that are more robust and defendable. CDA has a very specific set of aims."

As to the impulses behind this "paradigmatic shift" (O'Halloran 2004, 122), sometimes referred to as a "visual" or "multimodal turn" (Gibson et al. 2015, 274), several reasons have been identified. Although communication has always used multiple modes or semiotic systems, often simultaneously and in conjunction, leaving "the purely mono-modal text [as] an exception" (Stöckl 2004, 10), technological developments—in particular digital or (computer-)mediated forms of communication—have vastly increased the "possibilities of combining communication modes in the 'new' media" (Ventola et al. 2004). Clearly, such technological change must be seen not in isolation but linked to "considerable social change" (Jewitt 2009, 3). Inasmuch as contemporary digital environments increase the capacity and impact of multimodality on meaning-making (Androutsopoulos 2010; KhosraviNik and Unger 2015), it has also moved discourse analysts to consider the ways in which these modes semiotically function and combine in discourse (Bednarek and Caple 2017, 19).

The view that the change of culture constituted an impulse is sometimes seen in a wider historical frame. The early twentieth century's move towards a 'Gesamtkunstwerk' approach and the rise of film, television, and other mass media are thus understood as the necessary prefiguration of contemporary multimodality, also in terms of the literacy practices associated and growing with such media (O'Halloran et al. 2011, 110). Today, popular cultural products with massive global audiences construct and reflect social realities in ways that clearly demand discourse analysts' attention beyond the written word (Bednarek 2015, 63). Due to their spread and less accessible ways of constructing social reality, such data may even be more relevant than written text (Mautner 2016, 215). However, this juxtaposition can be misleading, for even written text is not mono-modal, comprising typography, layout, and materiality.

In this context, the increasing codification of semiotic resources described by Fairclough (1992) as "technologization" is also relevant, as it indicates processes of regulation, commodification, and marketization across modes as they become ever more interrelated and ubiquitous (Machin 2013b, 348). On the one hand, the challenge this represents is most evident in the multimodal nature of webpages that "interweave text, images, colour and other graphical material to create discursive contexts which may be difficult to identify or challenge" (Moran and Lee 2013, 373). On the other hand, such transformations are clearly ongoing and can affect all domains, as indicated by Zhang, Machin, and Song's analysis of a science webpage's shift to a social media-inspired 'scifopost' format (Zhang et al. 2015).

Other accounts, emphasizing the interdisciplinary nature of this endeavor, situate this particular trend within the larger frame of critical interest in media and culture from the 1970s onward, with Marxist scholars such as Adorno and Horkheimer leading the way. The work done at the Birmingham School of Cultural Studies, in particular by Raymond Williams and Stuart Hall, contributed much to the study of ideological structures in everyday culture from an anthropological point of view: as informed by and expressing a set of practices and beliefs constituting a socially negotiated understanding of how the world works (Hansen and Machin 2013, 152). More specifically, some have pointed to a connection between the weakening of disciplinary boundaries in the age of problem- or object-oriented research (O'Halloran and Smith 2011), suggesting that acceptability and spread of interdisciplinary work itself has been an enabling factor for discourse studies' integration of varied types of (non-linguistic) data (O'Halloran 2004, 122).

A further impetus to the study of multimodal discourse study, paralleling the technological developments mentioned above, is recognized in technologies enabling the collection, storage, and display of semiotically rich material as well as new multimodal annotation tools (O'Halloran et al. 2011, 110), data repositories, and interactive tools for data analysis (see Chapter 6 and the case studies of Part II). Ultimately, as CDS move to include non-linguistic forms of meaning-making, we must not be tempted by the charm of novelty, or even assume novelty, we need to demonstrate the advantage of such triangulation and of the specific tools we use.

3.2 The Language-Internal Argument/Triangulation in Linguistics

The narrowest bias with respect to data that CDS are often accused of is a focus on written, monologic language—although this still encompasses a wide range of language use, e.g. genres. This critique, framed within strictly linguistic terms, argues that by neglecting spoken language CDS have given us a very limited and skewed view of the discourses investigated. This bias is reproduced, for instance, in Antaki's (2008, 4) typological differentiation of forms of discourse analysis: Here, the critical approach to discourse is said to typically study official texts (such as party programs and commemorative speeches) as well as media texts and (published) interviews, whereas other forms of discourse analysis are linked to less official texts such as diaries, autobiographies, stories (elicited) interviews, ethnographic observations as well as audio and video recordings of social interaction. Yet, other forms of discourse analysis have focused on spoken language or even defined 'discourse' exclusively as spoken interaction.

In CDS, moves to broaden the range of linguistic data considered can take many forms. Several have involved either elicited interviews, group discussions, and naturally occurring conversations, bringing with them forms of Conversation Analysis (CA), or a combination of interviews and ethnographic observations in institutional settings, at public events, or with particular communities of practice. Both broad groups are briefly discussed below with respect to their main merits and challenges.

Despite their differences (Wooffitt 2005), CA and CDS share four basic principles: analysis of naturally occurring language, consideration of words in their co-text, attention to non-literal meaning or force, and the aim of revealing the social actions and consequences achieved through language use (Antaki 2008, 435). For Antaki, that means that both should be considered forms of discourse analysis, but it also implies a basic compatibility that some in CDS have sought to demonstrate and exploit. What CA brings to such an integration is its focus on the procedural analysis of talk-in-interaction, on how participants systematically organize their interactions to solve problems and collaborate in the production of meanings (Antaki 2008, 447). Thus, one potential context for integrating CDS and CA are studies on discourses that are associated with institutions or distinct communities of practice. Since members of such communities (e.g. a particular profession or institution) share stocks of interactional knowledge that relates intimately to the organization, values, and beliefs of the respective community, CA can give very local and deep insights into such discourses—particularly because this knowledge is often implicit or tacit, not to be found in official handbooks, regulations, and accounts. But in order to stay as close as possible to the speakers' life-world understandings, CA as such foregoes "interpretation from above" or "speculation about motives from below": no theory of society is adopted for the analysis, no pre-defined categories are applied (Antaki 2008, 15; Wooffitt 2005). This, then, is also the major point of friction with theory-heavy CDS, which typically goes into analysis with a pre-determined theoretical framework if not necessarily detailed categories. Possible solutions might be parallel analyses, the suspension of theoretical assumptions or, accepting a distinction between higher-level theory (e.g. about discourse and society) and assumptions about social interaction (e.g. about identity categories). Remarkably, the ground-breaking work on the discursive construction of national identities begun in the 1990s (Wodak et al. 1990, 1998) took a similar approach: eliciting group discussions and interviews alongside collecting official texts, analytical categories were formulated abductively.

More recently, online communication and in particular social media have sparked the development of specific approaches within or in conjunction with discourse studies—such as Susan Herring's computer-mediated discourse analysis (CMDA) and Jannis Androutsopolos's discourse-centered online ethnography (DCOE). As KohsraviNik and Unger (2015, 212) point out, such data—both their collection and their analysis—raise a number of challenges to established approaches in CDS. They go on to specify that "the differences in data types and new affordances" must be acknowledged and addressed on the macro-level before we can meaningfully engaging in micro-analysis (KhosraviNik and Unger 2015, 216). In other words, we cannot analyze language use on social media as if it were simply more of the same. In particular, the "fluid and dynamic nature of social media texts" renders standards approaches that first analyze (finalized) texts and then relate them to their context problematic. Their solution has been to adopt an observational, ethnographic approach, involving and confronting participants with material and observations that are usually avoided because they are difficult to integrate into text-based studies (KhosraviNik and Unger 2015, 231). This builds on but significantly extends the abductive tradition of the Discourse-Historical Approach (e.g. Wodak et al. 2009; Wodak 2011; Krzyżanowski 2010).

Also engaging with an online community, Potts (2015) studied an online community of practice formed around a gamer on YouTube. His channel constitutes a site where children and adolescents learn what it is to be masculine or feminine through legitimate peripheral participation. Triangulating her study with several datasets—63 YouTube videos, a corpus of 217,916 related comments, and an interview with the gamer featured in them—Potts gained insight into a number of perspectives within that community. On the one hand, the large set of comments required the use of corpus linguistic methods and allowed downsampling for closer linguistic analysis; on the other hand, even the videos were analyzed in terms of verbal interaction with only passing reference made to the gamers' in-game avatars' appearance.

Other studies that integrated ethnographic approaches (observations and often interviews) alongside written textual data have dealt with computer war games (Machin and Suleiman 2006), news narratives (Barkho 2011) and mental health settings (Galasiński 2011). While these studies also mention non-linguistic aspects—e.g. visual aspects of computer games—these are ancillary rather than integral to the approach. Their consideration does, however, suggest that in focusing on particular objects or problems, CDS may need to not only go beyond the linguistic in terms of data but rethink its fundamental understanding of discourse itself.

3.3 The Object- or Problem-Centered Perspective

In critical discourse studies, the analysis of different types of data, particularly non-linguistic data, is often framed in terms of an object- or problem-centered approach. If we want to study a particular phenomenon well or address a particular problem well, the argument runs, we need to study all of its aspects, or at least as many as possible, rather than stopping at the linguistic. If neither society nor discourse are purely linguistic, and some phenomena are in fact predominantly non-linguistic, this pushes discourse studies into new territory, seeking new tools.

Historically, CDS has privileged language as the principal means of communication, very nearly or downright equating language use with discourse, and has consequently studied discourse as a primarily linguistic phenomenon (Roderick 2018, 154–61). However, if the ultimate aim of critically studying discourse is to reveal the ways in which it constitutes, maintains, and transforms social reality and relations—including its many inequalities—such logocentrism is a severe limitation: to focus only on the linguistic elements risks ignoring a significant portion of the meaning potential of texts (Bednarek and Caple 2017, 24). Instances of inclusive object- or problem-centered studies are varied, including the representation of teachers as criminals in the news (Catalano and Gatti 2017), the construction of health and illness (Gibson et al. 2015) or visual metaphors (Bounegru and Forceville 2011; Feng and O'Halloran 2013; Feng and Espindola 2013). In the following, I draw on several examples to illustrate how such research designs have integrated data beyond the linguistic.

In their study on the performance and production of a European identity, Aiello and Thurlow (2006) proceed on the observation that "[i]n multilingual Europe, visual discourse may function as a cross-culturally strategic form of communication" and that "much in the way of intercultural exchange simply occurs outside of language" (Aiello and Thurlow 2006, 148–49). As a prerequisite for this function, they posit the perceptual and iconic availability of visual elements in discourse. Note that the reference to "visual discourse" might be mistaken to imply that there is an exclusively visual discourse and that therefore there might be purely linguistic, musical, architectural, etc. discourses as well. While this may be a useful shorthand, it is not a conceptually sound way of writing about discourse, not least because the different elements or modes of discourse (see below for the holistic and multimodal perspectives) are very much intertwined and interact with each other. Such conceptual isolation would therefore, in fact, be counter-productive to the aim of integrating different types of data into CDS.

Analytically, Aiello and Thurlow do not disregard the linguistic, but they successfully demonstrate that in European cities' bids for European Capital of Culture the visual elements of the discursive construction of Europeanness are surprisingly uniform across countries and decades. They highlight the iconic and symbolic meaning of recurring elements such as fireworks, children, and neoclassical buildings; the latter, in particular are used to index and invoke a sense of shared, specifically European "high culture" that privileges particular mythologies about culture and Europe (Aiello and Thurlow 2006, 158). Ultimately, however, their account betrays little interest in the interaction between the visual, linguistic and layout elements of their material, or even between the different forms of visuals such as photography, painting, and coloring.

Starting from a similar premise, Ledin and Machin (2017, 323) set out to reveal the ideas, values and priorities of neoliberal ideology informing a specific IKEA commercial for a kitchen. As with Aiello and Thurlow's (2006) analysis, the result might be called a case study, even if Ledin and Machin focus on a single text in greater detail. The commercial, they argue, presents the IKEA kitchen an aspirational form of elite space in which social status is performed through the deliberate use of semiotic resources, marking distinction and privilege. Activity/interaction, space, color, music and furniture are shown to mesh in this performance so as to regulate social behavior in terms of "self-management," "innovation" and "improved outcomes" (Ledin and Machin 2017, 323). This, the authors conclude, is commensurate with the (general, cultural) codification of the kitchen as a "high-prestige domestic space" very different from a functional space where people cook and eat. An important notion in the analysis is that of "rhyming." It is significant that their analysis hinges largely on the attention they give to the interaction between the various semiotic resources: Different semiotic resources "rhyme", they observe, to jointly code activities, colors, designs, and objects as coherent, or to mark differences across individual frames and scenes (Ledin and Machin 2017, 327; see also Kress and van Leeuwen 2002).

In studies that emphasize an object- or problem-centered approach, ethnographic methods have often been employed in order to get a firm grasp of the context. Both Machin and Mayr (2012, 216) and Krzyżanowski (2011a, 231) note the significance of integrating ethnography into problem-oriented and context-sensitive research on discourse as social practice. Krzyżanowski emphasizes fieldwork in understanding the (institutional) context of discursive practices, arguing that for contextualist CDS to live up to their own promise, the integration of ethnography is often a necessary complement to linguistic analysis (Krzyżanowski 2011a, 236). Perhaps the strongest stance on this point has been taken by Barkho (2011), who argues that the critical study of discourse is viable only if backed by ethnographic exploration for the contextualisation of linguistic data, especially in complex institutional settings. Indeed, the broadening and differentiation of the contextualist stance achieved by the multi-level definition of context offered in Reisigl and Wodak (2015) can be partly operationalized by ethnographic methods (Krzyżanowski 2011a, 231). In a conceptually significant move, this further allows linking the collection (and analysis) of data that could be situated on different contextual levels—socio-historical, situational, intertextual/interdiscursive, and co-textual—to well-established concepts such as *recontextualisation* and *interdiscursivity* (Richardson and Wodak 2009; Wodak and Fairclough

2010), thereby also suggesting an operationalization of context-to-text relationships (Krzyżanowski 2011a, 232).

Examples of such integrated research designs can be found in critical work on institutional discourses in the EU (Muntigl et al. 2000; Wodak 2011; Krzyżanowski 2010), where a combination of in-depth analyses of organizational contexts was tied in with detailed linguistic analyses of a range of materials. Specifically, such discourse-ethnographic research can offer nuanced and comprehensive insights into the constitution of new institutions and their discursive practices (Krzyżanowski 2011b). Similarly engaging with institutional discourses, Rogers (2011) integrates longitudinal ethnography into her "educational tracking" study of the effects of individuals' decisions within an educational system informed by neoliberal educational policies. Her approach thus also addresses the challenge of connecting micro-level analysis to macro-level context through triangulation: collecting and analyzing different types of data with an appropriate methodological combination.

Focusing on language policy, Johnson (2011) also integrates ethnography into CDS, combining the ethnographic examination of the process of policy-making and policy implementation with the analysis of policy documents. Without explicitly identifying and distinguishing context along the layers mentioned above, Johnson thus also demonstrates a research design capable of understanding interconnections between texts and discourses across multiple levels of policy creation, interpretation, and implementation. In effect, this offers insights into how US federal language policy (in Johnson's terms, the meso-level), itself embedded in political discourses (macro-level), is recontextualized in the bilingual education practice of the local school district of Philadelphia (micro-level). Johnson explicitly links his strategy of collecting and analyzing different types of data, giving him gain access to multiple perspectives, to the "perennial challenge" of "mak[ing] connections between the macro and the micro" (Johnson 2011, 267). While discourse analysis reveals links, ethnography is essential to understanding why these links are forged in particular ways, i.e. why language policies are recontextualized in divergent, often contradictory ways in particular contexts (Johnson 2011, 277).

Placing similar emphasis on what is traditionally considered 'context' in CDS, Norris (2004) offers an object-centered approach rooted in a multimodal perspective. The object, in this case, is defined as "the multiplicity of (inter)actions that a social actor engages in simultaneously" (Norris 2004, 101), including "embodied" as well as "disembodied modes" such as spatial arrangements or architectural layouts that persist in the absence of the social actor originating them (Norris 2004, 103). This particular approach is distinguished by its *heuristic* understanding of communicative modes as lacking stringent boundaries, often overlapping with each other, creating tension and even contradiction (see below).

3.4 The Holistic Perspective

Part of the challenge in integrating non-linguistic data into CDS is telling linguists that there is more to meaning-making than language. Stated simply, this observation is far from novel and the field of semiotics provides rich grounds for inspiration. From its conception, the field of semiotics, in aiming for a comprehensive view of all meaning-making through signs, is informed by the need to develop a holistic approach to communication. Several qualifications need to be added to this goal: not excluding any sign systems, taking into account the specific characteristics of different systems, and linking meaning-making to its social context. Both Saussure's (1916/1974, 16) call for a science that "studies the life of signs within society" and Barthes' (1957/1972, 112) rhetorical question as to "how many really non-signifying fields" we encounter each day both point to the ubiquity and social nature of meaning-making. Such a "holistic" approach to meaning-making (Preziosi 1986, 45) must also acknowledge the interaction between signs within texts (O'Halloran et al. 2011, 109).

Nonetheless, as the following passage by Aiello and Thurlow from 2006 attests, a broader view of communication still requires rather fundamental justification:

> Although it might seem out of place in a journal otherwise devoted to language/s, we see two good reasons why the study of visual discourse is an important consideration for linguists. First of all, no semiotic mode exists in isolation of other meaning-making practices. Language is only ever made truly meaningful and/or understandable in the context of paralinguistic

> and other nonverbal codes; in fact, in many instances written and spoken language are themselves the contextual 'background'. (Aiello and Thurlow 2006, 148)

The links of the problem- or object-oriented perspective to this holistic perspective are clear; yet with the former the methodological configuration adopted depends on and changes with the occasion, whereas the latter calls for a principled and consistent conceptualization of interrelated sign systems as used in communicative situations.

Thus, Theo van Leeuwen's programmatic "Ten Reasons why linguistics should pay attention to Visual Communication" takes a correspondingly strong stance on linguists' reticence to 'pay attention'. Among other things, van Leeuwen calls for the redefining of 'speech acts' as 'communicative acts' in which all the signs present determine communicative intent; for a renaming of genres as 'performed genres' if spoken and 'inscribed genres' if written, with language use being a possible but not necessary aspect of the stages that make up either type of genre; re-conceptualizing 'proposition' as potentially integrating language with other types of signs into a single syntagmatic unit; and recognizing typography and handwriting as "no longer" merely conveyer of linguistic meaning, but semiotic systems themselves. Such terminological and conceptual shifts, van Leeuwen (2004, 15) concludes, are necessary if CDS are to analyze discourses in their many and varied aspects, which often realize different—complementary or even contrasting—meanings. Before moving on to multimodal discourse analysis as the most coherent answer to this challenge, I discuss two studies that illustrate the holistic approach indicated above: Lim (2017) on gesture in classroom interaction and Krzyżanowska (2016) on monuments in public space.

The former convincingly demonstrates the inadequacy of research into classroom discourse which involves only language, leading to an impoverished understanding of interaction *as a whole*. Particularly gesture, Lim (2017) argues, cannot be overlooked to fully appreciate the meanings achieved through the orchestration of semiotic choices made by teachers. Although language is often dominant in classroom discourse, it is almost always co-deployed with other semiotic resources (Lim 2017, 1). His work achieves a holistic perspective by extending work on gesture undertaken by Martinec (2004) while integrating it into Systemic Functional Multimodal Discourse Analysis (see below).

In contrast, the latter engages with a form of meaning-making in which language is not dominant, even marginal, but which is itself ubiquitous and highly significant: As Abousnnouga and Machin (2011, 175) have noted, monuments mark that which our societies see as somehow outstanding and form an integral part of our everyday semiotic landscapes, contributing much to the spatial organization of cities, the moral order of societies, and the discursive construction of national identities by way of a shared past (see also Wodak et al. 2009). It is precisely because monuments use semiotic resources other than language—which appear to be more ambiguous and less fixed, and therefore less accessible to explication and critique—that they are able to institutionalize and naturalize discourses (Iedema 2003). Krzyżanowska's (2016) specific interest is in counter-monumental installations known in German as 'Stolpersteine', which translates roughly as 'stumbling blocks'. Since 1992, nearly 70,000 of these blocks have been embedded into the pavement or doorways in front of the former residences of victims of the Nazis.

Krzyżanowska's holistic approach draws attention to the spatial, material, linguistic, and cultural aspects of these monuments, but it also acknowledges their interconnections: Unlike most memorials, their placement is unobtrusive and only draws attention from close proximity, yet it ensures that contemporary inhabitants of those houses or spaces will notice the Stolpersteine on a daily basis. Their number and ubiquity, again unlike conventional monuments, embed this commemorative discourse in everyday space, where it can reach locals and tourists alike. In this spatial context, their material features are integral to their discursive effect: Their physical size is small enough to go unnoticed, yet large enough to hold key information (names, dates of birth and death, their fate at the hands of the Nazis); their rectangular shape is somber and tomb-stone-like, yet their rounded edges soften the gravity of their meaning; their material composition, brass, communicates durability and eternity while being non-intrusive, yet their smooth surface may also catch the sunlight and make them momentarily more visible; from the right angle, the plaques function like small mirrors that add a dialogic feature to commemoration. Typographically, the engravings utilize a somber, all-capitals font in two different sizes to give emphasis to names. Linguistically, the engravings individualize commemoration as opposed to hegemonic discourses that collectivize historical experience, but it also links the victims to their everyday lives, from which they were torn so ruthlessly (Krzyżanowska 2016, 465). Krzyżanowska is thus able to argue conclusively and in great detail that these are, indeed, counter-monuments inasmuch as they strategically recontextualize the lives and deaths of the victims outside of hegemonic discourses of commemoration.

3.5 The Multimodal Perspective

The holistic perspective of semiotics, in particular the approach called "social semiotics", has been integral to the development of the field of multimodality. The fact that it *is* a field—and as such offers the most comprehensive answer to the challenge of working with different types of data, while also comprising several distinct approaches as attested by an increasing number of introductory books and special issues (e.g. Machin 2007; van Leeuwen 2008; Machin and Mayr 2012; Machin and Abousnnouga 2013; Djonov and Zhao 2014; Zhao et al. 2018)—warrants a separate discussion. In the following, I give an overview of its most prominent strands of theorizing, shared tenets, and the possibilities they offer to CDS.

As to the field's theoretical foundations besides de Saussure and Barthes, systemic functional linguistics is one of its main inspirations. This concerns the definition of "culture as a set of semiotic systems, a set of systems of meaning, all of which interrelate" (Halliday and Hasan 1985, 4), jointly constituting "the 'reality' of the culture" (Halliday 1978, 123). At the same time, this view has also contributed much to CDS, which in turn has informed the emerging field of (critical) multimodal studies (O'Halloran et al. 2011, 110). Although the terminology varies, the following approaches to multimodality can be distinguished today: (1) contextual or *social semiotic* approaches; (2) grammatical approaches or *systemic-functional* multimodal discourse analysis; (3) *multimodal interactional analysis* with foundations in interactional sociolinguistics and intercultural communication; (4) *cognitive* approaches to multimodal metaphor based on cognitive linguistics and conceptual metaphor theory; and (5) *stylistic* approaches. Although all of these could conceivably be integrated into CDS, the first four have been most productive. At the same time, the fact that multimodality is branching off into relatively independent branches has been decried as fragmentation (Machin 2016, 322) and as counterproductive to Kress and van Leeuwen's (1996, 2001) aim to expand the critical analysis of discourse, conceptually and empirically, to non-linguistic data (Wang 2014, 265).

Central among the tenets shared by these approaches is the notion that "all discourse is multimodal" (Scollon and LeVine 2004, 1). Discourses are seen as realized not only in written or spoken language but through all forms of meaningful activity, including through entertainment media such as computer games and movies, through all aspects of everyday life such as fashion, toys, music, architecture, and spatial organization as well as through bodily hexis and physical interaction. The elements of meaning-making are considered *semiotic resources*, organized into *systems of meaningful choices* within each *mode* of communication, realized and combined with others in *genres*—the level at which many of them are recognizable as meaningful social action in everyday life (on multimodality and genre, see Bateman 2011). This entails an important distinction between mode and medium, even if no mode can exist without medium: Modes are semiotic systems of choices, a grammatical system in a sense; media are physical means of realization and distribution. This distinction helps to clarify that modes are always culturally determined and more or less conventionalized.

Especially the social semiotics approach to multimodality insists that a sign can exist in all modes of communication and is *made* rather than *used* by people. As Gunther Kress puts it, the sign-maker "brings meaning into an apt conjunction with a form, a selection/choice shaped by the sign-maker's interest" (Kress 2010, 62). In the broadest sense, then, approaches to multimodality are concerned with what people do with semiotic resources. But they are interested not only in analyzing a particular instance of meaning-making but the entire systems or repertoires of meaning potentials afforded by modes. Sign-makers are seen as selecting from these affordances according to their communicative needs and interests in a given context (Abousnnouga and Machin 2011, 178; Machin and Richardson 2012, 330).

Significantly, multimodal approaches hold that choices on all the aforementioned levels are infused by *ideology* and *power* (Machin 2013b, 347). The critical agenda informing the multimodal perspective is thus akin to CDS. And yet, because the field is diversifying, many of its leading figures have found it necessary to go back to that critical agenda and ask, in some form or other, how to "best approach the way that discourse and ideologies are disseminated generally simultaneously across different kinds of communicative modes and genres" or "how multimodal critical discourse studies (MCDS) can best embrace the questions and issues that are core to CDS" (Machin 2013b, 347).

It has often been acknowledged that much of the analytical impetus in the field of multimodality comes from, or was inspired by, the rigor of linguistic theorization, methodology, categorization, and systematicity (Machin 2013b, 349). Indeed, these principles clearly distinguish the multimodal perspective from what might be called "ad hoc" approaches informed by the problem- or object-oriented perspective (Baldry and Thibault 2006, 21, as quoted in Flewitt et al. 2009, 46). A key aspect in this is the multimodal understanding of the interrelationship between language and other modes as well as between modes in general: On the one hand, language is seen as part of a "multimodal ensemble" (Jewitt 2009, 14), making the mono-modal conception of discourse seem severely limited (Bolander and Locher 2014, 18); on the other hand, multimodality as such denotes "communicative artefacts and processes which combine various sign systems (modes) and whose production and reception calls upon the communicators to semantically and formally interrelate all sign repertoires present" (Stöckl 2004, 9). Since the meaning created through multimodal communication "is seen as multiplicative rather than additive", the "overall result is more than the sum of its parts" (Flewitt et al. 2009, 46).

While language may thus be the most important semiotic mode in a particular interaction, it rarely occurs in isolation and is often not merely "supported" by other modes. Rather, the multiplication of meaning leads to a multidimensional semantic space in which the propositional content of individual modes may be compressed, complemented, combined, duplicated for rhetorical effect, ornamented, inflected or even counteracted. Kress (2012, 378) argues that there are "meanings which cannot be spoken or written" or that people may choose to communicate non-linguistically for reasons that are worth investigating in their own right. This view is linked to the insight that modes occupy different 'reaches' with respect to their preferential use and the social meanings 'allocated' to them, and that this distribution varies between contexts, social groups, cultures or societies. With respect to speech, Kress (2012, 382) points to pitch-variation as "used in profoundly different ways by different social groups and languages, with profound effects on what a social group can or must do with this feature". As a result, the salience of specific modes varies between contexts both situational and cultural (Kress 2012, 383). Arguably, some modes may be used more effectively for manipulation than others: Image and sound, particularly music or song, have been discussed as effective means to achieving the desired ideological alignment and response in people (Hansen and Machin 2013, 160).

This key area of interest has been given many names: semiotic overdetermination (Roderick 2018), semiotic division of labor (van Leeuwen 2008), interaction between sign systems (Hansen and Machin 2013, 158), the inter-semiotic or inter-modal relationship (Roderick 2018) or simply intersemiosis (Jewitt 2009), and more specifically text-image relations (Bateman 2011). If pursued to its logical conclusion, this view rejects the idea—even as it appears implicitly in some work tagged as 'multimodal'—that individual semiotic modes can be analyzed as isolated carriers of meaning. Part of the interest here is which roles specific modes conventionally play (in particular situations, genres etc.): van Leeuwen (2008, 137) has hypothesized that, in many contexts in the Western world, language provides facts and explanations, while images provide connotative meanings, emotions, and interpretations. The ability of visuals to evoke affective responses is deemed to be significantly greater than that of language (Hansen and Machin 2013, 163; Jagodzinski 2013).

The potential deception here is that meanings seem to 'emanate' from the 'reality' depicted rather than from an act of signification. Barthes described this in the oft-quoted *Paris Match* example:

> I am at the barber's and a copy of Paris-Match is offered me. On the cover, a young Negro in a French uniform is saluting, with his eyes uplifted, probably fixed on a fold of the tricolour. All this is the meaning of the picture. But,

> whether naively or not, I see very well what it signifies to me: that France is a great Empire, that all her sons, without any colour discrimination, faithfully serve her flag. (Barthes 1957/1972, 116)

Significantly, such semiotic divisions of labor are historically and contextually specific, and CDS would do well to be aware of these in any analysis. Van Leeuwen (2008, 137) goes on to give a broad characterization of the division in "science and technology", where visualizations are regarded as the most comprehensive and explicit form of explanation, relegating language to the role of providing supplement, commentary or labels. For advertisements, he notes that the visual will similarly be dominant, if for very different purposes.

Other research has sought to map the intersemiotic relations at work in monuments, discussing as modes iconography, shape, size, typeface/typography, surface realization, material, and solidity (Abousnnouga and Machin 2011, 183). Here, too, one can observe the attempt to relate the choice of semiotic resources to experiential and cultural associations: roundness, for instance, is linked to the meaning potentials "smooth", "soft", "gentle", "emotional", "fluidity", "ease", and "organic"; angularity, in contrast, is associated with "harsh", "technical", "masculine", and "objectivity". Like monuments, music is regarded as a primarily non-linguistic form of communication, comprising modes such as pitch ranges, choice of notes, instrumentation, articulation, arrangements and rhythms. As such music has largely been neglected by critical discourse studies, at least partly because it is seen as a highly specialized, difficult field where few if any categories developed for language can be meaningfully applied (van Leeuwen 2012, 319). In their analysis of fascist music, Machin and Richardson (2012, 329) therefore aim to go beyond impressionistic description and "adopt the same rigour critical discourse analysts apply when analysing language and speech". They regard music as a multimodal ensemble that can realize socially determined meanings to express values, identities, and ideologies (van Leeuwen 2012, 327); by infusing ideological meanings with emotion, fascist music thus tries to naturalize relations of power and solidarity. As mentioned above, music is sometimes cited alongside image as particularly well suited to manipulation; however, unlike visual stimuli, sound actually enters the bodies of the audience, who literally resonate with the music. As such, Machin (2013a, 138) concludes, sound is more immersive than other modes and potentially more powerful.

Focusing on contemporary political songs, Screti (2013) similarly argues that these are important for transmitting ideological meanings by non-explicit means. In this, music engages the receiver in greater semiotic collaboration than other media by rhetorical devices such as rhyme, liturgical or magical effects (Screti 2013, 206). This is particularly pertinent to consensus building in collective rituals, among which national anthems, campaign anthems or counter-political songs stand out (Rheindorf and Wodak 2019). This insight is pertinent to critical studies of political discourses, in particular in election campaigns, inasmuch as such discourses are increasingly "contaminated" or "colonized" by other discourses and genres (Screti 2013, 209).

In directing attention to the way that semiotic resources, including but not limited to language, construct social reality, approaches to multimodality rely on the notions of representation and recontextualization, but the concept of "resemiotization" has also been suggested to indicate the shifting of propositions from one semiotic mode to another (Scollon 2006). As Iedema (2003, 47) has noted, such "transposition between different semiotics inevitably introduces a discrepancy that goes or points beyond the original", involving a semantic shift, as choices from different semiotic resources are not commensurate (Lemke 1998). Both recontextualization and resemiotization appear as transformations or deformations of discourse, informed by ideology, as many multimodal analyses have shown. Resemiotization is an important way for discourses to become naturalized and legitimized, and should accordingly draw significant attention from CDS. Since there is no easily identifiable process of resemiotization, research must trace how discourses (which are already multimodal) are transposed into new configurations of semiotic resources and to what effect (Machin 2013b, 351). Clearly, mechanisms of recontextualization such as abstraction, addition, substitution, deletion, and evaluation (van Leeuwen and Wodak 1999) are relevant to this, as are access to means of production, technological or media affordances as well as meso-level patterns and structures like 'register' or 'genre'. The notion of "recontextualization chains" (van Leeuwen 2008, 15) furthermore draws attention to the fact that meaning may undergo multiple such transformations across multiple contexts, registers or genres (see Chapter 4 on levels of discourse, specifically social fields of action).

An excellent case in point is Machin and Mayr's (2013) study on a "real crime" TV show that combines reporting with dramatized re-enactment. The genre makes a particularly apt case for demonstrating the effects of recontextualization: On the one hand, the reenactments personalize crime and construct criminal types as fundamentally different from consensual society—visually substituting the complexity of crime with the offender's sweaty, furtive, and repulsive exterior—while humanizing police work in the form of singularly committed detectives against the backdrop of collectivized and thorough policing. Such representations, the authors argue, ultimately serve to justify retributive discourses (Machin and Mayr 2013, 370).

The analysis of another contemporary television genre—The Biggest Loser, a reality TV show that dramatizes the struggle of its participants to lose weight as a competition—has delved deeply into the (post-)production process to reveal how different modes are used to conveying different, even contradictory meanings, one undercutting the other (Monson et al. 2016). On the explicit "surface", i.e. dialogue and other verbal elements, the show seems to empower its participants and to promote healthy behaviors, but its camera angles, amount of camera time, lighting and color, the candidates' clothing, and the post-production editing construct varying degrees of success and presents those unsuccessful at losing weight as "figures of abjection", weak of will and therefore undeserving. The show thus ultimately reinforces existing beliefs surrounding the character failings of fat people and the social value of fat bodies (Monson et al. 2016, 538).

In some cases, the identification of characteristic 'division of labor' between semiotic modes in specific media has been described as paradigmatic (or paradigm shifts). Such is the case with 'new writing', i.e. a recently emerged pattern of interaction between layout, spacing, visual elements like color, and language. A prominent example of this is the 'bullet list', a spatial form of organizing writing that "relies on visual-verbal interaction, rather than on verbal grammar or discourse-semantic structures, for creating cohesion and coherence, and is strongly fostered by technologies such as PowerPoint" (Djonov and van Leeuwen 2013, 14). This form of writing is paradigmatically 'new' in the sense that the type of coherence previously achieved in running text (i.e. cohesion, rhetorical composition) has been largely replaced by visuals, symbols, and spacing within the layout grid. Tables and lists are prime examples of how social reality can be constructed and legitimized in a specific way, i.e. in neoliberal management discourse (Ledin and Machin 2015, 466). The affordances of tables and lists allow the separation of items and recontextualize complex logical relations between elements through spatiality (Kress and van Leeuwen 2006). They abstract and reify the items in a paradigm, but they also serve to suppress the relationships between their components (Ledin and Machin 2015, 470).

More specific in their scope than the above-cited social semiotic approaches, cognitive metaphor approaches to multimodality began with Charles Forceville's seminal work on "pictorial metaphors" in the 1990s and have been applied in critical analyses of advertisements, cartoons, and films. Visual metaphors can play a key role in representational, interactive, and compositional meaning structures, particularly in conveying abstract meanings, which require the use of symbols, metonymies or metaphors (Feng and O'Halloran 2013, 320). In a symbolic attributive process (Kress and van Leeuwen 2006, 105), the visual mode will show the source domain while the linguistic co-text specifies the target domain by labeling the visual. The verbal label thus endows the image with a value, but cognitively that value is understood only in terms of the image (Feng and O'Halloran 2013, 320). Pictorial metaphors are thus a specific case of the interconnectedness of modes in meaning-making and can be used indirectly for ideological aims: In his study on media framings of the British Miners' Strike, Hart (2017, 25) found that the metaphorical interpretation of many images was realized only through intertextual references—either in the image itself or in accompanying text—establishing the source frame for the metaphor.

Also tracing the subtle ideological work that can be done multimodally, Mulderrig (2018) analyzed the "nudging" strategies in the UK government's "healthy living" campaign C4L. These draw on behavioral psychology to emotionally manipulate and persuade viewers to adopt healthier lifestyles in what she describes as a new form of "governmentality which uses subtle semiotic techniques to secure voluntary compliance with policy goals". Her data, a series of cartoon adverts, represents the human body as a site of battle by resemiotizing scientific, preemptive epidemiological discourse for an audience of children through visual metaphors. For instance, in depicting internal bodily processes of fat storage and arterial blockage, a "racing car" metaphor visually positions the audience in a way likely familiar to children from computer games (Mulderrig 2018, 39). These nudging strategies betray a biopolitics based on strongly emotional and moral judgments about how people should behave—and corresponding stigmatization of deviant behavior in parts of the population. In Foucauldian terms, they serve as "mechanisms of segregation and social hierarchization" in the interest of hegemony, reflecting the neoliberal paradox of fostering "free subjects" while also "managing undesirable behaviors" (Mulderrig 2018, 45).

Some studies in multimodality have tried to address a long-standing issue also present in CDS: the disconnect between 'discourse' and 'materiality'. The so-called discourse-design approach proposed by Ledin and Machin (2016, 16) conceptualizes design as the material realization of discourses in the sense of the concrete co-articulation of semiotic resources which have evolved in (or into) complex interrelationships, as structured wholes or multimodal ensembles. Combining ethnographic observations and interviews with analysis of the material design of toy guns, Machin and van Leeuwen (2009) show how children take up the discourses materialized in the toys' design in play. As interactive representations of war, they involve children in a specific "body politic", using the children's own playful activity to teach them about the social meanings of war.

Distinct from other approaches to multimodality is so-called multimodal interaction analysis as advocated in Norris (2004, 2011). Related to the nexus analysis approach of Scollon and Scollon (2004), this approach takes individual actions as its units of analysis, defining *action* as a social actor acting with or through multimodal mediational means in a particular situational context. Non-linguistic modes are thus studied as integral parts of interaction, characterized by the intricate and often subtle interplay between different semiotic resources such as intonation, pitch, facial expression, gesture, kinetics, posture, and proximity as well as cues in the interactants' immediate environment. Multimodal interaction analysis aims to gain insight into "how a variety of modes are brought into and constitutive of social interactions" (Jewitt 2009, 33). The challenge of relating micro-level analysis to macro-level context is here addressed by regarding a specific moment in social interaction as the "site of engagement", while larger activities involving multiple, repeated sites of engagement are seen as "nexus of practice". Through the relatively consistent ensemble of social processes the defines it, such a nexus can be related to its broader socio-political and cultural context (Norris 2011, 279). Empirically, this involves multiple stages of engaging with the field and its social actors in ways reminiscent of ethnographic approaches.

3.6 The Problem of Subjectivity

Like other forms of discourse analysis, multimodal approaches have been criticized as frequently relying on the analyst's intuition—at least in research practice—and failing to provide satisfactory, i.e. plausible and accessible accounts of how they arrive at specific interpretations. It is certainly true that some studies that use the label "multimodal" do little to explicate their analyses, while others seem to accept—even welcome—the absence of accountability: To quote but one example, Gibson et al. (2015, 284) assert that it "involves the same interpretive skills as any other qualitative research in psychology" and seek to justify this position by drawing on Gleeson's (2011, 316) resigned comment that "we have no rule books to support our interpretations and must fall back on a wider disparate range of texts and experiences to justify our interpretation of the image". Such attitude, of course, runs counter to several basic tenets of multimodality as elaborated above and therefore should not give rise to criticism against the approach as such.

Blatant subjectivity aside, the frameworks discussed above have frequently been challenged as being problematic in assigning specific meanings to semiotic resources (such as camera angles or positions in the visual space) based on introspection and observation rather than empirical evidence. Given that that "grammars" of modes other than language are arguably less conventionalized, we require empirical—perhaps experimental—evidence as to the effects of specific choices in specific contexts of communication (thus also taking into account, e.g., genre). To be sure,

Kress and van Leeuwen (1998, 218) acknowledged the major challenge to their approach in the epistemological status of assigning values to semiotic resources: "[H]ow can we know that left and right, and top and bottom, have the values we attribute to them, or more fundamentally, have any value at all?".

To address this impasse, Feng and Espindola (2013, 89) suggest looking to other areas of academic enquiry, such as cognitive linguistics or conceptual metaphor theory—but there is no reason, I would add, to stop there: many social sciences and humanities have much to offer regarding multimodality, and we should avoid reinventing the wheel (see Sect. 3.7). The evidence cited by Fend and Espindola relates to the experiential base of spatial-visual perception as well as their conventionalized use in everyday conceptual systems as "default" interpretations of, e.g., camera position or composition. They emphasize that these may be inflected by other elements or specific contexts of communication, highlighting the need for situated, contextualized analysis (see Sect. 3.10 on "tunnel vision" in multimodal approaches). The example they quote in support of this argument, however, is problematic and indicates its limitations: films scripts sometimes require a particular angle shot for the sake of consistency or continuity rather than for the purpose of expressing power relations (Feng and Espindola 2013, 96). While this is factually true, intent is not required for a particular semiotic resource to have a particular effect. Especially in non-fictional genres, this would otherwise render much of multimodal analysis void. To be fair, Fend and Espindola's objective is to conceptualize visual metaphors as *not* dependent on the immediate context of their use but on "physical and cultural experiences that are common to human beings or specific cultural communities" (Feng and Espindola 2013, 98).

Similarly, Hart (2016) turns to cognitive linguistics and conceptual metaphor theory for epistemological grounding, but he takes the argument much further. Arguing that not only is linguistic communication based on visual perception but that we can understand the linguistic mode through conceptual metaphors based on the visual/spatial mode. Among these, he examines two more closely: social relations are distance; stance is position/orientation in space (Hart 2016, 344). In other words, he not only affirms the social semiotic interpretation of key resources in the visual/spatial mode but concludes that findings from multimodal studies may well illuminate the ways in which language constructs knowledge and values.

3.7 Reinventing the Wheel

Although the study of multimodality as a field is generally seen as initiated by the groundbreaking work of Kress and van Leeuwen (1996, 2001) and O'Toole (1994), critical voices have pointed out that while their contributions were certainly original, they were hardly the first to study non-linguistic communication, in particular visual culture. In this view, the main achievements of multimodality have been to "open linguistics up to a whole new world", to introduce an array of interdisciplinary notions to discourse studies, and to infuse these with linguistics-like systematic rigor and systemic functional linguistics-informed conceptualizing. The downside of this, as Pauwels (2012) argues, is that multimodality thereby may well be following the tendency for different fields in visual research to 'reinvent the wheel' as they 'discover' new types of data but continue to operate in their own disciplinary networks.

Obviously, scholars in disciplines such as Cultural Studies, Media and Film Studies, Journalism, Visual Studies, Social Anthropology, Architecture, and Arts have spent many decades theorizing and analyzing many of the phenomena now studied under the rubric of 'multimodality'. There is certainly merit in engaging with these fields and their insights, so as not to ignore valuable insights (Machin 2013b, 348). However, we cannot simply disregard Pauwels' (2012) observation that scholars tend to find it difficult to explore methods beyond their own discipline, preferring those that emerge from within their own field, even where more suitable or mature approaches are available: familiarity with concepts, parallel terminologies etc. are unmistakably advantageous if the aim is, as the case may be, to convince linguistics 'that there is more than language'. As Machin (2013b, 348) points out, the ensuing development of new terminology and methods, many of which will parallel already existing ones, may appear rather arbitrary. From a sociology-of-science perspective, however, it may not be entirely avoidable.

There is another important caveat to avoiding 'reinventing the wheel' by adopting theories, concepts, methods or insights previously established in other fields: Different disciplines operate on different—sometimes fundamentally different—conceptions of both 'the world' and 'science'. This may show in terminology as well as in methodology. The theories, concepts, and insights they generate may thus be based on conceptions in conflict with not only multimodality but discourse studies at large. For instance, musicologists do not regard music as discourse and "refuse to deal with music meaning", as van Leeuwen notes with some frustration (van Leeuwen 2012, 320). Thus, some fields, such as cultural studies and some strands in film studies, may be closer to the theoretical makeup of multimodal approaches, in part because they share some of the same theoretical influences (e.g. Foucault); and their theories, concepts, and insights may be incorporated into a multimodal approach after little conceptual probing and testing for compatibility. In the case of other fields, however, the 'reverse engineering' necessitated by different epistemological traditions may come rather close to 'reinventing the wheel'.

3.8 Linguistic Imperialism

Arguably, multimodal approaches were so successful at telling linguists 'that there is more than language' because they approached non-linguistic modes *through* language, transferring a range of concepts and categories from language to very disparate modes. The underlying premise—that non-linguistic modes can be approached in ways not fundamentally different from established approaches to language—is undoubtedly appealing to linguists. To this date, scholars in the field still observe and maintain such disciplinary affiliations: Gibson et al. (2015, 274), for instance, observe that the most significant work in multimodal discourse analysis has been done *in* linguistics (and here they point to Kress and van Leeuwen). It would seem to follow that multimodal discourse analysis is, or can be, a subfield of linguistics. Given such affiliations/attributions of work in multimodality, it is perhaps not surprising that we also find criticism of "linguistic imperialism" in the field. Indeed, the relation between linguistic and multimodal approaches has recently been identified as one of two important challenges facing the field (Hart 2016, 335).

There is a general sense that linguistic approaches have influenced work in multimodality (Hart 2016, 335), although opinions differ on whether there has been influence in the other direction as well. While the former influence has no doubt been significant—and may well have been formative—some researchers have warned strongly against conceptualizing other modes analogous to language (e.g. Machin 2009; Stöckl 2004). Stöckl (2004, 18), for example, has argued that because of language's (perceived) dominance in society (or data), researchers tend to look at other modes in terms of language, asking which linguistic properties they have. This constitutes a "danger", in Stöckl's terms, because we might "overlook" important features that "lie beyond the scope of language".

As to what those features or affordances are, and how different they are from those of language, opinions vary. O'Halloran (2004, 127), for instance, holds that most modes are "fundamentally different to language" and that only those semiotic systems that have evolved from language or been developed based on language, such as mathematics or computer programming languages, resemble the grammaticality of language. Indeed, one reason why language may be seen as different from other modes is its symbolic nature, while many other modes are iconic in that they represent something through similarity. While no exact tally has been attempted, other scholars assert that most modes are meaningful only through cultural convention (Kress and van Leeuwen 2006). Explicit regulation and/or repetition in a given community embeds semiotic resources in our shared cultural conventions, forming associations such as those of certain musical sounds and patterns with emotions, attitudes and ideas (Machin and Richardson 2012, 330).

Chroniclers of the field of multimodal discourse analysis point out that the initial drive was "to seek out linguistic analogues in non-linguistic forms" (Roderick 2018, 161) and "to develop, *in the fashion of linguistics,* tools that could better allow us to describe how these nonlinguistic forms were being used to communicate ideas, attitudes, and identities" (Machin 2013b, 348, emphasis added). At the same time, this early work was informed by the drive to map the underlying repertoires of choices or meaning potentials rather than empirical study of data. As Machin (2013b,

349) points out, this drive and the concomitant principle of identifying *distinct* modes, to establish *boundaries* between modes and their *separate* rules, is evidence of the desire to apply linguistics models, principles and tools to nonlinguistic communication. This heritage still pervades multimodal approaches in the form of the idea that there is—or could be—a universal theory of meaning-making (Machin 2016, 326).

Tempting as the notion may be, it has been heavily criticized as a post hoc, self-referential mode of theorizing (Bateman et al. 2004) in which a system of choices is proposed (or derived from language) and then applied to exemplary data (Forceville 1999). Thus, it is unclear whether the result of the analysis is simply an interpretation justified by the use of terminology. This "grand theory" remains implicit in some multimodal work which assumes that all modes have a grammar in the sense of systems of choices; in such work, the identification of choices/resources in exemplary data appears little more than the result of "filtering" the data through a pre-determined set of semiotic options (Ledin and Machin 2018, 14; on underanalysis through "spotting features", see Antaki et al. 2003) or an exercise in obfuscation through technical description of mundane or subjective observations (Forceville 2010; Machin 2013b, 349; on underanalysis through "description", see Antaki et al. 2003).

Theo van Leeuwen has remained one of the strongest voices arguing that many of the concepts developed in the study of language, particularly grammar and text, are not unique to language and can be transferred to other modes. Researchers in visual communication should therefore "pay attention to linguists, as many linguistic concepts and methods are directly applicable to […] the study of visual communication" (van Leeuwen 2004, 16–18). Some of the most prominent and productive of such transfers have been social actors, transitivity, modality and cohesion (e.g. Machin and Mayr 2013, 356; Ledin and Machin 2018, 8). Indirect support for this view comes from cognitive linguistics, which suggests that language processing is not procedural—and thus unlike the perception of images, whose parts are perceived following Gestalt laws of organization—but sequential as an accumulation of parts and progressive dependencies. Drawing on this model, Hart (2016, 337) argues that meaning-making in language involves the construction of fully modal rather than amodal mental representations, flipping the relationship: language is cognitively multimodal, and therefore our understanding of language can be applied to other modes.

Meanwhile, some of the best work in multimodality has adopted a middle-ground position, taking inspiration from linguistics and its concepts but adapting them when applying them to other modes. Ledin and Machin's (2018) work on photography, for instance, takes its cue from (systemic functional) linguistic social actor and transitivity analysis but also introduces "canons of use"—a notion that partly echoes registers or genres as meso-level patterns structuring semiotic instantiation—in order to link semiotic features to cultural meanings so as to account for the affordances of photographs. They demonstrate that this is necessary, e.g. in the case of transitivity, because photographs cannot represent time but can only index time and movement and agency at a singular moment (Ledin and Machin 2018, 10).

3.9 The Notion of Mode as Equalizer

In extension of the above discussion, the very notion of "mode" has come under criticism as an "equalizing" force, i.e. conceptually equating different kinds of semiotic resources (Ledin and Machin 2016, 4). While this effect has been seen positively in the sense of "telling linguists" that other forms of meaning-making are as significant to discourse as language (Kress 2010, 104), the critical view holds that the different and specific affordances of semiotic resources should be foregrounded instead; only under this condition can research address the question of why specific modes are combined in a particular way and for specific ideological aims: Due to their different affordances, modes can be used to achieve different kinds of communicative tasks, creating meaning but also making/avoiding certain kinds of "epistemological commitments", such as including the perpetrator of a crime in its description. Language, in this perspective, typically brings the affordances of naming and establishing relations, while the visual brings spatial and size relations. Thus, different semiotic resources permit some aspects of the thing being recontextualized/resemiotized to be suppressed and others to be expressed specifically (Machin 2013b, 349–51; see above on the 'semiotic division of labor'). The role that the distribution of epistemological commitment plays in resemiotization clearly raises the stakes for the debate over the equalizing notion of 'mode'. Indeed, Ledin and Machin argue that resources are never of equal significance *in concrete use* and that the specificity of "affordances" should therefore be foregrounded to discover what can and cannot be done with the semiotic resources available in a given context (Ledin and Machin 2016, 4). In short, "equal significance" should not be taken to indicate "equal treatment" or "equal conceptualization" (Kress 2010).

The conceptual equalizing of modes may also have led researchers to neglect not only how modes collaborate in meaning-making but how they have evolved in and through such interaction in use, as when written, printed language is realized through forms of typography and spatial arrangement (see 'new writing'). Thus, owing to this "fundamental dependency" of modes on each other (Ledin and Machin 2015), to isolate them conceptually may forestall multimodal analysis before it even begins. In a different paper, Machin (2016, 327) proposes an affordance-driven approach to avoid the notion of mode altogether. It should be noted that this appears to be recent shift, as Machin and van Leeuwen's (2004) study of *Cosmopolitan* was still firmly rooted in the 'grand theory', applying (systemic functional) linguistic concepts to visual communication, and even Machin and Mayr (2012, 15) still emphasize that all communication should be seen as done through "a set of semiotic resources, options and choices".

The argument against the 'grand theory' of multimodality calls into question core principles of systemic functional linguistics, which informed the work of Kress and van Leeuwen (1996), O'Toole (1994), and others in their wake. In questioning whether the principles of SFL are able to yield reliable, relevant insights into multimodal discourse, Ledin and Machin (2018, 2) point to three problematic aspects of transferring SFL's principles to non-linguistic modes: (1) that all communication simultaneously constructs meaning in three 'metafunctions', (2) the 'systemic' modelling of paradigmatic choices, each of which has a distinctive structural realization, and (3) the assumption that all context and meaning can be derived from the semiotic text, resulting in a lack of empirical attention given to context. Regarding the first aspect, it has been objected that not all modes may fulfill all three metafunctions. As to the second, not all modes may parallel language in its underlying systems of choices. And finally, context cannot reliably be projected from a text without considering cultural conventions—which the researcher may or may not have access to but would need to explicate in the analysis.

3.10 Tunnel Vision: Ignoring Context

The final criticism raised above, i.e. that modes are analyzed as fixed systems of choices without the wider cultural and historical context (Machin 2016, 326), has a much broader base and relevance than transferring SFL—and thus ultimately language-based concepts to multimodality. Going back to Hodge and Kress (1988) or Kress (1989), it has been a corner stone of social semiotics that meaning-making be studied as situated and material phenomena in order to reveal the ideologies informing them. This is often interpreted as meaning that interpretation must draw on both immediate, cultural, and historical context (Hansen and Machin 2013, 158), paralleling three of the four context levels distinguished by Reisigl and Wodak (2015). It has also been interpreted as seeing discourses as social practice with not only one site of meaning-making but three: production, content, and consumption (Hansen and Machin 2013, 163). Specifically, multimodal discourse analysis has been criticized for a lack of concern with the "processes of the production of texts" (Machin and Mayr 2012, 10).

Such "tunnel vision" (Forceville 2010) in focusing only semiotic artefacts and the systems of choices underlying them falls short of connecting the micro-level analyses of meaning-making to the macro-level discussion of social context. It is with respect to this issue that (Ledin and Machin 2018, 6) propose the notion of "canons of use" at the meso-level, which they define in terms largely similar to 'register' or 'genre'—down to the notion that concrete texts are unique instantiations of such canons (Ledin and Machin 2018, 7). This is noteworthy insofar as both 'register' and 'genre' are well-established notions in SFL and might thus be seen as another—indeed meaningful—transfer of system functional concepts rather than a final answer to a fundamental critique.

3.11 Research Practice: Benefits and Pitfalls

Key issues in planning and conducting research in CDS that integrates a multi-data or multimodal perspective include:

- deciding on the units of analysis (e.g. text, mode, semiotic system),
- selecting the types of data to be collected and analyzed with respect to the research interests, aims or questions,
- defining each type of data in terms of how it relates to the other types of data and how each contributes to the overall aims,
- acknowledging common and specific traits of the data types (e.g. language but different methods of elicitation, spoken and written),
- looking into previous work not only in discourse studies/multimodality but other academic fields that may have insights to offer,
- paying attention to consistency/overlap between methods and conceptualizations of the different types of data,
- paying close attention to potential interdisciplinary frictions and incompatibilities in drawing on interdisciplinary work,
- deciding whether to separate semiotic modes involved in a given text and examine one or more modes, i.e. adopt an intrasemiotic or intersemiotic approach (Bednarek and Caple 2017, 19),
- deciding whether to analytically focus on individual modes or the interplay between multiple modes (e.g. viewing the text as a multimodal communicative act, van Leeuwen 2004),
- deciding whether to focus on patterns *across* texts (an intertextual or "text-as-corpus" perspective) or to focus on patterns *within* texts (an intratextual or "text-as-text" perspective) (Bednarek and Caple 2017, 19),[1]
- selecting appropriate methods for collecting, storing, *and* analyzing the different types of data chosen,

[1]Such topological distinctions can be very useful in planning research, but they need not be categorical and can also be used to distinguish different stages of a single research project (for more detail, see Bednarek and Caple 2017, 22–23).

- if a corpus approach is chosen, finding and setting up a suitable infrastructure for preparing, storing, retrieving, *and* annotating the multimodal corpus,[2]
- planning how to present the data and analysis, given that standard formats and lengths of research papers severely limit efforts to display the results of such complex analyses (O'Halloran 2004, 25), including copyright issues (but see Chapter 6 on visualization and interactivity).

References

Abousnnouga, Gill, and David Machin. 2011. "The Changing Spaces of War Commemoration: A Multimodal Analysis of the Discourses of British Monuments." *Social Semiotics* 21 (2): 175–96. https://doi.org/10.1080/10350330.2011.548640.

Adolphs, Svenja, and Ronald Carter. 2015. *Spoken Corpus Linguistics: From Monomodal to Multimodal.* Routledge Advances in Corpus Linguistics 15. New York: Routledge.

Aiello, Giorgia, and Crispin Thurlow. 2006. "Symbolic Capitals: Visual Discourse and Intercultural Exchange in the European Capital of Culture Scheme." *Language and Intercultural Communication* 6 (2): 148–62. https://doi.org/10.2167/laic234.0.

Allwood, Jens. 2008. "Multimodal Corpora." In *Corpus Linguistics: An International Handbook,* edited by Anke Lüdeling and Merja Kytö, 207–25. Berlin: Mouton de Gruyter.

Androutsopoulos, Jannis K. 2010. "Multimodal—Intertextuell—Hetero-Glossisch: Sprach-Gestalten in 'Web 2.0'-Umgebungen." In *Sprache Intermedial. Stimme Und Schrift, Bild Und Ton,* edited by Arnulf Deppermann and Angelika Linke, 419–46. Berlin: Mouton de Gruyter.

Antaki, Charles. 2008. "Discourse Analysis and Conversation Analysis." In *The Sage Handbook of Social Research Methods,* edited by P. Alasuutari, L. Bickman, and J. Brannan, 431–46. London: Sage.

[2]Several options are available today, including the Multimodal Corpus Authoring system (Baldry and Thibault 2006), the MCA Web Browser (Baldry and O'Halloran 2010), the Nottingham Multi-Modal Corpus (Adolphs and Carter 2015), as well as multimodal annotation software (e.g. Allwood 2008; Jimenez Hurtado and Soler Gallego 2013).

Antaki, Charles, Michael Billig, Derek Edwards, and Jonathan Potter. 2003. "Discourse Analysis Means Doing Analysis: A Critique of Six Analytic Shortcomings." *Discourse Analysis Online* 1. http://extra.shu.ac.uk/daol/articles/v1/n1/a1/antaki2002002-t.html.

Baldry, Anthony, and Kay L. O'Halloran. 2010. "Research into the Annotation of a Multimodal Corpus of University Websites: An Illustration of Multimodal Corpus Linguistics." In *Corpus Linguistics in Language Teaching*, edited by Tony Harris, 177–210. Bern: Peter Lang.

Baldry, Anthony, and Paul J. Thibault. 2006. *Multimodal Transcription and Text Analysis*. London and Oakville, CT: Equinox.

Barkho, Leon. 2011. "The Role of Internal Guidelines in Shaping News Narratives: Ethnographic Insights into the Discursive Rhetoric of Middle East Reporting by the BBC and Al-Jazeera English." *Critical Discourse Studies* 8 (4): 297–309. https://doi.org/10.1080/17405904.2011.601642.

Barthes, Roland. 1957. *Mythologies*. London: Jonathan Cape.

Bateman, John A. 2011. *Multimodality and Genre: A Foundation for the Systematic Analysis of Multimodal Documents*. 1st Paperback ed. Basingstoke, Hampshire: Palgrave Macmillan.

Bateman, John A., Judy Delin, and Renate Henschel. 2004. "Multimodality and Empiricism: Preparing for a Corpus-Based Approach to the Study of Multimodal Meaning-Making." In *Perspectives on Multimodality*, edited by Eija Ventola, Charles Cassily, and Martin Kaltenbacher, 65–87. Amsterdam and Philadelphia: John Benjamins.

Bednarek, Monika. 2015. "Corpus-Assisted Multimodal Discourse Analysis of Television and Film Narratives." In *Corpora and Discourse Studies: Integrating Discourse and Corpora*, edited by Paul Baker and Tony McEnery, 63–87. London: Palgrave Macmillan.

Bednarek, Monika, and Helen Caple. 2014. "Why Do News Values Matter? Towards a New Methodological Framework for Analysing News Discourse in Critical Discourse Analysis and Beyond." *Discourse & Society* 25 (2): 135–58. https://doi.org/10.1177/0957926513516041.

———. 2017. "Introducing a New Topology for (Multimodal) Discourse Analysis." In *Transforming Contexts: Papers from the 44th International Systemic Functional Congress*, edited by Phil Chappell and John S. Knox, 19–25. Wollongong: 44th ISFC Organising Committee.

Bolander, Brook, and Miriam A. Locher. 2014. "Doing Sociolinguistic Research on Computer-Mediated Data: A Review of Four Methodological Issues." *Discourse, Context & Media* 3 (March): 14–26. https://doi.org/10.1016/j.dcm.2013.10.004.

Bounegru, Liliana, and Charles Forceville. 2011. "Metaphors in Editorial Cartoons Representing the Global Financial Crisis." *Visual Communication* 10 (2): 209–29. https://doi.org/10.1177/1470357211398446.

Catalano, Theresa, and Lauren Gatti. 2017. "Representing Teachers as Criminals in the News: A Multimodal Critical Discourse Analysis of the Atlanta Schools' 'Cheating Scandal.'" *Social Semiotics* 27 (1): 59–80. https://doi.org/10.1080/10350330.2016.1145386.

Djonov, Emilia, and Sumin Zhao, eds. 2014. *Critical Multimodal Studies of Popular Discourse.* Routledge Studies in Multimodality 8. New York: Routledge.

Djonov, Emilia, and Theo van Leeuwen. 2013. "Between the Grid and Composition: Layout in PowerPoint's Design and Use." *Semiotica* 2013 (197): 1–34. https://doi.org/10.1515/sem-2013-0078.

Fairclough, Norman. 1992. *Discourse and Social Change.* Cambridge: Polity Press.

Feng, Dezheng, and Elaine Espindola. 2013. "Integrating Systemic Functional and Cognitive Approaches to Multimodal Discourse Analysis." *Ilha Do Desterro: A Journal of English Language, Literatures in English and Cultural Studies* (64). https://doi.org/10.5007/2175-8026.2013n64p85.

Feng, Dezheng, and Kay L. O'Halloran. 2013. "The Visual Representation of Metaphor: A Social Semiotic Approach." *Review of Cognitive Linguistics* 11 (2): 320–35. https://doi.org/10.1075/rcl.11.2.07fen.

Flewitt, Rosie S., Regine Hampel, Mirjam Hauck, and Lesley Lancaster. 2009. "What Are Multimodal Data and Transcription?" In *The Routledge Handbook of Multimodal Analysis*, edited by Carey Jewitt, 40–53. London: Routledge.

Forceville, Charles J. 1999. "Educating the Eye? Kress and van *Leeuwen's Reading Images: The Grammar of Visual Design* (1996)." *Language and Literature* 8 (2): 163–78. https://doi.org/10.1177/096394709900800204.

Forceville, Charles J. 2010. "Review of C. Jewitt (Ed.) *The Routledge Handbook of Multimodal Analysis.*" *Journal of Pragmatics* 42 (9): 2604–8. https://doi.org/10.1016/j.pragma.2010.03.003.

Galasiński, Dariusz. 2011. "The Patient's World: Discourse Analysis and Ethnography." *Critical Discourse Studies* 8 (4): 253–65. https://doi.org/10.1080/17405904.2011.601634.

Gibson, Alexandra Farren, Christina Lee, and Shona Crabb. 2015. "Reading Between the Lines: Applying Multimodal Critical Discourse Analysis to Online Constructions of Breast Cancer." *Qualitative Research in Psychology* 12 (3): 272–86. https://doi.org/10.1080/14780887.2015.1008905.

Gleeson, Kate. 2011. "Polytextual Thematic Analysis for Visual Data—Pinning Down the Analytic." In *Visual Methods in Psychology: Using and Interpret-*

ing Images in Qualitative Research, edited by Paula Reavey, 314–29. London: Routledge.
Halliday, Michael A. K. 1978. *Language as Social Semiotic: The Social Interpretation of Language and Meaning*. London: Arnold.
Halliday, Michael A. K., and Ruqaiya Hasan. 1985. *Language, Context and Text: Aspects of Language in a Social-Semiotic Perspective*. 3rd impr. Social Semiotic. Geelong: Deakin University Press.
Hansen, Anders, and David Machin. 2013. "Researching Visual Environmental Communication." *Environmental Communication* 7 (2): 151–68. https://doi.org/10.1080/17524032.2013.785441.
Hart, Christopher. 2016. "The Visual Basis of Linguistic Meaning and Its Implications for Critical Discourse Studies: Integrating Cognitive Linguistic and Multimodal Methods." *Discourse & Society* 27 (3): 335–50. https://doi.org/10.1177/0957926516630896.
———. 2017. "Metaphor and Intertextuality in Media Framings of the (1984–1985) British Miners' Strike: A Multimodal Analysis." *Discourse & Communication* 11 (1): 3–30. https://doi.org/10.1177/1750481316683291.
Hodge, Bob, and Gunther R. Kress. 1988. *Social Semiotics*. Ithaca, NY: Cornell University Press.
Iedema, Rick. 2003. "Multimodality, Resemiotization: Extending the Analysis of Discourse as Multi-semiotic Practice." *Visual Communication* 2 (1): 29–57. https://doi.org/10.1177/1470357203002001751.
Jagodzinski, Jan. 2013. "On the Problematics of Visual Imagery." In *Multimodality and Social Semiosis: Communication, Meaning-Making, and Learning in the Work of Gunther Kress*, edited by Margit Böck and Norbert Pachler. London: Routledge.
Jewitt, Carey. 2009. "What Is Multimodality?" In *The Routledge Handbook of Multimodal Analysis*, edited by Carey Jewitt, 14–27. London: Routledge.
Jimenez Hurtado, Catalina, and Silvia Soler Gallego. 2013. "Multimodality, Translation and Accessibility: A Corpus-Based Study of Audio Description." *Perspectives* 21 (4): 577–94. https://doi.org/10.1080/0907676X.2013.831921.
Johnson, David Cassels. 2011. "Critical Discourse Analysis and the Ethnography of Language Policy." *Critical Discourse Studies* 8 (4): 267–79. https://doi.org/10.1080/17405904.2011.601636.
KhosraviNik, Majid, and Johann W. Unger. 2015. "Social Media: Power, Resistance and Critique in Changing Media Ecologies." In *Methods of Critical Discourse Studies*, edited by Ruth Wodak and Michael Meyer, 3rd. ed., 205–33. London: Sage.

Kress, Gunther. 1989. "History and Language: Towards a Social Account of Linguistic Change." *Journal of Pragmatics* 13 (3): 445–66. https://doi.org/10.1016/0378-2166(89)90065-9.

———. 2010. *Multimodality: A Social Semiotic Approach to Contemporary Communication.* London and New York: Routledge.

———. 2012. "Thinking About the Notion of 'Cross-Cultural' from a Social Semiotic Perspective." *Language and Intercultural Communication* 12 (4): 369–85. https://doi.org/10.1080/14708477.2012.722102.

Kress, Gunther, and Theo van Leeuwen. 1996. *Reading Images: The Grammar of Visual Design.* 1st ed. London: Routledge.

———. 1998. "Front Pages: (The Critical) Analysis of Newspaper Layout." In *Approaches to Media Discourse,* edited by A. Bell and P. Garret, 186–219. Oxford: Blackwell.

———. 2001. *Multimodal Discourse: The Modes and Media of Contemporary Communication.* London: Arnold; New York: Oxford University Press.

———. 2002. "Colour as a Semiotic Mode: Notes for a Grammar of Colour." *Visual Communication* 1 (3): 343–68. https://doi.org/10.1177/147035720200100306.

———. 2006. *Reading Images: The Grammar of Visual Design.* 2nd ed. London: Routledge.

Krzyżanowska, Natalia. 2016. "The Discourse of Counter-Monuments: Semiotics of Material Commemoration in Contemporary Urban Spaces." *Social Semiotics* 26 (5): 465–85. https://doi.org/10.1080/10350330.2015.1096132.

Krzyżanowski, Michał. 2010. *The Discursive Construction of European Identities: A Multi-level Approach to Discourse and Identity in the Transforming European Union.* Sprache Im Kontext Bd. 35. Frankfurt am Main and New York: Peter Lang.

———. 2011a. "Ethnography and Critical Discourse Analysis: Towards a Problem-Oriented Research Dialogue." *Critical Discourse Studies* 8 (4): 231–38. https://doi.org/10.1080/17405904.2011.601630.

———. 2011b. "Political Communication, Institutional Cultures and Linearities of Organisational Practice: A Discourse-Ethnographic Approach to Institutional Change in the European Union." *Critical Discourse Studies* 8 (4): 281–96. https://doi.org/10.1080/17405904.2011.601638.

Ledin, Per, and David Machin. 2015. "How Lists, Bullet Points and Tables Recontextualise Social Practice: A Multimodal Study of Management Language in Swedish Universities." *Critical Discourse Studies* 12 (4): 463–81. https://doi.org/10.1080/17405904.2015.1039556.

———. 2016. "A Discourse–Design Approach to Multimodality: The Visual Communication of Neoliberal Management Discourse." *Social Semiotics* 26 (1): 1–18. https://doi.org/10.1080/10350330.2015.1089652.

———. 2017. "The Neoliberal Definition of 'Elite Space' in IKEA Kitchens." *Social Semiotics* 27 (3): 323–34. https://doi.org/10.1080/10350330.2017.1301797.

———. 2018. "Doing Critical Discourse Studies with Multimodality: From Metafunctions to Materiality." *Critical Discourse Studies* (April): 1–17. https://doi.org/10.1080/17405904.2018.1468789.

Lemke, Jay L. 1998. "Resources for Attitudinal Meaning: Evaluative Orientations in Text Semantics." *Functions of Language* 5 (1): 33–56. https://doi.org/10.1075/fol.5.1.03lem.

Lim, Victor Fei. 2017. "Analysing the Teachers' Use of Gestures in the Classroom: A Systemic Functional Multimodal Discourse Analysis Approach." *Social Semiotics* (December): 1–29. https://doi.org/10.1080/10350330.2017.1412168.

Machin, David. 2007. *Introduction to Multimodal Analysis.* London and New York: Hodder Arnold. Distributed in the U.S.A. by Oxford University Press.

———. 2009. "Multimodality and Theories of the Visual." In *The Routledge Handbook of Multimodal Analysis*, edited by Carey Jewitt, 181–90. London: Routledge.

———. 2013a. "Towards a Social Semiotics of Rhythm in Popular Music." *Semiotica* 2013 (197). https://doi.org/10.1515/sem-2013-0084.

———. 2013b. "What Is Multimodal Critical Discourse Studies?" *Critical Discourse Studies* 10 (4): 347–55. https://doi.org/10.1080/17405904.2013.813770.

———. 2016. "The Need for a Social and Affordance-Driven Multimodal Critical Discourse Studies." *Discourse & Society* 27 (3): 322–34. https://doi.org/10.1177/0957926516630903.

Machin, David, and Andrea Mayr. 2012. *How to Do Critical Discourse Analysis: A Multimodal Introduction.* Sage. http://public.eblib.com/choice/publicfullrecord.aspx?p=880803.

———. 2013. "Personalising Crime and Crime-Fighting in Factual Television: An Analysis of Social Actors and Transitivity in Language and Images." *Critical Discourse Studies* 10 (4): 356–72. https://doi.org/10.1080/17405904.2013.813771.

Machin, David, and Gill Abousnnouga. 2013. *The Language of War Monuments.* Bloomsbury Advances in Semiotics. London and New York: Bloomsbury.

Machin, David, and John E. Richardson. 2012. "Discourses of Unity and Purpose in the Sounds of Fascist Music: A Multimodal Approach." *Critical Discourse Studies* 9 (4): 329–45. https://doi.org/10.1080/17405904.2012.713203.

Machin, David, and Theo van Leeuwen. 2004. "Global Media: Generic Homogeneity and Discursive Diversity." *Continuum* 18 (1): 99–120. https://doi.org/10.1080/1030431032000181021.

Machin, David, and Usama Suleiman. 2006. "Arab and American Computer War Games: The Influence of a Global Technology on Discourse." *Critical Discourse Studies* 3 (1): 1–22. https://doi.org/10.1080/17405900600591362.

———. 2009. "Toys as Discourse: Children's War Toys and the War on Terror." *Critical Discourse Studies* 6 (1): 51–63. https://doi.org/10.1080/17405900802560082.

Martinec, Radan. 2004. "Gestures That Co-occur with Speech as a Systematic Resource: The Realization of Experiential Meanings in Indexes." *Social Semiotics* 14 (2): 193–213. https://doi.org/10.1080/1035033042000238259.

Mautner, Gerlinde. 2016. *Discourse and Management: Critical Perspectives Through the Language Lens.* Basingstoke: Palgrave Macmillan.

Monson, Olivia, Ngaire Donaghue, and Rosalind Gill. 2016. "Working Hard on the Outside: A Multimodal Critical Discourse Analysis of *The Biggest Loser Australia*." *Social Semiotics* 26 (5): 524–40. https://doi.org/10.1080/10350330.2015.1134821.

Moran, Claire, and Christina Lee. 2013. "Selling Genital Cosmetic Surgery to Healthy Women: A Multimodal Discourse Analysis of Australian Surgical Websites." *Critical Discourse Studies* 10 (4): 373–91. https://doi.org/10.1080/17405904.2013.813772.

Mulderrig, Jane. 2018. "Multimodal Strategies of Emotional Governance: A Critical Analysis of 'Nudge' Tactics in Health Policy." *Critical Discourse Studies* 15 (1): 39–67. https://doi.org/10.1080/17405904.2017.1382381.

Muntigl, Peter, Gilbert Weiss, and Ruth Wodak. 2000. *European Union Discourses on Un/Employment: An Interdisciplinary Approach to Employment Policy-Making and Organizational Change.* Vol. 12. Dialogues on Work and Innovation. Amsterdam: John Benjamins. https://doi.org/10.1075/dowi.12.

Norris, Sigrid. 2004. "Multimodal Discourse Analysis: A Conceptual Framework." In *Discourse and Technology: Multimodal Discourse Analysis*, edited by Philip LeVine and Ronald Scollon, 101–15. Washington, DC: Georgetown University Press.

———. 2011. *Identity in (Inter)action: Introducing Multimodal Interaction Analysis.* Trends in Applied Linguistics 4. Berlin, NY: De Gruyter Mouton.

O'Halloran, Kay L., ed. 2004. *Multimodal Discourse Analysis: Systemic-Functional Perspectives.* Open Linguistics Series. London and New York: Continuum.
O'Halloran, Kay L., and Bradley A. Smith. 2011. "Multimodal Studies." In *Multimodal Studies: Exploring Issues and Domains,* edited by Kay L. O'Halloran and Bradley A. Smith, 1–13. New York and London: Routledge.
O'Halloran, Kay L., Sabine Tan, Bradley A. Smith, and Alexey Podlasov. 2011. "Multimodal Analysis Within an Interactive Software Environment: Critical Discourse Perspectives." *Critical Discourse Studies* 8 (2): 109–25. https://doi.org/10.1080/17405904.2011.558687.
O'Toole, Michael. 1994. *The Language of Displayed Art.* Rutherford: Fairleigh Dickinson University Press.
Pauwels, Luc. 2012. "A Multimodal Framework for Analyzing Websites as Cultural Expressions." *Journal of Computer-Mediated Communication* 17 (3): 247–65. https://doi.org/10.1111/j.1083-6101.2012.01572.x.
Potts, Amanda. 2015. "'Love You Guys (No Homo)': How Gamers and Fans Play with Sexuality, Gender, and Minecraft on YouTube." *Critical Discourse Studies* 12 (2): 163–86. https://doi.org/10.1080/17405904.2014.974635.
Preziosi, Donald. 1986. "The Multimodality of Communicative Events." In *Frontiers in Semiotics,* edited by John N. Deely, Brooke Williams, and Felicia Kruse, 44–50. Bloomington: Indiana University Press.
Reisigl, Martin, and Ruth Wodak. 2015. "The Discourse-Historical Approach (DHA)." In *Methods of Critical Discourse Studies,* edited by Ruth Wodak and Michael Meyer, 23–61. London: Sage.
Rheindorf, Markus, and Ruth Wodak. 2019. "'Austria First' Revisited: A Diachronic Cross-Sectional Analysis of the Gender and Body Politics of the Extreme Right." *Patterns of Prejudice.*
Richardson, John E., and Ruth Wodak. 2009. "Recontextualising Fascist Ideologies of the Past: Right-Wing Discourses on Employment and Nativism in Austria and the United Kingdom." *Critical Discourse Studies* 6 (4): 251–67. https://doi.org/10.1080/17405900903180996.
Roderick, Ian. 2018. "Multimodal Critical Discourse Analysis as Ethical Praxis." *Critical Discourse Studies* 15 (2): 154–68. https://doi.org/10.1080/17405904.2017.1418401.
Rogers, Rebecca. 2011. "The Sounds of Silence in Educational Tracking: A Longitudinal, Ethnographic Case Study." *Critical Discourse Studies* 8 (4): 239–52. https://doi.org/10.1080/17405904.2011.601632.
Saussure, Ferdinand. 1916. *Course in General Linguistics.* London: Fontana Press.

Scollon, Ronald. 2006. "The Discourses of Food in the World System: Toward a Nexus Analysis of a World Problem." *Journal of Language and Politics* 4 (3): 465–88. https://doi.org/10.1075/jlp.4.3.07sco.

Scollon, Ronald, and Philip LeVine. 2004. "Multimodal Discourse Analysis as the Confluence of Discourse and Technology." In *Discourse and Technology: Multimodal Discourse Analysis*, edited by Philip LeVine and Ronald Scollon, 1–6. Washington, DC: Georgetown University Press.

Scollon, Ronald, and Suzanne B. K. Scollon. 2004. *Nexus Analysis: Discourse and the Emerging Internet.* London and New York: Routledge.

Screti, Francesco. 2013. "*Defending Joy* Against the *Popular Revolution*: Legitimation and Delegitimation Through Songs." *Critical Discourse Studies* 10 (2): 205–22. https://doi.org/10.1080/17405904.2013.764614.

Stöckl, Hartmut. 2004. "In Between Modes: Language and Image in Printed Media." In *Perspectives on Multimodality*, edited by Eija Ventola, Charles Cassily, and Martin Kaltenbacher, 9–30. Amsterdam: Benjamins.

van Leeuwen, Theo. 2004. "Ten Reasons Why Linguistics Should Pay Attention to Visual Communication." In *Discourse and Technology: Multimodal Discourse Analysis*, edited by Philip LeVine and Ronald Scollon, 7–19. Washington, DC: Georgetown University Press.

———. 2008. *Discourse and Practice: New Tools for Critical Discourse Analysis.* Oxford Studies in Sociolinguistics. Oxford and New York: Oxford University Press.

———. 2012. "The Critical Analysis of Musical Discourse." *Critical Discourse Studies* 9 (4): 319–28. https://doi.org/10.1080/17405904.2012.713204.

van Leeuwen, Theo, and Ruth Wodak. 1999. "Legitimizing Immigration Control: A Discourse-Historical Analysis." *Discourse Studies* 1 (1): 83–118. https://doi.org/10.1177/1461445699001001005.

Ventola, Eija, Charles Cassily, and Martin Kaltenbacher, eds. 2004. *Perspectives on Multimodality.* Amsterdam: Benjamins.

Wang, Jiayu. 2014. "Criticising Images: Critical Discourse Analysis of Visual Semiosis in Picture News." *Critical Arts* 28 (2): 264–86. https://doi.org/10.1080/02560046.2014.906344.

Wodak, Ruth. 2011. *The Discourse of Politics in Action: Politics as Usual.* Paperback ed. New York: Palgrave Macmillan.

Wodak, Ruth, and Norman Fairclough. 2010. "Recontextualizing European Higher Education Policies: The Cases of Austria and Romania." *Critical Discourse Studies* 7 (1): 19–40. https://doi.org/10.1080/17405900903453922.

Wodak, Ruth, Peter Nowak, Johanna Pelikan, Helmut Gruber, Rudolf De Cillia, and Richard Mitten. 1990. *"Wir Sind Alle Unschuldige Täter!": Diskurshis-*

torische Studien Zum Nachkriegsantisemitismus. 1. Aufl. Suhrkamp Taschenbuch Wissenschaft 881. Frankfurt am Main: Suhrkamp.

Wodak, Ruth, Rudolf de Cillia, Martin Reisigl, Karin Liebhart, Klaus Hofstätter, and Maria Kargl. 1998. *Zur Diskursiven Konstruktion Nationaler Identität.* 1. Aufl. Suhrkamp Taschenbuch Wissenschaft 1349. Frankfurt: Suhrkamp.

Wodak, Ruth, Rudolf de Cillia, Martin Reisigl, and Karin Liebhart. 2009. *The Discursive Construction of National Identity.* 2nd ed. Critical Discourse Analysis. Edinburgh: Edinburgh University Press.

Wooffitt, Robin. 2005. *Conversation Analysis and Discourse Analysis: A Comparative and Critical Introduction.* London and Thousand Oaks, CA: Sage.

Zhang, Yiqiong, David Machin, and Tao Song. 2015. "Visual Forms of Address in Social Media Discourse: The Case of a Science Communication Website." *Journal of Multicultural Discourses* 10 (2): 236–52. https://doi.org/10.1080/17447143.2015.1042384.

Zhao, Sumin, Emilia Djonov, Anders Björkvall, and Morten Boeriis, eds. 2018. *Advancing Multimodal and Critical Discourse Studies: Interdisciplinary Research Inspired by Theo van Leeuwen's Social Semiotics.* 1st ed. Routledge Studies in Multimodality 19. New York: Routledge.

4

Combining Analyses at Different Levels of Discourse

4.1 Introduction

Discourse being invariably regarded as a highly complex phenomenon, most efforts to theorize it have assumed that it is structured, ordered or organized in some form or fashion. And if discourse is organized or structured is some meaningful, recognizable way that affects how discourse is articulated, combined or inflected, it stands to reason that this structure should be factored into how we plan research with respect to data collection, analysis, and critique. In short, the structure of discourse—although primarily a theoretical issue—also has methodological implications. For some, this pertains mainly to issues of phenomenology (which phenomena exactly are we studying?), while others regard the structuredness of discourse as offering a way to link macro- to meso- or micro-level analysis, i.e. context to discourse, discourse to text, and text to specific linguistic or semiotic features. Yet other models foreground how the structure of discourse pertains to social structure and large-scale recontextualization processes, such as scientific discourse being popularized in educational material or the media, government policy being advertised in election

© The Author(s) 2019

M. Rheindorf, *Revisiting the Toolbox of Discourse Studies*,
Postdisciplinary Studies in Discourse,
https://doi.org/10.1007/978-3-030-19369-0_4

campaigns, laws being interpreted in court, public speeches being reported in the media, etc.

In his "brief academic autobiography", Teun A. van Dijk observed that in the 40 years of modern discourse studies, the number of "levels and dimensions" studied "have been multiplied" (2004, 39). It is a point well taken, all the more so for using the passive construction—it is not that levels have multiplied but that they have *been* multiplied as analytical categories. Van Dijk, however, is optimistic about this development, noting that while discourse analysis has become more complex it has also become empirically more precise. This hopeful observation also informs this chapter: that there is indeed a link between how we conceptualize 'levels of discourse' and the quality of our empirical work.

Existing approaches to the structure of discourse are varied, ranging from elaborate models to cursory mentions, from specific definitions to vague invocations of structuredness. The terminology used in these definitions also varies, but less so, creating an overlap of multiple conceptions for the same terms. Most of these invoke some sort of spatial and/or hierarchical structuring, ranging from Foucault's 'orders of discourse' to Jäger's 'discourse levels' or Linke's 'discourse types'. Of all the terms used, 'levels' is the most common and the most consistently used inasmuch as it is associated with distinct models of the structure of discourse. These fall into several broad categories, all of which make distinctions along a cline of abstraction, realization, and/or abstraction: (1) discourse as (super)structure, i.e. assuming a 'discursive level' as distinct from, e.g., a 'material', 'societal' or 'affective level', (2) levels of discourse as linguistic levels of realization, e.g. from phonetics, lexis, and grammar to meaning, (3) levels of discourse as text-and-talk or language use 'discourse' versus 'capital D Discourse', (4) levels of discourse as social action, analytically distinguished into semiotic artefacts, semiotic choices, discursive strategies, and macro-topics, and (5) levels of discourse distinguished broadly by reach, influence or power (e.g. institutional, public, and private) or by social fields of action (e.g. politics, media, and education).

Clearly, each of these broad frameworks, when adopted for a research design, is not only of great theoretical interest but also significantly affects questions of triangulation in data collection and analysis. The sections of this chapter therefore provide a concise overview of the ways in which the structuredness of discourse(s) has been conceptualized and operationalized in CDS. The final sections discuss which effects the most viable of these conceptualizations have on triangulation.

There are four conceptual aspects that run through this chapter, intersecting with its subsections. First, definitions of 'discourse' vary and with them varies the respective referent of structuredness. The term 'discourse' is used very differently by individual researchers and in different academic cultures (Wodak 2002, 8). It is used as an abstract noun to refer to the semiotic or meaning-making, to a dimension of the social or social reality; it is used as a countable noun to refer to specific discourses delineated by topic, quality, actors or fields; but it is also used to refer to concrete instances of situated language use, particularly spoken interaction (Fairclough et al. 2004, 4). Second, virtually all conceptions of the structuredness of discourse emphasize the interrelatedness rather than isolation of its structural elements. In doing so, most note or imply either a vertical or horizontal relationship between elements (Verschueren 2011, 123), i.e. hierarchical differentiation or equivalence of elements, or both. Third, models of discourse structure are conceptual, analytical distinctions and as such *create* levels of description, analysis or abstraction. Fourth, in conceptualizing discourse as structured, the terminology used introduces more or less pronounced metaphorical elements. Like all metaphors, these evoke mental representations and transfer some quality to the target, in the case of discourse structure primarily spatial notions of relatedness: a 'discourse strand' is something tightly woven and interconnected, perhaps slender and long, weaving through other matter; 'levels of discourse' are vertically related to each other, probably in a linear sequence or hierarchy, but each of them is *of discourse* or *of a discourse*; and so on and so forth. Like other conceptual metaphors, these can be immensely productive, but to be of theoretical value and methodological use, such terminology must be defined explicitly.

Major benefits of doing so are obtaining clear guidelines for operationalizing research aims, increasing validity of findings for a particular structural component, e.g. layers of discourse, and opening up new paths for triangulation, e.g. along a vertical or horizontal axis. With respect to the social distribution of power, Lamb (2013, 335–36) has argued along Foucauldian lines that CDS should "examine simultaneously multiple societal 'levels' in order to gain a fuller picture." Such an analysis can help avoid the limiting effects of tunnel vision or researcher bias in, e.g., only studying the 'level' of 'the political elite', 'the media', 'the extreme right' or 'civil society' in isolation.

4.2 Discourse as (Super)Structure: The Discursive Level

Some work in CDS refers to 'the discursive level', 'the discourse level' or 'the level of discourse'—note the definite article and singular—rather than to the internal structuring of discourse referenced by 'levels of discourse'. This use of 'level' raises two questions that are not, as a rule, addressed in these publications: (1) What is discourse a level of? and (2) What are the other levels? These questions are largely answered by discourse theories and are therefore addressed only briefly here.

Both questions are intertwined with each other as well as definitions of discourse itself. If 'the level of discourse' relates to social reality or reality as such, other—non-discursive—levels may be identified as "the material", "the psychological", "the affective" or even "the social" (e.g. Metten 2012, 43). Such a view is arguably most compatible with definitions of discourse as spoken or written language use in context and most at odds with holistic views of discourse as all meaning-making. It may also clash with views of the internal structuring of discourse, some of which regard discourse as comprising similarly labelled levels. Consider, for instance, approaches to multimodality covered in Chapter 3 that regard the physical, material reality of monuments are very much part of social semiotics.

To provide a few illustrative examples: When Berry (2004) analyzes how the Free Software Foundation and the Open Source Movement are "engaged in a struggle at the level of discourse", this presupposes other levels of potential struggle—even if none are discussed or mentioned in the study. When Carpentier and van Brussel (2012, 101) discuss the logics of contingency "at the level of discourse", they distinguish it from "the level of the social" and "the level of the interdiscursive". And Mckenna and Waddell (2006, 226), in studying the language use of an experienced parliamentarian deciding over refugees' asylum applications, conceive of "the level of discourse" as comprising "discursive sites", at which participants "control entry" and "determine appropriateness" of other participants' utterances, "creating and circumscribing the range of choices available to others".

Significantly, regarding discourse as a 'level' of something larger or, indeed, as superstructure based on materiality does not conceptually preclude viewing discourse as being internally structured, as having 'levels' of its own. Terminologically, however, it might be advisable to avoid the overlap or explicate the distinction.

4.3 Discourse as Structured Linguistic/Semiotic Realization

When 'discourse' is defined as language use or, more broadly, as meaning-making, its structuredness can be conceptualized as 'levels' or 'layers' in the expression or realization of meaning potential. Levels in this sense are typically situated on a cline of abstraction or complexity, e.g. comprising the lexical level, the sentence level, argumentation and other rhetorical forms, to the textual level and beyond, where concepts like genre or text type are often situated as mediating between text and discourse (Niehr 2014). The lowest or lower levels in such models are often referred to as 'micro' and include, for example, pronoun use, tense, metaphors, metonym, metaphor, anaphoric repetition, and nominalization (Slavíčková 2013, 377). The sentence level, sometimes discussed as part of the micro-level and sometimes separately, comprises grammatical phenomena like clause structure, transitivity, and passivation. The textual level has been referred to as 'meso-level' in terms of composition, rhetorics in general and rhetorical structure specifically, argumentation, calculated ambivalence, and reader orientation (Niehr 2014, 155). The discourse level or, in this hierarchy, the macro-level of analysis comprises patterns that extend across texts and is thus sometimes also referred to as the transtextual level (e.g. Spitzmüller and Warnke 2011). In between the textual and discourse level, some models include the intertextual level, i.e. relationships between individual texts (see below). In some accounts, only two 'levels', 'bands' or 'layers' are posited: Bax (2011), for instance, uses a model of discourse levels that distinguishes a micro-level of linguistic realization and a macro-level of concepts, pragmatics, and socio-cultural norms.

Methodologically, distinctions between these levels also mean that some linguistic methods or concepts may not be viable across them or may need to be adjusted. For instance, when studying argumentation on the level of discourse defined as a transtextual level, the influential Toulmin scheme of *fact-warrant-(backing)-rebuttal-conclusion* cannot simply be applied as on the textual level due to the many different linguistic forms of realizations encountered, including both explicit and implicit argumentation. A common solution has been to focus on argumentative patterns or topoi (Niehr 2014, 156) instead. This works particularly well in studies that use topical definitions of discourse (e.g. 'the discourse about refugees'), a vertical/hierarchical conception of discourse levels (e.g. 'official discourse' or 'public discourse'), a horizontal distinction by social fields (e.g. 'in the media' or 'legislative discourse') or a combination of these. Studies have consistently shown that such discourses, i.e. discourses defined in such terms, are characterized by a limited number of argumentative patterns or topoi (Niehr 2014, 156). At this level, combinations of qualitative and quantitative methods (see Chapter 2) offer a viable approach and can be used for the large-scale and/or diachronic study of argumentation patterns (e.g. Gabrielatos and Baker 2008; Wengeler 2003; Niehr 2014).

With respect to multimodal or semiotic approaches to discourse, the conception of hierarchically ordered levels of realization has been criticized for potentially treating phenomena under study 'as if' they were linguistic in nature, therefore transferring inappropriate assumptions about 'levels of realization' grounded in monomodal conceptions of discourse (see Chapter 3 on linguistic imperialism). As Bateman and Wildfeuer (2014, 181) demonstrate, linguistic and visual meaning-making are "fundamentally different at lower levels of descriptive abstraction", subsequently leading to distortions "at the more abstract levels of discourse". It is therefore necessary to question and reflect on whether a concrete conceptualization of discourse as structured in terms of levels of realization (or analytical abstraction) is, in fact, biased toward the linguistic. A much more general point to keep in mind with conceptions of discourse as structured by levels of realization is that they may but need not define discourse as social practice, as contextually situated action, as constitutive of social reality or knowledge, or as infused by and reproducing power relations.

4.4 Capital D Discourse

Although conceptions of discourse structure are not always easy to distinguish, a particularly clear contrast to the above is evident in notions of so-called 'capital D discourse'. The latter foreground the shaping of social reality through discourse (language use or, more broadly, semiotics; see Scollon and Scollon 2004, 4) and hence regard social reality as discursively constructed and maintained. A prominent example is James Paul Gee's definition of "Discourse with a capital 'D'" as the various ways in which human beings integrate the linguistic with the non-linguistic aspects of human experience, such as thought, action, interaction, emotion or belief, and the use of signs, tools, and other material objects to structure social reality, give meaning to it, organize society and regulate ways of knowing (Gee 1999, 13). This level of discourse, distinguished by capitalization of the term, is thus distinct from discourse as either written language use or face-to-face interaction (text and talk); irrespective of the specific terminology used, the ways in which the relationship of these levels can be conceived of is a key issue of the following sections.

One of the most elaborate and certainly popular articulations of such abstract levels of discourse can be found in the work of Alvesson and Karreman (2000). If an analogy were required, we might say they refer to language use as micro- and meso-levels of discourse, with rhetoric and other intra-textual phenomena situated on the meso-level. Grand discourse is defined as "an assembly of discourses, ordered and presented as an integrated frame" (Alvesson and Karreman 2000, 1133). It is thus the level at which ideology and power relations are at play, and it is also the level at which social reality is constituted. While Alvesson and Karreman concede that all levels are, in principle, linked, they discuss the Foucauldian projects of archaeology and genealogy with respect to the higher levels of discourse. Archaeology, in this view, aims to isolate the level of discursive practices and trace the changing rules that regulate discourse at the grand- and mega-level; genealogy, in contrast, in seeking to identify the power relations that structure, bind or differentiate discursive practices, does not separate the rules for the production of discourse from relations of power (Alvesson and Karreman 2000, 1126–28). They regard Foucault's own work as focused on mega discourse inasmuch as it privileges large-scale categories over detailed analysis in the treatment of empirical material (Alvesson and Karreman 2000, 1134).

By their own admission, in research practice the focus on higher levels of discourse in this sense typically means that micro- or meso-level discourse are not studied at all or merely cited for illustrative examples (on 'spotting features', see Chapter 2). This assessment is shared, among others, by Kwon, Clarke, and Wodak (2009, 276). Alvesson and Karreman (2000, 1134) correctly note that there is a "tension" between the different levels of discourse or rather between the respective analytical approaches, i.e. between studying discourse as emergent and locally constructed social interaction and approaching Discourse as the socio-political-cultural relationships among social groups and power interests (a similar tension as between conversation analysis and CDS, see Chapter 3). While Alvesson and Karreman treat this as discourse studies' very own Heisenberg uncertainty principle, there is no reason why a research project could not be designed in such a ways as to accommodate both approaches, e.g. in a modular fashion or by alternating between them.

Several scholars have acknowledged the need not only to distinguish levels (or sometimes layers) of discourse but also addressing their linkage in both conceptual and analytical terms. Sutherland (2005, 186), for instance, claims that theorizing at the level of grand discourses can be used as a "spring-board" for research on lower levels of discourse. More specifically, she argues that rhetoric, situated at the meso-level of discourse according to Alvesson and Karreman's model, provides a means of accessing discourses in their specificity, working as "the hinge [...] between micro discourse and macro Discourse" (Sutherland 2005, 197). A different approach is taken in Wodak (2002, 8), where the macro-level that has been identified as Discourse is elaborated in terms of Teun van Dijk's (1984, 1988) socio-cognitive theory of discourse as "a form of knowledge and memory", with the micro- and meso-levels identified as language use in texts.

There is a general consensus, if not in terminology, that a focus on either discourse or Discourse greatly affects the scope of one's perspective; but this relationship might also be reversed, allowing research interests or aims to affect the level at which we operate. Certainly, focusing on the level of grand discourses opens up different vistas—as evident in Vollmer's (2014) exemplary study of policy-making processes in terms of their historically contingent "meta-frames" at the level of Discourse. Policy-making in both the UK and Germany, Vollmer shows, discursively construct the phenomenon of irregular migration but also reflect wider discourses about immigration (which might be labelled grand discourses) and broader ideological frameworks concerning, inter alia, the role of the state (which might be labelled mega discourses). The broad politicization of immigration and the more specific criminalization of irregular migration studied by Vollmer operate on the level of policy but feed into the level of grand discourse: first, shifting "the irregular migrant" to "the enemy"; second, constructing a threat posed by irregular migration; and third, normalizing security politics as response to that threat. Moving to the level he calls "meta-frames", Vollmer situates these changes in long-standing, ideological conceptualizations of "man" and "the state"—both conservative and liberal—as they pertain to borders and the control of population movements. On this level, migrant populations are excluded via founding myths of the nation, in response to the narrative of migrants economically overburdening the true popolus as well as deceiving and undermining the state.

A widely used conception of discourse structure uses the macro-to-micro distinction, combining the notion of an abstract, higher-order level of discourse and multiple linguistic or semiotic levels of realization. The Discourse-Historical Approach posits a "discourse content" or "macro-topic" structure at the highest level of abstraction and analysis, formalizing a model of at least three interdependent levels of analysis—content, strategy, and semiotic means of realization—in which content is realized or actualized consecutively through the levels of both strategy and semiotics (Wodak et al. 2009). Depending on research aims and data, other levels of discursive practices may be included in the analysis, such as genre or argumentation.

4.5 Connecting Micro and Macro: Bringing in Agency and Social Actors

As indicated above, the conceptual and methodological difficulties inherent in linking macro- and micro-levels of discourse in contemporary CDS are foreshadowed in the juxtaposition of Foucault's "archaeology of all-pervasive power" and localized "genealogy of power" (Barrett 1991, 132–34). This tension is multiplied in approaches that insist on linguistic rigor in analyzing the minutiae of linguistic or semiotic realization. Several distinct approaches have elaborated their own attempts to bridge this gap between localized meaning-making and the relationships among social groups and power interests in society.

In particular for the *critical* aspect of CDS to get any purchase, detailed micro-level analyses of meaning-making must be conceptually and analytically tied to the larger socio-cultural-political realities that "constrain and shape" situated social interaction (Cicourel 2007, 735). The reverse is true for studies focusing on the macro-level, where the *analytical* aspect of CDS must provide solid footing in empirical data. Alvesson and Kareman refer to the respective risks as "conflating" situated meaning with discourse and separating discourse and meaning. As Kwon, Clarke, and Wodak (2009, 276) indicate, isolated micro-analyses tend to view power as tactical and localized, whereas macro-analyses risk treating power as pervasive but without locus. In both, the relationship between the agency of social actors and macro-level discourse is not adequately addressed.

For instance, Scollon and Scollon's nexus analysis explicitly seeks to unify micro- and macro-levels of analysis. Their approach is founded on the assumption that "broader social issues are ultimately grounded in the micro-actions of social interaction and, conversely, the most mundane of micro-actions are a nexus through which the largest cycles of social organization and activity circulate" (Scollon and Scollon 2004, 8). This is echoed, albeit in slightly different terms, in Kwon, Clarke, and Wodak's description of empirical triangulation between "micro-level discursive strategies" identified in specific texts and utterances and "macro topics of discourse that span across levels of context" identified in "historical sources and background knowledge on the social and political fields". Their declared aim in doing so is to illuminate the power dynamics and range of potentials of agents in the discursive practices of decision-making (Kwon, Clarke, and Wodak 2009, 273, 297). This adds to the general considerations of linking micro to macro a more specific concern for the interplay between individual agency and social structure or, as they refer to it, the "relative influence of agency and context" (Kwon, Clarke, and Wodak 2009, 274).

Methodologically, the integration of conversation analysis (Antaki 2008; Wooffitt 2005) or ethnography (Krzyżanowski 2011; Wodak 2011b; Iedema et al. 2004; Menz 1999) into CDS, as covered in Chapter 3, have been proposed as ways to address this issue. As rhetoric is generally seen as situated at a meso-level, analytical methods geared toward one or several elements of rhetoric have also been suggested as providing a link between micro- and macro-levels of discourse. One such element is narrative, which has been described as mediating the relationship between individuals and social groups (de Fina and Georgakopoulou 2012), and attendant methodology has been integrated into CDS on multiple occasions: the discursive construction of a shared, national history through commemorative practices (Wodak and de Cillia 2007), the intergenerationally shared narratives of survivors of National-Socialism and their children (Wodak and Rheindorf 2017), visual narratives (Bateman and Wildfeuer 2014), identity narratives in manager training (Andersson 2012), television and film narratives (Bednarek 2015), internal guidelines shaping news narratives (Barkho 2011), and so on and so forth.

Subtly inflecting Alvesson and Karreman's model, Andersson (2012, 575) defines macro-levels of discourse as "culturally standardized" or "aggregated similarities" that form "the contours and context that guide the construction of the micro discourse". Significantly, his paraphrase points to two significant complications in how the relationship between micro and macro is conceptualized. The first complication is arguably a misrepresentation of micro and macro discourses as local/global, as singular and collective or aggregated discourses, using a distinction not of kind but of scale or number. The micro-level then is simply discourses shared by few, in a particular site, whereas the macro-level is simply discourses shared by many or all. This leads Andersson (2012, 575) to conclude that "there is no clear distinction between global/macro and local/micro discourses; the global is part of the local, and the local is part of the global". This overlooks important differences in the respective discursive practices (with attendant media, genres etc.) that are a necessary part of the examples Andersson gives: If macro-level discourses reproduce social categories like class, gender, and nationality or role categories such as occupation and citizenship—subject positions that can be taken up, resisted or inflected by individuals—then the respective mechanisms (production, social context, power relations) must be substantially different (see the following sections). Empirically, this view leads Andersson to recognize both micro- and macro-level discourses in the same local practices, i.e. management training sessions: the macro-discourse position "manager" appears next to the micro-discourse position "veterinarian", "training" next to "profession" (Andersson 2012, 584). A similar problem is evident in Leitch and Davenport's (2007, 46) linking the levels of micro- and macro-analysis in terms of corpus linguistic keyword analysis, implicitly defining more general (and perhaps larger) corpora as macro-level discourse as opposed to specialized corpora. In short, the failure to distinguish levels clearly also makes it impossible to explicate their relationship.

The second complication arises from macro-level discourse being seen as 'context' of micro-level discourse. This terminological distinction seems to contradict Andersson's (2012, 575) assertion that there is no clear separation as well as his analytical practice of situating macro-level positions next to micro-level positions within data situated on what he regards the micro-level. Given the widely accepted view that "macro" indicates not just a more wide-spread but a more abstract or powerful level of discourse, it stands to reason that this level influences, shapes and constrains lower levels of discourse—but conceptually including it in the notion of "context" vis-à-vis situated social interaction on the micro-level is a far-reaching move that cannot not be glossed over. Andersson does not elaborate a model of text-context or discourse-context relationships that addresses the issue of multiple levels, but others have.

4.5.1 Discourse as Text in Context: Levels of Context

Indeed, *context* has been described as a key notion in CDS (Reisigl 2017, 53)—even if short-hand definitions of discourse as 'text in context' or 'language use in context' fall short of accounting for the relationship between discourse, its levels, and context. Several kinds or types of context are referenced in CDS, including cognitive, situational, (co)textual, social, political, and historical contexts—although sometimes only one of them and never all of them within the same model. Indeed, the links between various levels of analyses and contexts are often assumed rather than explicated (KhosraviNik 2010, 56). In the context of this chapter, only approaches that relate context to specific levels of discourse *and/or* posit levels of context as a means of triangulating the relationship between discourse and context are discussed.

The notion that context, like discourse, can be characterized in terms of a hierarchy of macro- to micro-levels distinguished either by abstraction, power, and/or reach, may well be regarded as an analogue to similar conceptions of levels of discourse. Thus, the previously quoted study by Kwon, Clarke, and Wodak (2009, 291–93) distinguishes the problems referenced by speakers in their data according to the micro-level context of interaction, meso-level organizational challenges, and macro-level labor market competition. It also differentiates between these contextual levels in terms of "scales of influence" and "impact", albeit not in the sense that the macro-level context always or necessarily outweighs the situational micro-level context. Even more importantly, these levels or layers of context are regarded as "heuristics", analytical tools to help locate discursive practices, to deconstruct their meanings, and to interpret the contexts' constraining and enabling influence on them.

A more formal and elaborate version of this model has been used in studies using the Discourse-Historical Approach. The model comprises four "levels" or "dimensions" of context, with some variation in the terminology: (a) the immediate, language-internal co-text of a linguistic or semiotic phenomenon or utterance, pertaining to thematic and syntactic coherence, lexical correspondence, collocations, connotations, implicatures, etc.; (b) the intertextual and interdiscursive relationship between utterances, texts or semiotic artefacts, genres, and discourses (see Sect. 4.5.1); (c) the context of situation as characterized by social factors and institutional frames that might include the degree of formality, place, time, occasion, addressees, interactive and political roles, political and ideological orientation, gender, age, profession, level of education, ethnic, regional, national, religious identities, etc.; and (d) the broader socio-political-cultural and historical context, taking into account "social fields of action" (see Sect. 4.8 below) as well as the history of relevant discourse topics, practices, institutions, etc. (Reisigl 2017, 53). Significantly, this context model provides a basis on which to situate data collected, e.g. ethnographic observations might be used to integrate the context of situation into the analysis. But it can also be used to explicate the relation or, indeed, partial intersection between discourse and context on the macro-level of analysis. In terms of analytical practice, this intersection relates to delineating the topical scope of discourses, segmenting discourses into periods or phases if a diachronic perspective is taken, determining the relationship between a given discourse and social structures or institutions (fields of action and attendant genres), and clarifying the relationship between adjacent or overlapping discourses (Reisigl 2007, 5).

Incidentally, although the DHA has always been a contextualist approach, the impulse to distinguish 'levels of context' aligned in some kind of hierarchy that parallels and intersects with 'levels of discourse' can be traced back to early work in the 1990s. Context, wrote Mitten and Wodak (1993, 206), had to be differentiated due to the many "layers of discourse" they had analyzed. In their case, that meant official norms on antisemitism in post-war Austria, national and international reporting of the Waldheim affair, and political statements made in this specific historical moment.

Providing a socio-cognitive account of "contextual control over discourse production and understanding" across "all levels and dimension of text and talk", van Dijk (2006a, 171) specifies this influence as the conditions of speech acts, the selection of appropriate topics as well as the de-selection of inappropriate topics (on 'conditions of the sayable', see below), the terms of changing topics, the distribution of knowledge in assertions and presuppositions, as well as many lexicogrammatical aspects and intonation. Van Dijk does so by postulating "context models" as socio-cognitive representations which effectively control an individual's "ways of speaking" in the sense of self-adapting to the communicative situation.

4.5.2 The Socio-cognitive Model of Discourse (Levels)

While not a discourse-context model in the conventional sense, van Dijk's approach to discourse integrates "context" on the socio-cognitive level. These mental representations of context, i.e. "context models", are assumed to control all levels and aspects of discourse production and discourse understanding. Categories familiar from text linguistics or pragmatics, such as genre, forms, style, variation, and communicative situation, are represented in such models as "setting", "participants" and "actions", and further specified as "time", "place", "identities", "roles", "aims", etc. (van Dijk 2004, 32). Significantly, context models can represent both large-scale contexts, such as institutions, and the local, situated social structure of interaction (van Dijk 2006b, 364).

Fundamentally, van Dijk's socio-cognitive approach posits that all social activity (including discourse and related textual artefacts) has a corresponding mental dimension, which in principle duplicates any "levels" of discourse as mental models involved in the production and interpretation of discourse (van Dijk 2004, 9). In assuming that ideology is both social and cognitive, this approach also offers a strikingly different way of linking the micro (cognitive, individual) and macro (social, collective) levels of discourse: "ideologies are the basic frameworks of organizing the social cognitions shared by members of social groups, organizations or institutions. […] They essentially function as the 'interface' between the cognitive representations and processes underlying discourse and action, on the one hand, and the societal position of interests of social groups, on the other hand" (van Dijk 1995, 17).

One example of this linkage through duality can be found in van Dijk's conception of "macrotopics" or "macrostructures", which he refers to as a "level". This topical level is not assumed to be necessarily expressed in discourse, and the fact that it is still inferable by people from cues is seen as evidence of a mental model of the macrotopics of a discourse. This effectively explains *presuppositions* as propositions contained not in text but in the corresponding mental model of discourse (van Dijk 2004, 10). Below the level of topics (in the sense of both complexity and realization), van Dijk posits, inter alia, a level of "semantic relations". If, in the discourse about “foreigners”, the macrotopic structure consist of a limited number of topics such as “cultural difference”, “deviance”, and “threats”, the level of semantic relations would comprise specific relations such discourses of “apparent denial” (e.g. “I have nothing against Jews, but…”) or “apparent concession” (“Not all Jews are greedy, but…”) (van Dijk 2004, 15).

In terms of the linguistic/semiotic side of the model, the “discourse levels” distinguished bear a strong resemblance to that of other models. To illustrate this with van Dijk’s own analysis of discourse about foreigners (van Dijk 2006b, 373), the following levels are listed in a top-down sequence: overall interaction strategies (e.g. positive self-presentation and negative other-presentation), macro speech acts or genres (e.g. accusation, defense), semantic macrostructures or topic selection (e.g. negative or positive topics), local speech acts that implement and sustain the global ones (e.g. statements), local meanings (e.g. positive/negative actions), lexicon (e.g. selected positive/negative words), local syntax (e.g. mood choice to de/emphasize agency or responsibility), rhetorical figures (e.g. hyperboles or euphemisms, metonymies or metaphors), expressions (e.g. acoustic or typographic emphasis), and ordering or arrangement (first to last, top to bottom).

Discourse analysts who have applied van Dijk’s scheme have sometimes loosely re-labelled these levels, as in the case of Cabrejas-Peñuelas’ (2017, 218) “content, lexis, topics, syntax, rhetoric, and order of discourse”, sometimes leading to terminological inconsistencies. Thus, when Cabrejas-Peñuelas states that she analysed extracts “at the syntactic, lexical and semantic and discourse levels” (2017, 218), she locates several of van Dijk’s discourse levels *outside* discourse.

While the levels of the mental models posited by van Dijk correspond roughly to linguistic levels on the one hand and to context levels on the other, “society”—the third key notion in his approach—is not similarly structured in the model. However, in his work on racism and ideology, there appears the notion of “the elite” and with it the assumption that it (re)produces the racism that is implemented and enacted in other social fields. There is thus at least an implicit, functional distinction between levels of society according to power-distinctions, albeit a controversial one in terms of unidirectional, top-down influence (Reisigl and Wodak 2005, 24; on different conceptions of social structure, see below).

The above-mentioned socio-cognitive definition of *presuppositions* as knowledge which is triggered in discourse, laid out by van Dijk only for mental models on the topic level of discourse, has been elaborated for all levels of discourse by Polyzou (2015). In short, presuppositions can be triggered on any or multiple levels of discourse—because communication requires large amounts of shared knowledge on a number of levels, from presuppositions on the lexical level through text and genre to pragmatics, context-related conventions and broad social norms (Polyzou 2015, 135). Thus, the typical structure and function of a genre may lead people to identify a particular element as 'exposition' or 'problem' without any explicit pointers, because it appears in the corresponding mental model's space. Analytically, Polyzou argues, this means that presuppositions that are not bound to specific triggers can still be identified through properties of the discourse. Apart from content conventionally associated with genres, Polyzou (2015, 131) also extends the notion to "commonplace implicit premises" or "inferable obligatory premises", i.e. "topoi" in Krzyżanowski and Wodak (2009a, 22), and to the "apparent denial" and "apparent concession" moves discussed by van Dijk: These, she argues, should be seen as part of our overall apparatus of processing discourse rather than specific knowledge of the specific assertions in question.

The socio-cognitive model has certainly been influential and it has been taken up in a wide variety of research contexts. It has perhaps been more productive conceptually than methodologically, as most empirical work using van Dijk's model has remained limited to textual data rather than attempting to explore the cognitive side.

4.5.3 Dimensions of Discourse Analysis: Norman Fairclough's Model

Norman Fairclough's approach to discourse structure differs somewhat from the above in that he proposes not layers but dimensions—not primarily of discourse but of discourse analysis. Remarkably, however, both distinctions have often been ignored in others' work drawing on Fairclough's model: there, the non-hierarchical "dimensions" become "levels", dimensions of analysis become levels of discourse, reifying the steps of an analytical procedure as the structure of the object of study. Significantly, Fairclough's model emphasizes linkages across dimensions, unlike some models that propose levels that can be studied independently.

Fairclough (1990, 1992, 1995, 2015) proposes that discourse analysis proceed along three dimensions—arguably corresponding to three dimensions of discourse, although there are some conceptual problems with that equivalence. The first dimension, sometimes referred to as the micro-level, is *textual analysis*: it entails the *description* of the formal properties of the texts chosen for study, comprising (as relevant) linguistic or semiotic analyses. The second dimension, sometimes referred to as meso-level, is *interpretation*. It focuses on the *discourse practices* related to the texts, in particular their production and reception, correspondingly viewing the text as both product and resource. The third dimension, sometimes labelled the macro-level, is *explanation*. It is concerned with the relationship between the broad sociocultural contexts in which these discursive practices are embedded.

Interestingly, these dimensions and corresponding analytical steps can also be approached in reverse sequence, yielding a slightly different perspective: The sociocultural context in which a particular 'discursive event' is produced comprises a network or nexus of practices formed through a particular political, institutional, economic, and social history. Power relations and ideologies infuse this dimension and the institutions, genres, and identities it gives rise to. The specific discursive practices that give rise to a text or group of texts may be those of policy, parliamentary debate or media reporting (i.e. genres, see also Koller 2012, 27) and present a unique locus for the production and reception of texts with respect to their form, function, and content within the broader sociocultural context. The textual dimension, finally, can only be understood in the context of the discursive practices that produced it and within the broader sociocultural context that informed those practices, giving meaning to the text. Meaning, thus, does not reside in the text alone, nor even in the discursive practices, but all three dimensions in conjunction. For research purposes, then, the three dimensions should be considered inseparable, which some work has missed in treating Fairclough's dimensions as container metaphors, with texts simply being "part of" discursive practices (Tracy et al. 2011, 247).

This interrelatedness has been demonstrated by numerous studies, including Rambe's analysis of the interplay between lecturers and students as well as among students in social networking environments. The study shows how such interactions are informed by both the immediate interactional context, i.e. emergent discursive practices, and the broader sociocultural context (Rambe 2012, 296). Significantly, such empirical analyses make use of the reciprocal relationship that allows us to approach the three dimensions from both directions (see above): the context of interaction structures the flow of interaction and, simultaneously, the interaction itself affords understanding of the context in which it is situated. As Jiwani and Richardson (2004, 242) argue with reference to both Fairclough and van Dijk, discursive phenomena studied in CDS, such as racism, are therefore always in evidence in all three dimensions (or levels) of discourse—the broad social context, situated discursive practices, and the texts produced in them—in ways "which are integrated and mutually self-supporting".

Care should be taken, however, not to conflate or confuse Fairclough's dimensions with other notions of 'discourse levels', as seems to happen in Bean and Stevens' study on reflections of pre-service and in-service teachers. Explicitly basing their approach on Fairclough's model, the authors refer to the three dimensions as "levels", but also distinguish "local", "institutional", and "societal" levels of discourse. Indeed, Bean and Stevens proceed to analyze their data for which "levels of discourse are present", meaning the local, institutional, and societal level (Bean and Stevens 2002, 212). This view of discourse structure does not correspond to Fairclough's, and their combination may well be contradictory or require additional theorization due to the doubling of the social as context/discourse level—aside from the terminological confusion.

4.6 Discourse as Levels of Social Action

Given the shared understanding of discourse as social action, the "levels of discourse" defined in Bhatia (2004) at first glance resemble Fairclough's dimensions. But Bhatia adds a fourth—genre—thus emphasizing the role of genres in professional contexts: Thus, professional discourse is seen as "operat[ing] within and across four somewhat different but overlapping levels": the textual, genre, professional practice, and professional culture. An arguably more significant difference is that all of these are seen as *practice* and as in relation of realization/instantiation: Any instance of communication can be analyzed as text, as representation of genre, as realization of professional practice, and as instance of culture (Bhatia 2010, 33).

This view has significant consequences for a range of other concepts in CDS. Just as Jiwani and Richardson (2004, 242) noted on Fairclough's and van Dijk's models of discourse structure, Bhatia's approach entails that discursive phenomena persist on all four levels: Racism or sexism are not restricted to one or two levels; nor can such phenomena suddenly appear on the textual or the sociocultural level if they are not in evidence on the other levels as well. Bhatia (2010, 34) explicates the consequences of her model for the concept of interdiscursivity as follows: Interdiscursivity thus comprises a variety of processes and practices that entail crossovers between properties on all four levels. These are viewed as "appropriation[s] of semiotic resources (which may include textual, semantic, socio-pragmatic, generic, and professional) across any two or more of these different levels". Of these, Bhatia is most interested in process on the level of genre, detailing the interdiscursive relations of "mixing", "embedding", and "bending" (Bhatia 2010, 34).

Providing empirical evidence of interdiscursivity, Bhatia identifies four such overlaps in his data, i.e. annual business reports: elements of accounting discourse, discourse of finance, public relations discourse, and legal discourse. While focusing his discussion on the genre level, Bhatia raises the issue of "integrity", i.e. discursive practices being compromised in terms of interdiscursivity. Similar perspectives have referred to such phenomena as "colonization" of discourses by other discourses (Iedema 2008, 389; Boje and Smith 2010, 313), and Bhatia also writes about the "territorial invasion" of fundraising discourse by the discourse of corporate advertising, threatening the integrity of the former (Bhatia 2010, 48). The terminology here is clearly not innocent, and whether one writes of discourse A as "appropriating" elements of discourse B or as being "invaded" by it should be carefully considered.

Conceptualizations of the internal structure of discourse thus also affect how we study inter-discursivity, or rather what we recognize as interdiscursive: discussions of thematic or topical overlaps are common, but Bhatia's model allows for a much deeper perspective.[1] While Bhatia conceived of levels of discourse as within a single discourse but conceptually cutting across social contexts, other work has conceived of levels of discourse in terms of each level referring to a different social context while also arranging these in a hierarchical relationship (see Sect. 4.7.3 below).

4.7 Levels of Discourse as Social/Geographical Hierarchy

While one might recognize a kind of hierarchy or scale in the above-cited models of dimensions or levels of discourse, if only in terms of analytical abstraction, other conceptions explicitly assume a social hierarchy of discourse levels. Common views distinguish, e.g., between "political", "public", "institutional", "academic", "media" and "private" or "individual" levels of discourse (e.g. Pühringer and Hirte 2015). The exact number and labels of levels distinguished vary, however, with some studies assuming only two levels and referring to the private as "micro" and to the institutional as "macro" (e.g. Kirvalidze and Samnidze 2016, 163), while others posit three levels in terms of general policy regarding deregulation of the public sector, specific educational policy, and policy implementation at individual schools (e.g. Arreman and Holm 2011, 226).[2]

Significantly, two scales coincide in this hierarchy: a scale of social, political or even legal power and a scale of geographical, spatial reach. There is potentially a third scale involved, though perhaps only indirectly for some studies, namely that of accessibility—this is foregrounded, however, in work that focuses on the 'public' to 'private' distinction. This may be modelled as a strict dichotomy or in a scalar, more nuanced manner as

[1] Like Bhatia, but fully integrating the sociological notion of "social fields of action", work in the DHA has looked at interdiscursivity/recontextualization across social fields (see Sect. 4.8 for social fields of action).

[2] There is clearly some overlap here with Alvesson and Karreman's (2000) four-level model of discourse (from micro-discourse in a specific micro-context to mega-discourse comprising universal ideas in an almost context-free way). Wastell (2003, 185) has discussed the relationship between their model and local/global distinctions.

discussed, e.g., by Jeffries (2003, 521), who posits "intermediate [levels] between the personal and the general culturally dominant". Such a distinction is relevant with respect to two major points: first, accessibility of data and data-collection methods and, second, the kinds of meaning-making, ideological struggles, and negotiations taking place on the different levels. In combination with a geographical national/local distinction, Jeffries can thus more precisely locate the discourse her data realizes within a multi-layered matrix.

4.7.1 Discourse Tracing

One of the less widely received approaches in CDS, termed "discourse tracing" by LeGreco and Tracy (2009), focuses on how discourse and discursive practices play out across micro, meso, and macro levels. Their definition of levels is illustrative at this point in my discussion because it seems to conflate rather than distinguish the geographical, abstraction, and topical scales mentioned above. The authors initially define "micro discourses" as "the local uses of text and language within a specific context", e.g. in their study of school menu policy a single school's menu and the ways in which students and staff used it; micro discourses when they are "linked across contexts" and seek to "coordinate practices across several local sites" are seen as "meso discourses"; and broad social narratives and systems of enduring thought, e.g. ideologies, are defined as "macro discourses" (LeGreco and Tracy 2009, 1525). As "levels" rather than "micro, meso, and macro discourses", these definitions strongly resemble Alvesson and Karreman's (2000) model.

However, the way LeGreco and Tracy operationalize discourse levels in their research deviates from their own definition: Rather than discourses that *are* micro, meso, and macro, they propose to study "how discourses operate across micro, meso, and macro levels". Their initial definition, which suggests a distinction of discourses, not of levels of the same discourse, based on geographical/spatial context or site, this research aim implies a topical distinction of discourses and a level distinction by context—otherwise discourses would not be able to operate *across* levels. And, indeed, this is how they implement their data collection strategy, i.e. triangulation by collecting data from multiple levels, based on the rationale that "discursive practices are constituted and enacted across micro, meso, and macro". In their study of school meal policy, such macro-level data are, inter alia, laws at the national level and media texts with wide reach; meso-level data are statewide regulations and info material; and micro-level data are individual school policies and interviews conducted by the researchers themselves (LeGreco and Tracy 2009, 1526–28).

4.7.2 Social Sites as Levels of Discourse

The so-called Duisburg School—a prominent approach to CDS in the German-language context—has arguably placed the structure of discourse at the center of its conception of discourse *and* its analytical practice. Combining Foucault's notion of discourse with the concept of "collective symbolism", Siegfried and Margarete Jäger among others have elaborated a detailed but accessible model of discourse's structuredness that has yet to receive adequate attention in the English-speaking research context.

The point of departure is the common enough assumption that discourses reproduce and affect social power relations, because they are socially institutionalized and conventionalized modes of communication. However, the resultant 'overall' or 'total' discourse of a given society is an incomprehensible tangle, a 'discursive swarming' or 'bustling' (from the German phrase 'diskursives Gewimmel'). This knotted mass, the approach posits, can only be comprehended by untangling the individual 'discourse strands'—an analytical concept introduce for this very purpose—which are defined as thematically interrelated *sequences* of 'discourse fragments', adding a longitudinal, potentially diachronic perspective. Each strand is thus defined by the development of a specific topic, e.g. 'refugees' or 'climate change', raised in texts that may contain fragments of multiple such strands. In other words, discourse fragments belonging to different discourse strands are combined in single texts. If that were the full extent of it, the Duisburg model would essentially be a spatially articulated model of thematic intertextuality with no grounding in social context.

However, this is where the model introduces "discourse levels" as a key element: the discourse fragments that make up the strands are conceptual-

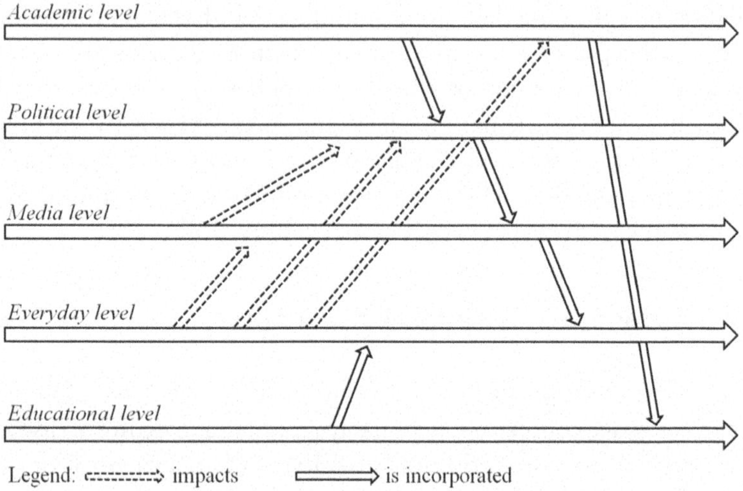

Fig. 4.1 Discourse levels model according to Siegfried Jäger (2015, 84)

ized as situated in and intersecting with contextually defined levels that are also described as "social sites". Examples of such levels/sites from various studies using this model include science, medicine, law, politics, media, education, everyday life, business life, and administration (S. Jäger 2015, 83). Thus, each discourse strand is contextually and historically embedded in social sites as the loci in which discourses can have an effect and from which individuals and group communicate when they produce texts (M. Jäger 2008, 380). These sites or levels constitute this model's contexts defined as material, cognitive, and normative infrastructures from which individuals speak and act, producing the texts in which discourse strands are realized. Each site thus also has its own historically shaped 'ways of knowing' and 'ways of doing' (Yıldız 2009, 33). While these levels are pictured as in a hierarchy (see Fig. 4.1), they are not described as macro- and micro-levels of discourse, nor as a geographical/spatial cline.

This qualification is significant insofar as discourse strands are said to 'appear' or 'manifest' only on these levels, as there is no 'outside' of such social sites. Given this definition of discourse levels, the model also assumes that these levels are interconnected, not only but also through such discourse strands. The analytical distinction, however, is intended to give appropriate weight to the social sites as sites of discourses' effectivity (M. Jäger 2008, 380). As we have seen with several other models, the Duisburg approach creates a matrix within which to locate discourses, using spatial and haptic/tactile metaphors: In developing research designs or subsequently describing them, all criteria can be used to define and delineate the object of research. In practice, this also includes a geographical-political component such as 'Germany'.

The model further posits that each level of discourse is highly interwoven, e.g. in the form of one medium picking up on or quoting news reported in other media, scientists drawing on other scientific publications etc. Siegfried Jäger (2015, 84) explicitly states that this quality justifies writing about 'the media discourse' or 'the discourse of the media', especially with respect to hegemonic media, as homogenous in central aspects. Indeed, Jäger elsewhere concluded that, in terms of the Duisburg model, the media must be regarded as contributing decisively to the construction of social reality insofar as they have an exceptionally strong impact on other levels of discourse (S. Jäger 2009, 306) and create or organize social consensus (Friedrich and Schultes 2013, 5). Moreover, all levels of discourse are conceptualized as related and interwoven with each other, as impacting and drawing on each other across levels. Thus, discourse fragments of scientific or political discourse can be incorporated on the discourse level of the media.

Empirically, the task of 'disentangling' this web that makes up the whole discourse of a society by bringing out individual discourse strands at the single discourse levels has been pursued mostly in terms discourse semantics, drawing on the notion of 'collective symbols'. Such metaphorical and synecdochic signifiers are immediately understood by all members of a speech community (Link 2013), such as natural disasters being used in the representation of immigration. For instance, the model has been analytically applied to the so-called 'headscarf debate' in Germany, an entanglement of two discourse strands (i.e. those on 'immigration' and 'women') on a least two levels of discourse (i.e. those of everyday and media). According to M. Jäger and S. Jäger (2007, 109), it is the entanglement of discourse strands that informs the dynamic of that debate. Ackermann et al. (2015, 98) extend this view by arguing that it is the discourse level of the media at or through which discourse strands are linked or intertwined. In a similar vein, Yıldız (2009, 34) argues that hegemonic discourses are "made" by social actors connecting categories and content they encounter at various levels of discourse, weaving heterogeneous discourse fragments into a coherent whole or "story line".

Other studies applying the Duisburg model have traced a range of such structural entanglements: between the discourse levels of politics, the everyday, and art history (Sachs 2011, 7); between discourses on the level of science and its popularization on the level of the everyday (Calsamiglia 2003, 140–43); and between the field of research into extremism, the Federal Office for the Protection of the Constitution, the press, and civic education (Ackermann et al. 2015, 35). As these examples show, research practice seems to invite a more focused definition of levels named, e.g., for a particular academic discipline or an intelligence service, even if this does not fully conform to the model. An even more liberal and contradictory interpretation of the model can be seen in Höly (2018, 63), who in studying the discourse of financial elites defines "the discourse level" as "management literature" as opposed to an unspecified non-discursive level of interviews conducted for the study. While a distinction might be made here—even in terms of levels according to the Duisburg model—, data elicited by researchers does not somehow exist outside "the level of discourse".

Apart from the media, the level of everyday discourse has recently been studied in terms of the Duisburg model, e.g. in terms of the recontextualization of scientific knowledge or the interweaving of racist or xenophobic discourse with established "markers" of "Islam" and "terrorism" (Friedrich and Schultes 2013, 10). Everyday discourse (also 'interdiscourse' or 'elementary discourse' in contrast to 'specialized discourses') presents a challenging but interesting case within this model, because it mixes other discourses and cannot be said to have institutionalized material, cognitive, and normative infrastructures like other levels of discourse. Waldschmidt et al. (2008, 317), however, argue that in constituting a particular kind of knowledge and experience of reality—i.e. 'everyday knowledge'—this level is of great importance in understanding the overall discourse of a society. Its relationship to other levels of discourse, it follows, cannot be described in similar terms as that between other levels: Rather, everyday discourse as a 'non-elaborated form of discourse' should be seen as engaged in a continual cycle of exchange with the other levels, i.e. 'elaborated forms of discourse'. This cycle, according to Link (2005, 91–92), moves new knowledge both "downwards" from specialized discourses, e.g. in science, to everyday discourse (a kind of "trickle-down effect") and "upwards" in the reverse direction.

Waldschmidt et al. (2008, 317–21) elaborate on this cycle by defining the specific type of everyday knowledge as constituted by everyday discourse. They describe it as based on subjective experience in everyday life but still structured and patterned (recipe-like typification, stereotypisation) as well as accidental (heavily impacted by singular events and coincidence). Such knowledge is based on 'lived experience', is highly personal, and its value is determined not by the norms of specialized discourses, e.g. scientific criteria, but by an individual's biographical relevance structures. Even collectively shared, everyday discourse and knowledge follow their own norms of legitimacy: the authenticity of personal experience or credible 'word of mouth'.

4.7.3 Layers and Levels: Hierarchical Discourse Structure in the DHA

Since the early 1990s, studies focusing on the discursive construction of antisemitism, racism, and national identity—which contributed substantially to the formation of the Discourse-Historical Approach—has referred to 'layers' and 'levels' of discourse to indicate their triangulation by collecting and analyzing data from different social contexts, not just genres or media. In terms of such research, of course, a narrow focus on one type of data from one social context would seem a major caveat, invalidating the claim to identifying *national* or *collective* identities.

In the seminal study of the "Waldheim Affair"—which was triggered by revelations about the then-candidate and later president of Austria, Kurt Waldheim, during WWII—Wodak (1990) and Wodak et al. (1994) indicate "the many layers of discourse" investigated: Wehrmacht documents concerning WWII in the Balkans, documents relating specifically to Waldheim's activities, interviews with Wehrmacht veterans who had served with Waldheim; Austrian newspapers' reporting (covering WWII in the Balkans, Waldheim's past, related historical research, and Waldheim's own explanation of his past); international newspapers' reporting (covering much the same topics); press releases and documents of the World Jewish Congress; public statements and interviews with Austrian politicians as well as the "common people" on all these topics (Wodak 2011a, 360–61; Wodak and Reisigl 1999, 187). In the case of Austria's post-war search for a new national identity, Wodak et al. (1998) showed the validation of Austrian distinctiveness through a reinforced homogenization of "us" versus "them" on "all levels of discourse" (Wodak and de Cillia 2007, 341). These studies, like many that have taken up the approach outlined therein, are informed by the aim to capture discourse across levels of social structure that might be set on a scale of official state representation, public (typically including politics, media, and academia), quasi-public, and private.

Apart from other research on national identities and racism, this approach of studying discourse from government policy to everyday talk has inspired work in healthcare, governance, and closely related fields (e.g. Stephens 2009; Bolam, Murphy, and Gleeson 2004). Interestingly, it has also been connected to a further distinction—not along a vertical or horizontal cline, but in terms "public" and "confidential" political discourse (Shenhav 2007), i.e. "frontstage" and "backstage" politics, to use Goffman's terminology in the sense of Wodak (2011b).

4.8 Discourse as Situated in Social Fields of Action

In addition to the above model of discourse levels oriented hierarchically along power relations of social structure, work in the Discourse-Historical Approach and elsewhere has developed a complementary model of horizontal distinction by "social fields of action". In this, as Blain (2005, 35) suggests, it may have taken a cue from Foucault's genealogy as discourse analysis that focuses on how discourses function in different fields of action.

Essentially, this model conceptualizes discourses as situated within and functionally related to specific social fields as "segments" of the respective social reality. Although discourses may intersect with several such fields, each field functions as the immediate social context of the discourse in question (Reisigl 2017, 52). This understanding of "field" draws on Bourdieu's notion of social fields as "social microcosms" that are distinguished by their own logic, rules, social roles, and power relations (Forchtner and Schneickert 2016, 296–97) as well as potentially different validity claims about truth and normative or moral correctness (Reisigl 2011, 479). In contrast to Bourdieu, however, the DHA emphasizes the social function of such fields in relation to the discursive practices situated in them (Reisigl 2011, 481–82). It is thus not surprising that this model has been combined with the notion of "communities of practice" (Lave and Wenger 1991), complementing it with the idea that social fields and their communities have access to and produce "normalized" knowledge that may not fully extend to other social fields (Kwon, Clarke, and Wodak 2009, 277).[3]

A second major influence on this model has been Girnth's (1996) work on political discourse, distinguishing the functions of "legislation, self-presentation, manufacturing of public opinion, developing party-internal consent, advertising and vote-getting, governing as well as executing and controlling as well as expressing (oppositional) dissent" (Reisigl and Wodak 2005, 36). Because politics is only one social field of action among many, this distinction is exemplary rather than exhaustive, as is the detailed mapping of these 8 functions with related genres in Reisigl and Wodak (2005, 38).

Broad examples of such fields have been identified as politics, the media, the economy, academia, medicine, legislation, etc. While these fields are more or less closely related to each other depending on their functions, this spatio-metaphorical distinction conceptualizes their interrelationship not as hierarchical or vertical, but horizontal. While social fields shape and affect discourses, discourses also influence discursive as well as non-discursive social practices and individual actions. In other words, discourses as a particular type of social practice are seen as producing, reproducing, and transforming the social fields in which they are embedded.

[3]There also seems to be a close conceptual affinity to nexus analysis, even if that approach is focused on a smaller scale of social practice; for an illustrative comparison, see Scollon and Scollon's (2004, 5–6) case studies of discourse in management meetings, academic classrooms, and legislative hearings.

This reciprocal relationship is a key analytical challenge but at the same time also a key goal of CDS using this model.

Similar to the Duisburg model, discourses are here seen as potentially moving across or intersecting with multiple fields. Thus, a discourse about a given topic can have its starting point in one field of action and "spread" to another (Reisigl and Wodak 2005, 36). When it intersects with another discourse, however, this always happens within a specific social field or fields of action. Such inter-discursive relations may be described in terms of several concepts: To see them as "textual chains" foregrounds the sequence or succession of thematically or/and functionally related texts, given by the particular configuration of practices in the social field(s) involved. Alternatively, they might be regarded in terms of the "hybridity" of practices or genres (see Bhatia 2010). And to discuss them as "interdiscursivity" emphasizes the particular "connection", i.e. overlapping, combination, colonization or invasion, of different discourses in particular analytical unit, e.g. text or corpus (Reisigl and Wodak 2005, 37).

Other work has looked at discourses on topics such as climate change or policy formation and used the 'social fields' model to discuss how discursively constituted social reality is recontextualized in and across different fields. In Sedlaczek (2017), for instance, the field-specific ways in which a religious magazine TV program and a service/consumer magazine program represent climate are studied. Both programs, being oriented towards different audiences, mediate between the scientific field and the religious and consumer field, respectively (Sedlaczek 2017, 493). For Hafez's (2017) study on Islamophobic populism, it is the social fields of law making, intersecting with the field of formation of public attitudes and opinions that is of critical interest. Studying the 2004 strategy of "branding" in the Romanian politician Băsescu's election campaign, Ieţcu-Fairclough (2009) relies on the notion of "field" to describe how this innovation cut across boundaries previously separating politics from the popular entertainment, commercial advertising and everyday life. And Turowski (2010, 21), in analyzing the formation of the so-called "third way" in social-democratic politics, combines the 'social fields' model with a hierarchical cline of abstraction, positing a level of political principles and theory, a level of political aims, and a level of practical policy implementation. Yet others draw on field distinctions primarily for the sake of triangulating their effort to grasp the "whole discourse" of a given society (Anagnostopoulos, Everett, and Carey 2013, 166).

A particularly prominent context of use for this model has been the study of 'normalization', i.e. the 'making normal' of once taboo topics, arguments or ways of speaking about topics. Such processes are usually highly political and may be regarded as altering the conditions and norms of 'the sayable'. While this is intrinsically a longitudinal phenomenon, i.e. pertains to discursive change, it is not necessarily a long-term phenomenon as such 'shifts' can also be abrupt (see Chapter 5), in particular through populism and/or mediatized politics. As Wodak (2015) has argued, racism and other ideolegemes of the extreme right have been and are becoming normalized across social fields. The model thus provides important conceptual tools for tracing the spread of political ideas, arguments, metaphors or terminology in what might otherwise simply appear to be "pervasive, diffuse forms" (Krzyżanowski and Wodak 2009a, 1–2; see also Hart 2018, 286; Musolff 2014).

4.9 Further Structural Concepts Applied to Discourse

4.9.1 Discourse as Core/Periphery

In modelling the Foucauldian notion of 'orders of discourse', Hedrén (1994) distinguishes between a discursive "core" and "periphery" by the degree to which statements are perceived as more or less natural, more or less correct or self-evident. The "core" is constituted by utterances that are considered self-evident and unquestionable, while the "periphery" of discourse comprises statements that are regarded as questionable or doubtful. Significantly, Hedrén also suggests that the periphery may present a hegemonic discourse's weak point, i.e. the best place to begin a critical analysis. Dekker Linnros and Hallin (2001, 392) have elaborated on this point through a case study on environmental concerns regarding the Öresund Bridge in Sweden: They argue that when two discourses overlap—in this case development and environmental discourses—the overlap will be of their peripheries and represent a discursive "band" of conflict. This conceptualization of discourse structure roughly corresponds to Diez's (2001, 15) notion of "geologically" structured discourse, i.e. discourse having "depth", its surface level being easier to change (and analyze) while its "deepest levels" represent deep-seated ideology.

4.9.2 Discursive Formations

Beyond discourse as an analytical unit, some authors have posited 'discursive formations' or 'discourse formations' as more or less tightly connected clusters of discourses. According to this conception, different discourses can center on or cluster around the same topic or object while having different rules (Diez 1999). This view, of course, precludes a purely topical definition of discourse and requires at least one other criterion for distinction, e.g. social fields, media or levels.

4.9.3 Discursive Sedimentation

To model the layered structure of discourse, foregrounding that discourses build up and change over time, Wæver (1998) posits discourse levels in a hierarchy according to their persistency. The metaphors of depth, surface, and sedimentation may make this view appealing for longitudinal or diachronic research.

4.9.4 Discursive Conduits

In her study on the discourse on "Gypsies, Travellers and Roma" in the institutions of the EU, Simhandl introduces the notion of "discursive conduits" to complement the Duisburg model (see above) to more fully conceptualize "the dynamic nature of discourse and reveal the entanglement of different strands" (Simhandl 2006, 111). More precisely, she argues that the notion is needed to name and incorporate that which "constrains and channels" discourses, delineating "what is sayable from what is not sayable". Analytically, interest is in the ways that discourses "silence" and "exclude", e.g. by "limiting and restricting authorities and experts to some groups, but not others, endorsing a certain common sense, but making other modes of categorizing and judging meaningless, impracticable, inadequate or otherwise disqualified" (Simhandl 2006, 109). Methodologically, Simhandl's approach tries to identify "interpretative patterns" that structure discourse. In her case study, two largely unarticulated assumptions or shared premises are identified as consecutive *conduits*: that "nomadism" is a "lifestyle" and that Roma are a minority essentially located in Eastern Europe (Simhandl 2006, 100–106).

4.9.5 Discursive Strands and Knots

In some work, the Duisburg model's spatial-tactile metaphor of 'discourse strands' has given rise to a further structural notion, 'discourse knots', to describe the entanglement of two discourses. Such entanglements parallel what might otherwise be describes as interdiscursivity within a single text or corpus of texts. If such knots become commonplace, Lassen (2018, 8) argues, they are identifiable as collective symbols, stereotypes or topoi. As such they may represent a short-hand way of invoking a shared understanding of a particular aspect of social reality or, to the discourse analyst, a point of interest and potential critique.

4.9.6 Cross-Level Discourses and Voices

Adding an agency- and social actor-centered consideration of power to the wide-spread interest in recontextualization and the ways discourses spread across levels or fields, Creed, Langstraat, and Scully (2002) point out that not all "voices" have the power to be heard across levels. In investigating cross-level discourses or patterns across the levels of discourse, they argue, one should therefore also look for the individuals and organizations that facilitate such transitions alongside terminology, ideas, arguments or texts.

4.10 Research Practice: Benefits and Pitfalls

For most research in CDS, the theoretical and conceptual framework adopted will have a significant impact on methodology in several respects. Adopting a particular view of the structuredness of discourse is likely to affect how we plan data collection, which data we collect, how we delineate or segment data into clusters or corpora, which categories and concepts we apply during analysis, how we interpret results with respect to social structure, and how we relate our insights into multiple 'levels of discourse' to each other. In particular, we should be aware that

- there is plethora of models of discourse structure in the field of CDS and even DS, some of them more elaborate than others,
- some of those models are more suitable to a particular research interest than others,
- the model of discourse structure adopted must correspond to, support, and add clarity to our research interests, research questions or aims,
- existing models of discourse structure can be distinguished in terms of whether, broadly speaking, they posit discourse as one level of social reality among others, see discourse as structured into levels of linguistic/semiotic realization, regard discourse as socially constructed ways of knowing, or as social practice,
- models may conceptualize discourse as hierarchically or horizontally structured, implying a particular view of social structure as well,
- models may assume levels of context that parallel levels of discourse and/or integrate higher levels of discourse as part of their context model,
- models may integrate other concepts as integral components of discourse structure that go beyond the linguistic, such as social practice, mental models and/or ideology,
- existing models may use the same terminology, most frequently 'levels', and may thus not be easy to distinguish,
- existing empirical work based on one of the most widely received models may, as I hope to have demonstrated above, extend or adapt the original model in problematic ways, eclectically combine several models or use inconsistent terminology,

- collection of textual data as well as complementary ethnographic, observational, etc. data will likely be affected by the model of discourse structure adopted, especially if it also implicates or models social structure,
- research interested in transversive or intersectional discourse phenomena such as recontextualization, normalization, interdiscursivity or the colonization of discourses must address the issue of discourse structure,
- terminologically, the metaphors used by different models may or may not offer an additional benefit to conceptualizing or visualizing, e.g. as "strands" and "knots" intersecting with 'levels' or 'fields' etc.,
- some models will suggest and others prescribe steps of analysis that run parallel to assumptions about discourse structure,
- the structure of discourse may be a marginal or central interest of a particular approach, and thus explaining how that structure affects, maintains or shapes discourses may be more or less integral to research adopting the respective model,
- consequently, adopting a particular model of discourse structure may suggest new research questions, steps of analysis or interpretation to our work,
- it may be possible to combine specific models without contradiction, especially vertical and horizontal ones, with levels of linguistic realization,
- and, insofar as strategies of triangulation rely on multiple sources of data being situated on different structural levels, strands etc., any claim that can be made as to the benefits of triangulation will depend on the model of discourse structure chosen (e.g. Krzyżanowski and Wodak 2009b).

References

Ackermann, Jan, Katharina Behne, Felix Buchta, Marc Drobot, and Philipp Knopp. 2015. *Metamorphosen des Extremismusbegriffes: diskursanalytische Untersuchungen zur Dynamik einer funktionalen Unzulänglichkeit.* Wiesbaden: Springer VS.

Alvesson, Mats, and Dan Karreman. 2000. "Varieties of Discourse: On the Study of Organizations Through Discourse Analysis." *Human Relations* 53 (9): 1125–49. https://doi.org/10.1177/0018726700539002.

Anagnostopoulos, Dorothea, Sakeena Everett, and Carleen Carey. 2013. "'Of Course We're Supposed to Move On, but Then You Still Got People Who Are Not over Those Historical Wounds': Cultural Memory and US Youth's Race Talk." *Discourse & Society* 24 (2): 163–85. https://doi.org/10.1177/0957926512469389.

Andersson, Thomas. 2012. "Normative Identity Processes in Managers' Personal Development Training." *Personnel Review* 41 (5): 572–89. https://doi.org/10.1108/00483481211249111.

———. 2015. *Politics of Fear: What Right-Wing Populist Discourses Mean.* Los Angeles: Sage.

Antaki, Charles. 2008. "Discourse Analysis and Conversation Analysis." In *The SAGE Handbook of Social Research Methods*, edited by P. Alasuutari, L. Bickman, and J. Brannan, 431–46. London: Sage.

Arreman, Inger Erixon, and Ann-Sofie Holm. 2011. "Privatisation of Public Education? The Emergence of Independent Upper Secondary Schools in Sweden." *Journal of Education Policy* 26 (2): 225–43. https://doi.org/10.1080/02680939.2010.502701.

Barkho, Leon. 2011. "The Role of Internal Guidelines in Shaping News Narratives: Ethnographic Insights into the Discursive Rhetoric of Middle East Reporting by the BBC and Al-Jazeera English." *Critical Discourse Studies* 8 (4): 297–309. https://doi.org/10.1080/17405904.2011.601642.

Barrett, Michèle. 1991. *The Politics of Truth: From Marx to Foucault.* Stanford, CA: Stanford University Press.

Bateman, John A., and Janina Wildfeuer. 2014. "A Multimodal Discourse Theory of Visual Narrative." *Journal of Pragmatics* 74 (December): 180–208. https://doi.org/10.1016/j.pragma.2014.10.001.

Bax, Stephen. 2011. *Discourse and Genre: Analysing Language in Context.* Basingstoke: Palgrave Macmillan.

Bean, Thomas W., and Lisa Patel Stevens. 2002. "Scaffolding Reflection for Preservice and Inservice Teachers." *Reflective Practice* 3 (2): 205–18. https://doi.org/10.1080/14623940220142343.

Bednarek, Monika. 2015. "Corpus-Assisted Multimodal Discourse Analysis of Television and Film Narratives." In *Corpora and Discourse Studies: Integrating Discourse and Corpor*, edited by Paul Baker and Tony McEnery, 63–87. London: Palgrave Macmillan.

Berry, David M. 2004. "The Contestation of Code: A Preliminary Investigation into the Discourse of the Free/Libre and Open Source Movements." *Critical Discourse Studies* 1 (1): 65–89. https://doi.org/10.1080/17405900410001674524.

Bhatia, Vijay K. 2004. *Worlds of Written Discourse: A Genre-Based View.* London: Continuum International.

Bhatia, Vijay K. 2010. "Interdiscursivity in Professional Communication." *Discourse & Communication* 4 (1): 32–50. https://doi.org/10.1177/1750481309351208.

Blain, Michael. 2005. "The Politics of Victimage: Power and Subjection in a US Anti-Gay Campaign." *Critical Discourse Studies* 2 (1): 31–50. https://doi.org/10.1080/17405900500052168.

Boje, David, and Robert Smith. 2010. "Re-storying and Visualizing the Changing Entrepreneurial Identities of Bill Gates and Richard Branson." *Culture and Organization* 16 (4): 307–31. https://doi.org/10.1080/14759551003769250.

Bolam, Bruce, Simon Murphy, and Kate Gleeson. 2004. "Individualisation and Inequalities in Health: A Qualitative Study of Class Identity and Health." *Social Science & Medicine* 59 (7): 1355–65. https://doi.org/10.1016/j.socscimed.2004.01.018.

Cabrejas-Peñuelas, Ana Belén. 2017. "Manipulation as an Ideological Tool in the Political Genre of Parliamentary Discourses." *Pragmatics* 27 (2): 207–34. https://doi.org/10.1075/prag.27.2.02cab.

Calsamiglia, Helena. 2003. "Popularization Discourse." *Discourse Studies* 5 (2): 139–46. https://doi.org/10.1177/1461445603005002307.

Carpentier, Nico, and Leen Van Brussel. 2012. "On the Contingency of Death: A Discourse-Theoretical Perspective on the Construction of Death." *Critical Discourse Studies* 9 (2): 99–115. https://doi.org/10.1080/17405904.2012.656372.

Cicourel, Aaron V. 2007. "A Personal, Retrospective View of Ecological Validity." *Text & Talk* 27 (5–6): 735–52. https://doi.org/10.1515/TEXT.2007.033.

Creed, Douglas W. E., Jeffrey A. Langstraat, and Maureen A. Scully. 2002. "A Picture of the Frame: Frame Analysis as Technique and as Politics." *Organizational Research Methods* 5 (1): 34–55.

Diez, Thomas. 1999. *Die EU lesen: diskursive Knotenpunkte in der britischen Eurodebatte.* Forschung Politikwissenschaft 31. Opladen: Leske + Budrich.

———. 2001. "Europe as a Discursive Battleground: Discourse Analysis and European Integration Studies." *Cooperation and Conflict* 36 (1): 5–38. https://doi.org/10.1177/00108360121962245.

Fairclough, Norman. 1990. "Technologization of Discourse." Lancaster: Centre for Language in Social Life, University of Lancaster. Mimeo.
———. 1992. *Discourse and Social Change*. Cambridge: Polity Press.
———. 1995. *Media Discourse*. London and New York: E. Arnold.
———. 2015. *Language and Power*. 3rd ed. London and New York: Routledge, Taylor & Francis Group.
Fairclough, Norman, Phil Graham, Jay Lemke, and Ruth Wodak. 2004. "Introduction." *Critical Discourse Studies* 1 (1): 1–7. https://doi.org/10.1080/17405900410001674489.
De Fina, Anna, and Alexandra Georgakopoulou. 2012. *Analyzing Narrative: Discourse and Sociolinguistic Perspectives*. Cambridge: Cambridge University Press.
Forchtner, Bernhard, and Christian Schneickert. 2016. "Collective Learning in Social Fields: Bourdieu, Habermas and Critical Discourse Studies." *Discourse & Society* 27 (3): 293–307. https://doi.org/10.1177/0957926516630892.
Friedrich, Sebastian, and Hannah Schultes. 2013. "Mediale Verbindungen—Antimuslimische Effekte Zu Den Gegenwärtigen Verschränkungen Des Islamdiskurses." *Journal Für Psychologie* 21 (1): 1–28.
Gabrielatos, Costas, and Paul Baker. 2008. "Fleeing, Sneaking, Flooding: A Corpus Analysis of Discursive Constructions of Refugees and Asylum Seekers in the UK Press, 1996–2005." *Journal of English Linguistics* 36 (1): 5–38. https://doi.org/10.1177/0075424207311247.
Gee, James Paul. 1999. *An Introduction to Discourse Analysis: Theory and Method*. London and New York: Routledge.
Girnth, Heiko. 1996. "Texte Im Politischen Diskurs: Ein Vorschlag Zur Diskursorientierten Beschreibung von Textsorten." *Muttersprache* 106 (1): 66–80.
Hafez, Farid. 2017. "Debating the 2015 Islam Law in Austrian Parliament: Between Legal Recognition and Islamophobic Populism." *Discourse & Society* 28 (4): 392–412. https://doi.org/10.1177/0957926517703223.
Hart, Christopher. 2018. "'Riots Engulfed the City': An Experimental Study Investigating the Legitimating Effects of Fire Metaphors in Discourses of Disorder." *Discourse & Society* 29 (3): 279–98. https://doi.org/10.1177/0957926517734663.
Hedrén, Johan. 1994. "Miljöpolitikens Natur" [The Nature of Environmental Politics]. *Linköping Studies in Art and Science* 110: 1–22.
Höly, Kristina. 2018. *Auf den Spuren der globalen Finanzelite*. Wiesbaden: Springer Fachmedien Wiesbaden. https://doi.org/10.1007/978-3-658-18769-9.
Iedema, Rick. 2008. "Embodying the Contemporary 'Clinician-Manager': Entrepreneurializing Middle Management?" In *Identity Trouble: Critical Dis-*

course and Contested Identities, edited by Carmen Caldas-Coulthard and Rick Iedema, 273–91. London: Palgrave Macmillan. http://public.eblib.com/choice/publicfullrecord.aspx?p=4331082.

Iedema, Rick, Pieter Degeling, Jeffrey Braithwaite, and Les White. 2004. "'It's an Interesting Conversation I'm Hearing': The Doctor as Manager." *Organization Studies* 25 (1): 15–33. https://doi.org/10.1177/0170840604038174.

Ieţcu-Fairclough, Isabela. 2009. "Branding and Strategic Maneuvering in the Romanian Presidential Election of 2004: A Critical Discourse-Analytical and Pragma-Dialectical Perspective." *Journal of Language and Politics* 7 (3): 372–90. https://doi.org/10.1075/jlp.7.3.02iet.

Jäger, Margarete. 2008. "Diskursanalyse: Ein Verfahren zur kritischen Rekonstruktion von Machtbeziehungen." In *Handbuch Frauen- und Geschlechterforschung*, edited by Ruth Becker and Beate Kortendiek, 378–83. Wiesbaden: VS Verlag für Sozialwissenschaften. https://doi.org/10.1007/978-3-531-91972-0_45.

Jäger, Siegfried. 2009. "Pressefreiheit Und Rassismus. Der Karikaturenstreit in Der Deutschen Presse. Ergebnisse Einer Diskursanalyse." In *Islamfeindlichkeit: Wenn Die Grenzen Der Kritik Verschwimmen*, edited by Thorsten Gerald Schneider, 305–22. Bielefeld: VS Verlag für Sozialwissenschaften.

———. 2015. *Kritische Diskursanalyse: eine Einführung*. 7., vollständig überarbeitete Auflage. Edition DISS, Bd. 3. Münster: Unrast.

Jäger, Margret, and Siegfried Jäger. 2007. *Deutungskämpfe: Theorie und Praxis kritischer Diskursanalyse*. 1. Auflage. Medien - Kultur - Kommunikation. Wiesbaden: VS, Verlag für Sozialwissenschaften.

Jeffries, Lesley. 2003. "Not a Drop to Drink: Emerging Meanings in Local Newspaper Reporting of the 1995 Water Crisis in Yorkshire." *Text—Interdisciplinary Journal for the Study of Discourse* 23 (4). https://doi.org/10.1515/text.2003.020.

Jiwani, Yasmin, and John E. Richardson. 2004. "Dicourse, Ethnicity and Racism." In *Discourse Studies: A Multidisciplinary Introduction*, edited by Teun A. van Dijk, 241–62. London: Sage.

KhosraviNik, Majid. 2010. "Actor Descriptions, Action Attributions, and Argumentation: Towards a Systematization of CDA Analytical Categories in the Representation of Social Groups 1." *Critical Discourse Studies* 7 (1): 55–72. https://doi.org/10.1080/17405900903453948.

Kirvalidze, Nino, and Nino Samnidze. 2016. "Political Discourse as a Subject of Interdisciplinary Studies." *Journal of Teachign and Education* 5 (1): 161–70.

Koller, Veronika. 2012. "How to Analyse Collective Identity in Discourse—-Textual and Contextual Parameters." *Critical Approaches to Discourse Analysis Across Disciplines* 5 (2): 19–38.

Krzyżanowski, Michał. 2011. "Ethnography and Critical Discourse Analysis: Towards a Problem-Oriented Research Dialogue." *Critical Discourse Studies* 8 (4): 231–38. https://doi.org/10.1080/17405904.2011.601630.

Krzyżanowski, Michał, and Ruth Wodak. 2009a. *The Politics of Exclusion: Debating Migration in Austria.* New Brunswick, NJ: Transaction Publishers.

———. 2006b. "Discourse and Manipulation." *Discourse & Society* 17 (3): 359–83.

Kwon, Winston, Ian Clarke, and Ruth Wodak. 2009. "Organizational Decision-Making, Discourse, and Power: Integrating Across Contexts and Scales." *Discourse & Communication* 3 (3): 273–302. https://doi.org/10.1177/1750481309337208.

Lamb, Eleanor C. 2013. "Power and Resistance: New Methods for Analysis Across Genres in Critical Discourse Analysis." *Discourse & Society* 24 (3): 334–60. https://doi.org/10.1177/0957926512472041.

Lassen, Inger. 2018. "Resisting Dehumanization: Citizen Voices and Acts of Solidarity." *Critical Discourse Studies* (February): 1–17. https://doi.org/10.1080/17405904.2018.1441038.

Lave, Jean, and Etienne Wenger. 1991. *Situated Learning: Legitimate Peripheral Participation.* Learning in Doing. Cambridge, UK and New York: Cambridge University Press.

LeGreco, Marianne, and Sarah J. Tracy. 2009. "Discourse Tracing as Qualitative Practice." *Qualitative Inquiry* 15 (9): 1516–43. https://doi.org/10.1177/1077800409343064.

Leitch, Shirley, and Sally Davenport. 2007. "Strategic Ambiguity as a Discourse Practice: The Role of Keywords in the Discourse on 'Sustainable' Biotechnology." *Discourse Studies* 9 (1): 43–61. https://doi.org/10.1177/1461445607072106.

Link, Jürgen. 2005. "Warum Diskurse Nicht von Personalen Subjekten „ausgehandelt" Werden. Von Der Diskurs- Zur Interdiskurstheorie." In *Die Diskursive Konstruktion von Wirklichkeit: Zum Verhältnis von Wissenssoziologie Und Diskursforschung,* edited by Reiner Keller, Andreas Hirseland, Werner Schneider, and Willy Viehöfer, 77–100. Konstanz: UVK Verlagsgesellschaft.

———. 2013. *Versuch über den Normalismus: wie Normalität produziert wird.* 5. Aufl. Göttingen: Vandenhoeck & Ruprecht.

Dekker Linnros, Hannah, and Per Olof Hallin. 2001. "The Discursive Nature of Environmental Conflicts: The Case of the Öresund Link." *Area* 33 (4): 391–403.

Mckenna, Bernard, and Neal Waddell. 2006. "Technologizing Inhumanity: A Discursive Practice." *Critical Discourse Studies* 3 (2): 211–28. https://doi.org/10.1080/17405900600908129.

Menz, Florian. 1999. "'Who Am I Gonna Do This With?': Self-Organization, Ambiguity and Decision-Making in a Business Enterprise." *Discourse & Society* 10 (1): 101–28. https://doi.org/10.1177/0957926599010001005.

Metten, Thomas. 2012. "Zur Analyse von Atmosphären in Diskursen. Eine Diskurslinguistische Untersuchung Kollektiver Befindlichkeiten Am Beispiel Des Vulkanausbruchs in Island." *Zeitschrift Für Angewandte Linguistik* 56: 33–65.

Mitten, Richard, and Ruth Wodak. 1993. "On the Discourse of Racism and Prejudice." *Folia Linguistica* 27 (3–4): 191–215.

Musolff, Andreas. 2014. *Metaphor, Nation and the Holocaust: The Concept of the Body Politic.* London and New York: Routledge.

Niehr, Thomas. 2014. *Einführung in die Politolinguistik: Gegenstände und Methoden.* UTB Sprachwissenschaften, Linguistik 4173. Göttingen Bristol, CT: Vandenhoeck & Ruprecht.

Polyzou, Alexandra. 2015. "Presupposition in Discourse: Theoretical and Methodological Issues." *Critical Discourse Studies* 12 (2): 123–38. https://doi.org/10.1080/17405904.2014.991796.

Pühringer, Stephan, and Katrin Hirte. 2015. "The Financial Crisis as a Heart Attack: Discourse Profiles of Economists in the Financial Crisis." *Journal of Language and Politics* 14 (4): 599–625. https://doi.org/10.1075/jlp.14.4.06puh.

Rambe, Patient. 2012. "Critical Discourse Analysis of Collaborative Engagement in Facebook Postings." *Australasian Journal of Educational Technology* 28 (2): 295–314.

Reisigl, Martin, and Ruth Wodak. 2005. *Discourse and Discrimination. Rhetorics of Racism and Antisemitism.* London and New York: Routledge.

Reisigl, Martin. 2007. "Projektbericht: Der Wiener Ansatz Der Kritischen Diskursanalyse." *Forum Qualitative Sozialforschung* 8 (2): 1–11.

———. 2011. "Grundzüge Der Wiener Kritischen Diskursanalyse." In *Handbuch Sozialwissenschaftliche Diskursanalyse*, edited by Reiner Keller, Andreas Hirseland, Werner Schneider, and Willy Viehöfer, 3rd ed., 1:459–98. Wiesbaden: VS Verlag für Sozialwissenschaften.

———. 2017. "The Discourse-Historical Approach." In *The Routledge Handbook of Critical Discourse Studies*, edited by John Flowerdew and John E. Richardson, 44–59. London: Routledge.

Sachs, Melanie. 2011. "Bericht Über Das Forum 'Wissenschaftsgeschichte Der Kunstgeschichte' Auf Dem Kunsthistorikertag 2011 in Würzburg." *Kunstgeschichte. Open Peer Reviewed Journal.*

Scollon, Ronald, and Suzanne B. K. Scollon. 2004. *Nexus Analysis: Discourse and the Emerging Internet.* London and New York: Routledge.

Sedlaczek, Andrea Sabine. 2017. "The Field-Specific Representation of Climate Change in Factual Television: A Multimodal Critical Discourse Analysis." *Critical Discourse Studies* 14 (5): 480–96. https://doi.org/10.1080/17405904.2017.1352003.

Shenhav, Shaul R. 2007. "Detecting stories." *Journal of Language and Politics* 6 (2): 177–200.

Simhandl, Katrin. 2006. "'Western Gypsies and Travellers'—'Eastern Roma': The Creation of Political Objects by the Institutions of the European Union." *Nations and Nationalism* 12 (1): 97–115.

Slavíčková, Tess. 2013. "The Rhetoric of Remembrance: Presidential Memorial Day Speeches." *Discourse & Society* 24 (3): 361–79. https://doi.org/10.1177/0957926512471762.

———. 2009b. "Theorising and Analysing Social Change in Central and Eastern Europe: The Contribution of Critical Discourse Analysis." In *Discourse and Transformation in Central and Eastern Europe*, edited by Aleksandra Galasińska and Michał Krzyżanowski, 17–39. London: Palgrave Macmillan. https://doi.org/10.1057/9780230594296_2.

Spitzmüller, Jürgen, and Ingo H. Warnke. 2011. "Discourse as a 'Linguistic Object': Methodical and Methodological Delimitations." *Critical Discourse Studies* 8 (2): 75–94. https://doi.org/10.1080/17405904.2011.558680.

Stephens, Christine. 2009. "Racism and Inequalities in Health: Notes Towards an Agenda for Critical Health Psychology." *Journal of Health Psychology* 14 (5): 655–59. https://doi.org/10.1177/1359105309104907.

Sutherland, Claire. 2005. "Nation Building Through Discourse Theory." *Nations and Nationalism* 11 (2): 185–202.

———. 2006a. "Discourse, Context and Cognition." *Discourse Studies* 8 (1): 159–77. https://doi.org/10.1177/1461445606059565.

Tracy, Karen, Susana Martinez-Guillem, Jessica S. Robles, and Kimberly E. Casteline. 2011. "Critical Discourse Analysis and (U.S.) Communication Scholarship Recovering Old Connections, Envisioning New Ones." *Annals of the International Communication Association* 35 (1): 241–86. https://doi.org/10.1080/23808985.2011.11679118.

Turowski, Jan. 2010. *Sozialdemokratische Reformdiskurse.* 1. Aufl. Wiesbaden: VS Verl. für Sozialwissenschaften.

van Dijk, Teun A. 1984. *Prejudice in Discourse an Analysis of Ethnic Prejudice in Cognition and Conversation.* Amsterdam and Philadelphia: J. Benjamins. http://site.ebrary.com/id/10517114.

———. 1988. *News as Discourse.* Hillsdale, NJ: L. Erlbaum Associates.

———. 1995. "Discourse Analysis as Ideology Analysis." In *Language and Peace*, edited by C. Schäffner and A. Wenden, 17–33. Aldershot: Dartmouth Publishing.

———. 2004. "From Text Grammar to Critical Discourse Analysis: A Brief Academic Autobiography." http://www.discourses.org/From%20text%20grammar%20to%20critical%20discourse%20analysis.html.

Verschueren, Jef. 2011. *Ideology in Language Use: Pragmatic Guidelines for Empirical Research.* Cambridge: Cambridge University Press. https://doi.org/10.1017/CBO9781139026277.

Vollmer, Bastian. 2014. *Policy Discourses on Irregular Migration in Germany and the United Kingdom.* http://public.eblib.com/choice/publicfullrecord.aspx?p=1837230.

Wæver, Ole. 1998. "Explaining Europe by Decoding Discourses." In *Explaining European Integration*, edited by Anders Wivel, 100–146. Copenhagen: Copenhagen Political Press.

Waldschmidt, Anne, Anne Klein, Miguel Tamayo Korte, and Sibel Dalman-Eken. 2008. "Diskurs im Alltag—Alltag im Diskurs: ein Beitrag zu einer empirisch begrundeten Methodologie sozialwissenschaftlicher Diskursforschung." Edited by GESIS-Leibniz-Institut Für Sozialwissenschaften. *Historical Social Research* 33 (1): Special Issue: Discourse Analysis in the Social Sciences. Starting Point and Frequency: Strong Year: 1979, Issues per volume: 4, Volumes per year: 1. https://doi.org/10.12759/hsr.33.2008.1.313-343.

Wastell, David G. 2003. "Organizational Discourse as a Social Defense: Taming the Tiger of Electronic Government." In *Global and Organizational Discourse about Information Technology*, 110, 179–95.

Wengeler, Martin. 2003. *Topos und Diskurs: Begründung einer argumentationsanalytischen Methode und ihre Anwendung auf den Migrationsdiskurs (1960–1985).* Reihe Germanistische Linguistik 244. Tübingen: Niemeyer.

Wodak, Ruth. 1990. "The Waldheim Affair and Antisemitic Prejudice in Austrian Public Discourse." *Patterns of Prejudice* 24 (2–4): 18–33. https://doi.org/10.1080/0031322X.1990.9970049.

———. 2002. "Aspects of Critical Discourse Analysis." *Zeitschrift Für Angewandte Linguistik* 36: 5–31.

———. 2011a. "Suppression of the Nazi Past, Coded Languages, and Discourses of Silence: Applying the Discourse-Historical Approach to Post-War Anti-Semitism in Austria." In *Political Languages in the Age of Extremes*, edited by Willibald Steinmetz, 351–79. Oxford: Oxford University Press.

———. 2011b. *The Discourse of Politics in Action: Politics as Usual*. Pbk. ed. New York: Palgrave Macmillan.

Wodak, Ruth, and Rudolf de Cillia. 2007. "Commemorating the Past: The Discursive Construction of Official Narratives About the 'Rebirth of the Second Austrian Republic'." *Discourse & Communication* 1 (3): 337–63. https://doi.org/10.1177/1750481307079206.

Wodak, Ruth, and Martin Reisigl. 1999. "Discourse and Racism: European Perspectives." *Annual Review of Anthropology* 28 (1): 175–99. https://doi.org/10.1146/annurev.anthro.28.1.175.

Wodak, Ruth, and Markus Rheindorf. 2017. "'Whose Story?'—Narratives of Persecution, Flight and Survival Told by the Children of Austrian Holocaust Survivors." In *Linguistic Diversity and Superdiversity: Sociocultural Linguistic Perspectives*, edited by Anna de Fina, Didem Ikizoglu, and Jeremy Wegner, 17–36. Washington, DC: Georgetown University Press.

Wodak, Ruth, Florian Menz, Richard Mitten, and Franz Stern. 1994. *Die Sprachen Der Vergangenheiten: Öffentliches Gedenken in Östereichischen Und Deutschen Medien*. 1. Aufl. Suhrkamp Taschenbuch Wissenschaft 1133. Frankfurt am Main: Suhrkamp.

Wodak, Ruth, Rudolf de Cillia, Martin Reisigl, Karin Liebhart, Klaus Hofstätter, and Maria Kargl. 1998. *Zur Diskursiven Konstruktion Nationaler Identität*. 1. Aufl. Suhrkamp Taschenbuch Wissenschaft 1349. Frankfurt: Suhrkamp.

Wodak, Ruth, Rudolf de Cillia, Martin Reisigl, and Karin Liebhart. 2009. *The Discursive Construction of National Identity*. 2nd ed. Critical Discourse Analysis. Edinburgh: Edinburgh University Press.

Wooffitt, Robin. 2005. *Conversation Analysis and Discourse Analysis: A Comparative and Critical Introduction*. London and Thousand Oaks, CA: Sage.

Yıldız, Safiye. 2009. *Interkulturelle Erziehung und Pädagogik: Subjektivierung und Macht in den Ordnungen des nationalen Diskurses*. 1. Aufl. VS Research. Wiesbaden: VS, Verl. für Sozialwiss.

5

From Synchronic to Diachronic Perspectives: Mapping Change Across Time

5.1 Introduction

Given that a key element of the critical study of discourse, starting with Foucault's *archeology* and *genealogy*, is its historical dimension and thus *change over time*, it is not surprising that several approaches to studying discursive change have been proposed. These moreover relate to other key issues covered in this book. Studying discursive change often multiplies the data to be analyzed, thus making CL methods an attractive choice of methodology (see Chapter 2). For instance, in studying how the British media's construction of refugees, asylum seekers, immigrants, and migrants changed between 1996 and 2005, a corpus of 140 million words promises more robust insights than the qualitative analysis of a few selected texts (see Gabrielatos and Baker 2008). As we trace such change over years, decades or even centuries, we may find that some of the most interesting changes occur across or between semiotic modes, i.e. involve the resemiotization of meanings (see Chapter 3). For example, changes in the mode of production, particularly in technology, as well as large-scale social change, have transformed the multimodal distribution of meaning-

© The Author(s) 2019

M. Rheindorf, *Revisiting the Toolbox of Discourse Studies*, Postdisciplinary Studies in Discourse,
https://doi.org/10.1007/978-3-030-19369-0_5

making in geographical maps and tourist brochures (see Hiippala 2015, Chapter 6). And as we critically examine how meaning is transformed through recontextualization across different social fields of action, our interpretations benefit from a robust conceptualization of the structuredness of discourse and society (see Chapter 4). For example, historical events or scientific findings may be recontextualized across the fields of politics, education, and the media, creating strikingly different effects (see Wodak et al. 2009; Achugar 2009).

Although discourse's changeability over time remains a central aspect of most approaches in CDS, its perhaps most poetic expression is Jäger and Jäger's (2007, 15) definition of discourse as "the flow of knowledge through time". Beyond their present existence, in other words, discourses always have a past and future. And while prognoses for the future of specific discourses remain difficult at best (Condit 2004), many scholars have made it an integral tenet to consider a discourse's history, even when their empirical analyses are focused on contemporary discourses. This is, for instance, clearly and programmatically expressed in the Discourse-Historical Approach, which mandates attention to the respective discourse's history at the very least as part of contextual analysis. A purely synchronic view of discourse is thus seen as a distorting isolation, but acknowledging a diachronic dimension is not the same as a diachronic analysis. This chapter discusses major methodological answers to this challenge.

Terminology, as is so often the case, is not consistent in this context. In addition to 'diachronic', 'historical', and 'longitudinal' are also used in the field—and with no clear distinction. Phenomena of change are often labelled as 'discursive change', but 'discourse change' and 'discoursal change' are also in evidence; while 'change' is generally used in the singular and in reference to large-scale or long-term developments, 'discourse shift' usually refers to small-scale, short-term developments and is sometimes used in the plural. Other terms may emphasize the abruptness of change (e.g. 'rupture', 'break' or 'discontinuity'), identify a particular type of change (e.g. 'technologization') or indicate a particular form and mechanism of change (e.g. 'mediatization'). Complementary terms relate to the absence of change as 'stability', 'continuity' or 'permanence'.

A more fundamental difference concerns whether we study discursive change in and of itself, in relation to social change, or even *as* social change. Since critical approaches to discourse studies assume a close relationship between discourse and society, a change in discourse must be connected to social change. Needless to say, theoretical assumptions as to the exact relationship between discourse and society greatly impact this issue. Specifically, the issue of which follows or causes which, while it cannot be resolved here, is a salient topic throughout this chapter. After discussing prominent conceptualizations of discursive change in relation to social change, this chapter covers approaches that operationalize diachrony as historical context of contemporary discourse, as two-point comparisons, and as gradual change or multi-point comparisons. Beyond this, the methodological implications of focusing on moments of crisis as catalysts for discursive change and/or relating local shifts to large-scale change are discussed. A separate section covers mechanisms that have been proposed as structuring, shaping or driving discursive change, including de- and recontextualization, normalization and colonization. The chapter concludes with a checklist of key conceptual and methodological issues in the diachronic study of discourse.

Running through these sections, the chapter addresses empirical studies of discursive change and their methodological contributions and limitations. In doing so, it becomes clear that there are frequently recurring objects of research when it comes to discursive change. These include discourses and social practices related to national identity, commemoration, AIDS, education, policy, climate change, political correctness or racism. While the structure of this chapter does not allow a focused discussion of these topical fields, they can safely be assumed to have impacted major conceptualizations of discursive change and the range of methodological tools available.

5.2 Social Change and Discursive Change

Numerous scholars have emphasized the close connection between social change and discursive change—an extension of the view that society and discourse are inextricably intertwined—and have built this tenet into their approaches. From one angle of the argument, the notion of discourse itself is so intimately related to a historical perspective that it cannot be conceived without a corresponding conceptualization of change (e.g. Landwehr 2010, 16). Diachronicity is thus seen as an intrinsic property of the concept of discourse inasmuch as it addresses the temporality of discourse: Language, like other modes of communication, at any given moment represents not only "the co-existence of socio-ideological contradictions" between "different socio-ideological groups in the present" but also "between the present and the past, between differing epochs of the past" (McKenna 2004). From another angle of the argument, processes of social change cannot be studied without taking into consideration discursive change, because macro-sociological structures (and thus also their changes) are related to social actors *through discourses*, i.e. through discursive practices situated in fields of social action (Krzyżanowski and Wodak 2009, 32). Foucault's conception of archeology as "writing a history of the social construction of a particular reality" acknowledged that discourses do not follow only discourse-internal logics and that discursive change—and social change—cannot be explained by analyzing only discourse. It follows that studies interested in explaining rather than simply documenting discursive change must pay attention to non-discursive context as well—keeping in mind that context itself is partly constituted by discourses and that its effects are mediated by discourses (Gasteiger 2008, 44).

Beyond these core assumptions lie many conceptual and methodological questions—questions that have been answered differently by various scholars (e.g. Eder 2006, 12; Landwehr 2010, 16). These include, first and foremost, three clusters of related questions: How can the temporal dimension of discourses be conceptualized and studied? How can the persistence and the change of a discourse and its exchange with other discourses be conceptualized and researched? A second set of pertinent question interrogates such processes of change, relating them to particular mechanisms, agency, and social structure: Which roles are played by social actors as producers, distributors, and recipients of discourses? Which possibilities of action are open to the subject within discourse, negotiating the constraining and enabling effects of the sayable? In the interaction between social actors and discourses, how are processes of change set into motion? While these may seem to be primarily theoretical questions, they have striking consequences for methodology and research design. A third set of related questions therefore pertains to the analytical tools appropriate to diachronic research aims or questions: How and on what level can change or stability, continuity or discontinuity be identified? How can data be compiled, segmented, and analyzed to describe discourse along a temporal axis? How can one distinguish different types, paces, scopes or strengths of change in discourse? How can change-initiating impulses be identified in either context or discourse, i.e. what drives social/discursive change?

A final issue concerns the direction of change or, as it were, the primacy of society or discourse: Do discursive changes reflect or follow social change, making them symptomatic of the former rather than powerful forces themselves? This particular question is often answered indirectly through empirical studies rather than on principal, theoretical terms. While Drury (2002) argues that for discursive change to occur there needs to be change in social relations first, the mutually constitutive relationship between discourse and society posited by Wodak et al. (2009) indicates that change can be driven by both, or rather in both directions. Indeed, most theoretical accounts allow for change to begin in non-discursive or discursive practices and then propagate in the other direction, respectively. Initially non-discursive change may, for instance, influence the means of production and thereby affect discourse; initially discursive change may transform the social reality of non-discursive practices, subject positions or field structure and thus instigate social change (Schmidt-Wellenburg 2013, 461). While determining the exact sequence (or point of origin) may well be an analytical impossibility, the discourse analyst may have to decide on a sequence of analysis, even if their procedure is ultimately cyclical (on deconstructing the interplay between discursive practices and social changes, see Krzyżanowski and Wodak 2009). Hence, we must avoid unintentionally creating the impression that the sequence of our analysis (or its textual presentation) captures the 'real' sequence of social/discursive change in the form of a strict, linear causality.

5.2.1 Analyzing the Relation Between Social Change and Discursive Change

Among the most articulate and well-balanced efforts to conceptualize the relationship between society and discourse for analytical practice is Wodak and Fairclough's (2010) integration of the former's discourse-historical approach with the latter's dialectical-relational approach. They emphasize that discourse is a social practice and thus not separate from social structures, social actors, and their agency. The dialectical relationship between society and discourse is thus not a mediation between antinomies but an intricate mesh of structures, practices, and the discursive strategies employed by individual or collective actors within them. Indeed, such agency and the strategies employed shape those structures and practices (aiming, e.g., to reproduce or transform) (Wodak and Fairclough 2010). Placing even more emphasis on individual agency, Lotz-Heumann (2010, 286–87) introduces the notion of "discursive actors", individuals who are able to initiate discursive change but not to enforce it. Such actors are distinguished by their social capital and position in social structure and may thus be able to shift the borders of the sayable or transfer elements of one discourse into another.

From Wodak and Fairclough's more cautious perspective, social conflict and the heterogeneity of positions in discourse are key drivers of social/discursive change. The dominance of hegemonic positions, by definition, is thus tenuous and achieved only temporarily. This perspective further suggests an analytical focus on intertextuality and interdiscursivity, more specifically on 'chains of texts' or 'chains of genres', as well as on discursive strategies and their effects over time. Taken to its conclusion, this perspective requires that diachronic analysis compare discourse across at least two moments in time. It does not allow for the analysis of single texts, or several, at a single point in time and then relating this to an assumed or received history of the respective discourse.

With respect to social structure, a necessarily context-sensitive analysis of discursive change must also be able to account for changes occurring differently in several fields, simultaneously or "at different times and with different speed". Such awareness of non-simultaneity is expressed, among other things, in the concept of *glocalization*: practices through which global processes are implemented, recontextualized, and thus changed on national or even more local levels (Wodak and Fairclough 2010). The notion also illustrates that, despite such differences, discursive discontinuities and continuities in different fields are not isolated from each other, and that the precise nature of their connection should be of particular interest to CDS. Prime examples of such a perspective are studies on policy implementation (e.g. Krzyżanowski and Wodak 2009; Katznelson and Bernstein 2017; Muntigl et al. 2000; Taylor 2004), the mediatization of politics (e.g. Carvalho 2008; Krzyżanowski 2018; Forchtner et al. 2013) or the popularization of science (e.g. Calsamiglia 2003; Molek-Kozakowska 2017; Seppänen and Väliverronen 2003). Providing a brief typology, Wodak and Fairclough (2010) suggest four main "points of entry" for researching social/discursive change: the emergence of discourses, the contestation/establishing of hegemonic discourses, the recontextualization of discourses in new social fields, and the implementation of discourses into other social practices (see below on recontextualization).

As pointed out above, this perspective represents a combination of the Dialectical-Relational Approach and the DHA; it is therefore worth devoting some space to a more in-depth discussion of both with respect to discursive change. Fairclough, whose work on social change and discourse has been seminal for CDS since the 1990s, argues the connection from the side of social change: Inasmuch as "social change entails change in social structures, social practices and social events", it entails "changes in genres and styles which affect how elements of discourse are articulated" (Fairclough 2006a). Change of social reality is thus, to the degree that it is realized through discourse, i.e. "realized through linguistic, semiotic and interdiscursive features of text" (Fairclough 2005). It should be noted that, like any analytical framework, Fairclough's dialectical-relational approach is partly shaped for a particular purpose and towards analyzing a particular range of phenomena, in this case the emergence of new forms of capitalism in late modernity and the increased potential of discourses to initiate social change (Chouliaraki and Fairclough 2007).

Several large-scale forms of emerging interdiscursivity or, rather, the colonization of discourses and their respective social fields have been the focus of this approach, among them globalization, democratization, commodification, technologization, securitization, and conversationalization.

Social and discursive hegemonies are contested and changed as various aspects of society, e.g. education, are re-spoken or re-written in terms of other orders of discourse, such as economics or everyday conversation. All of these developments describe ways in which discourses from one social field impinge on others not randomly but for functional purposes, evidencing changes in power relations in society. The discursive change identified as *conversationalization* thus indicates that professionals and bureaucracies find themselves increasingly unable to use traditional authoritative forms of interaction, having to engage clients and citizens in more dialogic and conversational modes. This trend has been identified by many studies and across various genres, perhaps most clearly for conversational styles in political communication. For instance, political discourse in the 1980s was found to be 'colonized' by everyday speech genres in order to achieve hegemony and increased legitimation for the voice of authority: This has been exemplified in a variety of speeches, including Margaret Thatcher's in the 1980s (Fairclough and Mauranen 1998) and David Cameron's in 2011 (Bennett 2013). For the UK, this body of work illustrates the elision of class from political discourse to the benefit of the ruling classes, but more recently also points to a growing moralization of class: The mainstream political response to the Occupy movement and the August 2011 British riots recontextualized civil unrest in neoliberal discourse, shifting the attention from the critique of capitalist-intrinsic inequality to the moral question of getting the right kind of capitalism.

Conversationalization, although it may facilitate more easy-going communication, also obscures the actual power relationships inherent in asymmetrical institutional interactions by suggesting an equality of conversational rapport. Unlike truly diachronic analyses like the study by Fairclough and Mauranen mentioned above, some publications drawing on Fairclough's approach only analyze single data points, i.e. conduct synchronous analyses which they then relate to an already assumed picture of large-scale transformations, with their own analysis simply "demonstrating the point" in an exemplary fashion (Blommaert and Bulcaen 2000). Blommaert (2008) has identified this "snapshot approach" to diachrony as a serious flaw in such studies.

Significantly, Fairclough (2003) elaborates his view of change to include, as a necessity, the "formation of (relative) permanences", i.e. stable formations or continuities opposite to and restricting change. In short, although discourses are continuously negotiated, they are not so fluid as to be chaotic; the structure of discourse must be "orderly" enough to be effective. A key role in this is played by the "relative permanences" of institutions and organizations in a given society, forming networks of practices. These develop "internal rigidities", which Fairclough (2003) links to the notion of *habitus*, and which may be linked to further sociological notions such as *field* and *communities of practice*. Thus, a given discourse's susceptibility to change is assumed to be dependent on the respective resistance of (institutional and habitual) structures on the one hand and on the agency of social actors on the other (Mills 2003). Elaborating the change/permanence dialectic, Krzyżanowski (2013b, 105) introduces a distinction between *overt* and *covert* change/permanence, observing that these forms may be strategically deployed: "overt discursive continuity allows social actors to produce discourses which remain seemingly unchanged while in fact already effectively recontextualizing elements of other discursive practices", thus keeping positions seemingly within the limits of the sayable; in contrast, "covert discursive continuity [...] shows discourse as profoundly changing while in fact retaining many of its former features", thus presenting social actors with a means to, e.g., respond to scandalisation or demonstrate a willingness to change.

The nuanced position of the dialectical-relational approach is sometimes simplified in its application by assuming that a particular discourse is 'influenced' by social structures and therefore 'reflects' society as well as its change. At best, this is a one-sided view; at worst, it assumes an automatic and unmediated symptomatic relationship between society and discourse (e.g. in Al-Momani 2016). In Blommaert's (2008) words, discursive novelty cannot be automatically projected onto social change, based not on analysis but simply on the assumed symptomatic relationship between discourse and society. This critique potentially applies to Chouliaraki and Fairclough's (2007) aim of demonstrating how social change already identified by scholars like Giddens, Harvey or Habermas is *instantiated* in discursive practices. The issue, then, is ultimately one of demonstrating such *discursive instantiation* of social change *at a particular site, a particular social field, and over a particular period of time* in order to establish a robust link. Along the same lines, Angus (2004) has argued that while local discursive change (or "shifts") may be closely analyzed, studies are rarely able to explain them in relation to social change, giving rise to a sense of "linear effects" labelled variously as the "colonization", "borrowing", "migrating" or "travelling" of discourses. In the context of education, this may concern discourses of accountability, market organization, managerialism, and effectiveness, whose effects outside of discourse are rarely analyzed at the sites of educational practice where discursive data is obtained. Among other things, that may lead to a reification of such processes and a neglect of resistant practices.

As to conceptions of potential tensions between social structure/practice and discourse, Bebbington et al.'s (2004) study of potential changes in the discourse of lending policy in documents of the World Bank shows that such a powerful institution's permanences (i.e. its mission statement, political, economic, and organizational structures) constrain not only the possible effects of discursive change where it might otherwise stimulate social change (Bebbington et al. 2004, 51) but also discursive change itself (Bebbington et al. 2004, 58). Such an approach is in line with Carvalho's (2008) call for greater attention to the influence of fields like politics or the media on discursive practices, especially when aspects of particular discourses are recontextualized into new fields.

5.2.2 Recontextualization and Change

Originally defined by Basil Berstein as a principle of pedagogy for appropriating other discourses, recontextualization has become a key concept in CDS, particularly with respect to discursive and social change. Although recontextualization takes place whenever social practices, including discursive practices, are represented in text, it is particularly pertinent to how some fields, such as the media and politics, construct social reality to serve their agenda. The notion was elaborated for the analysis of anti-immigration policies and legitimation strategies of bureaucracies, specifically the linguistic transformations of intertextually related documents which realize recontextualization (van Leeuwen and Wodak 1999) and, somewhat differently, to describe the transformation of genres (Chouliaraki 1998; Chouliaraki and Fairclough 2007), the potential of organizational discourses (Iedema and Wodak 1999; Kwon et al. 2009) or policy implementation (Muntigl et al. 2000).

Chouliaraki and Fairclough (2007) insist that the relationships between discourses are dialectic: as one practice attempts to colonize another, it can also be rejected, transformed or appropriated by the other. The actual effects of recontextualization on power relations or social structures are specific to each case and cannot be known in advance. It is an often-neglected complication that recontextualization is not strictly a textual process: it can affect all social practices, many of which—being discursive practices—also produce texts. Recontextualization does manifest in the intertextuality and interdiscursivity of texts, and can thus be investigated concretely by analyzing texts, but it is not exhausted on the textual level. In addition to linguistic analyses, therefore, other methods, prominently ethnographic observation, may be used (see Chapter 3). Textually, recontextualization is often realized in the mixing of elements from the colonizing and colonized, the appropriating and the appropriated practice or field. The arising forms of hybridity (see Bhatia in Chapter 3) display characteristic tensions, contradictions, and antinomies (Wodak and Fairclough 2010).

From a methodological point of view, the assumption that discursive change is expressed through hybridity and works through mechanisms of recontextualization can, according to Kopytowska (2015), translate into three analytical aims: (1) analysis of the social fields of action in which discursive events are embedded, (2) using diachronic data to examine discourse as changing diachronically, (3) focusing on the manifestation of recontextualization in terms of intertextuality and interdiscursivity.

5.2.3 Diachrony as the Study of Recontextualization

In research practice, recontextualization is involved in and often conceptually subsumed under more specific processes and practices such as the construction of collective memory. Inasmuch as it continuously negotiates between historical records and current socio-political agendas, the construction of collective memory works by recontextualization, in the process shifting interpretations, selectively emphasizing, suppressing, and elaborating different aspects of the historical record (Achugar 2009, 539).

In other contexts, recontextualization relates to field- or even media-specific practices, such as the de-contextualization of 'image bites' for their later use in other broadcasts, i.e. their strategic recontextualization. Kaufer et al. (2012) have shown in detail how the recontextualization of the same footage of Hillary Clinton over newscasts spanning 20 months from August 1998 to June 2000 manipulates impressions of entirely different news stories: NBC extracted images of Clinton's troubled face at a memorial service, seemingly under the anguish of indecision, and then re-used them to comment on her husband's affair with Monica Lewinsky, the impeachment hearings, and her own Senate run.

The popularization of science is another social practice that hinges on recontextualization: Beyond general considerations of style, this involves rhetorical strategies to generate or enhance the newsworthiness of scientific insights. In a case study of articles devoted to environmental issues in the popular magazine New Scientist, published between 2013 and 2014, Molek-Kozakowska (2017) traces how the field-specific emphasis on newsworthiness criteria (novelty and superlativeness, timeliness and impact, negativity and positivity) might impact the public understanding of environmental science. Drawing on the notion of "socioscientific issue" to denote "societal dilemmas with conceptual, procedural, or technological links to science", Stewart (2009) traces discursive change in textual chains across different fields. Controversies across science and public discourse can thus be analyzed as multidirectional intersections of scientific and nonscientific discourse. Among the effects of such socioscientific controversies, Stewart not only identifies changes in public perceptions of scientific issues but also points out that criticism emerging in media discourse has led scientists to delegitimize such criticisms in the context of subsequent publications in scientific journals.

However, there are also social practices in which discourse follows patterns of recontextualization that involve more or less set sequences of genres that can be described as more or less stable and institutionalized "genre chains" (Zappettini and Unerman 2016). Policy implementation is one such practice, as Taylor (2004) has shown through a case study of how the way equity issues are addressed changes along a genre chain in policy implementation: In Queensland's 2010 education reform strategy, subtle discursive shifts have marginalized social-democratic positions on active citizenship and public education. Despite the close link between institutions and genres, the relation between genres and discourses are never rigidly fixed, and the hybridization of genres alongside discourses is sometimes seen as a prime indicator of discursive struggle for hegemony (Zappettini and Unerman 2016).

5.3 Conceptualizing Discursive Change: Mechanisms and Patterns

Several theoretical accounts of discursive change include more or less constant or universal mechanisms or conditions for discursive change, such as social crises or a cycle built into the structuredness of discourse itself. Emphasizing contingency, several studies have concluded that periods of social/discursive instability represent catalysts for change, seemingly endowing individual or collective social actors with heightened agency and the capacity to "develop diverse and competing strategies for change" that, once implemented, "can lead to structural change" (Krzyżanowski and Wodak 2009, 26).

An almost contrary view regarding discursive change assumes a constant and universal mechanism that informs the structural relationship between elaborated, hegemonic discourses and everyday discourses. In the interplay between these levels, Linke (2005, 91–92) posits an unceasing and generative cycle in both directions. This dynamic is assumed to move elaborate and objectified knowledge "downwards" into everyday discourses and to move subjective and socially emphasized knowledge "upwards" into elaborated discourses (e.g. into academia or politics), which may lead to new conflicts and the production of new knowledge there.

Given the bearing that distinctions between macro- and micro-levels of structure (see Chapter 4) have on conceptions of discourse, it bears mentioning that virtually all levels of linguistic/semiotic realization have been the focus on empirical studies on discursive change. Among the most common are lexical and semantic changes, processes related to metaphors, and changes in argumentative patterns or topoi. Beyond these, however, discursive change is often discussed as being driven by, or operating on, specific mechanisms such as discursive strategies, legitimization, interdiscursivity or hybridity. The following brief subsections each discuss one such mechanism, but these concepts can be found at work in virtually all of the work covered in the later sections of this chapter.

5.3.1 Conceptual and Terminological Change

Conceptual history or *Begriffsgeschichte* has been an influential approach for CDS, and it certainly exemplifies the analytical, interpretative weight put on the relation between discourse and society, and thus also between discursive change and social change: Historical semantics are assumed to change with social structure, fulfilling a constitutive social function but only because they are so intricately intertwined with social reality, in turn making them a point of access for analysis. As Reinhart Koselleck put it: Without shared notions, there is no society; at the same time, those notions are grounded in political-social systems that are far more complex than key notions can reflect individually (Koselleck 1989). Processes of terminological change that are of interest to CDS include the extension or generalization of notions, the "jumping" of notions into other semantic contexts (metaphors), and the abrasion of the metaphorical character of such terms through habitualization (Koselleck 2010).

Sometimes, such terminological change is subtle and takes place within a rather narrow semantic field, such as the "learnification" of educational discourse and practice (Biesta 2015), i.e. the transformation of education into "lifelong learning". Corresponding policies examined by Biesta have come with a systematic discursive shift from pupils or students to "learners", from teaching to "facilitating learning", "creating learning opportunities" or "delivering learning experiences", and from schools to "learning environments" or "places for learning". Such terminological shifts can be strategic and well planned, but they can also be chaotic, leading to the overlexicalization of specific semantic fields, e.g. when political discourse impinges upon the limits of the sayable (Rheindorf and Wodak 2018).

5.3.2 Normalization

Many studies have explored the normalization of neoliberal, racist or extreme-right ideolegemes, topoi or terminology through discourse. Jürgen Linke's (2013) seminal work is more or less explicitly acknowledged in these, and it remains the most elaborate theorization of normalization in CDS. At its core, the concept denotes the discursive process(es) through which a marginal or even taboo position comes to be redefined not just as acceptable but as the normal, unmarked state. Conceptually, normalization is thus related to, if not identical with, shifting or changing hegemonic discourse—and I would argue the notions of overt/covert continuity and discontinuity should prove useful here.

Empirically and thus also of methodological relevance, several studies have identified specific changes or shifts as ongoing or completed processes of normalization, often measuring 'normal' by spread and frequency, by acceptance/lack of contestation, or by the left-center-right positioning of political actors endorsing a particular position. Such processes have been identified in the political fields of several countries, including Austria, Switzerland, France, and the UK (Wodak et al. 2013). But they are also in evidence in the fields of medicine and health-care, business and management, or finance (de Cock et al. 2012). From a diachronic perspective, normality is maintained, contested, and changed discursively; it inevitably involves power relations and is thus never neutral with respect to whose interests it serves.

5.3.3 Colonization

Despite its seemingly self-evident applicability to the interaction between two or more discourses, the notion of colonization is complicated not just by potential reciprocity between discourses (colonization being met with appropriation) but by variations of the underlying model of discourse it implies. According to Fairclough (2013a), three basic models need to be distinguished to specify the meaning of the processes and effects of "colonization". In terms of research design and methodology, each of these models allows us to foreground different aspects: (1) The "code model" assumes a "stable local order of discourse" characterized by "naturalized conventions instantiated in practice". Colonization here means an external influence that can be described as "unilinear colonization". (2) The "hegemonic model" views discursive practice as articulation in Ernesto Laclau's sense: colonization by another discourse hence signifies the disarticulation of existing configurations in the colonized discourse and the concomitant re-articulation in new configurations. Colonization viewed in this model describes struggles over discursive hegemony. (3) The "mosaic model" emphasizes the consequential space for negotiation or play in combining and mixing discourse elements in new ways: Where social struggles prevail or social order is fluid, conventions can no longer be taken as given and social actors can/must negotiate, sometimes radically, which discourse elements are to be drawn upon.

Ayer's (2005) study of the colonization of community colleges in the United States by neoliberal practices is framed within the hegemonic model: The author describes the change as a shift from a community-based social practice focused on the needs of learner systems to a market-based social practice focused on the needs of business and industry. As community college education is re-articulated as a means of human capital development, a new hegemony is established.[1] Clearly, education is not the only public institution charged with advancing or safeguarding the interests of citizens that has become increasingly colonized by consumerist practices, giving rise to the "citizen consumer" even where the public service frame is maintained (Livingstone et al. 2007).

The so-called "democratization" of the transnational, corporate economy through Corporate Social Responsibility (CSR) programs has often been framed in terms of the code model, positing a unilinear form of colonization. As corporations ostensibly take on global problems by accepting responsibility for society, the practices of business may be said to become colonized by practices of governance. However, an argument can made that as a process of "neoliberalization", there is an element of highly selective and opportunistic appropriation at play as well, evidenced by the

---

[1] On the larger change of educational discourse from a democratic model to a consumerist framework, see Fairclough (2013b). For more detailed analyses of specific aspects of this change, see Mulderrig (2008, 2011a, 2011b) on the educational policies of UK governments and parties between 1972 and 2005.

"short-termism" and precariousness of many CSR projects that ultimately aggravate rather than alleviate the problems they ostensibly sought to address (Brei and Böhm 2014).

Sharing much of the frame of the "hegemonic model", a critical view of colonization inspired by the work of Habermas and Bourdieu would distinguish between field-immanent and inter-field conflicts. Colonization here denotes a "distortion" resulting from the diminishing autonomy of one social field and its logic as it becomes colonized by another field (Forchtner and Schneickert 2016). A social field's autonomy or lack therefore can thus be used as a measure of its colonization by other fields.

5.3.4 Structuration

In similar contexts, concepts such as framing, agenda setting or structuration have been applied in CDS to denote effective means of changing a specific discourse. Of these, structuration is the strongest concept in that it exceeds local framing (a primarily textual effect) in that it sets the conceptual terms of a particular debate, discourse strand or textual chain.

In tracing the continuities and discontinuities in the representation of the greenhouse effect in the UK between 1985 and 2000, Carvalho (2005) concluded that the British government's discourse had a strong and almost constant effect of structuration on the press's discourse. Using discursive strategies to shift responsibility, British governments have transformed the greenhouse effect from a strictly scientific problem, first, into a controversial political matter and, then, into an object of regulation dominated by techno-corporatist governance.

5.3.5 Mediatization

A common type of interdiscursive relation is that of mediatization. More precisely, it denotes the colonization of the discursive practices of a social field of action such as science or politics by the discourses, practices, and logics that are characteristic of the media. In this sense, then, mediatization goes well beyond mediation or reporting, as it projects the logic and mechanisms of modern mass media into the other field and at least partly changes its practices.

For example, in her diachronic study of war memoirs, Chouliaraki (2014) links the change from the dispassionate perspective of the civilian-turned-soldier, dominated by estrangement and anti-war skepticism, to the compassionate perspective of the professional witness, dominated by meta-irony, not only to the changing nature of war but to the mediatization of warfare itself.

5.3.6 Hybridization

As a general mechanism or effect of discursive change, the hybridization of discourses has been called the most important and overriding process of change (Chouliaraki and Fairclough 2007). Methodologically, this suggests a parallel analytic focus on intertextuality/interdiscursivity as well as on changing relations of power evident in conflicting discursive elements as, e.g., educational practices are colonized by managerial and economic practices. Chouliaraki and Fairclough hypothesize that any broad trend exists in a complex relationship with its opposite: colonization with appropriation, globalization with localization, and reflexive consciousness with ideological naturalization. Hybridization is a feature of these relationships and has guided analyses of concrete discursive changes such as the commodification or marketization of higher education (Fairclough 1993), the conversationalization of media and political discourse (Fairclough 2010), broad changes in the ideology of capitalism (Chiapello and Fairclough 2002), and globalization in Central and Eastern Europe (Fairclough 2006b).

5.3.7 Discursive Strategies and Topoi

Highlighting the agency of collective or individual social actors, discursive change may also be driven by strategies employed by them. Strategies in this sense refer to plans of action that may vary in their degree of elaboration, may be located at different levels of mental organization, and may range from automatic to highly conscious (de Cillia et al. 1999).

However, *discursive* strategies are distinguished from *rhetorical* strategies and other linguistic or semiotic levels of realization in that they relate directly to discourses. Thus, they can be categorized as being directed at *constructing*, *transforming*, *destroying* or *maintaining* specific discursive positions such as a particular aspect of national identity or collective past (Wodak et al. 2009).

Such a perspective is often linked to more specifically identified topoi or argumentative patterns that social actors draw on to achieve their aims. Thus, Achugar (2007, 524–25) identifies "practices that contribute to the maintenance, reproduction or change of particular interpretations of the past" as mechanisms behind the continuities and discontinuities in the Uruguayan military's narrative of their own identity and positioning vis-a-vis other social actors. Even more radically, Séville (2017) approaches discursive change through the changing dominance of topoi or arguments: German Chancellor Angela Merkel's slogan "There is no alternative" can thus be regarded as key to an argumentative strategy to vindicate the financial aid rendered to Greece during the Eurozone crisis after 2010.

5.3.8 Legitimization

Although legitimization has been observed in several social fields, political discourse is arguably the clearest case. Indeed, Paul Chilton (2004) hypothesized that political discourse has an inherent legitimizing function. While some studies on legitimization apply the concept in a strictly synchronic fashion, the very notion implies a process, a change of both discursive and non-discursive social practice: a policy, measure or position *becomes legitimized* through discourse, either in advance or retrospect, or *fails to become legitimized*. In either case, there is an implication of discursive struggle (van Leeuwen and Wodak 1999).

A case in point is Filardo's (2008) diachronic study of the ways in which Northern Irish political parties have depicted and (de)legitimized the 1998 Agreement and the resumption of devolved government to Northern Ireland in 2007. This period covers the entire process of implementation, including the establishing and suspension of the devolved Assembly. The strategies of legitimization identified at the outset are distinct for each party but become similar towards 2007, when opposed ideological aspects are suppressed in favor of the creation of a new and common imagined community.

5.3.9 Technological Change

An argument can also be made for technological developments as a significant impetus to discursive change, directly impacting as it often does the means of production, distribution, and reception of texts. Most prominently, this has concerned digital technologies including online media and, in particular, social media. Horsti (2015), for instance, makes a compelling argument that technology-driven transformations in the media environment shaped the success of the anti-immigration movement in Finland from 2003 to 2013, shifting political discourses from what was essentially centripetal mass communication to a centrifugal communication system involving multiple platforms.

5.4 Diachrony as Historical Context

Some work in CDS emphasizes the importance of the historical dimension of discourse for the interpretive process without analyzing diachronic discourse data. While this is certainly a viable approach, it needs to be distinguished from diachronic or longitudinal analysis—terminologically, conceptually, and methodologically.

The basic argument for this perspective is that our understanding of any aspect of discourse is greatly enriched, and may even depend on, our knowledge of its history. At those times that our analytical focus is on a single point in time, such history becomes 'historical context' and may be researched through literature rather than our own empirical work. The reasons for this may be pragmatic, a limitation on resources, or interdisciplinary boundaries; we may simply not have the sociological, economic or medical training to research a given discourse's history. This approach has been given great viability and visibility in the form of Wodak's Discourse-Historical Approach (Wodak et al. 2009), which elaborates the conceptual and methodological aspect of conducting research in this form while not precluding the analysis of diachronic data. The former addresses the historical dimension of discursive acts by integrating information on the historical background in which discursive events are embedded. The latter explores the ways in which the positions, practices or genres related to a particular discourse change diachronically.[2]

Despite the prominence of the DHA, the historical contextualization of discourse analyses is wide-spread beyond this particular framework. For instance, Marchi and Partington's (2012) "historical perspective" on European identity provides historical context before analyzing Italian and UK media's texts published between 2007 and 2009; despite the range of three years in that sample, they do not develop a longitudinal perspective on the data. Likewise, Cooper et al.'s (2017) contrastive analysis of national and regional Australian media reporting on refugees and asylum seekers over a period of ten months, despite focusing on a period characterized by key events such as the reintroduction of Temporary Protection Visas, does not directly relate the reporting to significant events but to a historical context outside the period analyzed. Treating Scottish devolution as a milestone, Dekavalla (2010) studies the construction of national identity in the news coverage of policy issues during the first two general elections after devolution, 2001 and 2005, as one dataset. The news during the 1999 election, which serves as the historical contrast to show change after devolution, is brought in only through other researcher's publications. Costelloe (2014) takes a similar approach in the critical analysis of news reporting on incidents of urban violence in the French banlieues in 2005: There is consideration of the discursive practice's historical context from 1970s to the 2000s, but no diachronic analysis. As with the other examples cited here, the texts analyzed stem from a time identified, with the help of contextual insights, as a time of crisis, in this case resulting in the declaration of a state of emergency and the introduction of curfews. While integrating such historical information is clearly valuable, it highlights a

[2] Hyatt (2005) proposes a contextualist, historical approach that differs slightly from the DHA in its definition of four levels of context: immediate socio-political context of the moment; medium-term socio-political context or mores of a period (e.g. Thatcherism); contemporary individuals, organizations, and structures of socio-political relevance; and epoch or era with its respective epistemological framework for knowledge.

limitation: If the identification and, indeed, critique of discursive change is to be made on the comparison of two points in time, but only one of these is actually analyzed through data, the comparison may rest on very shaky ground: The insights we draw on regarding the historical data may rest on entirely different procedures of data collection and analysis, including different disciplinary epistemologies.

Rather than a systematic analysis, Anaïs (2013, 127) suggests a 'genealogical' approach to diachrony: Revisiting Foucault, she proposes integrating the genealogical method into the DHA, emphasizing the contingency of discursive events. This entails assembling data not systematically and focused on specific themes, media or fields and looking for a story from beginning to end, or imposing such a logic on the data, but assembling an "archive" that is open-ended, with no effort to tell "the whole story". Instead, it would focus on texts situated at "ruptural moment[s] in time" to trace the emergence and "eruptions" of discourses generated by the interplay of power relations. Analytically, this would foreground the "relational aspect of discourse", its tendency to articulate with other discourses. With its non-systematic collection of data and embrace of contingency, it could also present a way of reading for silences and counter discourses in unexpected places, avoiding the presumption of knowing in advance (Anaïs 2013, 134). Needless to say, such an analysis would itself be highly contingent on chance. A prime example of recent CDS that fits Anaïs' call for genealogy is Koller's (2008) diachronic survey of conceptions of the lesbian community as they have appeared in lesbian-written texts in the 40 years since the Stonewall riots of 1969. Starting with the 1970s, Koller analyzes texts identified as influential and/or representative of the time period, amply supplemented by documents from historical archives and interviews with self-identified lesbians.

5.5 Operationalizing Diachrony: Periodization and Data Segmentation

Elaborating the role of history in empirical studies following the DHA, Reisigl (2017) distinguishes three broad alternatives: (1) Taking a single discourse fragment as the analytic focus, then reconstructing its "prehistory" and relating past to present in terms of recontextualization; (2) analyzing a diachronic series of thematically or/and functionally connected discourse fragments, then reconstructing their respective historical contexts and interrelationships; (3) focusing the analysis on how different social actors, situated in different social fields of action, discursively construct the past, thereby revealing different norms, epistemes etc. in the respective discourses. Although these three approaches can also be combined, they give very different meanings to "historical": the first treats history as context for a synchronic analysis, the second analyzes a discursive diachrony, and the third focuses on the contemporary construction of history in discourse.

With a greater focus on data segmentation for diachronic analysis[3]—the second type above—Marchi (2018) notes the apparent lack of reflection on the methodological implications of dealing with temporal variables. Periodization, she highlights, is often taken to be a neutral instrument for organizing data, when in reality the division of time into distinct periods inevitably affects the entire analysis, bringing with it assumptions about the nature of change. Building on Stanyer and Mihelj's (2016, 273) basic tripartite typology—(a) tracking the development of a chosen phenomenon over time, (b) comparing two moments in time, and (c) focusing on turning points defined a priori as critical junctures, comparing before and after—Marchi (2018) adds the notions of bottom-up and top-down data segmentation. Taken together, these typologies yield the following options for operationalizing diachrony:

1. comparing data between two or more distinct moments in time
2. tracking change over continuous chronological data
3. segmenting data by turning points as they emerge from the data (internal variability)
4. segmenting data by trigger events determined a priori (contextual historical data)
5. segmenting data by standardized spans (e.g. by calendar, years/months/weeks)

[3]To better capture the short time-span involved in modern diachronic studies (see also Carvalho 2008), the term "brachychrony" has been suggested instead of diachrony (Mair 2015).

6. segmenting data by text-lifecycle based on the periodicity of a text type (e.g. daily editions of a newspaper)

In any of these options, the granularity of the analysis is determined by the number of time-points at which data is analyzed and the proportion of these sampling points to the length of the period covered. The following sections roughly follow this typology.

5.5.1 Diachrony as Two-Point Comparisons

If diachronic analysis is intrinsically comparative, comparing data from at least two different time points is a prerequisite for diachrony (Marchi 2018). The low granularity of such studies, however, need not be a disadvantage to tracing change, especially if they are conceptualized as before-and-after comparisons that attempt to track the effects of a particular event or period on discourse. In other words, and relating to the above-discussed issue of the directionality of social and discursive change, this kind of research design is most likely to be used to study the effects of social change on discourse. Such change and the related discursive changes can be, inter alia, deeply personal and biographic, media-related or highly political and public.

Situated on the personal end of that spectrum, Varjonen et al.'s (2013) longitudinal study on ethnic identity construction in the context of ethnic Finns uses focus group data from before and after their migration from Russia to Finland. Analyzing category labels, rhetorical devices, interpretative repertoires, and other discursive resources used by these migrants to account for their identities, the authors conclude that participants emphasized their Finnish identity in Russia pre-migration (2008). In contrast, they explicitly problematized their Finnish identity post-migration (2010), stating that ethnic Finnish migrants could not be Finnish in Finland.

Operating with data from two broad periods to establish a two-point comparison (1900–1930 and 2000–2005), Mcmanus (2009) indicates society's changing attitudes towards medicine as reflected in Patient Information Leaflets. Drawing on Halliday's transitivity model, the author identifies significant differences in the two samples as reflections of the changing view of medicine in "Western culture": Whereas the 1900–1930 texts are dominated by "medicines" and "medical conditions", patients are paramount in their modern counterparts, represented as being actively involved in their own treatment alongside medical professionals.

In the field of media, a large number of studies have conducted two-point comparisons, increasingly also using CL methods on sizable corpora. Comparing the genre of environmental reportage in UK newspapers from 1990 and 2014, Aronsen (2016, 104) found a shift of agency and responsibility from humans to nature in the construction of causation, sentience, and agency. Similarly studying British newspapers, Toolan's (2016) analysis of discourses on wealth inequality is methodologically interesting because it demonstrates the difficulties of sampling data for phenomena that are typically dispersed across texts that focus on other topics. Comparing samples from 1971 and 2012/2013, Toolan faces the dilemma mentioned above: How can we know if the discursive changes observed in two-point comparisons do not only reflect social change but have also advanced such change by reshaping mainstream common-sense thinking?

Notable work using this approach has also been done in the field of policy, including practices related to policy implementation and evaluation. Comparing two essential texts of the Norwegian educational system, Bubikova-Moan (2017) contrasts the changing construction of the "multilingual child" in 1995 and 2010. She finds a significant discursive shift in the discourse on childhood, breaking away from the traditional conceptualization of preschool as a play-based arena associated with care and moving towards emphasizing formal education and colonization by discourses on integration/immigration that advocate active interference and duty-based methodology. Also exploring discursive change through two texts related to educational policy, in this case on multilingual education in California, Katznelson and Bernstein (2017) contrast policy propositions from 1998 and 2016: The former uses a language-as-problem frame, presenting bilingual education as a threat to children's and the nation's well-being, whereas the latter represents multilingual education as key to students' future economic success as well as to the nation's continued global economic advantage. In the discursive strategies identified in both, the authors detect discourses of neoliberalism, global human capital, and linguistic instrumentalism. This raises the critical question whether policies framed within one discursive regime (e.g., neoliberalism) can serve the aims of another: Multilingualism, when promoted by neoliberalism, may still serve to improve equity, plurality, and social justice.

An even larger body of work using two-point comparisons has dealt with political discourses, often in the form of party programs, manifestos, and speeches. Edwards' (2012) analysis of the construction of in-groups in the 2005 and 2010 manifestos of the British National Party is a case in point: The comparison reveals how the far-right party has adopted a moderate tone to appeal to a wider electoral base by increasingly disguising the racially constructed in-group behind its ostensibly inclusive discourse of nationhood. This particular study explicitly acknowledges the two-point conundrum of identifying cause and effect relations on the basis of discursive change identified through analysis. Krzyżanowski's (2013a) discussion of the Austrian Freedom Party barely fits into the two-point category: It uses more continuous data, but still categorizes it into two periods (the 1990s and 2000s), which are then compare to identify shifts in the party's rhetoric and arguments. These changes are interpreted, on a historical scale, as "responses" to "the changing national and, to some extent also international, political conditions" (Krzyżanowski 2013a, 135). Interestingly, these shifts have not been complete but have led to paradoxical discursive continuities/discontinuities as a defining characteristic of contemporary right-wing populism as it seeks to appeal to different sections of the electorate.

5.5.2 Moments of Crisis

Using continuous data for a short and clearly demarcated period, studies on 'crisis discourse' have seen a sharp rise in interest since the early 2000s, including many investigations of 9/11 and other terrorist attacks, the financial crisis, the Eurozone crisis, and the so-called refugee crisis of 2015/2016 (Krzyżanowski and Forchtner 2016, 256). Methodologically, these studies share a focus on a trigger event determined a priori by contextual knowledge: The moment of crisis and disruption is already known, either through non-discursive events (such as war, accidents, loss of life, etc.) and/or through the discursive construction of the respective moment as 'crisis' by politics, the media, etc.

This approach can be seen at work, for instance, in Beelitz and Merkl-Davie (2012), who analyze the attempt by Vattenfall, a Swedish state-owned energy company, to restore organizational legitimacy after an incident in one of its nuclear power plants in 2007. Their corpus of corporate documents relating to the incident during a six-month period after the incident can be considered a 'textual chain' due to the high level of intertextuality. The texts analyzed tell the story of how Vattenfall negotiated the confidence crisis following the incident by redefining its relationship with its stakeholders in terms of openness, transparency, and CSR (Beelitz and Merkl-Davies 2012, 113).

Under the label of "comparative-synchronic analysis", Carvalho (2008) argues for tracing short-term textual chains for mediatized politics, cross-referencing news outlets, and checking original documents, such as reports or policy documents, to allow for a better assessment of the media's transformations of previous documents. To narrow down the potentially vast scope of such an approach, Carvalho suggests to focus only on "critical discourse moments" as "particularly important times in the social construction of an issue", rather than random sampling. In short, the notion of 'crisis' may need to be combined with other approaches in the process of data collection.

This is also the case in Griesser's (2018) two-point comparison of crisis moments in German labor market policy, the AFG reform of 1969 and the Hartz IV reform of 2005. The study identifies discursive shifts in the images of unemployed people, i.e. from an insecure and vulnerable human being confronted with an all-powerful and unpredictable market process, indicating the necessity of social protection and support by the state, to "transgressors" and "scroungers" that refuse to use existing opportunities. Similarly, Domínguez (2015) compares the Spanish press' use of visual metaphors at two connected moments of crisis in what he terms the "evolution" of oil slick cartoons. The first data sample stems from publications following the oil slick on Spanish shores caused by a tanker in 2002; the second sample relates to the related court decision in 2013. Both caused deep political crises, but while the oil slick metaphor of "chapapote" was initially connected to the physical reality caused by the tanker, it has since become metaphorical for something sticky, complex, disgusting, and difficult to manage.[4]

5.5.3 Diachrony as Multi-Point Comparison or Continuous Data

No categorical distinction can be made between multi-point comparisons or the longitudinal analysis of continuous data. Even a considerable amount of data may still give a relatively grainy picture, and the analytical grasp of discourse is never complete. However, we can think of the granularity of the data analyzed as situated on a continuum between two, three or n points. The relevance of that gradation can only be established in relation to the research question and the number of data points hypothetically available. In collecting data from a daily newspaper, obtaining data from each day can be considered continuous—or at least high granularity, if the newspaper's online edition also updates or revises its article during the day. Although most such studies set out to identify discursive change, some also find continuity (e.g. Duncan 2014).

Among studies that demonstrate substantial change is Achugar's (2009) examination of the discursive development of collective memory in Uruguay, based on texts chosen for their production at key historical moments from the beginnings of the dictatorship in 1976 until 2009. Her work is thus a combination of contextual data sampling (key moments) and the bottom-up approach to data segmentation. Achugar divides the discourse into three periods: (1) 1976–1978, when the Uruguayan military's discourse is contested by international accusations of violations of human rights; (2) 1984–1996, when the discourse is contested by internal groups through plebiscites, demonstrations, and court challenges; and (3) 1999–2004, when their discourse is challenged by international and national groups demanding the prosecution of military officers accused of human rights violations (Achugar 2009, 524).

[4]A similar study on exclusionary representations of welfare recipients in Australia, i.e. Gunders (2012), paints a much more fine-grained picture, using 95 speeches by six ministers between 1998 and 2011. Gunders' conclusions are bolder, positing that these speeches facilitated the implementation of punitive welfare measures by constructing welfare recipients as a threat to the economic and moral wellbeing of ordinary Australians.

Focusing on the historical development of the notion of 'extremism' in Germany, Ackermann et al. (2015) illustrate the potential of combining the multi-point comparison with a contrastive analysis of discourse in different social fields of action. Prominent discursive events through several decades are analyzed to show a change from questions of defining politically marginal, extremist ideologies towards social order and, increasingly, towards violence against people and property. This shift is found across discourses in the fields of legislation, politics, policy, intelligence, and civic education. In some ways a counterpart to that study, Filardo-Llamas (2013) provides a diachronic account of the changing extremist discourse of the IRA between 1998 and 2013, a significant period of the Northern Irish peace process. The analysis of 39 IRA statements shows efforts to discursively legitimize first violent and then non-violent political actions as means of achieving a united Ireland—closely connected to the context of the peace process, the waning political prominence of the IRA, and Sinn Fein's growing power. Similarly, Amer (2012) traces how political speeches and declarations by the Palestinian Hamas' have changed between 1968 and 2007, gradually accommodating notions of human rights, international law, social reform, political pluralism, and individual rights and freedoms. Although this can be read as a diminishing gap between Hamas and Fatah, we cannot know whether these discursive shifts might be tactical or driven by a more fundamental political rethinking.

In the field of corporate communication, Laine (2010) has demonstrated the viability of a multi-point comparison across 20 years. The study investigated the "discourse of sustainability" in social disclosures published by Finnish companies, detecting a gradual shift from constructions of sustainability as a difficult-to-achieve aim to a feasible objective that requires no major restructuring of the current economic paradigm.

While the above studies used a dozen or a few dozen texts across decades—which might count as continuous data for, e.g., business reports published annually—media like newspapers by their very nature afford a much denser stream of data. Approximating continuous chronological data from the BBC News website from 2001 to 2007 (a corpus 1.9 million words in 3269 articles), Al-Hejin (2015) combines qualitative and corpus-based methodologies to investigate the semantic macrostructures associated with Muslim women and the discursive strategies employed in the representation of the hijab. On the one hand, arguments against face veils in the UK were identified in "key" texts and traced through textual chains of BBC articles: allegedly impeding integration by expressing "separateness from the rest of society"; forming a physical barrier to communication; and being not an Islamic requirement but merely a cultural practice. On the other hand, CL methods helped show the wider social trend away from an orientation towards "multi-culturalism" towards "integration". Significantly, these results allow Al-Hejin to link this change, or at least its acceleration, to the London 7/7 bombings in 2005 (Al-Hejin 2015, 36).

5.5.4 Diachrony from the Bottom Up

A substantially different type of data segmentation uses patterns as they emerge from analysis by some criteria of internal variability, be it text number, lexical frequencies or argumentative patterns. This approach is often used with CL methods (e.g. Baker 2010; Potts 2015), particularly the corpus-driven approach (see Chapter 2), but is open to purely qualitative analyses as well (see Chapter 10). It should also be noted that such internal segmentation is often applied after cut-off points, i.e. a chronological beginning and ending, have already been determined—randomly, by availability, or by means of contextual knowledge.

The latter is in evidence in a number of studies on economic discourses during or after the onset of the global financial crisis of 2008. Rather than focusing on the moment of crisis (or a narrowly defined timespan), such work aims to observe not only immediate shifts but more or less lasting re-orientations of relevant discourses. This is in evidence in de Ville and Orbie's (2014) account of how the European Commission (EC) has re-aligned its discourse on free trade during the Eurozone crisis (2008–2012) to legitimate free trade. Based on their results, the authors post four consecutive periods of change, each characterized by a dominant strategy of legitimation: from defensive, over offensive-desirable and offensive-necessary towards necessary-but-not-sufficient. Providing a close look at media coverage of the financial crisis between 2007 and 2009, Hartz (2012) segments the narrative of a "defense of the market economy" into four periods, each corresponding to different legitimation strategies. The total of 8343 articles are thus interpreted as a successive re-normalization of an initially problematized economic order: "before the crisis", "having a temperature", "days of revelation", and "in defense of freedom".

Going by the basic measure of the number of news items mentioning "political correctness", a number of studies have periodized the discursive history of political correctness (Johnson et al. 2003). Extending such work with a qualitative analysis, Johnson and Suhr (2003) note that quantitative methods alone would not have allowed them to discover that the unexpected increase in the term's usage in a corpus of German newspaper articles between 1995 and 2000 is due to debates over historical consciousness within the broader context of Germany's particularly problematic sense of nation and national identity in the light of its National Socialist past. Following a similar logic, KhosraviNik (2015) first conducted a diachronic CL analysis, establishing "hot spots" in his media data covering Iran's nuclear program in terms of number of articles per month (2004 and 2007). Guided by these, the study then focused qualitative analysis of legitimation topoi within one such period, giving a detailed perspective within the previously established longitudinal frame.

The methodological reasoning in Carvalho's (2005) analysis of the continuities and discontinuities in the representation of the greenhouse effect in the UK between 1985 and 2000 is less clear: To be sure, three phases are identified in terms of the frequency of articles that cover climate change (1985–1990, initial rising trend; 1991–1996, recession; and 1997–2000, a second sharp rise). However, this observation is not linked to the procedure for data segmentation, but the author points out that these three phases correspond to the mandates of three different prime ministers. With respect to the cut-off points, there is a similar ambiguity: at one point, they are linked to prime ministers and, at another point, to crucial international scientific meetings in the field of climate change. While the methodological approach may have been either of those or, indeed, a combination, the publication does not clearly state so.

5.5.5 Diachrony Structured by Contextual Knowledge

Especially when dealing with longer periods or timeframes, CDS often adopt a strategy of data segmentation (and collection) that follows previously established contextual knowledge. Needless to say, how that knowledge is established or where it is obtained may strongly impact the quality and usefulness of such an approach to segmentation.

In studying the discursive construction of national identity, for instance, it has become a widely accepted practice to collect data on days of national significance, such as commemorative or anniversary occasions (e.g. Wodak et al. 2009), or to examine data from a period linked to specific 'debates' pertaining to one or the other aspect of national identity (e.g. Wodak 1990). Piwoni (2012) demonstrates that such debates can structure or parallel discursive change across three decades (1980–2010): Several "snapshots of historical moments" are selected for highly salient debates on German national identity and then analyzed through textual data centered on these. While some of these might be considered crises, Piwoni does not argue their selection as such: the so-called Historikerstreit (historians' row), the debate over German reunification before and after reunification, the so-called Walser-Bubis controversy over Germany's past, the so-called Leitkultur-debate in 2000, and the debate over newly invigorated patriotism during the soccer world championship in 2006.

A similar approach, if on a more narrow timescale, is followed by Sowinska and Dubrovskaya (2012), who segment their Polish and Russian media reporting on the US anti-ballistic missile shield in Poland into three periods based on contextual information: (1) by the signing the US–Poland agreement in 2008, (2) President Obama's visit to Russia in 2009, and (3) Obama's decision to withdraw from the agreement later the same year.

5.5.6 Diachrony by Calendar

Calendar dates, i.e. decades, years, months, weeks or even days, are a convenient external criterion for data segmentation. As such, they are both free of potential researcher bias (of which segmentation based on contextual knowledge or crisis-focused studies are sometimes accused) and standardized (which makes the segmentation reproducible and facilitates cross-study comparison). However, data segmentation by calendar can be crude and, more importantly, insensitive to the dynamics of discourse; and in the case of long time intervals, the low granularity obtained for point-to-point comparison may obscure changes of a smaller scale.

With an average granularity of approximately 20 data points per time interval, Marshall et al. (2014) analyzed the link between fatherhood and masculinity in 131 ads from the UK magazine Good Housekeeping, using standard calendar decades (1950–2010). They found that the 1950s cast the father as the provider, the 1960s as relaxing at home, the 1970s as the family man, the 1980s as emotionally engaged, the 1990s as the new family man, the 2000s as absent, and in 2010 as invisible. While this allows for easily relating results to other studies in terms of a history-by-decades, no questions are raised as to whether—or why—key discursive shifts around fatherhood would so neatly coincide with calendar decades.

Analyzing almost fully continuous data in one of the largest CDS projects incorporating CL methodology to date, Gabrielatos and Baker (2008) used calendar-based segmentation to develop a diachronic perspective on the discursive construction of refugees, asylum seekers, immigrants, and migrants. They divided the 140-million-word corpus of UK press articles (1996–2005) into 10 sub-corpora by calendar year, thus creating a more manageable number of diachronic points of comparison while retaining, at least hypothetically, the option of zooming in on any of those years by switching to a month-, week- or even day-based segmentation. Staying within the annual frame, Gabrielatos and Baker provided a CL operationalization corresponding to the notion of discursive stabilities/permanences in the form of constant collocates or "c-collocates". In that study, a given collocate is considered "consistent", if it appears as collocate in at least seven of the ten annual sub-corpora—though that number could be adjusted to facilitate other research questions. In the case of Gabrielatos and Baker, their parameters[5] lead them to conclude that only a small percentage of the collocates were consistent and that the

[5]That study used a threshold frequency, in each annual sub-corpus, of five occurrences for collocates of "refugees", "asylum seekers", and "immigrants", and of three occurrences for collocates of "migrants".

vast majority of collocates for refuges, asylum seekers, and immigrants were related to specific events (Gabrielatos and Baker 2008, 11). Significantly, this approach can be used to obtain a picture of the "core semantic attributes" of any given term and thus reveal "the incremental effect of discourse" (Baker 2006, 13). The other collocates are interpreted as "seasonal", i.e. related to singular events identified in the context, as were the sharp rises ("spikes") in the number of articles published per month. The latter were taken to indicate temporary media interest in refugees triggered by wars, natural disasters, and terrorist attacks, as well as elections and new legislation (Gabrielatos and Baker 2008, 18).

5.5.7 Discursive Shifts as Local, Strategic Responses to Change

In order to establish a distinction between discursive 'change' and 'shift', Krzyżanowski (2013b, 105–6) defines the latter as primarily based on recontextualization, allowing "for the simultaneous promulgation of different types of practices", entailing the creation of new and hybrid discourses. Largely in correspondence with previous usage of the term 'change', Krzyżanowski defines discursive change—note the general singular—as those "broader changes and dynamics" discussed by Fairclough (e.g. commodification). In contrast, "discursive shifts"—note the plural—are defined as "more or less localized responses to those [broader] changes constructed in dynamics of discursive practices of selected individual or collective actors". *Change* is thus defined as a macro-level category, while *shift* is suggested to allow for the actual observing of change in discourse at the micro-level, grasping what are actually multidimensional and multidirectional changes. For Krzyżanowski, this distinction coincides with an important point: Shifts can be empirically analyzed "diachronically", while change suggests a "historical" perspective. I do not take this to mean that "change" occurs too slowly to actually observe in data, but that the concept is generally—if not necessarily—employed in such a way as to render it historical (background, context, or a previously proven reality) rather than the analytical focus of empirical studies. It is also noteworthy that Krzyżanowski defines shifts as individual and collective actors' "responses" to broader changes. Although this makes sense in terms of scale, it does not fully account for the relationship between change and shifts, or address the relationship between social change and discursive change: Theorizing must still address, for instance, whether there are social shifts (or shifts in social structure) that correspond to discursive shifts, just as social change corresponds to discursive change.[6]

Methodologically, this conceptual distinction between change and shift also situates discursive change as a particular kind of *context*, i.e. a broader, perhaps even global trend in discourses to which the local data to be analyzed may or may not respond by instantiating, inflecting or resisting change. This conceptualization is no doubt well suited for top-down processes such as those favored by neoliberalism, globalization and other transnational changes (Krzyżanowski 2016), which nonetheless require accommodation via different context-specific discursive shifts (Krzyżanowski 2013b). Significantly, shifts in this sense cannot be identified independent of larger changes and require either a complementary analysis of discursive change or referencing changes established by other work (Krzyżanowski and Forchtner 2016, 256).

From this angle, much can be said in favor of seeing discursive shifts as a form of strategy or "strategic enactment" (Krzyżanowski 2018, 77–78), particularly in the field of politics. Discursive shifts associated with politicization of immigration by the Polish PiS party in the context of the European 'refugee crisis' of 2015/2016 seem to confirm this pattern, as they propagated discursively formed imaginaries as part of an orchestrated move. Notably, the corresponding re-definition of discursive change departs from Fairclough's seminal definition as "a significant shift in the social functioning of language" (Fairclough 1992, 6), situating it at the macro-level of global or transnational imaginaries or framings of public discourses. Referentially and terminologically, however, Krzyżanowski maintains the link to many if not all of the previously discussed forms of discursive change, e.g. economization, securitization, radicalization.

The characterization of shifts as both local and strategic integrates agency, inasmuch as shifts are actor-specific responses toward social, polit-

[6]Some work has used the term "discursive shift" dismissively and in contrast to ideological or programmatic changes, i.e. "real change", using "shift" to describe a merely superficial change without substance (e.g. Küçükali 2014, 103).

ical, and economic macro-level transformations, and opens up the notion of discursive struggle on a global-to-local scale. Noting that shifts may be aimed at abrupt, gradual or even perpetuating goals, Krzyżanowski's (2018, 78) approach is particularly well-suited to discursive practices situated in fields characterized by strong interactions between global and local actors, such as some political discourses and their mediatization, or transnational organizations and policy implementation (Krzyżanowski 2013b). In the case of the Polish PiS, the strategic politicization of immigration has been helped greatly by mediatization and the logic of global social media, which have been deployed not only to reinforce and disseminate political argumentation but to create "the semblance of a polyphonic political discourse that suggests that the expressed opinions are not only the party's but part of a widely shared set of views". Social media may thus be characterized as vital to politically driven discursive shifts on controversial topics, as today's political actors seek to test or shift the limits of the sayable (Krzyżanowski 2018, 93).

While directing public opinion like that may be a political goal with respect to elections, distracting from scandals or internal affairs, it is often also a strategic step towards new legislation, legitimizing particular policies or measures. Such contexts are clearly of great interest to CDS due to their often far-reaching consequences, but they also provide rich empirical data in the form of strong textual chains, genre chains, recontextualizations that cross social fields and often throw into stark relief the different norms and habitus of such fields. This is demonstrated, for instance, by Blackledge's (2009) study of the discursive shifts that, following the English 'race riots' of 2001, led to the naturalization and acceptance of racialized monolingual language ideology in the form of the Nationality, Immigration and Asylum Act of 2002. Blackledge was able to show how such racialization of language is strategically employed to explain and maintain social inequality, while at the same time allowing British media and politics to maintain the positive self-image of the UK as liberal and democratic. In this research design, the end-point of discursive shifting in new legislation is thus situated in a 'chain' of genres cutting across multiple social fields and discourses.

A different type of textual chain is found in the development of the so-called "Bush Doctrine" security strategy: presented and widely accepted as the United States of America's response to 9/11, Dunmire (2009) has convincingly argued that it constitutes a form of covert discursive continuity with post-Cold War attempts to legitimize a security strategy which sanctions preventive war. The argumentative shift allowed by 9/11 is thus revealed to be the legitimating device that enabled the Bush Administration to sanction a security policy aiming to maintain US global supremacy, presenting it as the inevitable response to 9/11 and overtly disconnecting it from its cold-war antecedents.

Indeed, the ways in which 9/11 was seized upon by the US administration have been the subject of much work in CDS. Comparing national security strategies of 1996 and 2006 with respect to the link between poverty and international security, Lorenzo-Dus and Marsh (2012) argue that 9/11 accelerated rather than created a new paradigm for the securitization of poverty. Like Dunmire, they demonstrate the legitimating role given to the terrorist attacks for naturalizing the link between free market policies, poverty alleviation, and threat tackling. In the specific discursive shift identified, this link is argued via topoi of usefulness and humanitarianism, but relies on (a) demonizing poverty as linked to tyranny, (b) metaphorically representing poverty as an illness or trap from which the poor are unable to escape on their own, and (c) presenting it as a security threat insofar as it is contributes to security threats. Interventionist responses, even military ones, are thus legitimized as moral imperatives in line with the USA's discursively maintained self-image as a beacon of liberty, justice, and freedom.

Several other researchers have examined discursive shifts in local/national responses to the so-called refugee crisis of 2015/2016 which, taken together, reveal both commonalities and contrast. For Sweden, Torstensson (2016) has examined shifts in the Swedish government's discursive representation of refugees in late 2015. Since the decision to close the borders and implement one of Europe's toughest border control regimes is an unprecedented reversal of Swedish migration policy, Torstensson theorizes that it constitutes a form of transgression that can be traced to contradictory or inconsistent elements on the linguistic level, such as overlexicalization. Using an legitimation- and topoi-focused approach, Kissová (2017) identifies a very clear-cut shift of migrant's representation in Slovakia before and after the EC decided to relocate 120,000 people in September 2015. While refugees had previously been represented as deserving of help and acceptable to Slovakia, they were now constructed as undeserving and unacceptable, their rejection legitimized by identifying them as 'non-Christian' and therefore not only alien but dangerous to 'Christian Slovakia'. Christianity thus became the central signifier distinguishing the Slovakian 'us' from the refugee 'other', much like in other European countries, as a mobilizing tool for nationalist and anti-European Union sentiment.

5.6 Research Design and Research Practice

Inasmuch as the diachronic study of discourse is built into virtually all conceptualizations of discourse encountered in CDS, the empirical analysis of discursive change and stability has taken many forms and shapes. Over the last few decades, several distinct approaches have emerged from the plethora of individual studies, although this has not yet led to a clear typology of diachronic CDS. Although this chapter has sought to make some small contribution to this aim, it must ultimately focus on methodological tools available for the diachronic study of discourse. As with other issues, their viability remains closely tied to conceptualizations of discourse, discursive change, and other key notions such as social actors, agency, and social fields of action.

In planning and designing research into the diachronic dimension of discourse, we should therefore:

- clarify the fundamental relation between discourse and society in general, and between discursive change and social change,
- specify what we mean by change and stability, respectively, as well as any complementary notions such as shift in relation to the former,
- distinguish between internal and inter-discursive change,
- clarify what constitutes description, explanation, and critique with respect to the diachronic dimension of discourse,
- decide whether and which mechanisms of discursive change/stability we posit within our model, as well as how to empirically study such mechanisms,

- decide the empirical role of diachrony in our study, specifically how the diachronic dimension will be analytically integrated, i.e. as historical context or empirical comparison,
- decide on strategies of data collection, storage, and annotation that adequately operationalize the chosen conceptualization of diachrony and periodization,
- operationalize the diachronic dimension in terms of periodization and data segmentation, keeping in mind criteria such as granularity as well as the interpretative impact of different analytical framings such as 'crises',
- choose appropriate analytical categories and methods, or combinations of methods, to handle the amount of data, keeping in mind criteria such as granularity and the possible need for additional data to provide a sufficiently 'thick' description of context, related social practices, and social actors involved,
- and develop adequate means of representing the diachronic dimension of discourse, specifically with respect to change/stability, possible links, and correspondences to contextual factors and events.

References

Achugar, Mariana. 2007. "Between Remembering and Forgetting: Uruguayan Military Discourse About Human Rights (1976—2004)." *Discourse & Society* 18 (5): 521–47. https://doi.org/10.1177/0957926507079632.

———. 2009. "Constructing the Past and Constructing Themselves: The Uruguayan Military's Memory of the Dictatorship." *Critical Discourse Studies* 6 (4): 283–95. https://doi.org/10.1080/17405900903181051.

Ackermann, Jan, Katharina Behne, Felix Buchta, Marc Drobot, and Philipp Knopp. 2015. *Metamorphosen des Extremismusbegriffes: diskursanalytische Untersuchungen zur Dynamik einer funktionalen Unzulänglichkeit.* Wiesbaden: Springer VS.

Al-Hejin, Bandar. 2015. "Covering Muslim Women: Semantic Macrostructures in BBC News." *Discourse & Communication* 9 (1): 19–46. https://doi.org/10.1177/1750481314555262.

Al-Momani, Kawakib. 2016. "Discourse Change in a Changing Society: A Critical Discourse Analysis of Political Advertisement in Jordan Before and After the Arab Spring." *Círculo de Lingüística Aplicada a La Comunicación* 65 (0): 3–43. https://doi.org/10.5209/rev_CLAC.2016.v65.51980.

Amer, M. Mosheer. 2012. "The Discourse of Homeland: The Construction of Palestinian National Identity in Palestinian Secularist and Islamist Discourses." *Critical Discourse Studies* 9 (2): 117–31. https://doi.org/10.1080/17405904.2012.656374.

Anaïs, Seantel. 2013. "Genealogy and Critical Discourse Analysis in Conversation: Texts, Discourse, Critique." *Critical Discourse Studies* 10 (2): 123–35. https://doi.org/10.1080/17405904.2012.744321.

Angus, Lawrence. 2004. "Globalization and Educational Change: Bringing About the Reshaping and Re-norming of Practice." *Journal of Education Policy* 19 (1): 23–41. https://doi.org/10.1080/0268093042000182618.

Aronsen, Ingunn. 2016. "Ideology and Change: A Systemic Functional Approach to the Climate Discourse in the British Press." Dissertation, Oslo: University of Oslo.

Ayers, D. Franklin. 2005. "Neoliberal Ideology in Community College Mission Statements: A Critical Discourse Analysis." *The Review of Higher Education* 28 (4): 527–49. https://doi.org/10.1353/rhe.2005.0033.

Baker, Paul. 2006. *Using Corpora in Discourse Analysis*. Continuum Discourse Series. London and New York: Continuum.

———. 2010. "Will Ms Ever Be as Frequent as Mr? A Corpus-Based Comparison of Gendered Terms Across Four Diachronic Corpora of British English." *Gender and Language* 4 (1). https://doi.org/10.1558/genl.v4i1.125.

Bebbington, Anthony, Scott Guggenheim, Elizabeth Olson, and Michael Woolcock. 2004. "Exploring Social Capital Debates at the World Bank." *Journal of Development Studies* 40 (5): 33–64. https://doi.org/10.1080/0022038042000218134.

Beelitz, Annika, and Doris M. Merkl-Davies. 2012. "Using Discourse to Restore Organisational Legitimacy: 'CEO-Speak' After an Incident in a German Nuclear Power Plant." *Journal of Business Ethics* 108 (1): 101–20. https://doi.org/10.1007/s10551-011-1065-9.

Bennett, Joe. 2013. "Moralising Class: A Discourse Analysis of the Mainstream Political Response to Occupy and the August 2011 British Riots." *Discourse & Society* 24 (1): 27–45. https://doi.org/10.1177/0957926512463634.

Biesta, Gert. 2015. "What Is Education for? On Good Education, Teacher Judgement, and Educational Professionalism." *European Journal of Education* 50 (1): 75–87. https://doi.org/10.1111/ejed.12109.

Blackledge, Adrian. 2009. *Discourse and Power in a Multilingual World.* Amsterdam and Philadelphia: John Benjamins.

Blommaert, Jan. 2008. "Book Review: Norman Fairclough, Language and Globalization." *Discourse & Society* 19 (2): 257–62. https://doi.org/10.1177/0957926507085954.

Blommaert, Jan, and Chris Bulcaen. 2000. "Critical Discourse Analysis." *Annual Review of Anthropology* 29: 447–66.

Brei, Vinicius, and Steffen Böhm. 2014. "'1L = 10L for Africa': Corporate Social Responsibility and the Transformation of Bottled Water into a 'Consumer Activist' Commodity." *Discourse & Society* 25 (1): 3–31. https://doi.org/10.1177/0957926513503536.

Bubikova-Moan, Jarmila. 2017. "Constructing the Multilingual Child: The Case of Language Education Policy in Norway." *Critical Discourse Studies* 14 (1): 56–72. https://doi.org/10.1080/17405904.2016.1190389.

Calsamiglia, Helena. 2003. "Popularization Discourse." *Discourse Studies* 5 (2): 139–46. https://doi.org/10.1177/1461445603005002307.

Carvalho, Anabela. 2008. "Media(Ted) Discourse and Society: Rethinking the Framework of Critical Discourse Analysis." *Journalism Studies* 9 (2): 161–77. https://doi.org/10.1080/14616700701848162.

Carvalho, Anabela. 2005. "Representing the Politics of the Greenhouse Effect." *Critical Discourse Studies* 2 (1): 1–29.

Chiapello, Eve, and Norman Fairclough. 2002. "Understanding the New Management Ideology: A Transdisciplinary Contribution from Critical Discourse Analysis and New Sociology of Capitalism." *Discourse & Society* 13 (2): 185–208. https://doi.org/10.1177/0957926502013002406.

Chilton, Paul A. 2004. *Analysing Political Discourse: Theory and Practice.* London: Routledge.

Chouliaraki, Lilie. 1998. "Regulation in 'Progressivist' Pedagogic Discourse: Individualized Teacher-Pupil Talk." *Discourse & Society* 9 (1): 5–32.

Chouliaraki, Lilie. 2014. "From War Memoirs to Milblogs: Language Change in the Witnessing of War, 1914–2014." *Discourse & Society* 25 (5): 600–618. https://doi.org/10.1177/0957926514536830.

Chouliaraki, Lilie, and Norman Fairclough. 2007. *Discourse in Late Modernity: Rethinking Critical Discourse Analysis.* Transferred to Digital Printing. Critical Discourse Analysis Series. Edinburgh: Edinburgh University Press.

Condit, Celeste M. 2004. "The Meaning and Effects of Discourse About Genetics: Methodological Variations in Studies of Discourse and Social Change." *Discourse & Society* 15 (4): 391–407. https://doi.org/10.1177/0957926504043706.

Cooper, Samantha, Erin Olejniczak, Caroline Lenette, and Charlotte Smedley. 2017. "Media Coverage of Refugees and Asylum Seekers in Regional Australia: A Critical Discourse Analysis." *Media International Australia* 162 (1): 78–89. https://doi.org/10.1177/1329878X16667832.

Costelloe, Laura. 2014. "Discourses of Sameness: Expressions of Nationalism in Newspaper Discourse on French Urban Violence in 2005." *Discourse & Society* 25 (3): 315–40. https://doi.org/10.1177/0957926513519533.

de Cillia, Rudolf, Martin Reisigl, and Ruth Wodak. 1999. "The Discursive Construction of National Identities." *Discourse & Society* 10 (2): 149–73. https://doi.org/10.1177/0957926599010002002.

de Cock, Christian, Leanne Cutcher, and David Grant. 2012. "Finance Capitalism's Perpetually Extinguished Pasts: Exploring Discursive Shifts 2007–2011." *Culture and Organization* 18 (2): 87–90. https://doi.org/10.1080/14759551.2011.636612.

de Ville, Ferdi, and Jan Orbie. 2014. "The European Commission's Neoliberal Trade Discourse Since the Crisis: Legitimizing Continuity Through Subtle Discursive Change." *The British Journal of Politics and International Relations* 16 (1): 149–67. https://doi.org/10.1111/1467-856X.12022.

Dekavalla, Marina. 2010. "Tax, War and Waiting Lists: The Construction of National Identity in Newspaper Coverage of General Elections After Devolution." *Discourse & Society* 21 (6): 638–54. https://doi.org/10.1177/0957926510381222.

Domínguez, Martí. 2015. "Evolution of Metaphors: Phylogeny of Oil Slick Cartoons in Spanish Press." *Discourse & Society* 26 (2): 184–204. https://doi.org/10.1177/0957926514556208.

Drury, John. 2002. "'When the Mobs Are Looking for Witches to Burn, Nobody's Safe': Talking About the Reactionary Crowd." *Discourse & Society* 13 (1): 41–73. https://doi.org/10.1177/0957926502013001003.

Duncan, Philip T. 2014. "Remembering the Future: Temporal Tensions in the Discursive Construction and Commemoration of Israel." *Critical Discourse Studies* 11 (4): 416–40. https://doi.org/10.1080/17405904.2014.890946.

Dunmire, Patricia L. 2009. "'9/11 Changed Everything'. An Intertextual Analysis of the Bush Doctrine." *Discourse & Society* 20 (2): 195–222. https://doi.org/10.1177/0957926508099002.

Eder, Franz X. 2006. "Historische Diskurse Und Ihre Analyse." In *Historische Diskursanalysen: Genealogie, Theorie, Anwendungen*, edited by Franz X. Eder, 9–23. Wiesbaden: Springer VS.

Edwards, Geraint O. 2012. "A Comparative Discourse Analysis of the Construction of 'in-Groups' in the 2005 and 2010 Manifestos of the British

National Party." *Discourse & Society* 23 (3): 245–58. https://doi.org/10.1177/0957926511433477.

Fairclough, Norman. 1992. *Discourse and Social Change*. Cambridge: Polity Press.

———. 1993. "Critical Discourse Analysis and the Marketization of Public Discourse: The Universities." *Discourse & Society* 4 (2): 133–68. https://doi.org/10.1177/0957926593004002002.

———. 2003. "'Political Correctness': The Politics of Culture and Language." *Discourse & Society* 14 (1): 17–28. https://doi.org/10.1177/0957926503014001927.

———. 2005. "Critical Discourse Analysis in Trans-Disciplinary Research on Social Change: Transition, Re-scaling, Poverty and Social Inclusion." *Lodz Papers in Pragmatics* 1 (1): 37–58.

———. 2006a. "Critical Discourse Analysis and Change in Management Discourse and Ideology: A Transdisciplinary Approach to Strategic Critique." In *Discourse and Enterprise: Communication, Business, Management and Other Professional Fields*, edited by Fernando Ramallo, Lorenzo Anxo, and Xoán Paulo Rodríguez-Yáñez. München: Lincom.

———. 2006b. *Language and Globalization*. London and New York: Routledge.

———. 2010. *Media Discourse*. Repr. London: Bloomsbury Academic.

———. 2013a. *Discourse and Social Change*. Reprinted. Cambridge: Polity Press.

———. 2013b. "Critical Discourse Analysis and Critical Policy Studies." *Critical Policy Studies* 7 (2): 177–97. https://doi.org/10.1080/19460171.2013.798239.

Fairclough, Norman, and Anna Mauranen. 1998. "The Conversationalisation of Political Discourse: A Comparative View." *Belgian Journal of Linguistics* 11: 89–119. https://doi.org/10.1075/bjl.11.06fai.

Filardo, Laura. 2008. "A Comparative Study of the Discursive Legitimation of the Agreement by the Four Main Northern Irish Political Parties throughout Time." *Ethnopolitics* 7 (1): 21–42. https://doi.org/10.1080/17449050701846634.

Filardo-Llamas, Laura. 2013. "'Committed to the Ideals of 1916'. The Language of Paramilitary Groups: The Case of the Irish Republican Army." *Critical Discourse Studies* 10 (1): 1–17. https://doi.org/10.1080/17405904.2012.736396.

Forchtner, Bernhard, Michał Krzyżanowski, and Ruth Wodak. 2013. "Mediatisation, Right-Wing Populism and Political Campaigning: The Case of the Austrian Freedom Party (FPÖ)." In *Media Talk and Political Elections in Europe and America*, edited by M. Ekström and A. Tolson, 205–28. Basingstoke: Palgrave.

Forchtner, Bernhard, and Christian Schneickert. 2016. "Collective Learning in Social Fields: Bourdieu, Habermas and Critical Discourse Studies." *Discourse & Society* 27 (3): 293–307. https://doi.org/10.1177/0957926516630892.

Gabrielatos, Costas, and Paul Baker. 2008. "Fleeing, Sneaking, Flooding: A Corpus Analysis of Discursive Constructions of Refugees and Asylum Seekers in the UK Press, 1996–2005." *Journal of English Linguistics* 36 (1): 5–38. https://doi.org/10.1177/0075424207311247.

Gasteiger, Ludwig. 2008. "Michel Foucaults interpretative Analytik und das unbestimmte Ethos der Kritik." In *Kritik mit Methode? Forschungsmethoden und Gesellschaftskritik*, edited by Ulrike Freikamp, Matthias Leanza, Janne Mende, Stefan Müller, Peter Ullrich, and Heinz-Jürgen Voß, 33–52. Texte / Rosa-Luxemburg-Stiftung 42. Berlin: Dietz.

Griesser, Markus. 2018. "Images and Imaginaries of Unemployed People: Discursive Shifts in the Transition from *Active* to *Activating* Labour Market Policies in Germany." *Critical Social Policy* 38 (2): 387–406. https://doi.org/10.1177/0261018317727481.

Gunders, Lisa. 2012. "Immoral and Un-Australian: The Discursive Exclusion of Welfare Recipients." *Critical Discourse Studies* 9 (1): 1–13. https://doi.org/10.1080/17405904.2011.632136.

Hartz, Ronald. 2012. "Reclaiming the Truth of the Market in Times of Crisis: Course, Transformation and Strategies of a Liberal Discourse in Germany." *Culture and Organization* 18 (2): 139–54. https://doi.org/10.1080/14759551.2011.636617.

Hiippala, Tuomo. 2015. *The Structure of Multimodal Documents: An Empirical Approach.* Hoboken: Taylor and Francis. http://public.eblib.com/choice/publicfullrecord.aspx?p=2065294.

Horsti, Karina. 2015. "Techno-Cultural Opportunities: The Anti-Immigration Movement in the Finnish Mediascape." *Patterns of Prejudice* 49 (4): 343–66. https://doi.org/10.1080/0031322X.2015.1074371.

Hyatt, David. 2005. "Time for a Change: A Critical Discoursal Analysis of Synchronic Context with Diachronic Relevance." *Discourse & Society* 16 (4): 515–31.

Iedema, Rick, and Ruth Wodak. 1999. "Introduction: Organizational Discourses and Practices." *Discourse & Society* 10 (1): 5–19.

Jäger, Margret, and Siegfried Jäger. 2007. *Deutungskämpfe: Theorie und Praxis kritischer Diskursanalyse.* 1. Auflage. Medien - Kultur - Kommunikation. Wiesbaden: VS, Verlag für Sozialwissenschaften.

Johnson, Sally, Jonathan Culpeper, and Stephanie Suhr. 2003. "From 'Politically Correct Councillors' to 'Blairite Nonsense': Discourses of 'Political Correctness' in Three British Newspapers." *Discourse & Society* 14 (1): 29–47. https://doi.org/10.1177/0957926503014001928.

Johnson, Sally, and Stephanie Suhr. 2003. "From 'Political Correctness' to 'Politische Korrektheit': Discourses of 'PC' in the German Newspaper, Die Welt." *Discourse & Society* 14 (1): 49–68. https://doi.org/10.1177/0957926503014001929.

Katznelson, Noah, and Katie A. Bernstein. 2017. "Rebranding Bilingualism: The Shifting Discourses of Language Education Policy in California's 2016 Election." *Linguistics and Education* 40 (August): 11–26. https://doi.org/10.1016/j.linged.2017.05.002.

Kaufer, David, Shawn J. Parry-Giles, and Beata Beigman Klebanov. 2012. "The 'Image Bite,' Political Language, and the Public/Private Divide: NBC News Coverage of Hillary Clinton from Scorned Wife to Senate Candidate." *Journal of Language and Politics* 11 (3): 336–56. https://doi.org/10.1075/jlp.11.3.02kau.

KhosraviNik, Majid. 2015. "Macro and Micro Legitimation in Discourse on Iran's Nuclear Programme: The Case of Iranian National Newspaper *Kayhan*." *Discourse & Society* 26 (1): 52–73. https://doi.org/10.1177/0957926514541345.

Kissová, Lenka. 2017. "The Production of (Un)deserving and (Un)acceptable: Shifting Representations of Migrants Within Political Discourse in Slovakia." *East European Politics and Societies: And Cultures*, 1–24.

Koller, Veronika. 2008. *Lesbian Discourses: Images of a Community*. Routledge Studies in Linguistics 9. New York: Routledge.

Kopytowska, Monika. 2015. "Mediating Identity, Ideology and Values in the Public Sphere: Towards a New Model of (Constructed) Social Reality." *Lodz Papers in Pragmatics* 11 (2). https://doi.org/10.1515/lpp-2015-0008.

Koselleck, Reinhart. 1989. "Begriffsgeschichte Und Sozialgeschichte." In *Vergangene Zukunft. Zur Semantik Geschichtlicher Zeiten*, edited by Reinhart Koselleck, 107–29. Frankfurt am Main: Suhrkamp.

———. 2010. "Die Verzeitlichung Der Begriffe." In *Begriffsgeschichten. Studien Zur Semantik Und Pragmatik Der Politischen Und Sozialen Sprache*, edited by Reinhart Koselleck, 77–85. Frankfurt am Main: Suhrkamp.

Krzyżanowski, Michał. 2013a. "From Anti-Immigration and Nationalist Revisionism to Islamophobia: Continuities and Shifts in Recent Discourses and Patterns of Political Communication of the Freedom Party of Austria (FPÖ)." In *Right-Wing Populism in Europe: Politics and Discourse*, edited by Ruth Wodak, Majid KhosraviNik, and Brigitte Mral, 135–48.

———. 2013b. "Policy, Policy Communication and Discursive Shifts: Analysing EU Policy Discourses on Climate Change." In *Analysing New Genres in Political Communication*, edited by Piotr Cap and Urszula Okulska, 101–35. London: Bloomsbury Academic.

———. 2016. "Recontextualisation of Neoliberalism and the Increasingly Conceptual Nature of Discourse: Challenges for Critical Discourse Studies." *Discourse & Society* 27 (3): 308–21. https://doi.org/10.1177/0957926516630901.

———. 2018. "Discursive Shifts in Ethno-Nationalist Politics: On Politicization and Mediatization of the 'Refugee Crisis' in Poland." *Journal of Immigrant & Refugee Studies* 16 (1–2): 76–96. https://doi.org/10.1080/15562948.2017.1317897.

Krzyżanowski, Michał, and Bernhard Forchtner. 2016. "Theories and Concepts in Critical Discourse Studies: Facing Challenges, Moving Beyond Foundations." *Discourse & Society* 27 (3): 253–61. https://doi.org/10.1177/0957926516630900.

Krzyżanowski, Michał, and Ruth Wodak. 2009. "Theorising and Analysing Social Change in Central and Eastern Europe: The Contribution of Critical Discourse Analysis." In *Discourse and Transformation in Central and Eastern Europe*, edited by Aleksandra Galasińska and Michał Krzyżanowski, 17–39. London: Palgrave Macmillan. https://doi.org/10.1057/9780230594296_2.

Küçükali, Can. 2014. "Discursive Strategies of Instrumentalizing History in Mainstream Turkish Political Discourse: The Case of the Negative Other Presentation of the CHP." *Journal of Language and Politics* 13 (1): 98–119.

Kwon, Winston, Ian Clarke, and Ruth Wodak. 2009. "Organizational Decision-Making, Discourse, and Power: Integrating across Contexts and Scales." *Discourse & Communication* 3 (3): 273–302. https://doi.org/10.1177/1750481309337208.

Laine, Matias. 2010. "Towards Sustaining the Status Quo: Business Talk of Sustainability in Finnish Corporate Disclosures 1987–2005." *European Accounting Review* 19 (2): 247–74. https://doi.org/10.1080/09638180903136258.

Landwehr, Achim. 2010. "Diskurs Und Wandel. Wege Der Historischen Diskursforschung." In *Diskursiver Wandel*, edited by Achim Landwehr, 11–28. Wiesbaden: Springer VS.

Link, Jürgen. 2005. "Warum Diskurse Nicht von Personalen Subjekten "ausgehandelt" Werden. Von Der Diskurs- Zur Interdiskurstheorie." In *Die Diskursive Konstruktion von Wirklichkeit: Zum Verhältnis von Wissenssoziologie Und Diskursforschung*, edited by Reiner Keller, Andreas Hirseland, Werner Schneider, and Willy Viehöfer, 77–100. Konstanz: UVK Verlagsgesellschaft.

———. 2013. *Versuch über den Normalismus: wie Normalität produziert wird.* 5. Aufl. Göttingen: Vandenhoeck & Ruprecht.

Livingstone, Sonia, Peter Lunt, and Laura Miller. 2007. "Citizens, Consumers and the Citizen-Consumer: Articulating the Citizen Interest in Media and Communications Regulation." *Discourse & Communication* 1 (1): 63–89. https://doi.org/10.1177/1750481307071985.

Lorenzo-Dus, Nuria, and Steve Marsh. 2012. "Bridging the Gap: Interdisciplinary Insights into the Securitization of Poverty." *Discourse & Society* 23 (3): 274–96. https://doi.org/10.1177/0957926511433453.

Lotz-Heumann, Ute. 2010. "Wie Kommt Der Wandel in Den Diskurs? Der Kurort Und Der Wandel Der Landschaftswahrnehmung in Der Sattelzeit." In *Diskursiver Wandel*, edited by Achim Landwehr, 281–308. Wiesbaden: Springer VS.

Mair, Christian. 2015. "Parallel Corpora: A Real-Time Approach to the Study of Language Change in Progress." *Diacronia* 1.

Marchi, Anna. 2018. "Dividing Up the Data: Epistemological, Methodological and Practical Impact of Diachronic Segmentation." In *Corpus Approaches to Discourse: A Critical Review*, edited by Charlotte Taylor and Anna Marchi, 174–96. London: Routledge.

Marchi, Anna, and Alan Partington. 2012. "Does 'Europe' Have a Common Historical Identity?" In *European Identity: What the Media Say*, edited by Paul Bayley and Geoffrey Williams, 118–49. Oxford: Oxford University Press.

Marshall, David, Teresa Davis, Margaret K. Hogg, Tanja Schneider, and Alan Petersen. 2014. "From Overt Provider to Invisible Presence: Discursive Shifts in Advertising Portrayals of the Father in *Good Housekeeping*, 1950–2010." *Journal of Marketing Management* 30 (15–16): 1654–79. https://doi.org/10.1080/0267257X.2014.945471.

McKenna, Bernard. 2004. "Critical Discourse Studies: Where to from Here?" *Critical Discourse Studies* 1 (1): 9–39. https://doi.org/10.1080/1740590041000l674498.

Mcmanus, Jennifer. 2009. "The Ideology of Patient Information Leaflets: A Diachronic Study." *Discourse & Communication* 3 (1): 27–56. https://doi.org/10.1177/1750481308098763.

Mills, Sara. 2003. "Caught Between Sexism, Anti-Sexism and 'Political Correctness': Feminist Women's Negotiations with Naming Practices." *Discourse & Society* 14 (1): 87–110. https://doi.org/10.1177/0957926503014001931.

Molek-Kozakowska, Katarzyna. 2017. "Communicating Environmental Science Beyond Academia: Stylistic Patterns of Newsworthiness in Popular Science

Journalism." *Discourse & Communication* 11 (1): 69–88. https://doi.org/10.1177/1750481316683294.

Mulderrig, Jane. 2008. "Using Keywords Analysis in CDA : Evolving Discourses of the Knowledge Economy in Education." In *Education and the Knowledge-Based Economy in Europe*, edited by Bob Jessop, 149–69. Educational Futures: Rethinking Theory and Practice 24. Rotterdam: Sense Publlications.

———. 2011a. "Manufacturing Consent: A Corpus-Based Critical Discourse Analysis of New Labour's Educational Governance." *Educational Philosophy and Theory* 43 (6): 562–78. https://doi.org/10.1111/j.1469-5812.2010.00723.x.

———. 2011b. "The Grammar of Governance." *Critical Discourse Studies* 8 (1): 45–68. https://doi.org/10.1080/17405904.2011.533570.

Muntigl, Peter, Gilbert Weiss, and Ruth Wodak. 2000. *European Union Discourses on Un/Employment: An Interdisciplinary Approach to Employment Policy-Making and Organizational Change*. Vol. 12. Dialogues on Work and Innovation. Amsterdam: John Benjamins. https://doi.org/10.1075/dowi.12.

Piwoni, Eunike. 2012. *Nationale Identität im Wandel*. Wiesbaden: VS Verlag für Sozialwissenschaften. https://doi.org/10.1007/978-3-531-18740-2.

Potts, Amanda. 2015. "How Can Computer-Based Methods Help Researchers to Investigate News Values in Large Datasets? A Corpus Linguistic Study of the Construction of Newsworthiness in the Reporting on Hurricane Katrina." *Discourse & Communication* 9 (2): 149–72.

Reisigl, Martin. 2017. "The Discourse-Historical Approach." In *The Routledge Handbook of Critical Discourse Studies*, edited by John Flowerdew and John E. Richardson, 44–59. London: Routledge.

Rheindorf, Markus, and Ruth Wodak. 2018. "Borders, Fences, and Limits—Protecting Austria from Refugees: Metadiscursive Negotiation of Meaning in the Current Refugee Crisis." *Journal of Immigrant & Refugee Studies* 16 (1–2): 15–38. https://doi.org/10.1080/15562948.2017.1302032.

Schmidt-Wellenburg, Christian. 2013. "Diskursiver Wandel Im Fadenkreuz von Wissenssoziologischer Diskursanalyse Und Feldanalyse. Der Aufstieg Der Managementberatung." In *Methodologie Und Praxis Der Wissenssoziologischen Diskursanalyse. Band 1: Interdisziplinäre Perspektiven*, edited by Reiner Keller and Inga Truschkat, 451–80. Wiesbaden: Springer VS.

Seppänen, Janne, and Esa Väliverronen. 2003. "Visualizing Biodiversity: The Role of Photographs in Environmental Discourse." *Science as Culture* 12 (1): 59–85. https://doi.org/10.1080/0950543032000062263.

Séville, Astrid. 2017. "From 'One Right Way' to 'One Ruinous Way'? Discursive Shifts in 'There Is No Alternative.'" *European Political Science Review* 9 (3): 449–70.

Sowinska, Agnieszka, and Tatiana Dubrovskaya. 2012. "Discursive Construction and Transformation of 'Us' and 'Them' Categories in the Newspaper Coverage on the US Anti-Ballistic Missile System: Polish Versus Russian View." *Discourse & Communication* 6 (4): 449–68.

Stanyer, James, and Sabina Mihelj. 2016. "Taking Time Seriously? Theorizing and Researching Change in Communication and Media Studies: Taking Time Seriously?" *Journal of Communication* 66 (2): 266–79. https://doi.org/10.1111/jcom.12218.

Stewart, Craig O. 2009. "Socioscientific Controversies: A Theoretical and Methodological Framework." *Communication Theory* 19: 124–45.

Taylor, Sandra. 2004. "Researching Educational Policy and Change in 'New Times': Using Critical Discourse Analysis." *Journal of Education Policy* 19 (4): 433–51. https://doi.org/10.1080/0268093042000227483.

Toolan, Michael. 2016. "Peter Black, Christopher Stevens, Class and Inequality in the Daily Mail." *Discourse & Society* 27 (6): 642–60.

Torstensson, Emelie. 2016. "'My Europe Does Not Build Walls': The Swedish Government's Discourse Change in the Refugee Issue." Master Thesis, Jönköping, Sweden: Jönköping University.

van Leeuwen, Theo, and Ruth Wodak. 1999. "Legitimizing Immigration Control: A Discourse-Historical Analysis." *Discourse Studies* 1 (1): 83–118. https://doi.org/10.1177/1461445699001001005.

Varjonen, Sirkku, Linda Arnold, and Inga Jasinskaja-Lahti. 2013. "'We're Finns Here, and Russians There': A Longitudinal Study on Ethnic Identity Construction in the Context of Ethnic Migration." *Discourse & Society* 24 (1): 110–34. https://doi.org/10.1177/0957926512463632.

Wodak, Ruth. 1990. "The Waldheim Affair and Antisemitic Prejudice in Austrian Public Discourse." *Patterns of Prejudice* 24 (2–4): 18–33. https://doi.org/10.1080/0031322X.1990.9970049.

Wodak, Ruth, Rudolf de Cillia, Martin Reisigl, and Karin Liebhart. 2009. *The Discursive Construction of National Identity*. 2nd ed. Critical Discourse Analysis. Edinburgh: Edinburgh University Press.

Wodak, Ruth, and Norman Fairclough. 2010. "Recontextualizing European Higher Education Policies: The Cases of Austria and Romania." *Critical Discourse Studies* 7 (1): 19–40. https://doi.org/10.1080/17405900903453922.

Wodak, Ruth, Majid KhosraviNik, and Brigitte Mral. 2013. *Right-Wing Populism in Europe: Politics and Discourse.*London, New Delhi, and New York: Bloomsbury.

Zappettini, Franco, and Jeffrey Unerman. 2016. "'Mixing' and 'Bending': The Recontextualisation of Discourses of Sustainability in Integrated Reporting." *Discourse & Communication* 10 (5): 521–42.

6

Visualization, Interactive Visualization, and Open Science

6.1 Introduction

Interest in visualization as a tool in linguistics has been growing noticeably for more than two decades. The reasons identified for this development are numerous and include increased computing power, the availability of ever larger amounts of linguistic data (in digital form, on the web, and in dedicated public corpora), the adoption of text processing algorithms (e.g. for topic modeling), the increased availability of easy-to-use software for visualization, the possibilities of wide distribution of high-quality graphics on the web as well as online interactivity (Kucher and Kerren 2015, 117). In contrast to illustration, visualization promises to support the processing, analysis, and understanding of information both during analysis and in subsequent publication (Therón et al. 2014, 154). The field of visualization—with its subfields of data visualization (DataVis), information visualization (InfoVis), and Visual Analytics—combine technical and creative aspects of visualization and is, of course, much wider than its application in linguistics. Language data and the information gained through analyzing it has been recognized as quite distinct from the types

© The Author(s) 2019

M. Rheindorf, *Revisiting the Toolbox of Discourse Studies*,
Postdisciplinary Studies in Discourse,
https://doi.org/10.1007/978-3-030-19369-0_6

of data and information that visualization experts commonly focus on, e.g. statistical and geospatial data. The specific concern with visualizing language has more recently been dubbed Linguistic Information Visualization or LInfoVis (Culy et al. 2011, 485).

To date, visualization in linguistics—specifically visualizations of linguistic data and analytical abstractions based on such data—remains limited, although it has been established in areas that process large data sets and/or rely heavily on quantitative methods, such as NLP and CL. The strong link between quantitative methodology and visualization thus seems to have carried over into linguistics in general, and into CDS in particular, where it is mainly studies that integrate CL methods that employ some forms of visualization. As Anthony (2018, 197) observes, "[d]iscourse analysts are much less likely to use bar charts, line charts, scatter plots and other visualization techniques that are commonly used in quantitative data analysis". However, Anthony's assessment that discourse studies "have traditionally not used data visualization to represent the underlying complex relations between people and language" (Anthony 2018, 199) is linked, in part, to a narrow definition that identifies visualization closely with "automatic generation" of images as well as reliance on "quantitative data". It is one of the aims of this chapter to re-visit such underlying assumptions, particularly with respect to the consequence that visualization would seem to reinforce the divide between qualitative and quantitative methodology.

6.2 Visualizations in CDS

Publications in CDS tend to rely on text-based explanations, supplementing them with extracts or examples from the material analyzed. Less frequently, diagrams or infographics are used to visualize central findings, theoretical constructs or models of language practice. Interestingly—and here the distinction between published texts and CDS as research practice is crucial—these textual tendencies have been identified as a possible reason for accusing CDS of "cherry picking" (Anthony 2018, 200) inasmuch as readers of such publications might question the representativeness of extracts chosen for their illustrative qualities. Indeed, a strongly limited set of extracts and/or examples is unlikely to capture the full complexity of the data. In any context, visualizations can help to express this complexity, in particular relational qualities. Anthony here singles out "diagrams" and "infographics" as visuals created manually, even if on a computer, rather than automatically generated; by definition, such visuals have to be updated manually when applied to different data (on differences between infographic and data visualization, see also Hagley, n.d.). Anthony's conclusion that the absence of an automatic update option "limits their utility", requires some qualification: While it does limit the adaptability and increases the time required to (re)create such visuals, it does not limit their analytical or explanatory power.

Although Corpus Linguistics are also known to use long explanatory passages interspersed with source text extracts, the integration of CL seems to raise the chances for visualization in CDS—the most popular of which are KWIC concordance displays and charts that display data clusters or trends. On the one hand, the display of multiple, ordered extracts in KWIC concordance layouts represents a borderline case of visualization (Anthony 2018, 202); certainly, the spatial arrangement and possible color-coding represents information value beyond the linguistic. However, such displays suffer from similar limitations as more conventional forms of presenting linguistic evidence, as they are typically highly selective and avoid "noisy" or non-illustrative concordance lines (Anthony 2018, 202). This may well be necessary due to space constraints, but it remains a form of cherry picking nonetheless. On the other hand, the data charts used in corpus-based CDS are often line charts that display the number of articles in the corpus on a time axis, showing the development for set timeframes such as years, months or weeks (e.g. Gabrielatos and Baker 2008, 18). While this can be an effective form of visualization, its potential is clearly limited. More rarely, CL-based studies employ more sophisticated—but also less intuitive and less widely recognized—visualizations such box plots, scatter plots or heat maps (see below).

6.3 Visualization as External Cognition

The field of visualization is concerned with the use and design of visual representations to support or amplify human cognition. It tends to focus on computer-supported and, increasingly, also on interactive forms of visualization (Card et al. 2007). As a scientific field in its own right, visualization is not only technical but also experimental, seeking to optimize the ways in which visualization engages the human visual system's special capabilities for pattern recognition (Culy and Lyding 2010, 257). Since the seminal semiotic work on visualization of Bertin (1967), theoretical discussions of data visualization have largely focused on cognition and perception in order to derive parameters for designing visualization (e.g. Evergreen 2016; Knaflic 2015; Teate 2015; Few 2009; Tufte 2001).

Key concepts and definitions are therefore application-driven and oriented towards optimization of design options. On the most basic level, visualizations are defined as based on non-visual data and producing an image that is recognizable and comprehensible (Anthony 2018, 198; Kosara 2007). The final aspect is the one that is open to experimentation and optimization: effective and efficient visualization must enable the observer to learn something new about the data or learn it more effectively than by studying the same data in its raw form (Kosara 2007). This quality is often referred to as "visual efficiency", describing how quickly, accurately, and effortlessly the information is conveyed through the respective visualization (Anthony 2018, 198).

More contentiously, much work on visualization interprets this potential for improved pattern recognition and exploration as a form of "external cognition" (Scaife and Rogers 1996). The term controversially suggests that human cognition or a part of cognition can be 'externalized' through cleverly exploiting the potential of visualization. Factually, it refers to the ways in which internal and external representations interact when human beings perform perceptual and cognitive tasks; in this context, visualization as external representation can facilitate cognitive 'offloading' insofar as it diverts work from the cognitive to the perceptual system and thus reduces the cognitive effort required to solve a problem (Rogers 2005; Penn et al. 2009). This underlying observation links the basic limitations of human cognition to our creativity in devising tools to overcome those limitations, the tool in question being visualization:

> The power of the unaided mind is highly overrated. Without external aids, memory thought, and reasoning are all constrained. But human intelligence is highly flexible and adaptive, superb at inventing procedures and objects that overcome its own limits. The real powers come from devising external aids that enhance cognitive abilities. (Norman 2003, 43)

More specifically, visualizations can be useful if and insofar as they allow researchers and their readers to 'communicate ideas', 'see old things in new ways', 'create and discover ideas or knowledge', 'detect patterns' or 'find abstractions'. These goals of visualization are often referred to as presentation, confirmatory analysis, and exploratory analysis (Mayer 2013).

Visualization can thus not only reduce the cognitive effort for understanding complex information but open up entirely new ways of seeing information; but it can do so only because of the perceptual capabilities of human beings, more specifically attention mechanisms for monitoring, pattern detection, adaptivity, and perceptual inference (Card et al. 2007; Penn et al. 2009). To make the most of this potential, understanding the way we process visual information is key. The type of information processing that occurs during reading text has been described as 'controlled processing': It is detailed and conscious but, due to its seriality, slow, affords relatively low capacity, and is relatively easily inhibited. While visualizations often include controlled processing, they also seek to activate its counterpart, 'automatic' or 'preattentive processing': This type is unconscious and superficial, but due to its parallel nature fast, affords high capacity, and is not easily inhibited. It allows us to 'see things at a glance' and creates the impression of individual items 'popping out'. Spacing, or rather the distribution of information across the space of the visualization, is key to automatic processing.

The possibility of such 'external cognition' is further extended by adding an interactive dimension, i.e. providing information in a manipulable medium that allows, among other things, controlling, alternating or combining views such as overview/context and detail/focus as well as visually stratifying various aspects of the data in one display (Tufte 2001;

Card et al. 2007; Culy and Lyding 2011; Lyding and Culy 2012). This can be achieved by means of a picture-in-picture display or an integrative dashboard. As in non-interactive visualization, the use of space is a key resource, inspiring the "mantra" of "overview first, zoom and filter, then details-on-demand" (Shneiderman 1996, 336). Indeed, nany design-oriented approaches take a cue from the importance of the spatial dimension and define all data visualization as "maps" and the process of creating visualizations as "mapping data to visuals" (Murray 2013, 12, 67; see also Bostock et al. 2011).

Basic tenets underlying the design of visualizations include *data transparency and integrity* (Lopez-Bigas 2013), which addresses many of the concerns raised by Anthony (2018). This principle entails indicating what if any information is not included, providing ways of reconstructing or supplementing such information outside the visualization, allowing the reader to recognize and track any transformations, simplifications or abstractions of the information provided (whether before or during the reader's interaction with the visualization).

Among the varying sets of concrete criteria that have been proposed to guide the design or evaluation of visualization, the functional approach taken by Miksch and Aigner (2014) is among the most integrative and well suited to the purposes of CDS. It posits a triangle of concerns: data, users, and tasks. These are related to each other in functional terms by the criteria or qualities of (a) *expressiveness*, (b) *effectiveness*, and (c) *appropriateness*. The quality of expressiveness depends on showing no more or less than the information required for the intended task(s), based on computational or other analyses of the data. Linking data and users, effectiveness is focused on the degree to which a particular visualization manages to exploit the cognitive capabilities of the human visual system to provide intuitively recognizable and interpretable visual representations ('automatic processing', see above). Finally, appropriateness refers to the benefits/drawbacks of using a particular visualization—rather than text, numbers, etc.—to represent the data, specifically with respect to achieving the intended task(s) (Fig. 6.1).

These relations translate into questions that can guide the design process, e.g. 'Who are the intended users of the visualization?', 'What are the characteristics of the data?', 'What kinds of data do these users usu-

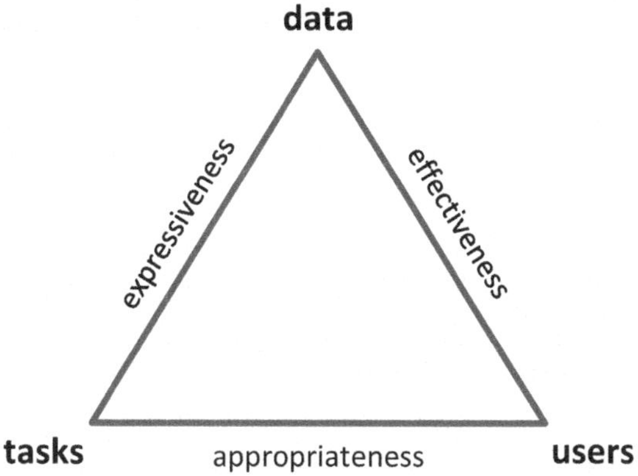

Fig. 6.1 Interactive visual analytics (Miksch and Aigner 2014, 286) (Note that Miksch and Aigner [2014] situate their work in the field of Visual Analytics [or VA], taking a view that strongly emphasizes the aim of visualizations to aid the information discovery process from large volumes of complex and heterogeneous data or information)

ally work with?' and 'Which tasks will the users need or want to perform on the data?' (Miksch and Aigner 2014, 286). As several of these points depend on characterizing *datasets* and *tasks*, typologies for both have been developed (e.g. Shneiderman 1996; Brehmer and Munzner 2013; Schulz et al. 2013). A widely accepted distinction defines datasets and their internal relations as *lists*, *clusters* or *sets* (containing items), as *tables* (items, attributes), *networks* or *trees* (items/nodes, links, attributes), *fields* (grids, positions, attributes) or *geometry* (items, positions) (Munzner 2015, 20).

In the case of linguistic data, this formal typology has to accommodate the more specific types of written and spoken data. Beyond text extracts and computed quantitative data, such as frequency or dispersion, linguistic data might include related extra-textual data or metadata (e.g. time or place) as well as manifold linguistic annotations (categorizations, e.g. genre; analytically imposed hierarchies, e.g. the compositional structure of linguistic units; relational data, e.g. the strength of collocational association between words; parallel layered data, e.g. parts-of-speech categories). In short, visualization in CDS will frequently involve multiple data layers

(Lyding and Culy 2012), indicating a need for interactive, manipulable visualizations.

For tasks, although typologies vary, core distinctions include tasks such as *present, explore subsets/examples, find similarities/differences, visualize parameter distributions, visualize parameter variations, visualize outliers, gain overview, find relations/correlations*, and *search for features* (Schulz et al. 2013). Other task taxonomies distinguish actions such as *focusing on a region of interest, highlighting/encoding individual items or regions* (e.g. by color or size), *tagging or grouping elements into clusters or categories, reconfiguring items into a different arrangement, comparing items or groups by visually juxtaposing them, gaining an overview, monitoring to observe changes over time, showing more or less detail*, and *uncertainty tackling by visualizing uncertainty in data* (Kucher and Kerren 2015, 119; Penn et al. 2009, 269–73). Other typologies distinguish tasks along in terms of three broad *goals* (*consume*, i.e. present, discover, generate, verify, enjoy; *search*, i.e. look up, browse, locate, explore; and *query*: identify, compare, summarize) and, separately, *actions* (i.e. select, navigate, arrange, change, filter, and aggregate) (based on Brehmer and Munzner 2013, 2382).

6.4 The Role of Visualization

Anthony (2018), virtually the only and certainly the most up-to-date publication on visualization in Discourse Studies, defines data visualization as "an automatically generated visual representation of real or simulated non-visual data that communicates information about that underlying data in a readable and recognizable way". He thus distinguishes data visualization categorically from diagrams (graphics that explain arrangements, relations or operations) and infographics (which represent and explain relations in "visually striking and often persuasive manner"), both of which Anthony defines as "created manually, perhaps aided by a computer" (199). The key distinction to Anthony, then, is not so much the type of data or the visualization but the relation between the data and the visualization, and the automatic/manual process of transforming the former into the latter. The observation that changing diagrams or infographics that were created manually in order to represent different data "usually" involves much

Table 6.1 A segregated view of visualization (based on Lengler and Eppler, n.d.)

Data visualization	Visual representation of (mostly) quantitative data in schematic form
Information visualization	The use of interactive visual representations of data to amplify cognition data is transformed into an image, it is mapped to screen space the image can be changed by users as they proceed working with it
Concept visualization	Methods to elaborate (mostly) qualitative concepts, ideas, plans, and analysis
Strategy visualization	Use of visuals in the analysis, development, formulation, communication and implementation of strategies
Metaphor visualization	Visual metaphors position information graphically to organize and structure information; convey insights about the represented information through the key characteristics of the metaphor employed
Compound visualization	Complementary use of different graphic representation formats in one single schema or frame

work, whereas automatically generated graphics are easily recreated for different data (Anthony 2018, 199), thus becomes the cornerstone of his narrow definition of data visualization.

Given the wider perspective introduced in the previous section, I would argue against such a narrow definition of 'data visualization' or 'visualization of linguistic data'. As all visualization imposes not only types of visualization but also categories, in this case linguistic or discourse-analytical categories, visualization is not merely a tool for displaying results but a tool for analysis—and can even the visualize the analytical process itself. In other words, the kind of data visualized is never entirely 'raw' in the first place, and it can—and should—also include information generated explicitly through analysis, e.g. results, intermediate steps, and analytical abstractions based on data. Such a broad understanding of visualization encompasses all of the sometimes segregated fields of visualization (see Table 6.1). More importantly, it also corresponds to the aim of making Discourse Studies more accessible. And it abandons the positivist pretense that visualization can somehow make data accessible in an immediate and raw fashion, that is, without transforming it by imposing the analyst's view. In this sense, visualization should always be seen as, and should acknowledge that it is, an analytical and interpretative tool.

From a more general perspective, many of the tasks identified as achievable through visualization are elements of analytical processes in CDS, such as recognizing structure, patterns, rules or constraints. It follows that visualization can be used as a tool, and may even prove to be "an indispensable tool" (Godfrey et al. 2016, 214) at various steps of analysis: during initial exploration, hypothesis generation, categorization, contrastive or longitudinal analysis, and finally the presentation of discovery.

6.5 Established Forms of Visualization

Despite the importance of understanding the affordances of human visual perception and cognition, and despite the value of establishing general criteria, in practice those designing visualizations will often look towards well established forms of visual representation first. In relation to these more general considerations, of course, each of these forms has its advantages and disadvantages. In other words, established forms or types are suitable for specific types of data, data relations, and aims. While this chapter cannot hope to provide an exhaustive catalogue of types of visualization (but see Lengler and Eppler, n.d.; Tory and Moller 2004), the following presents an overview of forms that can be useful in CDS.

The following alphabetical list follows common practice in naming types of visualization but also gives alternative labels. It also contains some suggestions as to what type of CDS-related information they might be used for.

- Arc diagrams *visualize connections and relationships between multiple items; usually limited to one type of relationship (e.g. between social actors as represented in discourse).*
- Area graphs (also area charts) *are a variant of line graphs that displays multiple lines, colors the area between axis and lines, and may either "overlap" or "stack" these lines so that quantities are added to show proportional*

values (e.g. different variants of a lexical item as individual lines, adding up to a total number) as changing over a period of time.

- Bar charts (also stacked bars, stacked-to-grouped bars) *to indicate quantities, proportions, and developments and facilitate comparisons (e.g. between lexical items, frequencies in different time periods or datasets).*
- Box plots *visualize groups of numerical data through quartiles or ordinal scales, can also include "whiskers" to indicate variability; allow quick comparison of distributions between several datasets (e.g. discourses, media, corpora).*
- Bubble charts *display three dimensions of data, with each "bubble" representing a triplet of linked data points, two through its location on the grid (e.g. time and place) and one through its size (e.g. word frequency); optionally, color or labeling can encode a fourth dimension (e.g. social actor, discourse level).*
- Cartograms (also Dorling cartograms) *map some geographically coded information onto an actual map of, e.g. a country or continent, thus displaying geographical distribution (e.g. of words forms, dialects); may distort the actual dimension of the geographical regions to indicate the relative weight or frequency of the information mapped onto it.*
- Chord diagrams *display multiple interrelationships between multiple items, effectively visualizing a matrix, typically in a radial layout (unlike the arc diagram).*
- Circle packing (also circular treemaps) *displays hierarchical relationships by representing each level in the hierarchy as containment in one circle; what would be branch in a tree is thus represented as one circle; circle size and color can encode additional dimensions of information (e.g. discursive strategies, functions, lexical items and their frequencies).*
- Dendograms (also treemaps) *display hierarchical relationships and can use various formats, ranging from the technical to the biological, to show hierarchical clustering of items.*
- Edge bundling (also hierarchical edge bundling) *displays connections between items of hierarchical networks (e.g. groups of social actors, types of media or discourses).*
- Heatmaps (also shading matrices) *display data by encoding the individual values are represented as colors according to a pre-determined color*

scheme, e.g. from "cold" blue to "hot" red (e.g. frequencies of lexical items or collocations).

- Line charts (also line graphs) *display a series of data points connected by straight lines; often used to present changes over time or time segments (e.g. grouped by year/month/week), where different segmentations may give a very different impression of peaks/spikes (Anthony* 2018*) in the data (e.g. of the number of articles containing a search term).*
- Matrices *are visualizations (like tables) only insofar as they spatially arrange data so as to indicate correspondences.*
- Networks (also graphs and force-directed graphs) *show networks, i.e. items in a group and the relationships between them; the number, type or strength of the relationships can be also be encoded* (as done, e.g. in Social Network Analysis; besides increasingly popular collocation networks, adaptations for sociolinguistics and discourse studies have been suggested by De Liddo et al. 2011).
- Sankey diagrams (also alluvial diagrams) *are a type of flow diagram that visualize changes in quantity, category or quality (e.g. voter migration, change of rhetorical strategies or lexical items) between two or more points in time.*
- Scatter plots (also scatter graphs, scatter charts or scatter diagrams) *display data points, usually containing two values, along Cartesian coordinates (e.g. time and number/frequency of linguistic items, articles published) (for scatter plots and linguistic data, see Kessler* 2017*).*
- Stream graphs *are a type of stacked area graph displaced around a central axis, resulting in a flowing, organic shape.*
- Treemaps (also trees, radial trees, node-link trees) *display hierarchical information as a set of nested shapes, typically rectangles or tree branches, where size may indicate weight and color usually indicates a group or subgroup in the hierarchy (e.g. discursive strategies and rhetorical/ linguistic realizations, functions, lexical items and their frequencies).*

6.6 Visualizations of Linguistic/Discourse Data

Regarding the question of how visualization can benefit CDS, we must keep in mind that this concerns information not only about language (linguistic data) but about other modes of meaning making as well as time, place, sociodemographic variables etc. Inasmuch as these data are quantified or quantifiable, the distinction may not affect the type of visualization that can be useful; this changes, however, if we consider qualitative and conceptual information as well. Relevant as it is to these considerations, Linguistic Information Visualization or LInfoVis—defined as the application of information visualization to language and its use (Lyding and Culy 2012)—may thus not fully correspond to the interests of CDS.

That said, the debate on how language can be visualized—other than graphemically—is highly relevant to CDS. Visualizing language has its specific challenges, as Penn et al. (2009) point out, but LInfoVis also inherits many of the common challenges of visualization: occlusion through overlapping items (the issue of 'screen real estate'), the difficulty of choosing appropriate visual variables for mapping information onto two-dimensional space, issues of color differentiation and perception, maintaining consistency within one or multiple visualizations in the same text ('graphical integrity'), and beyond that usability for interactive visualizations. Specific challenges for visualizing language include graphemical representations, both individual lexical items and text excerpts, insofar as text readability depends on size, orientation, font, and cluttering—more so than with non-linguistic items (Penn et al. 2009, 329). Of all challenges, the issues of visual scalability and limited screen real estate have likely been the strongest factor in forcing a divide between the visualization of qualitative and quantitative data, resulting in a strong bias towards the latter: Data, as Godfrey et al. (2016, 214) point out, has to be compacted before visualization techniques can be applied, because space is always limited—both on screen and on the page. Data that can be reduced to numerical values while still 'representing' the raw data is thus easier to visualize than data that cannot; compacting qualitative data must take different routes: abstraction, categorization, exemplification, etc.

On the practical side of the issue, particularly regarding quantitative data, researchers in CDS can draw on an increasing number of software options for visualization. These range from ready-made suites for generating a particular type of visualization, which emphasize ease-of-use, to bare programming languages like R (Gries 2013), Ajax, Java or javascript distributions such as D3.js (Bostock 2017; Bostock et al. 2011). The advantage of coding one's own visualizations from the bottom up is that each aspect of the visualization to be designed can be modified and controlled (e.g. axis scaling or transparency, coloring, and size of visual objects), but acquiring familiarity with a programming language takes considerable time and effort. Custom-built visualizations, which would be the forte of programming languages like R, also have the potential disadvantage of not being immediately recognizable (Anthony 2018, 206), simply because they do not conform to one of the common types outlined above.

More specialized data visualization software packages like Tableau (e.g. Dancy-Scott et al. 2018), Infogram, Chartblocks, Datawrapper, Plotly or RAW (Fahad and Yahya 2018) may offer an alternative to bare-bones programming. To many, however, more readily available (and already purchased) software like Libre Calc or Microsoft Office (specifically as integrated in Excel, more limited in Word or PowerPoint) will be the first plausible point of contact with visualization. These tools offer a limited degree of control over visual parameters but integrate most of the well-established forms of visualization discussed above.

Given the notable bias of existent forms of visualization towards quantitative data—which for CDS suggests that studies that integrate some tools of CL may be more open to visualization—it is likely that the CL software already used for analysis is able to generate some types of visualization. Corpus-based and, more specifically, corpus-driven studies, which emphasize the hypothesis-free exploration of data, can benefit strongly from visualization at the exploratory stage of analysis (Culy and Lyding 2010, 258). Both AntConc and WordSmith can generate bar code dispersion plots and kwic concordance displays. The online tools associated with corpus.byu.edu can generate time-series graphs and heat maps to visualize search results (Davies 2018). In addition, there are also dedicated visualization tools that can be easily combined with corpus tools, such as Cone (Gullick 2010) or GraphColl (Brezina et al. 2015), both standalone tools for creating collocation networks. Designed to represent multidimensional corpus data using a two-dimensional display, the tool Parallel Coordinates and its offshoot, Structured Parallel Coordinates (Culy et al. 2011), place data on vertical axes, lining them up horizontally. Each axis is assigned a different dimension of data (to be determined) and can express either categorical or numerical data. The data points are thus mapped onto different axes are visually connected by colored lines. While these tools include a number of interactive features, e.g. adjusting scales, highlighting parts of the data or selecting a part of an axis (Lyding et al. 2012, 45–47), they are not intuitive.

Finally, there are purpose-built visualization tools for the analysis of multimodal or visual data in discourse analysis, such as Kaleidographic (Bednarek and Caple 2017), which not only allows the input of (pre-categorized) data but also its manipulation over time through a "play" function, and the SIDGrid infrastructure for annotating, archiving, and analyzing multi-modal, multi-measure time series data (Levow et al. 2006, 2007).

As O'Halloran et al. (2011, 109) point out, multimodal CDS may be a particularly fertile context for developing and using interactive software—including visualization techniques—because such tools facilitate something that is integral to the multimodal perspective: the application, exploration, and correlation of various analytical perspectives and/or different levels of analysis. However, that same argument can easily be extended to other strands of CDS in terms of triangulation: Where visualization in general, and interactive visualization in particular, affords additional perspectives or facilitates access to additional perspectives, it can aid triangulation for researchers as well as readers. In fact, it can open up the research process to the reader.

Beyond professional and strongly computer-driven tools for visualization, there are, of course, the singular and purpose-built visualizations that researchers have devised to visualize a particular dataset, result, model or concept. While these would all fall outside of Anthony's (2018) narrow definition of visualization, dismissing them would impoverish our view of visualization in CDS and certainly cut off creative potential. Take, for instance the "discursive map" produced by Dekker Linnros and Hallin (2001, 393) to visualize the environmentalist discourse on the Öresund bridge. It is, at heart, a network of "story-lines" (and subordinated arguments) that uses spatial distribution and non-directed links to map the interrelationships between individual data points identified in their qualitative analysis. Three story-lines converge to support the claim that the Öresund link is a "threat to fertile earth", i.e. that of (1) regional inequality, (2) fertile earth, and (3) lack of knowledge. Each of these is broken down into smaller narratives (what others might identify as topoi), which are themselves interlinked to show parallelism (e.g. between "exploitation of gravel", "exploitation of water", and "exploitation of fertile earth") as well as hierarchy (e.g. all of the former are linked to "limited natural resources") as well as non-directional associations (e.g. the former is linked to "population growth"). This creates a dense map of analytical abstractions, which meets key criteria of visualization to facilitate, on the cognitive side, automatic processing and provides an overview while also indicating patterns. Technically, it is little more than spatially distributed phrases and linking lines, but it is nevertheless a productive visualization. As such, it certainly has its shortcomings, but these are due neither to the absence of quantitative data nor to its improvised graphics. The non-directionality of the links raises questions as to the conceptual status of the relationships. The descriptive text describes this as a form of development: "From this discursive core, different themes or story-lines have developed" and goes on to add a diachronic dimension: "Some of these have remained unchanged over the years, while others have been excluded, toned down or incorporated in the discourse". The paper does not analyze this in more detail, thus leaving the visualization partially unelaborated.

Another example of a custom-made visualization without any automatic or quantitative elements is Marshall et al.'s (2014) visualization of how discourses of masculinity in portrayals of fatherhood have developed between 1950 and 2010. The figure is framed top and bottom by two arrows, running from left to right, that indicate the timescale as well as the change from "provider to invisible presence" and a general "fragmentation of stable cultural scripts". In between, the visualization indicates a change (a) from hegemonic masculinity to hegemonic hybrid or multiple masculinities and (b) an opening up of the breadwinner and provider role towards a nurturing and caring, emotionally engaged, and responsible and accessible father. This "opening-up" is visualized as a triangle

Fig. 6.2 Border-related terminology in mediatized politics 2015–2016 (Rheindorf and Wodak 2018, 27)

with its narrow point in 1950 and its broader base in 2010. Clearly, the spatial arrangement of elements is the most important aspect of this visualization; the arrows certainly support expressing the directionality of the development, as does the triangle element. However, the opportunities for automatic processing are minimal in this case.

Take, as a final example, the following manual visualization of border-related terminology (nouns only) as used in mediatized politics during the so-called refugee crisis of 2015–2016 (Rheindorf and Wodak 2018). This particular dataset was used because it captured the over-lexicalization of the semantic field that occurred when Austrian politicians tried to euphemize the closing of borders, to be achieved through the building of fences or walls. And it was chosen for visualization because the terms semantically relate to space as bordered, i.e. space as divided into an inside and outside by the border, stopping or allowing flows etc. As this is an abstract space—i.e. not an actual location or region, but rather 'the Austrian border'—the area graph in Fig. 6.2 does not use a geographical map of Austria but an abstract representation of bordered space. Informed by theories on the social construction of borders, this space was divided into four regions:

the 'inside' defined by the border, the 'outside' defined by the border, the 'border' as a barrier against threatening movements, and 'openings' in that barrier as well as 'controlled movements' associated with such openings. The lexical items identified through CL methods were then mapped onto the respective regions randomly. The size of their lettering encodes their frequency in the corpus (similar to a word bubble), but the stark differences between frequencies would either have led to illegible lettering for the less frequent terms or have forced us to set a cut-off point, thus limiting the data that could be visualized. To circumvent this issue, we mapped the frequencies to an incremental scale, ensuring that even low-frequency items would be legible. Clearly, this compromise is only tenable if the actual frequencies are presented or made retrievable for the reader.

6.7 Interactive Visualization

Static or non-interactive visualizations face some limitations that are becoming painfully obvious in the age of digital media and online publishing. They can offer only pre-composed "views" of data, often necessitating multiple static visuals to present the desired variety of perspectives on or arrangements of the same information. They are also limited with respect to the number of data dimensions that can be presented simultaneously, on the two-dimensional surface, again requiring multiple visuals. Interactive visualizations promise to overcome these limitations, if not categorically, than at least by mitigation. The immediate benefit for the research context, then, is that interactive visualization can empower readers/viewers to explore the data for themselves (Murray 2013). To some, this is tantamount to a fundamental change of how researchers approach and understand data (Card et al. 2007). The wider promise in the context of the Digital Humanities, however, is that such interactive visualization will be key to assuring digital access to cultural heritage in general and to textual cultural heritage in particular (Therón et al. 2014, 153; Terras et al. 2016).

Like visualization as such, interactive visualization is perhaps easiest applied to CDS approaches that integrate CL methods or other quantitative methods (Therón et al. 2014, 154). First, these are more likely to be already familiar with some form of visualization; second, many forms of visualization are built to display quantitative information; third, many corpus-analytic tools and online corpora integrate not only visualizations but interactive visualizations. While corpus-related visualization was long focused on presenting search results (Culy and Lyding 2010), interactivity now increasingly supports exploratory tasks. While standalone corpus analysis tools such as AntConc and WordSmith include interactive visualizations which can be used by the individual researcher, e.g. in the form of interactive dispersion plots or heatmaps, these cannot be shared or published.

Of the tools that are designed for both researcher and audience, the majority seems to operate on the word level, i.e. word semantics, collocations, etc. Examples include DocuBurst (Collins 2007), a tool that visualizes semantic information of document content at the lexical level in a preset format: a radial, space-filling layout that allows the interactive tasks of zoom, filter, and details-on-demand. The so-called Word Trees (Wattenberg and Viegas 2008) is a technique for the visualization and interactive exploration of keyword in context lines displayed as tree structures. Despite their potential, such interactive visualizations often fall short on the scientific side, i.e. they lack a linguistic foundation. As Culy and Lyding (2010, 259) point out, Word Trees does not, in fact, use any kind of the linguistic categorization, annotation or analysis (e.g. part-of-speech tagging to distinguish homographs).

A smaller number of tools are built on a solid analytic basis and integrate more functionality. This includes the commercial data-mining suite Leximancer, which visualizes "high level concepts" from text collections, displaying their conceptual relation, frequency, and intra-textual context (Leximancer Pty Ltd. 2018). It displays multiple views or perspectives simultaneously in a "dashboard" format (Atapattu and Falkner 2016), integrating several interlinked "windows" that display specific but interrelated information. In contrast, text structures—although amenable to visualization (e.g. the dependency trees used in Rhetorical Structure Theory or RST; see, e.g., Mann 2018)—have so far rarely been represented in interactive visualizations.

Similarly using a dashboard concept to integrate different levels of abstraction into a single screen, DAViewer might be described as a "discourse parser" or "visualization system" for discourse structure (in the sense of RST). In terms of its design, it is both singular and exemplary: It offers multiple visual forms of representation of the structure trees, i.e. as (a) icicle plot, (b) dendrogram, (c) vertical compact view, and (d) horizontal compact view. Moreover, the dashboard's individual panels interrelate and are mutually complementary. Panel (1) shows an overview of statistics about the respective dataset; panel (2) shows in detail the full structure as the result of the analysis; panel (3) shows the basic properties of the currently selected data; panel (4) allows the user to annotate the data and edit notes; panel (5) shows the content of the active document as parsed; and panel (6) provides a search option for querying keywords and structures for the data displayed in the second panel. The panels are connected not just by providing different views and tools for the analysis but through interactive elements: selecting a tree in the analysis panel also brings up the corresponding text (Zhao et al. 2012).

The frontend interfaces of online corpora, too, have increasingly integrated interactive visualizations—what McEnery and Hardie (2012) refer to as "fourth-generation" corpus analysis tools. One particularly popular form is the "word cloud" enhanced with a simple "select and display" function, linking either to concordances of the selected item or more detailed analytical results (e.g. DWDS, Berlin-Brandenburgische Akademie der Wissenschaften 2018).

Although the notion of "tasks" in the context of visualization denotes any perceptual or related action open to the reader and is thus not necessarily predicated on interactivity, the majority of the tasks outlined in Sect. 6.3 are greatly enhanced through interactivity—and some are made possible only by a manipulable medium. Indeed, this matches the core definition of Visual Analytics as combining the intuition of human readers with the processing power of computers, the "external cognition" facilitated by visualization, and interactive environments that afford a variety of tasks (Keim et al. 2008). In terms of interaction techniques, many tasks involve a form of selection (Lyding and Culy 2012), which may trigger different responses such as highlighting, zooming or displaying additional information.

With interactivity, general concerns of user-friendliness or usability also become relevant (McEnery and Hardie 2012), taking the technical criteria and expertise required well beyond visualization as such. Unless existing tools are used to create them within the pre-defined limits of templates, i.e. corresponding to established forms of visualization with known strengths and suitability (see Sect. 6.5), interdisciplinary collaboration between discourse analysts and DataVis, InfoVis or Visual Analytics specialists thus seems the best approach to exploring interactive visualization in CDS. Existing interactive visualizations of linguistic or discourse data are not only rare, they often also fall short of offering or integrating multiple perspectives onto the data, e.g. lexical and structural levels of text, qualitative and quantitative results, or descriptive, explanatory, and critical perspectives. However, the 'dashboard' concept as exemplified by software like Leximancer or DAViewer seems ideally suited to integrating multiple views of the same data, be they different levels of data (e.g. corpus, text, lexis) or levels of analytical abstraction (e.g. contextual information, discourse macro-topics, keyword spread, argumentation patterns, collocation patterns). Since not all levels can ever be displayed simultaneously, the dashboard design would either have to carefully select which parts of the data are crucial and help to mutually inform each other (Culy and Lyding 2010) or to offer the user the option to select and modify which information is displayed in which window.

It is worth pointing out that the interactive transition between perspectives within the same visualization space (e.g. Vivid D 2014), but even more so the parallel display of perspectives within a dashboard, can realize for the reader what analytical tools began to deliver to researchers in the 1990s. It can maintain the link between different levels of abstraction, e.g. between an individual instance of communication and patterns of language use characterizing a community of speakers (Tognini-Bonelli 2004, 11); it can equally maintain the integrity of texts by linking different levels of abstraction, e.g. excerpts to full-text displays or audio recordings and frequency information based on the transcript corpus, and it offers a way of breaching the barrier between quantitative and qualitative perspectives on the same data (Wegerif and Mercer 1997, 277).

From a design perspective, intuitive interaction with the visualization itself is preferable to interaction via menus or buttons, where possible. In particular, interactive tasks like *rearrange*, *select*, *highlight*, *tag*, and *group* are best linked to the relevant items within the visualization space itself via click or drag-and-drop actions. In such cases, care must be taken to avoid occlusion issues resulting from the user's interaction with the visualization space, e.g. through creating repulsion- and attraction-like effects between elements as seen in force-directed graphs (e.g. d3noob 2015).

6.8 Visualization, Open Data and Open Science

With respect to triangulation, visualization as a different mode than text-based descriptions, explanations or discussions does not simply offer another form of representing information, it exploits different cognitive and perceptual capabilities. Interactivity adds to this the ability to switch, combine, and integrate perspectives—which can be defined as different layers of data, levels of abstractions, sequential steps of analysis, or even alternative versions of categorization systems. I would argue that, while none of this takes power or authority away from the researcher, it does shift the relationship and interaction between researcher/writer and reader/user. More specifically, it has the potential to open up the research space to the reader/user and connects visualization to the aims and strategies of Open Science initiatives, including Open Data and Open Access (e.g. Bartling and Friesike 2013).

There is, to date, no clear or coherent agenda in any strands of CDS to embrace Open Science, even though some of its principles are shared by critical approaches to discourse analysis. The openness of the research process and accessibility of results, in particular, relate to the fourth step of critique, *political action*, as defined by Fairclough (2018), the research-based *interventions* advocated by Reisigl and Wodak's (2015) and Reisigl's (2017) conception of *prospective critique* as application-oriented and practical action. These are not defined as academics-designed measures carried out in the field or implemented top-down, but as active engagement with social actors as part of the research program. They are, however, in each case, defined as the final step of the research process and thus confine "openness" to a late stage, when most of the groundwork and analysis has already been done. In this, they differ from the bottom-up approach of citizen science programs, which seek to involve members of the public at an early stage of the research process.

The use of visualization in CDS relates to Open Science at the very least in terms of data transparency: Ensuring links between publications, specifically visualizations, and underlying data, would meet a core demand of Open Science (Foster 2018). A second, related aspect is the use of open data repositories, ideally institutional repositories that can safeguard the long-term preservation and integrity of the data (re3data 2018; Strasser 2015). In many studies, this particular point will require rigorous anonymization of elicited data (e.g. interviews) and may prove problematic regarding copyright issues (e.g. newspaper or media texts), which still leaves the option of publishing metadata (e.g. data type, quantities, time, place) and various analytical abstractions (e.g. categorizations, results from different stages of analysis). A third aspect relates to the use of open-source software and open interfaces (Foster 2018), which already seems feasible if still limited with respect to software for visualization as such and for creating and publishing interactive visualizations on the web (D3.js being a prime example, see Bostock et al. 2011). Fourth, as indicated above, interactive visualization can open up the research process not only in the sense of transparency and allowing alternative views that would be excluded, if only for reasons of space, from a written account; it can allow the reader/user to *view*, *rearrange*, and thereby *explore* the data on their own.

6.9 Research Design and Research Practice

Although some literature on visualizations starts from the premises that only quantitative data can be visualized and that only fully automatic visualization is effective, the wide field of CDS offers an equally wide range of opportunities for visualization that meet its core criteria: exploiting perceptual and cognitive capabilities to provide overviews, alternative views, reveal patterns and discover abstractions. This holds true for both qualitative data and more or less manually created visualizations, offering options beyond well-established forms of visual representation. In some cases, these forms will be a good starting point for researchers in CDS to experiment with visualization, particularly of quantifiable data; in other cases, a more open and creative approach to visualization will be required, particularly for concepts, models, metaphors and high-level abstractions of a more theoretical nature (e.g. field-structure, interrelated levels of discourse, and processes of normalization).

Different considerations apply to interactive visualization insofar as the minimum level of additional expertise required is different: It is relatively easy to use standard software to create a line graph, but freely designing interactive visualizations requires programming skills. Some specialized software eliminates this by offering pre-set forms, and a specialized JavaScript distribution like D3.js can significantly reduce the effort and learning curve. The fact remains, however, that interactive visualizations will typically call for collaboration with specialists in the fields of DataVis, InfoVis or Visual Analytics. As this may require not only involve planning and collaboration but funding, and should be seen as part of the research process—possibly even an early stage, such as data exploration, rather than as an element of publishing final results, it is critical that some thought be given to visualization strategies early on.

In planning and designing (interactive) visualization as part of our research, we should therefore:

- consider the options for (interactive) visualizations with respect to the dataset(s) and data type(s) involved in the research,
- consider the role visualization might play for the research process and at what stage,
- decide which levels of abstraction and/or analysis might be amenable for visualization, in which combination, and for which target audience,
- such considerations should include possible benefits such as (a) maintaining links between levels of abstraction, methods, data, and results, (b) maintaining the integrity of the text, (c) giving an overview, (d) providing alternative perspectives, (e) allowing the reader/user to perform specific tasks, some of which may require interaction techniques,
- ensure a match between data, audience, and tasks in terms of appropriateness, expressiveness, and effectiveness,
- decide on the basic composition and components of the visualization, if interactive, e.g. individual but manipulable views, multiple sequential

views to be selected and individually displayed, or multiple simultaneous views in a dashboard or picture-in-picture format,
- decide on a strategy for data transparency with respect to the planned visualizations,
- decide anonymization and copyright issues with respect to publishing data and/or metadata as part of or in conjunction with the visualizations,
- decide on a data repository, where applicable, for publishing data and/or metadata related to the visualizations,
- consider the technical options presented by existing software and the level of expertise required for using them,
- decide on whether to design and implement the (interactive) visualizations on our own or in collaboration with specialists,
- decide on specific software tools for creating the (interactive) visualization,
- provide sufficient time and opportunity for testing and revising the visualization, especially if interactive, before publication.

References

Anthony, Laurence. 2018. "Visualisation in Corpus-Based Discourse Studies." In *Corpus Approaches to Discourse: A Critical Review*, edited by Charlotte Taylor and Anna Marchi. 1st ed., 197–224. Oxon and New York: Routledge. https://doi.org/10.4324/9781315179346.

Atapattu, Thushari, and Katrina Falkner. 2016. "A Framework for Topic Generation and Labeling from MOOC Discussions." *MOOC Discourse Analysis* (blog). https://blogs.adelaide.edu.au/cser/mooc-discourse-analysis/.

Bartling, Sönke, and Sascha Friesike, eds. 2013. *Opening Science: The Evolving Guide on How the Web Is Changing Research, Collaboration and Scholarly Publishing*. Heidelberg: SpringerOpen.

Bednarek, Monika, and Helen Caple. 2017. "Introducing a New Topology for (Multimodal) Discourse Analysis." In *Transforming Contexts: Papers from the 44th International Systemic Functional Congress*, edited by Phil Chappell and John S. Knox, 19–25. Wollongong: 44th ISFC Organising Committee.

Berlin-Brandenburgische Akademie der Wissenschaften. 2018. "DWDS. Digitales Wörterbuch Der Deutschen Sprache. Das Wortauskunftssystem Zur Deutschen Sprache in Geshichte Und Gegenwart." https://www.dwds.de/.

Bertin, Jacques. 1967. *Sémiologie Graphique: Les Diagrammes, Les Réseaux, Les Cartes.* Paris: Gauthier-Villars.

Bostock, Michael. 2017. "Data-Driven Documents." https://d3js.org/.

Bostock, Michael, Vadim Ogievetsky, and Jeffrey Heer. 2011. "D^3 Data-Driven Documents." *IEEE Transactions on Visualization and Computer Graphics* 17 (12): 2301–9. https://doi.org/10.1109/TVCG.2011.185.

Brehmer, Matthew, and Tamara Munzner. 2013. "A Multi-level Typology of Abstract Visualization Tasks." *IEEE Transactions on Visualization and Computer Graphics* 19 (12): 2376–85. https://doi.org/10.1109/TVCG.2013.124.

Brezina, Vaclav, Tony McEnery, and Stephen Wattam. 2015. "Collocations in Context: A New Perspective on Collocation Networks." *International Journal of Corpus Linguistics* 20 (2): 139–73. https://doi.org/10.1075/ijcl.20.2.01bre.

Card, Stuart K., Jock D. Mackinlay, and Ben Shneiderman. 2007. *Readings in Information Visualization: Using Vision to Think.* Nachdr. The Morgan Kaufmann Series in Interactive Technologies. San Francisco, CA: Morgan Kaufmann.

Collins, Christopher. 2007. "Docuburst: Radial Space-Filling Visualization of Document Content." Knowledge Media Design Institute, Umiversity of Toronto, Technical Report KMDITR-2007-1.

Culy, Chris, and Verena Lyding. 2010. "Visualizations for Exploratory Corpus and Text Analysis." In *Proceedings of the 2nd International Conference on Corpus Linguistics, CILC-10, April 6–9, 2011, Coruña, Spain*, 257–68. Coruña: University Coruña.

———. 2011. "Corpus Clouds—Facilitating Text Analysis by Means of Visualizations." In *Human Language Technology: Challenges for Computer Science and Linguistics: 4th Language and Technology Conference, LTC 2009, Poznan, Poland, November 6–8, 2009*, edited by Zygmunt Vetulani, 351–60. Heidelberg: Springer.

Culy, Chris, Verena Lyding, and Henrik Dittman. 2011. "Structured Parallel Coordinates: A Visualization for Analyzing Structured Language Data." In *Proceedings of the 3rd International Conference on Corpus Linguistics, CILC-11, April 6–9, 2011, Valencia, Spain*, 485–93. Valencia: Universitat Politécnica de Valéncia.

d3noob. 2015. "Directional Force Layout Diagram with Varying Link Opacity." December 14. http://bl.ocks.org/d3noob/5155181.

Dancy-Scott, Nicole, Gale A. Dutcher, Alla Keselman, Colette Hochstein, Christina Copty, Diane Ben-Senia, Sampada Rajan, Maria Guadalupe Asencio, and Jason Jongwon Choi. 2018. "Trends in HIV Terminology: Text Mining and Data Visualization Assessment of International AIDS Conference Abstracts over 25 Years." *JMIR Public Health and Surveillance* 4 (2): e50. https://doi.org/10.2196/publichealth.8552.

Davies, Mark. 2018. "BYU-BNC: Based on the British National Corpus from Oxford University Press." https://corpus.byu.edu/bnc/.

Dekker Linnros, Hannah, and Per Olof Hallin. 2001. "The Discursive Nature of Environmental Conflicts: The Case of the Öresund Link." *Area* 33 (4): 391–403.

De Liddo, Anna, Simon Buckingham Shum, Ivana Quinto, Michelle Bachler, and Lorella Cannavacciuolo. 2011. "Discourse-Centric Learning Analytics." In *LAK '11: Proceedings of the 1st International Conference on Learning Analytics and Knowledge, February 27–March 1, 2011, Banff, Alberta, Canada*, 23–33. Association for Computing Machinery. http://dl.acm.org/citation.cfm?id=2090116.

Evergreen, Stephanie. 2016. "Updated Data Visualization Checklist." *Evergreen Data: Intentional Reporting & Data Visualization* (blog) (May). http://stephanieevergreen.com/wp-content/uploads/2016/10/DataVizChecklist_May2016.pdf.

Fahad, S. K. Ahammad, and Abdulsamad Ebrahim Yahya. 2018. "Big Data Visualization: Allotting by R and Python with GUI Tools." In *2018 International Conference on Smart Computing and Electronic Enterprise (ICSCEE)*, 1–8. Shah Alam: IEEE. https://doi.org/10.1109/ICSCEE.2018.8538413.

Fairclough, Norman. 2018. "CDA as Dialectical Reasoning: Critique, Explanation and Action." In *The Routledge Handbook of Critical Discourse Studies*, edited by John Flowerdew and John E. Richardson, 13–25. London: Routledge.

Few, Stephen. 2009. *Now You See It: Simple Visualization Techniques for Quantitative Analysis.* Oakland, CA: Analytics Press.

Foster. 2018. "Foster: The Future of Science Is Open." https://www.fosteropenscience.eu/.

Gabrielatos, Costas, and Paul Baker. 2008. "Fleeing, Sneaking, Flooding: A Corpus Analysis of Discursive Constructions of Refugees and Asylum Seekers in the UK Press, 1996–2005." *Journal of English Linguistics* 36 (1): 5–38. https://doi.org/10.1177/0075424207311247.

Godfrey, Parke, Jarek Gryz, and Piotr Lasek. 2016. "Interactive Visualization of Large Data Sets." *IEEE Transactions on Knowledge and Data Engineering* 28 (8): 2142–57. https://doi.org/10.1109/TKDE.2016.2557324.

Gullick, David. 2010. *Cone*. https://github.com/UCREL/collocation-network-explorer/.

Hagley, Jack. n.d. "What's the Difference Between an Infographic and a Data Visualisation?" https://www.jackhagley.com/What-s-the-difference-between-an-Infographic-and-a-Data-Visualisation.

Keim, Daniel A., Florian Mansmann, Jörn Schneidewind, Jim Thomas, and Hartmut Ziegler. 2008. "Visual Analytics: Scope and Challenges." In *Visual Data Mining*, edited by Simeon J. Simoff, Michael H. Böhlen, and Arturas Mazeika, 76–90. Berlin, Heidelberg: Springer. https://doi.org/10.1007/978-3-540-71080-6_6.

Kessler, Jason. 2017. "Scattertext: A Browser-Based Tool for Visualizing How Corpora Differ." In *Proceedings of ACL 2017, System Demonstrations*, 85–90. Vancouver, Canada: Association for Computational Linguistics. https://doi.org/10.18653/v1/P17-4015.

Knaflic, Cole Nussbaumer. 2015. *Storytelling with Data: A Data Visualization Guide for Business Professionals*. Hoboken, NJ: Wiley.

Kosara, Robert. 2007. "Visualization Criticism—The Missing Link Between Information Visualization and Art." In *2007 11th International Conference Information Visualization (IV '07)*, 631–36. Zurich, Switzerland: IEEE. https://doi.org/10.1109/IV.2007.130.

Kucher, Kostiantyn, and Andreas Kerren. 2015. "Text Visualization Techniques: Taxonomy, Visual Survey, and Community Insights." In *2015 IEEE Pacific Visualization Symposium (PacificVis 2015): Hangzhou, China, 14–17 April 2015*, edited by Shixia Liu, Gerik Scheuermann, and Shigeo Takahashi, 117–21. Piscataway, NJ: IEEE.

Lengler, Ralph, and Martin J. Eppler. n.d. "A Periodic Table of Visualization Methods: Version 1.5." Accessed December 11, 2018. http://www.visual-literacy.org/periodic_table/periodic_table.html.

Levow, Gina-Anne, Susan Duncan, and David McNeill. 2006. "Multi Modal Discourse Investigation with SIDGrid." http://faculty.washington.edu/levow/papers/ATI.pdf.

Levow, Gina-Anne, Sonjia Waxmonsky, Bennett Bertenthal, David McNeill, Mark Hereld, Sarah Kenny, and Michael E. Papka. 2007. "SIDGrid: A Framework for Distributed, Integrated Multimodal Annotation, Archiving, and Analysis." http://faculty.washington.edu/levow/papers/ATI.pdf.

Leximancer Pty Ltd. 2018. "Leximancer Manual: Version 2.23." https://info.leximancer.com/.

Lopez-Bigas. 2013. "Thread 4: Data Discovery, Transparency and Visualization." *Nature Genetics*, 45 (10) (October). https://doi.org/10.1038/ng.2789.

Lyding, Verena, and Chris Culy. 2012. "Visualizing Linguistic Data: From Principles to Toolkits for Doing It Yourself." Presented at the *AVML Conference*, York.

Lyding, Verena, Ekaterina Lapshinova-Koltunski, Stefania Degaetano-Ortlieb, Henrik Dittman, and Chris Culy. 2012. "Visualising Linguistic Evolution in Academic Discourse." In *Proceedings of the EACL 2012 Joint Workshop of LINGVIS & UNCLH, Avignon, France, April 23–23, 2012*, 44–48. Vancouver, Canada: Association for Computational Linguistics.

Mann, William C. 2018. "Rhetorical Structure Theory." http://www.sfu.ca/rst/.

Marshall, David, Teresa Davis, Margaret K. Hogg, Tanja Schneider, and Alan Petersen. 2014. "From Overt Provider to Invisible Presence: Discursive Shifts in Advertising Portrayals of the Father in *Good Housekeeping*, 1950–2010." *Journal of Marketing Management* 30 (15–16): 1654–79. https://doi.org/10.1080/0267257X.2014.945471.

Mayer, Thomas. 2013. "Interactive Visualizations of Linguistic Data." Conference presentation, Bochum, Germany, October 22. http://th-mayer.de/bochum2013/#/.

McEnery, Tony, and Andrew Hardie. 2012. *Corpus Linguistics: Methods, Theory and Practice.* Cambridge: Cambridge University Press. https://corpora.lancs.ac.uk/clmtp/answers.php?chapter=7&type=questions.

Miksch, Silvia, and Wolfgang Aigner. 2014. "A Matter of Time: Applying a Data–Users–Tasks Design Triangle to Visual Analytics of Time Oriented Data." *Computers & Graphics* 38 (February): 286–90. https://doi.org/10.1016/j.cag.2013.11.002.

Munzner, Tamara. 2015. *Visualization Analysis and Design.* A. K. Peters Visualization Series. Boca Raton: CRC Press, Taylor & Francis Group, CRC Press is an imprint of the Taylor & Francis Group, an informa business.

Murray, Scott. 2013. *Interactive Data Visualization for the Web.* 1st ed. Sebastopol, CA: O'Reilly Media.

Norman, Donald A. 2003. *Things That Make Us Smart: Defending Human Attributes in the Age of the Machine*, 16. Reading, MA: Perseus Books.

O'Halloran, Kay L., Sabine Tan, Bradley A. Smith, and Alexey Podlasov. 2011. "Multimodal Analysis Within an Interactive Software Environment: Critical Discourse Perspectives." *Critical Discourse Studies* 8 (2): 109–25. https://doi.org/10.1080/17405904.2011.558687.

Penn, Gerald, Sheelag Carpendale, and Christopher Collins. 2009. "Interactive Visualization for Computational Linguistics: Tutorial at ESSLLI-09." Tutorial presented at the ESSLLI-09. http://esslli2009.labri.fr/documents/carpendale_penn.pdf.

re3data. 2018. "Re3data.Org—Registry of Research Data Repositories." https://www.re3data.org/.

Reisigl, Martin. 2017. "The Discourse-Historical Approach." In *The Routledge Handbook of Critical Discourse Studies*, edited by John Flowerdew and John E. Richardson, 44–59. London: Routledge.

Reisigl, Martin, and Ruth Wodak. 2015. "The Discourse-Historical Approach (DHA)." In *Methods of Critical Discourse Studies*, edited by Ruth Wodak and Michael Meyer, 23–61. London: Sage.

Rheindorf, Markus, and Ruth Wodak. 2018. "Borders, Fences, and Limits—Protecting Austria from Refugees: Metadiscursive Negotiation of Meaning in the Current Refugee Crisis." *Journal of Immigrant & Refugee Studies* 16 (1–2): 15–38. https://doi.org/10.1080/15562948.2017.1302032.

Rogers, Yvonne. 2005. "New Theoretical Approaches for Human-Computer Interaction." *Annual Review of Information Science and Technology* 38 (1): 87–143. https://doi.org/10.1002/aris.1440380103.

Scaife, Mike, and Yvonne Rogers. 1996. "External Cognition: How Do Graphical Representations Work?" *International Journal of Human-Computer Studies* 45 (2): 185–213. https://doi.org/10.1006/ijhc.1996.0048.

Schulz, Hans-Jorg, Thomas Nocke, Magnus Heitzler, and Heidrun Schumann. 2013. "A Design Space of Visualization Tasks." *IEEE Transactions on Visualization and Computer Graphics* 19 (12): 2366–75. https://doi.org/10.1109/TVCG.2013.120.

Shneiderman, Ben. 1996. "The Eyes Have It: A Task by Data Type Taxonomy for Information Visualizations." In *Proceedings 1996 IEEE Symposium on Visual Languages*, 336–43. Boulder, CO: IEEE Computer Society Press. https://doi.org/10.1109/VL.1996.545307.

Strasser, Carly. 2015. "Research Data Management: A Primer." NISO: National Information Standards Organization. https://www.niso.org/publications/primer-research-data-management.

Teate, Renee. 2015. "Principles of Data Visualization for Exploratory Data Analysis." Presented at the *UVA SYS 6023 Cognitive Systems Engineering*. https://www.becomingadatascientist.com/wp-content/uploads/2015/05/Principles-of-Data-Visualization-for-Exploratory-Data-Analysis-ppt.pdf.

Terras, Melissa, Julianne Nyhan, and Edward Vanhoutte, eds. 2016. *Defining Digital Humanities a Reader*. London: Routledge.

Therón, Roberto, Carlos Seguín, Laura de la Cruz, and María Vaquero. 2014. "Highly Interactive and Natural User Interfaces: Enabling Visual Analysis in Historical Lexicography." In *Proceedings of the First International Conference on Digital Access to Textual Cultural Heritage—DATeCH '14*, 153–58. Madrid, Spain: ACM Press. https://doi.org/10.1145/2595188.2595215.

Tognini-Bonelli, Elena. 2004. "Working with Corpora: Issues and Insights." In *Applying English Grammar: Functional and Corpus Approaches*, edited by Caroline Coffin, Ann Hewings, and Kieran O'Halloran, 11–24. London: Arnold.

Tory, Melanie, and Torsten Möller. 2004. "Rethinking Visualization: A High-Level Taxonomy." In *IEEE Symposium on Information Visualization*, 151–58. Austin, TX: IEEE. https://doi.org/10.1109/INFVIS.2004.59.

Tufte, Edward R. 2001. *The Visual Display of Quantitative Information.* 2nd ed. Cheshire, CT: Graphics Press.

Vivid D. 2014. "Smooth Transitioning Between Tree, Cluster, Radial Tree, and Radial Cluster Layouts." June 1. http://jsfiddle.net/VividD/3TkJj/show.

Wattenberg, Martin, and Fernanda B. Viegas. 2008. "The Word Tree, an Interactive Visual Concordance." *IEEE Transactions on Visualization and Computer Graphics* 14 (6): 1221–8. https://doi.org/10.1109/TVCG.2008.172.

Wegerif, Rupert, and Neil Mercer. 1997. "Using Computer-Based Text Analysis to Integrate Qualitative and Quantitative Methods in Research on Collaborative Learning." *Language and Education* 11 (4): 271–86. https://doi.org/10.1080/09500789708666733.

Zhao, Jian, Fanny Chevalier, Cchristopher Collins, and Ravin Balakrishnan. 2012. "Facilitating Discourse Analysis with Interactive Visualization." *IEEE Transactions on Visualization and Computer Graphics* 18 (12): 2639–48. https://doi.org/10.1109/TVCG.2012.226.

7

Case Study 1: Retold Narratives of Holocaust Survivors and Their Children

7.1 Introduction: The Original Study

This case study revisits research on the narratives of Holocaust survivors as passed on and retold by their children, so-called intergenerational narratives (previously published, in part, in Wodak and Rheindorf 2017; Berger and Wodak 2018). More than 70 years after the end of World War 2, and despite the tremendous archiving efforts of institutions like the Survivors of the Shoah Visual History Foundation, the question of who and how to pass on and perpetuate the stories of survival, flight, and persecution told by survivors of the Holocaust is being asked with renewed urgency. Austria as a country to which very few of those persecuted ever returned, in large part because the state failed to encourage and facilitate such return, represents a special context for the study of such intergenerational narratives.

The original study was part of a larger research effort focused on the children of Viennese returnees who had been persecuted by the Nazis for, among other reasons, being Jewish and/or political dissidents. Their biographies differ greatly and reach well beyond Europe, including exile in France, Belgium, England, China, or the Soviet Union, joining the

© The Author(s) 2019

M. Rheindorf, *Revisiting the Toolbox of Discourse Studies*,
Postdisciplinary Studies in Discourse,
https://doi.org/10.1007/978-3-030-19369-0_7

international brigades in Spain, enlisting in one of the Allied Armies or the Jugoslav Freedom Battalion, imprisonment in concentration camps, and many other forms of resistance and persecution. Those who returned from exile after 1945 were not, as a rule, welcomed in Austria; the Austrian post-war consensus was not to discuss Nazi atrocities, not to acknowledge collective responsibility or guilt, and not to openly discuss the many stolen (i.e., Aryanized) homes, goods, or professional positions (Berger 2007; Knight 2000; Ziegler and Kannonier 1997).

The larger research project combined discourse analysis with psychological and historiographical perspectives. Data was collected in the form of family histories, photographs, and 39 semi-standardized biographical interviews with second-generation returnees. The interviews focused on their life stories, their relationships with their parents, and the stories they told about their political activism, the war, persecution, and the Holocaust. Part of the overall results was a general characterization of the group of interviewees, their shared experiences and differences: Some of the interviewees were born in Austria, some in exile. In some of these countries, they were relatively safe during their childhood, while in others (e.g., France) they survived the first years of their life in hiding and under false names. Some lived through a particularly grueling time, their communist parents falling victim to Stalinist terror in the Soviet Union or deportation to Siberia.

Most of the interviewees were born after 1945, many growing up without grandparents. While their childhood was in many ways characterized by social marginality, it was an intellectually privileged environment for most. They also share the experience that their parents saw themselves not so much as victims but as victors in the struggle against fascism. In that context, they also placed great hope in their children as carrying on that fight, shaping the future of the world. Such topics, grand as they may seem for childhood, were ubiquitous in their families, with friends, and with their wider social circles—especially the child and youth organizations in which most of the interviewees were also socialized. Most of them described their immediate environment's general stance on the traumatic past, i.e., persecution, imprisonment, resistance, years of war in Allied or underground armies, as one of silence. Such things were rarely if at all spoken about in the family or youth organizations. Indeed, this resem-

Table 7.1 Demographic details on interviewees

	No. of interviewees
Total	29
Male	19
Female	10
Jewish	20
Parent(s) fled into exile	20
Parent(s) imprisoned	15
Parent(s) active in the resistance	23
Born 1939–1944	14
Born 1945–1946	3
Born 1947–1953	12

bled the general postwar silence surrounding the narratives of the victims as well as the perpetrators (Schröter 2013; Wodak 2011), although, of course, the reasons for such silence varied significantly. To a large extent, they confirmed having carried on their parents' mission in their own way: Toward the end of the 1960s, almost everyone in the group was active in the student movement, many in leading roles. And although none of them entered party politics, they all became active, politically engaged members of civil society. For an overview of some demographic data of the interviewees, see Table 7.1.

The original discourse study analyzed the *narratives* told by these children of returnees, now aged between 60 and 75 themselves, about their parents' lives as well as their *framing* and *retelling* of the stories their parents had told them. In doing so, the original study pursued several questions related to the larger project: Does the marginal position of the returnees and their families in post-war Austria manifest linguistically in their narratives? Might those narratives be said to constitute a shared but group-specific discourse about the war, persecution, and the Holocaust? How does this group's discourse relate to and differ from Austria's mainstream, hegemonic discourses about the war, persecution, and the Holocaust? How do the children deal with and position themselves to their parents' narratives in their retelling? Are intergenerational traumata evident in these retold stories? To answer these questions, the original study used a combination of quantitative and qualitative methods in analyzing the interviews. The semi-structured interviews were conducted by experienced interviewers, recorded, and then transcribed in their entirety.

Conceptually, the focus on inter-generational narratives of Holocaust survivors required a more specific theoretical framework than general discourse theory. This framework combined theories on individual and collective memory, trauma, and narrative. Work in collective memory and story-telling has shown that the analysis of narratives (including narrative structures, linguistic patterns, the representation of actors and their actions) allows insight into socially grounded and shared "collective stories" (Heer et al. 2008). On the individual level, very personal, traumatic events are recounted, narrativized in particular ways, effectively placing fragmentary, incomprehensible events in a more coherent framework that is not simply individually but socially meaningful. In consequence, it has been noted, members of a social group with a shared past—irrespective of whether they know each other personally—use similar narratives or similar repertoires of narrative elements to give meaning to this past. In this sense, narratives relate to discourses as shared social practice of meaning-making, in this case making sense of the traumatic past of the parents' generation. Marginal as well as hegemonic histories alike are the result of a social process through which social groups decide which stories about past events can carry their values and perception of the world (Heer et al. 2008).

The history emerging from biographical interviews as a post-factum and meaning-infused narrative is thus always a construction, making this type of data an intriguing subject for CDS regarding the collective construction of history in discourse. Conceptually, collective memory can thus be approached as a collection of narratives that are significant for the historical trajectory of a specific group, giving the capacity to relive these shared memories on the occasion of rites, celebrations, and public festivities (Halbwachs 1992). Significantly, this applies to social groups of various sizes, ranging from transnational commemorative communities to nations, ethnic groups, and the family as a unit of social cohesion (e.g., Achugar 2016; De Fina 2003a; Welzer 2001; Keppler 1994).

The first analytical step was quantitative, using CL tools to identify semantic macrostructures in the interviews. Macrostructures, as defined by van Dijk (2009, 4–5), inform the global coherence of discourses in the sense of constituting the semantic basis for a range of pragmatic aspects such as implicit and explicit categorizations, tacit knowledge, conclusion rules, and narrative settings. While the semantic macrostructures of a single text can be reconstructed by qualitative analysis of same text (van Dijk 2009), corpus-linguistic analyses provide an alternative approach in the case of more extensive material. In the original study, semantic macrostructures were operationalized as semantically grouped frequency and keyword lists, the latter using a reference corpus of biographical interviews also conducted in Austria, using WordSmith software. Clustered into semantic fields, the items of the frequency and keyword lists indicate, respectively, the dominant topics of the corpus and its distinct features vis-à-vis other biographical narratives.

The clusters obtained on the basis of the keyword list indicated the keyness of (1) family, especially mother, father, and grandparents; (2) references to the narrative situation itself; (3) political terms, organizations, and figures; (4) events and experiences related to persecution, emigration, flight, and return; and (5) historical reference points such as dates, places, and events. In contrast, work, career, and personal life played a subordinate role, evident in negative keyness values. The original study also noted the remarkable homogeneity of these semantic macrostructures across the corpus: The lexical items with the highest overall keyness occur in 100% of the interviews, and more than 50% of the words with significant keyness occur in over 66% of the interviews (see the companion website Revisiting the Toolbox for comprehensive results).

To address the methodological issue that neither frequency nor keyness alone provide a reliable measure of the salience of sematic macrostructures—an item occurring only 5 times can have higher keyness than one occurring 500 times; and very frequent items can be equally frequent in both corpora—the original study also calculated the keyness/frequency ratio. This ratio gives a value between 1 (the highest ratio possible, i.e., frequency matching keyness 100%) and 0 (the lowest ratio possible, i.e., frequency being identical in both corpora). The original study thus suggested a methodological solution to gaining a more robust understanding of salient macrostructures. For example, while close family members appear with very high frequencies in both corpora, this is not surprising for biographical interviews.

The items on the resulting list were again clustered into semantic fields, yielding the following salient groups with a ratio of 1:

1. political organizations, movements, and parties, represented in part metonymically by historical figures and leaders (e.g., Marx, Stalin, Kreisky);
2. Jewishness/being Jewish;
3. persecution, imprisonment, and death (and the places associated);
4. emigration, flight (and the places associated);
5. Nazis, the Gestapo, and National Socialism as such; and
6. identity and the self in relation to country/nation, family, heritage, and politics.

Significant at a ratio between 0.75 and 1 were the semantic fields of

7. fear;
8. memory, memories, and remembering;
9. resistance, struggle, and fight;
10. return, arriving, and having survived;
11. the invasion and annexation of Austria; and
12. extended family.

These findings confirm that, in terms of semantic macrostructures, the inter-generational discourse of children of Holocaust survivors is indeed marginal, but they also indicate in which ways: in terms of political engagement, Jewish identity, the persecution of the interviewees' parents by the Nazis, and explicit identity constructions in relation to Austria.

However, the CL analyses reported above engaged with the data as they would with any type of linguistic material, neglecting their special properties *as narrative* and *as narratives of a traumatic past* specifically. In investigating collective constructions of the past through narrative, more or less consistently established interpretations of connections between people, places, events, and actions in time should be an analytic focus. One of the key findings of previous work on Holocaust narratives (Schiffrin 2002, 2003) is that Holocaust narratives, precisely because they are intertextually linked and generic narratives, may present a partial solution to having no words to express trauma: "Because of the radical break between trauma and culture, victims often cannot find categories of thought or words to contain or give shape to their experience" (Schiffrin 2002, 313).

With Holocaust narratives, even more so than in most other narrative situations, the authenticity and credibility of the story, as well as of the person telling the story, rest on a believable claim to personal experience and thus on a correspondingly positioned and performed narrative voice. One principal way of creating such authentic positioning has been termed 'story ownership': Embedding narratives into accounts of how the story was *experienced* or *received by a first-hand witness* increases the story's plausibility (De Fina and Georgakopoulou 2012, 137). In case of the original study, the qualitative analysis of all accounts into which the narratives about the Holocaust, persecution, flight, and return of the interviewees' parents are embedded showed them to be accounts of the circumstances of their *knowing* or rather *not-knowing*. This distancing is often realized in ways that are antithetical to positive story ownership as described by De Fina and Georgakopoulou (2012), e.g., through *disclaimers* such as 'I don't really know,' 'I was not there to see it myself,' or 'I actually know very little'. In fact, the original study characterized this characteristic type of narrative framing as "story dis-ownership" (Wodak and Rheindorf 2017).

The disclaimers identified are, indeed, "story openings" and as such "consequential for what is going to come" (De Fina and Georgakopoulou 2012, 49). Remarkably, the interviewees continually foregrounded the situation and conditions of re-telling their parents' stories: These conditions are presented like a veil of not-knowing or not-knowing-well, of partly remembering and not-having-been-told, framing the narratives as meta-commentary. In some cases, it was the parents who commanded not just confidence or silence, but *not knowing*, as one of the interviewees recounted the words of his mother. This pattern is remarkably consistent, regardless of whether parents told much or very little, as illustrated by the following two excerpts:

> It was a topic, not only but still largely in a very general form. The concrete story I know very little. I know that my parents fled from Austria in June 1938 and actually meant to go to France, but went via Italy. They did send their whole luggage to France, as far as I know, but my mother went to the

> Swiss consul in Italy. Why, I don't know, however, and she bribed him with jewelry, as she told me, and thereby got entry into Switzerland. Then my parents spent the wartime from 1938 to 45 in Switzerland. My father was lucky not being imprisoned like most others. I really don't know anything specific, it was never this concrete.
>
> My mother told me things and then: "Seal of silence, you may never speak about this, you may never mention this." [...] "You must not do anything to know, this someone or that someone came back." But we did not go into this afterwards, because we said this exceptional situation should not revisited after the war. "But it was him and it was her, but you may never know this".

Such paradoxical, indeed impossible commands can be read as undermining the position of the narrators, their claim to authenticity and ability to bear witness in retelling their parents' stories; however, their inclusion of these commands in the interviews can also be read as augmenting their authenticity in telling the story of how they were told those stories. In short, the original study concluded that there were at least three levels to the interviewees' positioning: in relation to their own life stories, in relation to their parents' life stories, and in relation to the experience of being told by their parents.

In all three positionings, the original study identified cases of "narrative affectivity" (De Fina and Georgakopoulou 2012, 65) created, e.g., through performing the voice of another person such as the mother in the above example. Such narrative affectivity not only emphasizes the narrative segment but also charges it emotionally and gives it coherence by involving the narrator as a character in the story. Occasionally, this affect will be maintained and thus expand a particular story into a "scenic narrative" (Wodak 1986). In scenic narratives, the interviewees perform the incident by reenacting the experience via direct quotations and elaborating the complication of the story. This leads to a polyphonous performance, containing many voices: voices of parents, perpetrators, victims, and bystanders. Many emotions are expressed, via intonation, code-switching, hesitation, pause, or indeed, by embarrassed laughter or crying. The teller relives the experience as told by their father or mother. The original study moreover found such scenic narratives to lack the typical *orientation* at the outset and *coda* at the end, i.e., the disclaimers creating story dis-ownership. In summary, scenic narratives seem to be the exception to the story dis-ownership generally characterizing the interview data, piercing what might be termed a "narrative veil" (Wodak and Rheindorf 2017).

For the most part, the interviewees' telling of their parents' narratives of persecution conforms to the pattern of "retold" narratives in terms of language use: they are short, succinctly formulated, largely devoid of detail, and abstract (e.g., people are typified and functionalized rather than individualized or named). They are also "generic" in the sense that they use culturally established, shared, and thus discursively available narrative patterns and phrasings (Schiffrin 2006, 275; De Fina and Georgakopoulou 2012, 149; Baynham 2005, 15). The original study found several generic stories in the data, working as metonymic representations of Nazi atrocities and cruelty. In one of these stories, for example, one of the SS guards in a concentration camp takes a prisoner's cap away, throws it over the outer fence, and then cruelly threatens to shoot the prisoner if he does not climb over the fence to retrieve it, an ostensible escape attempt for which he will likely be shot as well. Since both of the prisoner's actions will give the SS guard a reason to murder him, the narrative presents the prisoner as caught in a lethal double bind.

As previously noted, the initial CL analysis had indicated the prominence of particular places and dates in the interview data. To follow up on this, the original study pursued both quantitative and qualitative analyses of temporal and spatial references in the narratives. Conceptually, it drew on Bakhtin's notion of the *chronotope* as "a unit of analysis for studying language according to the ratio and characteristics of the temporal and spatial categories represented" (Bakhtin 2011, 425). Insofar as the concept links narrative patterns to social structure, the chronotope provides a compelling frame to discuss the complex interplay between group-specific experiences and discourses on the one hand and personal narratives on the other hand. The chronotope of a particular narrative is defined by the way in which the linguistic form of the telling of events takes "deforms" the chronological or spatial events (Bakhtin 2011, 113), e.g., by flashbacks, spatial or temporal omissions and distortions, or hypothetical scenarios.

In any narrative, so Bakhtin's key assumption, the construction of meaning must negotiate time and space, creating a particular chronotope which, insofar as it is socially meaningful and shared, can be read as an "index" for that particular social group (Bakhtin 2011, 258). This observation highlights the significance of narratives as social practice through which memories are made accessible and shared, thus bridging individual and collective memory. Among members of a social group, a shared chronotope is seen as plausible, common sense, even natural. More recent discourse-analytical approaches, specifically van Dijk's socio-cognitive approach (van Dijk 2009), suggest that all linguistic expression is based on, and to some degree reflects, previous filtering of perception or memory through cognitive schemata. Perceptions are fitted, understood, and remembered according to these internalized schemata, which would be evident in patterns like the chronotope. Such schemata are seen as largely acquired through socialization (Reisigl and Wodak 2001, 2015), which parallels Bakhtin's notion of an indexical relation between narrative and society.

A closer quantitative and qualitative analysis of all narrative passages shows that, when it comes to World War 2 and the Holocaust in contrast to events before and after, very few specific temporal references (e.g., dates) are used; most temporal references are vague and relational (e.g., "then," "back then," "now," "later," "before," "after"). This pattern is consistent across all interviews: the narratives contain specific dates leading up to and including 1938, a date that represents the beginning of persecution and indicates a significant rupture in normal spatio-temporal experience (De Fina 2003b). The same is true for dates after 1945, the end of the war, after which the narratives return to more specific time references. In the interval, however, the narratives lack temporal specificity but link to a plethora of specific and generic places ("the camp" or "a camp"). The original study interpreted these as "places outside of normal time", specifically outside of official historical chronology and military history. Many of these places take on metonymic meaning in the narratives, condensing all movement of the parents' flight into a sequence of stops without a journey connecting them (Wodak and Rheindorf 2017).

The loss of time can also be measured quantitatively, showing peaks at biographically significant dates (1938, 1945, and 1968) as well as the absence of absolute temporal reference between 1938 and 1945 (see Fig. 7.1). Within the temporal boundaries of 1938 and 1945, virtually all temporal reference is relative, vague, or expressed indirectly through spatial

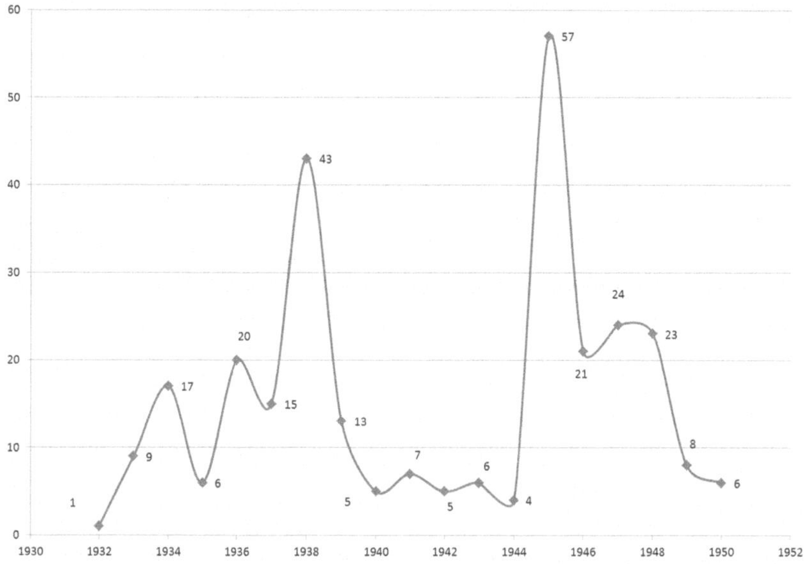

Fig. 7.1 Specific time references in the interview corpus by year

reference. Even flight and persecution are thus metonymically expressed as spatial categories, as *being in prison* or *being at Morzinplatz* (the Gestapo headquarters in Vienna).

With respect to the conventional view of narrative, in which the narrator seems in control of the telling and orientation sections (prominently time and place), this matches De Fina's (2003b) work on disorientation in narrative. Narrators who are lost in the sense that they struggle, and often fail, to reconstruct complex spatial and time in their stories, will show different linguistic behavior. The original study also identified transitions from time-oriented to time-less narratives, from oriented to disoriented story-telling. In the following excerpt, the interviewee invests great effort in giving precise dates, but abruptly loses time-orientation with the reference "before Hitler invaded".

> She left home very early and was very young then as she worked in this communist something, there, there, and did all sorts of things. She then after 1934, I assume, I don't know, no, that must have been around 1935,

> 1936, there she was then locked up as a communist, the communists were already illegal then, since 1934, but that must have been a little later. She was born in 1913, so she was, I think, 24 or so, that would have been 1936 or so then, yes, that's about right. She then, relatively shortly before Hitler invaded, was released and that is why at once—she was known because of that and would have been in danger—and she then, with a forged passport that she got from the party, went first to Switzerland, which she felt was terrible, because she was working in the house of some rich Jewish family there, but my mother is so not into housework things that I cannot imagine that at all. She found that terrible, she hates Switzerland since then and then she went to England and there she worked in this Austrian Center, where they also had a magazine and there she sort of began with her journalistic work, which she then later continued.

Alternating between quantitative and qualitative perspectives, the original study concluded that the inter-generational narratives of persecution in the interview data represented a type of communal discourse shared by second-generation returnees, and that it constituted a marginal discourse in the sense that it differed substantially from hegemonic discourses about World War 2 and the Holocaust in Austria. In interdisciplinary collaboration with the project team's psychiatrist, instances of story dis-ownership, scenic narratives, and the loss of time orientation were identified as traces of inter-generational trauma (Berger and Wodak 2018).

7.2 Revisiting the Study

In retrospect, the original study suffered from a key limitation connected to the conceptual relation between *narrative* and *discourse*. From its earliest forms, such as Russian formalism, narratology has worked with (and sometimes against) the premise that socially shared narratives involve archetypal characters, settings, and actions (Propp 1968). Fairy tales or folk tales may be the simplest and clearest cases of this, but novels, news stories, and autobiographical accounts among others have been shown to follow similar, if less constrained patterns. More recently, individual contributions have sought to operationalize narrative on the level of discourse (e.g., Bubenhofer et al. 2014; Franzosi 1998; Franzosi et al. 2012), sometimes integrating some form of quantification *and* visualization. This relation can be conceptualized, e.g., on the level of recurring or conventionalized roles, actions or plot, narrator positioning or linguistic patterns. While the latter two were addressed in the original study, no attention was given to roles or actions: Some key actors no doubt emerged from the frequency and keyword lists, but these were grouped, first, as lexical items and, second, as semantic groups—rather than for the roles they fulfilled in the respective narrative. Clearly, there is a substantial difference there, as the same item, e.g., "soldier" can appear equally in the role of a perpetrator, bystander, helper or even victim. This may be considered a critical shortcoming of the original study insofar as narratology since its beginnings has been interested in recurring roles and plots as socially shared and meaningful patterns.

Revising the study should therefore integrate analyses on the level of roles or plots. Conceptually, these have to be limited to narratives of persecution rather than the entire interview material. Methodologically, a combination of qualitative and quantitative perspectives will be necessary to (1) identify roles and plot elements, (2) quantify them across narratives to identify discourse patterns, and (3) visualize the emerging patterns for further interpretation and analysis. Both methodologically and visually, suitable approaches will have to be found, adapted or developed to overcome the key challenge of previous approaches: to achieve a suitable level of detail in the linguistic analysis while maintaining a broad overview of the discourse-level patterns.

A second, if related, limitation of the original study lies in its treatment of the interviewees' narrative "I", i.e., the roles they play in their own narratives. This was, of course, partly covered in terms of positioning, showing story dis-ownership and narrative veiling, but it remained limited to this particular perspective and qualitative analyses. In short, the narrators may well be engaged in other actions, take on different roles in their own narratives than those of being-told and telling.

The revised study should therefore include a more comprehensive analysis of the narrative "I" in terms of roles and actions, separately as well as within its more general focus on recurring roles. As above, a suitable integration of qualitative and quantitative methods will have to be developed in order to operationalize this dimension of narrative on the level of discourse.

7.3 The Revised Study: Results and Discussion

In revising the study, some changes were made on the conceptual and methodological level to accommodate the new analytical aims. First, previous work on narrative that looked at patterns of roles and actions in a larger set of data rather than single narratives was consulted. Here, the work of Franzosi (1998) and Franzosi et al. (2012) proved particularly inspirational: Unlike classical narratology (Bal 1997, Chapter 4), Franzosi's original approach has the advantage that, although no automatic analysis is possible, the categorization of roles and actions into types which can then by quantified allows a relatively large amount of textual data to be analyzed, thereby revealing patterns in the links between roles across texts. Finally, the visual representation of these roles and their interrelations as a node-link graph provides a useful if limited overview.

Franzosi developed his approach, to which he refers as Quantitative Narrative Analysis (QNA), based on the sociological method of Social Network Analysis (SNA, see Scott and Carrington 2011). SNA is typically used to investigate social structures like kinship, businesses or friendship networks through systematically mapping those networks based on various types of data, including ethnographic interview data. As a Visual Analytics method, it depicts social structures as so-called *sociograms*, i.e., node-link graphs (nodes being individual actors in the field; connecting lines or links representing the relationships or interactions between). In some cases, the intensity or strength of the relationship is quantified and appended to the line as a number or visually mapped as a *weighted link* in the form of its line strength.

Characteristic limitations of SNA and its visualization are, firstly, that only one relationship level is mapped at a time, e.g., farmer A having given advice to farmer B, farmer B having given advice to farmer D, etc. For an overview of multiple types of relationships, one must therefore draw multiple graphs. Secondly, the directionality of relationships is typically distinguished as *indegree* (number of links coming into a specific node) and *outdegree* (number of links going out from a specific node) and may be visualized in separate graphs or by using curved edges in a single graph. Available space and occlusion through multiple links or link types is a clear limitation here, even if curved links are used to avoid immediate occlusion: If the relationship between farmer A and farmer B were investigated on 6 different levels—e.g., advice, manual help, lending money, sharing equipment, familial relation, and trade—and in both directions, the resulting 12 links would need 6 different degrees of curving and occupy considerable space, which in a network of dozens of farmers would lead to substantial occlusion and visual incomprehensibility.

Franzosi (1998), a sociologist interested in media representations of sociological phenomena, adapted SNA for the analysis of newspaper reports on lynch mobs in the US state of Georgia between 1875 and 1930. Key shifts here are that Franzosi approaches his data as narratives to be analyzed as such, highlighting the constructedness of such accounts; that he is aware of the role of the medium and social context in which these narratives are constructed; and that by delimiting the data by topic and field, Franzosi is effectively investigating narrative at the discourse level. Although not developed within a CDS framework, the approach thus seems viable for integration or adaptation. Like most narratological approaches, Franzosi's does not identify all individual persons as actors, but identifies their "roles", thereby greatly reducing the number of nodes in the network. Likewise, he focuses only on the key relationships or actions between these nodes, i.e., those relations and actions that inform the narrative pattern (i.e., "plot") of the newspaper texts.

To obtain an overview of how lynch murders were narrativized by newspapers at the time, Franzosi categorizes the central actors as *victims*, *perpetrators*, and *police*—note that centrality needs to be established quantitatively rather than inferred. Similar to the original study's aggregation of items on the frequency list into semantic groups, quantified roles are here aggregated into the three central roles. Franzosi does the same for actions, based on verbs and verb phrases used, grouping them into broad categories, such as "attacking" or "movement", and quantified them. As in standard SNA, the resulting network graph only depicts one of the central relations/actions at a time, e.g., "attacking", necessitating a different visualization for each action type and dropping any role from the network that does not have a relationship of the respective type. For instance, if "police" do not "attack" anyone, they will not be represented in the network for the relation "attack". This greatly impoverishes the visual efficiency of the network. While Franzosi visualizes the frequency of these relations through the line strength of the links, he follows standard SNA practice of not indicating directionality in the graph and simply aggregates relations. Thus, if "mob" attacks "police", and "police" also attacks "mob", the frequencies are simply added. Clearly, this severely limits reduces and analytic applicability of the visualization.

From a linguistic point of view, Franzosi's analysis of textual data is limited primarily by the fact that his "role" and "action" categories neglect crucial lexico-grammatical patterns and are derived from his previous understanding of the material rather than a corpus-based analysis. To counteract these limitations, the revised study turned to the existing linguistic frameworks of van Leeuwen's (1996) *Social Actor Analysis* and, more broadly speaking, *Systemic Functional Linguistics*. These seem to be an excellent fit for making this particular type of narratological approach—one that is interested in inventorying recurring actors, places, and relations between them—work on the level of discourse rather than individual texts. Based on the frequency lists already obtained through CL methods, qualitative Social Actors Analysis was used on concordances to group key entities according to their roles in the narratives. Interestingly, agency in the narratives is not limited to human beings: [events], [places], and [stories] are among the entities that most frequently interact with the social actors [parents], [perpetrators], [helpers], and [narrative I]. Each of these categories comprises a number of different linguistic nominations and descriptors and could, if needed, be differentiated further, e.g., [parents] into [mother] and [father] or [perpetrators] into [Nazis], [soldiers], etc. Since these are based on the frequency lists and concordances already obtained in the original study, quantification of the role categories is the next step (see Table 7.2).

Even at the simplest level, this analytical step confirms the expected centrality of the interviewee's parents and the strong involvement of the narrative I, places, and stories—as opposed to the relative backgrounding of perpetrators.

In order to map the network of relations between these roles across all interviews, all verbs and verb phrases connecting any two of them were manually identified, categorized according to the "verb process" categories of Systemic Functional Linguistics (van Leeuwen 1995, 1996, 2008; van

Table 7.2 Role categories and their frequencies in the interview corpus

Role category	Aggregated frequency	Examples
Parents	1641	Mother, father, parents, parent, step-father
Narrative I	1418	I, me, myself
Perpetrators	84	Nazis, regime, Hitler, soldiers, Wehrmacht, SS, Gestapo, guards
Helpers	169	Friends, acquaintances, relatives, strangers, neighbors
Events	331	The war, the attack, the beginning, the shooting, the end
Places	958	Vienna, Berlin, Morzinplatz, Dachau, Maly Trostinez, Auschwitz
Stories	583	The story, his story, their stories, those things, telling

Table 7.3 Matrix for verb-process relations between roles

	Parents	Narrative I	Perpetrators	Helpers	Events	Places	Stories
Parents	–	535	–	–	113	758	221
Narrative I	121	–	–	–	–	–	473
Perpetrators	48	–	–	–	196	–	–
Helpers	169	–	–	–	–	–	–
Events	218	–	–	–	–	–	–
Places	–	–	–	–	–	–	–
Stories	–	–	–	–	–	–	–

Leeuwen and Wodak 1999), and then quantified (see Table 7.3). In SFL, verb process categories are used to distinguish any form of action or event that is expressed through a verb. These include material processes ("The soldiers shot them"), verbal processes ("She never told me"), mental processes ("She struggled with the memory"), and relational processes ("He was in prison"). Using this broad distinction, the following matrix gives an overview of how the roles interact in the interviewees' narratives of flight, persecution, and the Holocaust.

In terms of visualization, the matrix form of Table 7.3 would be better suited to a case with large numbers of nodes and relations; for a case such as this, i.e., narratives with a small number of roles which, out of 8 possible link types, relate to each other in no more than 3 ways at the same time, a node-link graph provides better visual efficiency for tasks like *overview*, *compare*, and *explore* (see Chapter 6). In this case, the visual links have to carry three types of information: link direction, link type, and link frequency. While direction is reliably indicated by simple arrows (although there are other options, see Holten et al. 2011), link type and frequency can present something of a challenge. Link type can be expressed through different colors, different line types (solid, dotted, etc.), but since these are not conventional or known to the readers, this option would require adding a legend, thereby reducing visual efficiency. A different option is to append labels to identify the link types, which in the case of a relatively small number of links is preferable. Finally, link frequency can be visualized through the relative line strength of the respective links; however, in case of greatly varying frequencies—say between 1000 and 1—the numerical values have to be mapped onto a gradient rather than expressed directly in line strength. Especially in this case, the reader will not be able to carry out precise comparisons, thus limiting task performance. Alternatively, the numerical values for link frequency can also be appended to the respective links. Figures 7.2 and 7.3 illustrate these options, using manually created visualizations.

Both visualizations clearly indicate the centrality of [parents] in the narratives' interactional network. They interact most often with the [I] of the narrators (and here as telling them [stories] as well as caring for them) and with [places] (being in places and travelling to places). Less frequently, they think of, remember or are haunted by [events] in the past. They are also the recipients, beneficiaries or victims of actions by [helpers] and [perpetrators]. Among the links between other roles, [perpetrators] are linked to [events], much more frequently in fact than to [parents]—indeed, it is a regular pattern in the narratives for [perpetrators] to indirectly link to [parents] by causing [events] which then affect [parents]. The [I] of the narrating interviewees, in turn, is linked mainly to [stories] by remembering or thinking about them, and less often telling them; finally, they are also linked to [parents] by asking for information.

The quality of the narrative I's positioning is addressed more specifically by the second extension of the study. Having completed the quantitative analysis above made a closer look at the verb processes connecting the narrators to stories, their parents, and other (non-key) entities relatively easy.

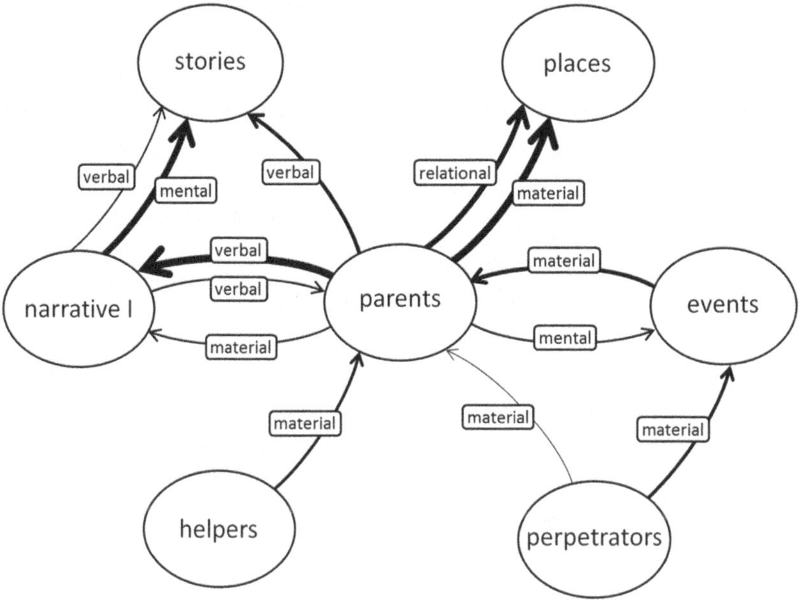

Fig. 7.2 Network for roles (link strength visualized, link type appended)

The impression of a 'narrative veil' being constructed through the ways in which the narrators relate to their parents' stories is confirmed by concordancing focused on the first-person pronouns in the data (Table 7.4).

The range of verb processes identified indicates that the narrators are preoccupied with mental processes, particularly knowing and not knowing, as well as material processes related to researching their parents' stories and verbal processes related to asking or talking about those stories. Collocational patterns also confirm that verbs of *knowing* and, to a lesser degree, of *telling* are often negated or limited: approximately 45 and 28% of their use, respectively.

The revised study thus achieves several broad goals in complementing the original research. First, it establishes an interdisciplinary integration of conceptual and methodological tools drawn from narratology, CL, and SFL within the discourse-analytic framework. Second, it demonstrates that narrative patterns on the discourse level can be mapped as a network or node-link graph to gain an overview of how roles interact. Consistent

Table 7.4 Number and examples for verb processes for [narrative I] by type

Processes	Examples for [narrative I] as *agent*	Examples for [narrative I] as *recipient*
Mental (403)	Find, find out, discover, have no answer, not get the point, have a general impression, have the feeling that, still not understand, not knowing, not understanding, not having information, knowing, believing, thinking, not remembering, remembering, having the impression that, prefer, not notice much, not seeing, not needing, having enough, knowing enough, not knowing anything, having no memory of, not looking back, not being able to forget, sense, feel, not delving into history, to engage with, to confront, not being aware of, have an opinion, ask oneself, to wonder, to be sure	Having occupied me, being preoccupied by, having been given a load to bear, having had to bear
Verbal (155)	Talk, tell, say, speak, mention, deal with, question, ask, sing	Having been told, not having been told, having had to listen
Material (177)	Research, investigate, search, March, write a book, send by mail, go to England, search for, find, look at, visit Dachau, drive, read	Being taken care of, being taken to
Relational (40)	Be, have	

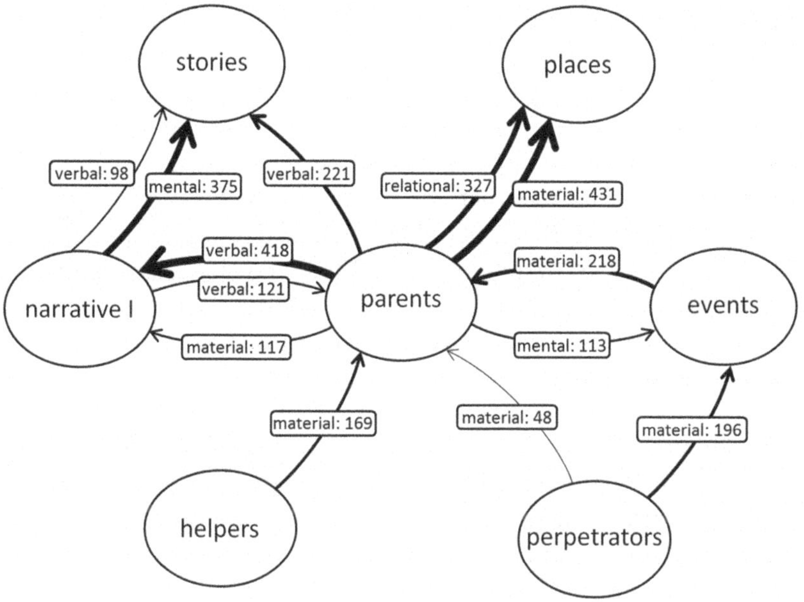

Fig. 7.3 Network for roles (link strength visualized and appended, link type appended)

patterns emerge from the interviewee data, confirming and deepening the original study's qualitative analyses. Thirdly, the revised study adds a layer of detail to the way the interviewees position themselves in and through their narrations, i.e., with respect to their parents' stories, with respect to being told (or not told) those stories, and with respect to retelling them in the context of the interview situation. The overall consistency of these results also confirms that the group shares a marginal discourse positioned not outside but in relation to dominant Austrian discourses on World War 2 and the Holocaust.

7.4 Research Design and Practice

The case study presented here focuses on a very specific, contextualized discourse: the intergenerational narratives of survivors who returned to

Austria after 1945, as passed on and retold by their children. It approaches the data collected through biographical interviews as a window onto the discourse of a social group that not only shares similar family histories but can be considered marginal to Austrian society. Integrated qualitative and CL methodology offer a way to demonstrate such marginality empirically through semantic macro-structures. Narrative, in this case study, represents a level of analysis that is not often integrated into conceptualizations of discourse in CDS, despite its undoubtedly crucial role in individual and collective memory and identity constructions.

With respect to research design and practice, this case study's discussions indicate that we should

- not dogmatically rely on qualitative or quantitative methods alone, especially in analyzing higher-level linguistic patterns such as narrative,
- ensure an adequate match between the conceptual and analytical level of the research design, as not every method or category system is adequate in a particular research context,
- in interdisciplinary research contexts, strive for joint analyses but note that other discipline's concepts, such as 'trauma', may be outside the epistemological limits of CDS or the particular linguistic, multimodal or ethnographic methods we use,
- be aware that judgments as to the hegemonic, marginal, resistant or subaltern positon of discourses, or positions in discourse, can be made only in relation to reference points and by situating data in their social context,
- use multiple forms of visualization during the research process, as tools of analysis, rather than just to display results,
- consider visual efficiency, data transparency, and user tasks in either choosing an established form of visualization or designing a custom-made one, and
- consider whether static or interactive visualizations best serve the tasks the readers should be able to perform as well as the depth of information we want to provide access to.

References

Achugar, Mariana. 2016. *Discursive Processes of Intergenerational Transmission of Recent History: (Re)Making Our Past.* Basingstoke: Palgrave Macmillan.

Bakhtin, Michail M. 2011. *The Dialogic Imagination: Four Essays.* Translated by Michael Holquist and Caryl Emerson, 18 paperback printing. University of Texas Press Slavic Series 1. Austin, TX: University of Texas Press.

Bal, Mieke. 1997. *Narratology: Introduction to the Theory of Narrative.* 2nd ed. Toronto and Buffalo: University of Toronto Press.

Baynham, Mike. 2005. "Network and Agency in the Migrations Stories of Moroccan Women." In *Dislocations/Relocations: Narratives of Displacement,* edited by Mike Baynham and Anna De Fina, 11–35. Manchester: St. Jerome.

Berger, Ernst (ed.). 2007. *Verfolgte Kindheit: Kinder Und Jugendliche Als Opfer Der NS-Sozialverwaltung.* Wien: Böhlau.

Berger, Ernst, and Ruth Wodak. 2018. *Kinder Der Rückkehr: Geschichte Einer-marginalisierten Jugend.* Wiesbaden: Springer VS and Springer Fachmedien Wiesbaden.

Bubenhofer, Noah, Nicole Müller, and Joachim Scharloth. 2014. "Narrative Muster Und Diskursanalyse: Ein Datengeleiteter Ansatz." *Zeitschrift Für Semiotik* 35 (3–4): 419–44.

de Fina, Anna. 2003a. *Identity in Narrative: A Study of Immigrant Discourse.* Studies in Narrative 3. Amsterdam: Benjamins.

———. 2003b. "Crossing Borders: Time, Space, and Disorientation in Narrative." *Narrative Inquiry* 13 (2): 367–91. https://doi.org/10.1075/ni.13.2.08def.

de Fina, Anna, and Alexandra Georgakopoulou. 2012. *Analyzing Narrative: Discourse and Sociolinguistic Perspectives.* Cambridge: Cambridge University Press.

Franzosi, Roberto. 1998. "Narrative Analysis—Or Why (and How) Sociologists Should Be Interested in Narrative." *Annual Review of Sociology* 24 (1): 517–54. https://doi.org/10.1146/annurev.soc.24.1.517.

Franzosi, Roberto, Gianluca De Fazio, and Stefania Vicari. 2012. "Ways of Measuring Agency: An Application of Quantitative Narrative Analysis to Lynchings in Georgia (1875–1930)." *Sociological Methodology* 42 (1): 1–42. https://doi.org/10.1177/0081175012462370.

Halbwachs, Maurice. 1992. *On Collective Memory.* Translated by Lewis A. Coser. The Heritage of Sociology. Chicago: University of Chicago Press.

Heer, Hannes, Walter Manoschek, Alexander Pollak, and Ruth Wodak (eds.). 2008. *The Discursive Construction of History: Remembering the Wehrmacht's War of Annihilation.* Basingstoke, UK and New York: Palgrave Macmillan.

Holten, Danny, Petra Isenberg, Jarke van Wijk, and Jean-Daniel Fekete. 2011. *An Extended Evaluation of the Readability of Tapered, Animated, and Textured Directed-Edge Representations in Node-Link Graphs.* Hong Kong: IEEE Press. https://hal.inria.fr/inria-00548180/document.

Keppler, Angela. 1994. *Tischgespräche: Über Formen Kommunikativer Vergemeinschaftung Am Beispiel Der Konversation in Familien.* 1. Aufl. Suhrkamp Taschenbuch Wissenschaft 1132. Frankfurt am Main: Suhrkamp.

Knight, Robert. 2000. *"Ich Bin Dafür, Die Sache in Die Länge Zu Ziehen": Die Wortprotokolle Der Österreichischen Bundesregierung von 1945 Bis 1952 Über Die Entschädigung Der Juden.* 2nd ed. Wien: Böhlau.

Propp, Vladimir. 1968. *Morphology of the Folktale.* Translated by Lawrence Scott, vol. 9, 2nd ed., Publications of the American Folklore Society. Austin: University of Texas Press.

Reisigl, Martin, and Ruth Wodak. 2001. *Discourse and Discrimination: Rhetorics of Racism and Antisemitism.* London and New York: Routledge.

———. 2015. "The Discourse-Historical Approach (DHA)." In *Methods of Critical Discourse Studies,* edited by Ruth Wodak and Michael Meyer, 23–61. London: Sage.

Schiffrin, Deborah. 2002. "Mother and Friends in a Holocaust Life Story." *Language in Society* 31 (3): 309–53. https://doi.org/10.1017/S0047404502020250.

———. 2003. "We Knew That's It: Retelling the Turning Point of a Narrative." *Discourse Studies* 5 (4): 535–61. https://doi.org/10.1177/14614456030054005.

———. 2006. *In Other Words: Variation in Reference and Narrative.* Studies in Interactional Sociolinguistics 21. Cambridge, UK and New York: Cambridge University Press.

Schröter, Melani. 2013. *Silence and Concealment in Political Discourse,* vol. 48. Discourse Approaches to Politics, Society and Culture (DAPSAC). Amsterdam and Philadelphia: John Benjamins Publishing Company.

Scott, John, and Peter J. Carrington (eds.). 2011. *The Sage Handbook of Social Network Analysis.* London and Thousand Oaks, CA: Sage.

van Dijk, Teun A. 2009. "Semantic Macro-Structures and Knowledge Frames in Discourse Comprehension." In *Cognitive Processes in Comprehension,* edited by Marcel A. Just and Patricia Carpenter, 3–32. New York: Psychology Press.

van Leeuwen, Theo. 1995. "Representing Social Action." *Discourse & Society* 6 (1): 81–106. https://doi.org/10.1177/0957926595006001005.

———. 1996. "The Representation of Social Actors." In *Text and Practices: Readings in Critical Discourse Analysis*, edited by Carmen Rosa Caldas-Coulthard and Malcolm Coulthard, 32–70. London: Routledge.

———. 2008. *Discourse and Practice: New Tools for Critical Discourse Analysis.* Oxford Studies in Sociolinguistics. Oxford and New York: Oxford University Press.

van Leeuwen, Theo, and Ruth Wodak. 1999. "Legitimizing Immigration Control: A Discourse-Historical Analysis." *Discourse Studies* 1 (1): 83–118. https://doi.org/10.1177/1461445699001001005.

Welzer, Harald (ed.). 2001. *Das soziale Gedächtnis: Geschichte, Erinnerung, Tradierung*, 1st ed. Hamburg: Hamburger Edition.

Wodak, Ruth. 1986. *Language Behavior in Therapy Groups.* Berkeley: University of California Press.

———. 2011. "Suppression of the Nazi Past, Coded Languages, and Discourses of Silence: Applying the Discourse-Historical Approach to Post-War Antisemitism in Austria." In *Political Languages in the Age of Extremes*, edited by Willibald Steinmetz, 351–79. Oxford: Oxford University Press.

Wodak, Ruth, and Markus Rheindorf. 2017. "'Whose Story?'—Narratives of Persecution, Flight and Survival Told by the Children of Austrian Holocaust Survivors." In *Linguistic Diversity and Superdiversity: Sociocultural Linguistic Perspectives*, edited by Anna de Fina, Didem Ikizoglu, and Jeremy Wegner, 17–36. Washington, DC: Georgetown University Press.

Ziegler, Meinrad, and Waltraud Kannonier. 1997. *Österreichisches Gedächtnis: Über Erinnern Und Vergessen Der NS-Vergangenheit.* Böhlaus Zeitgeschichtliche Bibliothek, Bd. 25. Wien: Böhlau.

8

Case Study 2: Normalization of Populist Terms in Political Discourse and Beyond: The 'Unwillingness to Integrate'

8.1 Introduction: The Original Study

This case study revisits work done in an extensive research project on the discursive construction of national identities in Austria[1] and has been partially published as Rheindorf (2017, 2018a, b). The project's aim was to develop the first longitudinal perspective on changing constructions of national identities based on similar datasets across 20 years, using similar methods for data collection and analysis, within the same theoretical and conceptual framework. The introduction to this case study will briefly outline this larger study before presenting the case study in its original form and then follow the general structure of all case studies in this volume: a critical discussion of the original study, highlighting limitations and suggesting changes, revising the study and discussing its results, and finally drawing general conclusions for research design and practice.

The larger project drew on the theoretical framework of the DHA for its understanding of discourses as always historically embedded, as mutually

[1] FWF-funded project P27153, The discursive construction of Austrian identity/ies 2015: A longitudinal perspective, began on January 1, 2015 and concluded on June 30, 2018.

© The Author(s) 2019

M. Rheindorf, *Revisiting the Toolbox of Discourse Studies*,
Postdisciplinary Studies in Discourse,
https://doi.org/10.1007/978-3-030-19369-0_8

constitutive with social contexts, and as sites of struggle over power (Reisigl and Wodak 2015). More specifically, the project's framework conceptualized national identities as plural, discursively constructed, and therefore historically changeable. To map these constructions, the study design emphasized data collection on multiple levels of discourse, in distinct fields of social action, e.g. public discourses such as politics (parliamentary politics, election campaigns, state representation), the media (print, television, radio, social media, advertisement) as well as quasi-private discourses (data elicited through group discussions and interviews), complemented with ethnographic observations (at rallies and commemorative events). Similar data had been collected in parallel projects in 1995 (Wodak et al. 1998) and 2005 (de Cillia and Wodak 2009; Wodak et al. 2009), opening up the possibility of a robust longitudinal comparison.

In data collection, the project focused on five conceptual dimensions of national identities that had been inductively developed and refined in related projects since 1995: the construction of (1) a Homo Nationalis in terms of typical traits, dispositions, and behaviors; (2) a shared culture, including traditions, religion, values, and language(s); (3) a shared past narrated as the origin and story of a people and country; (4) a shared political present and future rooted in that past, emphasizing continuity and unity; and (5) a national body conceptualized as national territory, borders, artefacts of the built environment such monuments and public spaces, as well as the bodies of national heroes (Wodak et al. 2009). For an overview of all data collected in that project as well as related publications, see the companion website Revisiting the Toolbox.

Analytically, the project matched the very varied data with a combination of linguistic methods ranging from CL to argumentation analysis, but maintained an exploratory approach to all aspects of the data throughout the project's duration. Thus, due to circumstances beyond our control, the global events of 2015—most prominently migration and the so-called 'refugee crisis'—entered into the research as very prominent topics. It was in this general context that the original study reported here was undertaken, seizing the opportunity of analyzing a migration-related political debate as it unfolded.

Discursive constructions of national identities relate to migration in several ways, as migration intersects with all five of the above-mentioned dimensions: (1) Migrants are constructed as different from the Homo Nationalis, as Homo Externus, in terms of essentialised traits; (2) they are constructed as not sharing 'our' culture, traditions, values or language; (3) migrants are constructed as having a separate past; (4) as threatening 'our' present and future; and (5) migrants are defined by physically crossing 'our' borders into the national territory. The first and second of these dimensions are of particular importance to the case study inasmuch as discursive constructions of national identities often emphasize national uniqueness and (inner) homogeneity, backgrounding or downplaying heterogeneity and difference within the population. At the same time, such constructions also focus on differences to members of other nations, often resorting to stereotyping of entire populations or groups (de Cillia and Wodak 2009; Wodak et al. 2009). Discourses on 'migration' and, more specifically, on 'integration' cut across the above-mentioned concerns: They focus on the manner and, even more prominently, the regulation and control of migration in general and, specifically, the production of potential new citizens through processes of integration (i.e. citizenship qua integration) (de Cillia 2012; Perchinig 2010). In doing so, the hegemonic discourses on integration and citizenship invariably construct a homogenous national Self and an external Other (Wodak et al. 2009); the degree to which they do so and the categories and norms they employ in this Othering—be they cultural, racial, ethnic, religious, economic, educational etc.—are highly relevant from the perspective of CDS as they serve to legitimize and regulate access to rights and representation.

The original study approached the debate over 'integration' as a prime example of mediatized politics. The study combined qualitative and quantitative methods in analyzing a corpus of 280 news articles published in the course of four weeks, a corpus delineated as a *discourse strand* in terms of an initiating event, topical continuity, strong intertextual links, and a limited group of social actors (Jäger 2001; Wodak 2002a, b; Achtenhagen and Welter 2008). What is more, there were indications that said discourse strand had caused a notable discursive shift in introducing a previously taboo term, "Integrationsunwilligkeit" [unwillingness to integrate], into media discourse. While the term was in evidence as having been used on the World Wide Web for approximately ten years, its use

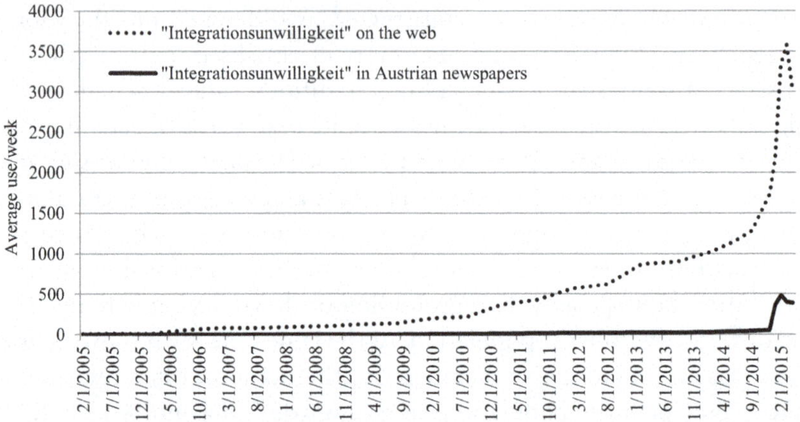

Fig. 8.1 Average frequency/week of "Integrationsunwilligkeit" in Austrian web domains and national newspapers (2005–2015) (To plot these graphs, raw frequencies were taken for three-month intervals and then calculated for an average/week to smoothen the graphs. Data were obtained by Google Search Tools and Search Console for Austrian domains, preventing the calculation of words per million ratios. While this approach does not provide exact data, the trend it indicates seems sufficiently clear)

there also received a significant boost through the debate in early 2015 (see Fig. 8.1).

The initiating event, which established the central issue of the debate, occurred one day after the terrorist attacks on Charlie Hebdo and a Jewish supermarket in Paris (January 7, 2015) in the form of an interview given by the governor of the Austrian state of Styria, Franz Voves. The original study concluded that this interview and the legislative initiative that followed determined the course of the following debate, shifting political discourse on migration with respect to the notion of 'integration'. In the interview, Voves decried the terrorist attacks and linked them to the alleged failure of European and Austrian politics to tackle enforce 'integration':

> These truly dramatic terror attacks on an editorial office in Paris lead me to say very clearly that politics in Europe has been turning a blind eye for far too long, that is, when people come to Europe, come to Austria, who are religiously motivated in trying to subvert our values, and then openly

show and live this attitude in front of us native Austrians, Europeans, in their neighborhoods, and thereby show absolutely no willingness to really want integration, there we should re-align our rule of law differently. (ORF 2015)

In the course of the interview, Voves sought to legitimize his own actions as a necessary reaction to the attacks. Positioning himself as a man of action and in opposition to European politics, he boldly advocated a change in the rule of law. His rhetorics here bear some closer scrutiny, as he repeatedly alternated between "Austria" and "Europe", listing both in an unusual construction without conjunction that suggests equivalence or a repair. This can be read as pars-pro-totem: What applies to Europe also applies to Austria. Indeed, it is crucial to the link between terrorism in France and integration in Austria. This, the original study showed, became a common feature of the mediatized debate that followed, as did Voves' characterization of migrants as the reason for terrorism, but terrorism read not as violence but as an attempt to "subvert our values". Note, however, that to Voves, as in the ensuing debate, this subversion is simply a lack of displaying the "willingness" to integrate. Within the discourse strand, it thus appears that Voves' statements in the interview began to shift the attention from a possible lack of integration to an allegedly lacking "display" of "willingness" to integrate. Significantly, he did so from a nativist perspective: While Voves' initial use of "our" in relation to values was ambiguous, he then clarified that "our values" are those of "native Austrians" only, thereby including migrants with Austrian citizenship in his blanket suspicion of the migrant Other. Because their numbers were ever growing, he continued, and because "the people" could "feel" that something was "wrong", politicians needed to act by introducing new criminal laws to enforce integration. And although this was ultimately the responsibility of the federal government and parliament, he was going to launch a legislative initiative at the state level.

To understand this bold statement, the original study turned to the socio-political and situational context. At the time, Voves was campaigning for his reelection as governor, but even so it was unusual. Political parties in Austria have long instrumentalized migration for political gain, most glaringly in the case of the Freedom Party (Freiheitliche Partei Österreichs or FPÖ) (Forchtner et al. 2013; Krzyżanowski 2013). However, Voves was a prominent member of the Social Democratic Party (Sozialdemokratische Partei Österreichs or SPÖ), which has traditionally been more welcoming of migration and taken a strong stance against the FPÖ's xenophobic and often racist election campaigns (but see Wodak 2018). Voves' law-and-order stance and appeal to "the people", then, appear to have been part of a populist strategy: playing not only on fear and distrust of foreigners, in particular Muslim migrants, but also playing on the well-worn drama of regional politics fighting against the true elites in the federal government and, even worse, in Brussels (Wodak 2015; Rheindorf 2019).

Tracing the development of the debate, the original study found little media reaction to this interview other than it being reported, largely verbatim, in several local and national newspapers. Controversy only began when Voves launched his legislative initiative in the regional parliament of Styria as Resolution 3237/6 on January 20, 2015 (Landtag Steiermark 2015), which passed the vote due his party's majority. Elaborating the pattern of the interview, the resolution linked the terrorist attacks in Paris to a lack of integration of migrants in Austria and called for the drafting of legal definitions for new statutory offenses under the heading of "Integrationsunwilligkeit"—the unwillingness to integrate. The resolution's authors may well have had some qualms about presuming that the as-yet-to-be-defined transgressions could be subject to legal consequences, as the document puts the legal term for offenses, *Tatbestände*, in quotation marks to indicate awareness of its inappropriateness. In contrast, the utterly undefined term "Integrationsunwilligkeit" was not treated with such care (Rheindorf 2018a).

In essence, the resolution argued that people of "other faiths", implying not Christian, are likely to undermine "our" values and become terrorists, but failed to explain how these things are supposed to be linked, except by being "other". It further linked security to the integration of migrants, defining the latter as a precondition for the safety of Austrians. After naming "health, welfare, education, and youth" as areas where integration is allegedly most lacking, the resolution focused on schools and the perceived failure of Muslim children to display the expected "willingness to integrate". In procedural terms, the resolution created a commission of legal experts charged with deliberating the issue and defining new crimes under the heading of "Integrationsunwilligkeit". One year later, this commission concluded that any such laws would be in violation of the Austrian constitution (for a detailed analysis of the resolution's rhetorics, see Rheindorf 2018a, 2017).

Part of their reasoning was based on the stark unsuitability of the term "Integrationsunwilligkeit" in the legal context; indeed, it was one of the most contentious aspects of the debate that followed the resolution. Taking a closer look at the compound's semantics, the original study concluded that "Integrationsunwilligkeit" combines the desired "Integration" as something that a migrant (i.e. someone who has not fully integrated yet, thus lacking the reified integration) can be either willing or unwilling to undertake, but it also implies that integration cannot and will not happen without such willingness. The compound's head "unwilligkeit" denotes the contrariness or absence of such willingness and furthermore reifies it as an abstract quality (via the suffix "-keit"). Shifting attention away from "Integration" as comprised of observable actions or behaviors, the term thus denotes an interior quality or attitude. The stems "-willig" and "-willigkeit" have connotations of submission on the part of the person having said quality, rather than aggressive dominance on the part of the person (here political actors presuming to speak for Austrian society) demanding said quality. Historically, the word traces back to military service in a feudal context (Grimm and Grimm 1965) as well as sexual submission (Reddemann 2005). While it does not spell out any consequences, its use often carries the threat of force in the case of non-compliance.

The successful passing of the resolution sparked media interest and political debate, constituting mediatized politics insofar as this was politics not only using but depending on the mechanisms and logic of modern media (Strömbäck 2008). When such a political issue is heavily mediatized, it also means that politics is largely conducted frontstage (Wodak 2011) and that media carry a substantial responsibility for how such public debates play out. To tackle this type of data, the original study integrated CL analyses of related news articles. Having access to the larger project mentioned above, I was able to operationalize the *discourse strand*, in CL terms, as a specific strand within the discourse on "integration": The project compiled a corpus of 3202 texts (1,866,424 words) from 11 national newspapers to represent that discourse. The discourse strand on

"Integrationsunwilligkeit" could thus be investigated through a *subset of data* within that larger corpus. In short, the CL perspective added to the definition of discourse strand the criterion of *high keyness values* (distinctive elements in the subcorpus, using the entire corpus as reference). The notion of discourse strand thus became the original study's conceptual counterpart to the CL practice of studying thematically and/or temporally bounded subcorpora. This delimitation facilitated a focused contextualisation of the discursive shift around "Integrationsunwilligkeit", allowing me to analytically zoom in, as it were, on specific changes in patterns of language use and the normalization of previously taboo terms.

The subcorpus representing the discourse strand on "Integrationsunwilligkeit" comprised 280 texts (290,440 words) published between January 20 and February 5, 2015. Beginning with a simple lexical analysis to identify terminology related to "Integration", the original study found numerous compounds containing **integration**: Beside the prominent notions of "integrationsunwillig" (unwilling to integrate) and "Integrationsunwilligkeit" (unwillingness to integrate) as well as the respective counterparts "integrationswillig" (willing to integrate) and "Integrationswilligkeit" (willingness to integrate), this included related notions of "Integrationsverweigerung" (refusal to integrate), "Integrationsprobleme" (integration problems), "Integrationsdefizite" (integration deficits) or "Integrationsmangel" (lack of integration). To varying degrees, these qualities were also embodied by social actors defined by their lacking integration, e.g. "Integrationsverweigerer" (people who refuse to integrate). Austrian "Integrationspolitik" (politics or policies of integration) and the "Integrationsminister" (Minister for Integration) are the only social actors represented in this group of compounds without a negative denotation (Table 8.1).

The original study's next step was a keyword analysis in relation to the reference corpus representing the discourse on integration in Austrian print media of 2015, using WordSmith 7.0 standard settings for log likelihood (max. p-value 0.0000001, max. wanted 500, min. frequency 3). Results show the discourse strand to be distinguished by the dominance of Social Democratic politicians (largely on the provincial level), school children and their parents (accused of being unwilling to integrate and identified as problems), radical Islam and terrorism, punishments of var-

Table 8.1 Compounds formed with **integration** by normalized frequency

Compounds	Normalized frequency (pmw)	Spread in %
Integrationsunwillige	826.33	82
Integrationsunwilligkeit	771.24	78
Integrationsminister	399.39	39
Integrationsdebatte	309.39	32
Integrationsverweigerung	268.55	25
Integrationsverweigerer	192.81	20
Integrationsunwillig	141.165	14
Integrationsprobleme	89.52	9
Integrationswilligkeit	75.75	7
Integrationspass	65.42	5
Integrationspolitik	51.65	5
Integrationsmängel	27.54	2
Desintegrationstendenzen	13.77	1
Ausländerintegration	13.77	1
Nichtintegration	13.77	1

ious kinds as well as teachers and other actors associated with school (see the companion website Revisiting the Toolbox for the full results on keywords).

Based on these quantitative results, the original study then integrated an analysis of the macro-topics, employing qualitative aggregation of lemmata in semantic fields with respect to salient social actors and social fields of action, before quantifying the presence of these groups and their characterization. Overall, social actors represented in the discourse strand comprise a narrowly defined set of people, groups, and institutions. According to the logic of the debate, and at least partly prefigured by the argument put forth in Resolution 3237/6, these fall into three major categories:

1. political actors calling for, debating or opposing strict measures (1378 mentions);
2. those accused of an unwillingness to integrate (691 mentions);
3. and those called on to facilitate integration and to discipline the unwilling in the school context (317 mentions).

The dominance of the first group shows a focus on political debate over a lack of integration rather than on the lack itself, confirming that this was an instance of mediatized politics (Strömbäck 2008; Preston 2009; Forchtner et al. 2013).

The composition and representation of the three aggregated groups is of particular interest. (1) The vast majority of political actors associated with the debate over the unwillingness to integrate are *Social Democrats* (821 mentions, present in 75% of texts), followed by the *People's Party* (384 mentions, present in 60%), which dominates the overall discourse on integration; marginal roles are played by political actors of opposition parties, i.e. the far-right Freedom Party (81 mentions, present in 31%), the left Greens (41 mentions, present in 9%) and the liberal NEOs (13 mentions, present in 8%). These findings strongly support the conclusion that this particular debate over stricter measures against foreigners was not, as in previous decades, carried by the far-right FPÖ or even the center-right ÖVP, but by populist elements in the center-left SPÖ.

(2) Those suspected and accused of being unwilling were mainly *school children*. Familial relations play an important role as this group is also represented as *families* and *parents*. Other common forms of representation emphasize their alterity as *migrants, immigrants, Turks, foreigners, Muslims* or other *minorities*. Beyond that, this group is often reduced to the quality of being unwilling in the nominalized forms "Integrationsunwillige" and "Integrationsverweigerer". Significantly, the original study's complementary collocation analysis revealed that the quality of being "unwilling to integrate" is attributed exclusively to school children and their parents; furthermore, that the attributing is most frequently done by Social Democrats (direct or reported speech) and, increasingly so over the period under investigation, the respective newspaper itself (no direct or reported speech). The reified "unwillingness to integrate" is also frequently connected to punishments and demands for the former, but not to offenses or behaviors (see the companion website Revisiting the Toolbox for full results on collocational patterns).

(3) The third major group of social actors, i.e. those called on to facilitate integration or punish the unwilling, is represented as *teachers, pedagogues*, and *school administrators*. In addition, this group includes *institutions of child and youth welfare, social workers, psychologists* and other experts. Remarkably, *law-enforcement, courts*, and *the police* only figure in a very minor role.

In summary, the original study successfully integrated a cycle of qualitative and quantitative analyses to capture the dynamics of the political debate as a discourse strand, from the initiating event to the remarkably quick reification of the unwillingness to integrate through media. The representation of social actors in the data indicated a narrow focus on the punishment of transgressions committed by school children and their families, as discussed mostly by SPÖ and ÖVP politicians, to be carried out by institutions of education and welfare.

8.2 Revisiting the Study

In the following, the original study design will be discussed with respect to its limitations relating to the five methodological chapters—triangulation through the integration of quantitative and qualitative methods in CDS, working with multiple datasets, contrasting different levels of discourse, and visualization. These critical discussions will end with suggestions for revision which, where feasible, were carried out in the *revised study*. The following section will then report and discuss the results of the revised study design.

Arguably the most fundamental limitation of the original study concerns the empirical focus on a short-term discursive shift around terminology and the underlying assumption that this term represents the normalization or breaking of a taboo. Although the original study's operationalization of *discourse strand*, in combining a qualitative, contextualist analysis with CL methods, proved conceptually and empirically robust (Rheindorf and Wodak 2017; Rheindorf 2018a), it also highlighted the limitations of isolating discursive shifts from larger diachronic perspectives. Figure 8.1, as much as it confirms the impact of the mediatized debate over "Integrationsunwilligkeit", also shows that the term has a history of increasing usage for years before that—if not in the media, then perhaps in other fields of social action. *The revised study, then, would need to look beyond the initiating event, not just as historical context but empirically. While no complete archeology of the term is feasible, available data from related fields of social action could be investigated for usage of "Integrationsunwilligkeit" and terminological variations. Since this is, essentially, a lexical issue, CL methods should be sufficient to clarify whether and to which extent the discursive shift relates to the normalization of a taboo term. Obvious fields of social action related to the political demands for punitive measures against migrants who appear unwilling to integrate are politics, legislation, and jurisprudence. An extended study should identify specific discourses in those fields, compile data to represent the diachronic dimension of these discourses—at least ten years as suggested by Fig. 8.1. Beyond determining* whether *similar terminology had been used before, the revised study might also look into* how *it was used by different actors in the respective social fields and their discourses.*

It could also be argued that the original study failed to investigate in more detail how the media related to the controversial political assertions, such as the alleged connection between terrorism and school children's misbehavior, or political demands for new laws in reporting them, i.e. reproducing or rejecting the key contentions voiced by political actors. *Although this perspective may ultimately have to be quantified to provide an overview, it is essentially a qualitative research question. The revised study should therefore expand the qualitative analysis of the news articles to include the key rhetorical links suggested by the texts triggering the debate, i.e. Voves' interview and Resolution 3237/6: (a) the alleged link between terrorism and migrants', specifically migrant children's, unwillingness to integrate, (b) the usefulness of legal measures, specifically criminal law, to enforce integration and thereby reduce the risk of terrorism, and (c) changing current laws on integration to prevent possible terrorist attacks in the future as a responsible and necessary response by politicians. Such a perspective would effectively test whether the news media reaffirmed, if only by repetition, the highly problematic claims made for populist reasons during an election campaign period.*

8.3 The Revised Study: Results and Discussion

In revising the study, no changes are made to the theoretical-conceptual framework, but the amount of data analyzed is extended significantly—quantitatively but also diachronically, extending the revised study's analytical perspective more 15 years into the past. Methodologically, the study is complemented by argumentation analysis.

First, publicly available datasets are identified that would adequately represent relevant discourses in pertinent fields of social action. For *politics*, the stenographic protocols of all debates of the Austrian Nationalrat (henceforth *parliamentary debates*) since 1998 are available in digital form. Prepared and compiled into a machine-processable corpus, the 757 debates amount to more than 56 million words of running text. For *legislation*, all legal texts and supplementary materials for asylum, naturalization, foreigners, residency, and related proceedings (AsylG, StbG, FrG, FPG, NAG, BFA-VG) as well as related government drafts and parliamentary motions as provided by the Austrian parliament since 1998 are included. The 154 texts of this corpus come to over 1.8 million words of running text. For *jurisprudence*, the revised study includes all publicly available appeal rulings pertaining to the legal areas of asylum, naturalization, foreigners and residency (AsylG, StbG, FrG, FPG, NAG, BFA-VG) as provided by the digital information system of the Austrian government (Bundesministerium für Digitalisierung und Wirtschaftsstandort 2019). Because different courts have presided over relevant matters in the course of the past decades, the appeal rulings come from the Federal Asylum Senate, Asylum Court, and Federal Administrative Court; final appeal rulings come from the Constitutional Court and Supreme Administrative Court. In general, appeal rulings rather than first decisions had to be used, because the latter are not generally made public. For an overview of all corpora used in the revised study, see Table 8.2.

The results of the CL analysis for the legal framework confirm that neither "Integrationsunwilligkeit" nor any of its morphological variants occur in existing or previous legislation and related documents. However, an expanded search for compounds including **integration** shows that closely related terminology does have a history in Austrian legislation. This history begins with the FPÖ's campaigns for a stricter immigration regime in the mid-1990s and its subsequent negotiations with their coalition partner in government, the ÖVP. Documents drafted during this process included the term "Integrationsbereitschaft" (i.e. readiness to integrate, though sometimes translated as "willingness", e.g. Scheibelhofer 2012, 326), often qualified as "mangelnd" (i.e. lacking). For instance, a law drafted by the ÖVP suggested that citizenship should not be given away to foreign nationals showing "Anzeichen mangelnder Integrationsbere-

Table 8.2 Corpora in the revised study

Number of words and texts in the corpora and subcorpora				
	Texts		Words	
	Number	% of corpus	Number	% of corpus
Print media on *Integration*	3202	100	1,866,424	100
– on *Integrationsunwilligkeit*	280	8.75	290,440	15.56
Legislation	154	100	1,839,676	100
Jurisprudence since 1998	107,859	100	371,432,223	100
– Constitutional Court VfGH	612	0.57	859,142	0.23
– Supr. Admin. Court VwGH	18,450	17.11	21,989,610	5.92
– Fed. Asylum Senate UBAS	3508	3.25	7,886,341	2.12
– Asylum Court AsylGH	49,507	45.90	184,760,821	49.74
– Fed. Admin. Court BVwG	35,782	33.18	155,936,309	41.99
Parliamentary debates	757	100	56,023,108	100

itschaft", i.e. "signs of lacking readiness to integrate" (Regierungsvorlage 1998, 1283 BlgNR 20.GP, Österreichische Bundesregierung 1998). The same document refers contrastively to the welcome "Integrationsneigung" (inclination to integrate) of citizens of EU member states or recognized refugees, exempting these from the general suspicion that migrants are likely to resist integration.

The Nationality Law that was passed in 1998 and first introduced language requirements as conditions for attaining citizenship refers to "Merkmale" (signs) and "Grade" (degrees) of integration, but refers neither to the will or the readiness to integrate. Later amendments, most recently in 2011, did not change or add to the terminology in this regard, nor did the plethora of amendments and regulations passed since then (Perchinig 2010; Stern and Valchars 2013a, b).

Remarkably, the revised study's results with respect to jurisprudence are strikingly different. Although no terminology associated with "Integrationsunwilligkeit" is established in Austrian legislation, the institutions that have held first-appeal authority over the relevant legal matters since 1998 made relatively frequent reference to such notions. This includes the Bundesasylsenat (Federal Asylum Senate) from January 1, 1998 to June 30, 2008, the Asylgerichtshof (Asylum Court) from July 1, 2008 to December 31, 2014, and since January 1, 2015 the Bundesverwaltungsgericht (Federal Administrative Court). A close look at the appeal rulings reveals a differentiated picture: The Asylum Senate in over ten years of practice used the term "integrationswillig" a total of 3 times, always in positive contexts attesting the applicant the will to integrate in 2003, 2005, and 2006. It also used the terms "integrationsbereit" (ready to integrate) and "Integrationsfähigkeit" (ability to integrate) in similar contexts in 1999 and 2002, respectively.

The Asylum Court, in contrast, in its less than seven years of existence, used the negative terms "integrationsunwillig", "Integrationsunwilligkeit", and "Integrationsunwille", in a total of eight rulings between 2008 and 2011. With much higher frequency, however, it referred to the absence of "Integrationswilligkeit" (581), "integrationswillig" (91), and "Integrationswille" (96) as well as "Integrationsbereitschaft" (165) and "Integrationsfähigkeit" (46). While little can be inferred from these results as to why the rulings of the Asylum Court used such terms much more frequently than its predecessor court, it is certain that there was no corresponding change in legislation.

The Federal Administrative Court, which replaced the Asylum Court four years ago at the time of writing, seems to have continued this trend. It has used the term "Integrationsunwilligkeit" in fifteen rulings and very frequently referred to the absence of "Integrationswilligkeit" (352), "integrationswillig" (451), and "Integrationswille" (371) as well "integrationsbereit" (29) and "Integrationsbereitschaft" (52). In terms of the overall pattern, it thus seems as if reference to a "will" to integrate, but most frequently to its absence or lack, has been increasing and replacing references to an "ability" or "readiness" to integrate, despite the absence of these terms from relevant laws.

Plotted as normalized frequency (per million words) on a line graph at annual intervals, the above results shows the striking increase of all related terms beginning with 2008, peaking in 2011, most notably of terms denoting the "will" to integrate. The compounded negated forms, i.e. "integrationsunwillig" and "Integrationsunwilligkeit", have seen sharply increased use only since 2015. Prior to the discourse strand investigated in the original study, use of the terms in jurisprudence, although limited, is clearly attested by the data (Fig. 8.2).

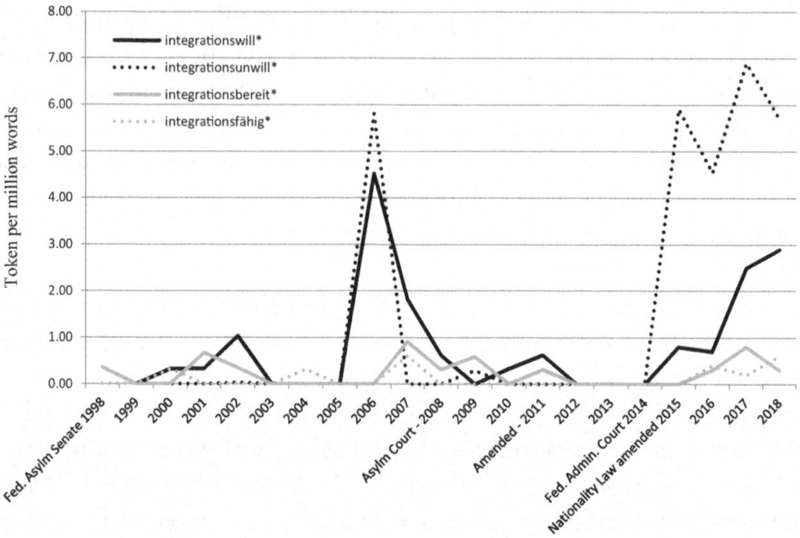

Fig. 8.2 Terminology denoting 'willingness', 'unwillingness', 'readiness', and 'ability' to integrate in appeal rulings related to asylum, nationality and residency (1998–2018)

The revised study's findings for the rulings of Austria's supreme courts, which are the final courts of appeal in matters related to nationality, residence, and asylum, provide a stark contrast. Jurisprudence of the Austrian Supreme Administrative Court (VwGH) since 1998 refers to lacking willingness to integrate exclusively in its discussions of the decisions appealed against, i.e. it does not use any of the terms in its own reasoning. For instance, in a prominent appeal which referred to the applicant as "absolut integrationsunwillig" (absolutely unwilling to integrate) because he had not completed any language courses, the Supreme Court harshly criticized this vague and unfounded conclusion and repealed it for its counterfactual argument (VwGH 2008/21/0075). The Supreme Administrative Court likewise has not used such terminology other than in summaries of rulings appealed against. In summary, the Supreme Court and Constitutional Court avoid terms not established in relevant legislation in arguing their own decisions on appeal. In contrast to the decisions by administrative institutions and the first-order appeals against them, the Supreme Courts use the terminology of the relevant laws (e.g. VfGH U613/10): “Integrationsbemühungen” (efforts to integrate), “Integrationsgrad” or “Grad der Integration” (degree of integration), and “Integrationskriterien” (criteria for integration). Thus, their rulings emphasize positive or measurable phenomena rather than the absence of willingness.

While the original study only analyzed a specific, short-term instance of mediatized politics, and concluded from the evident controversy that the term “Integrationsunwilligkeit” had previously been a taboo in Austrian politics, the revised study takes a long-term diachronic look at political discourse in the form of parliamentary debates since 1998. Remarkably, the revised study finds some instances of “Integrationsunwilligkeit” and related terms, although more isolated than in jurisprudence (see Fig. 8.3). Considering that the frequencies of the noun “Integration” (62.57 pmw), the verb “integrieren” (7.71 pmw) and the adjective “integriert” (16.82 pmw) attest to the fact that integration is a salient topic in parliamentary debates for the last 20 years, references to the willingness and unwillingness to integrate (0.55 and 0.36 pmw) or to the readiness and ability to integrate (0.2 and 0.07 pmw) are marginal. Nonetheless, these occurrences prior to the mediatized debate in early 2015 warrant a closer analysis. As shown in Fig. 8.3, there are first minor peaks of usage in 2001 and 2002; a major peak in 2006; and minor peaks in 2009 and 2011. Remarkably, all related terms had disappeared between 2011 and 2015.

All minor peaks are related to legislative initiatives for stricter naturalization and asylum regimes. The major peak, however, is not. In the parliamentary debate of May 24, 2006, the opposition parties used an Urgent Enquiry, i.e. a formal written enquiry that must be answered by the government, to address a statement made by the Minister of Interior Affairs Liese Prokop (ÖVP). In the context of her election campaign, Prokop had claimed that 45% of Muslims living in Austria were “integrationsunwillig” (unwilling to integrate) and therefore a “tickende Zeitbombe” (ticking time-bomb) waiting to go off. In the debate that day as well as in the two following debates on June 21 and 22, members of the governing ÖVP and FPÖ/BZÖ (a rebranded splinter group of the FPÖ) defended that claim, if not its wording. Members of the opposition parties, including the SPÖ, were outspoken in their rejection of the insinuations of an unwillingness to integrate. The major peak in Fig. 8.3 is thus the

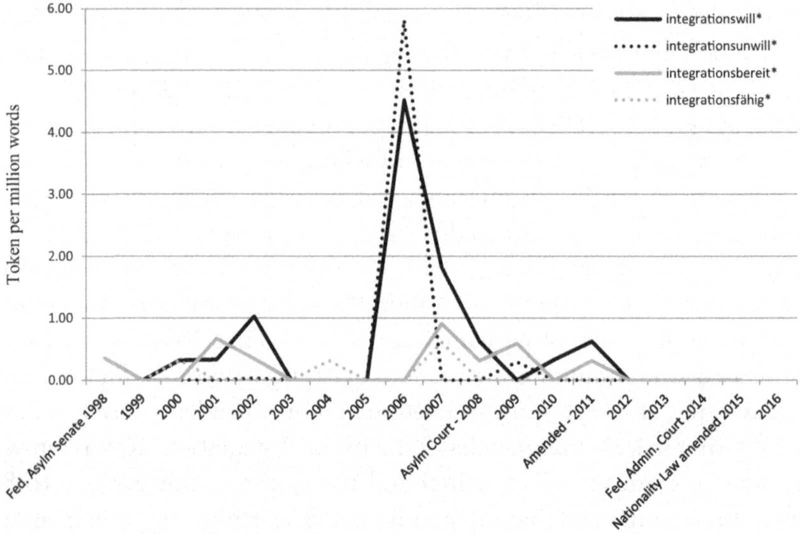

Fig. 8.3 Terminology denoting 'unwillingness', 'readiness', and 'ability' to integrate in parliamentary debates (1998–2018)

effect of a clear opposition, led by the SPÖ, to counter the implications of the term. This opposition seems to have been effective for the following years, until Voves (a prominent member of the SPÖ) triggered the controversy that firmly established it in political and media discourse. While the revised study thus does not show that "Integrationsunwilligkeit" had never been used before, it confirms its marginality prior to the mediatized debate studied in the original study.

The second major revision of the study is a closer look at the extent to which the media in 2015 reproduced the key rhetorical links suggested by Voves' interview and Resolution 3237/6. Argumentation analysis encompasses all 280 texts included in the original study with respect to (a) the alleged link between terrorism and migrants' unwillingness to integrate, (b) the usefulness of legal measures to enforce integration and thereby prevent terrorism, and (c) changing current laws on integration as responsible and necessary response by politicians. Using MAXQDA software, the two-layered coding scheme seen in Tables 8.3 and 8.4 is applied: Content is coded for the three pairs of elements linked by Voves and Resolution

Table 8.3 Arguments in the mediatized debate

Content codes	Spread	Spread in %
(a) Threat of terrorism and radicalization	268	95.7
(a) Migrants' unwillingness to integrate	280	100.0
(b) Legal measures to enforce integration	274	97.9
(b) Preventing terrorism	253	90.4
(c) Changing current laws on integration	244	87.1
(c) Necessary response by politicians	238	85.0

Table 8.4 Argumentative links in the mediatized debate

Link codes	Spread for (a)	Spread for (b)	Spread for (c)
– Link explicit	30% (84)	6.8% (19)	20.4% (57)
– Link implied	53,2% (149)	47.1% (132)	41.8% (117)
– Link explicitly questioned	12,5% (35)	18.2% (51)	16.1% (45)
– No link	*4,3% (12)*	*27.9% (78)*	*21.8% (61)*

3237/6; links are coded for their explicit/implicit reproduction and questioning in the newspaper articles.

Coding results for the spread of the three content pairs confirm the strong topical and structural cohesion of the discourse strand as well as the texts' intertextual ties with the two initiating texts. Coding the type of link is not always a clear-cut process, especially with implied links: These are often non-causal conjunctions such as "und" (and) or simple association by contiguity, with the two elements of their pair being mentioned a sequence (of items in a list, of sentences or paragraphs) that would imply causality or consequence. The following example illustrates this type of association:

> On Tuesday, Franz Voves proposed in the Styrian state parliament to task experts with "legally defining statutory offenses of unwillingness to integrate". Niessl also demands that people who go into jihad should be stripped of their citizenship: "Anyone who goes to war and fights should lose their citizenship." (Kurier, January 21, 2015)

In this article, published relatively late in the debate, the association is created not by reproducing the claims advanced by Voves or Resolution

3237/6, but by juxtaposing them with the statements of Governor Niessl, another prominent Social Democrat. Like Voves, Niessl was at the time campaigning for reelection as Governor and seized the populist opportunity offered by the debate about terrorism and integration. The conjunction "also" here links the two issues lexically, but the more important choices on the part of the newspaper were to include these statements, to put them in this order, and to do so without addressing the alleged link explicitly.

Quantitatively, the results for link types indicate that implicit links are pervasive in the corpus. Combined with explicit links, over 83% of the articles link the threat of terrorism and radicalization to migrants' unwillingness to integrate; nearly 54% link legal measures to enforce migration and preventing terrorism; and more than 62% present changes to current laws on integration as a necessary response by politicians. This means that the link underlying the entire debate, the assumption that migrants' unwillingness to integrate is linked to terrorism, is reproduced the most and questioned the least, while the two instrumental, goal-oriented links are less widely accepted.

Beyond this general characterization of the debate, we might also ask if these links change in the course of the debate, i.e. if there is a discursive shift not only terminologically but in the way the three claims are recontextualized. To obtain a measure of this development, the link type frequencies are aggregated for each day in the period under investigation and then visualized as a stacked line graph (Fig. 8.4).

As the raw figures do not reveal much in terms of the link type ratio's development over time, a second stacked line graph normalizes their frequency for the number of articles published on the respective day (Fig. 8.1). Here, the relative increase of explicit links (and no links) emerges clearly, as does a slight decrease in implicit links (Fig. 8.5).

Although conducted on a relatively small scale, the revised study's diachronic analysis of argumentation is able to show how overall media reporting follows and gradually normalizes highly contested relations—between terrorism and integration, between stricter laws for migrants and successful prevention of terrorism, and between the call for politicians to respond to terrorism and changing the legal framework for migrants. Notably, the most normalized connection seems to be the

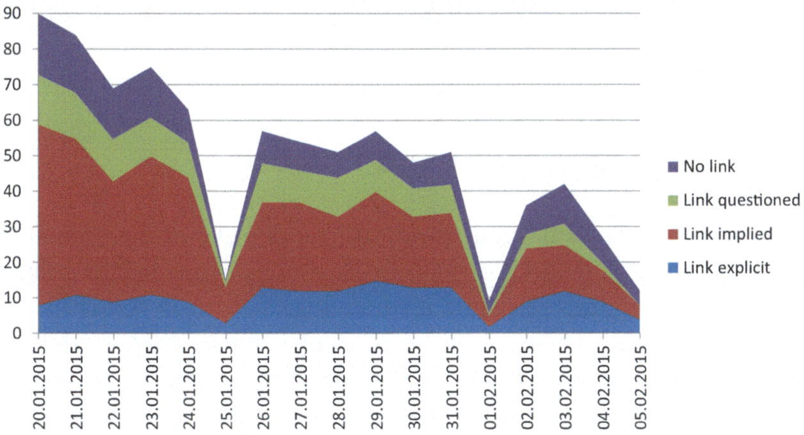

Fig. 8.4 Aggregated link types per day (20.1.2015–5.2.2015)

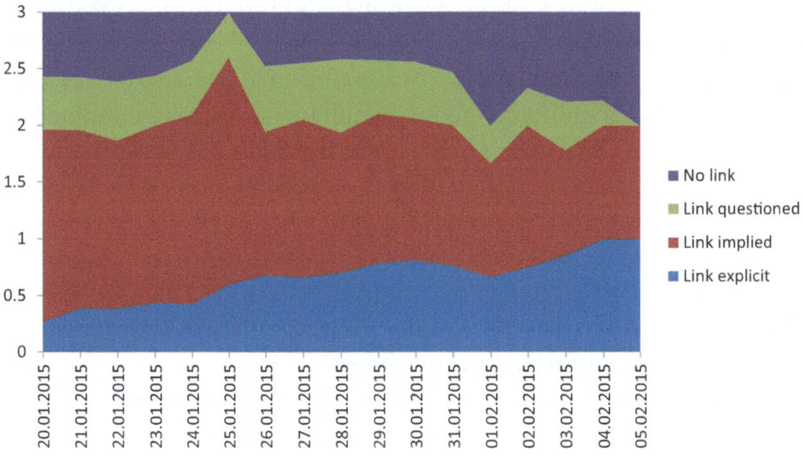

Fig. 8.5 Aggregated link types per day (20.1.2015–5.2.2015), normalized for number of articles

underlying claim that an 'unwillingness to integrate', if left unpunished, will lead to (religious) radicalization and terrorism.

8.4 Research Design and Practice

The study of short-term discursive shifts, in particular of the normalization of contested terms and concepts in the context of mediatized politics, highlights several conceptual and methodological issues in contemporary CDS. This chapter has used the revision of previous work to demonstrate the critical aspects of (1) operationalizing the notion of *discourse strand* empirically, specifically for corpus compilation and CL analysis, (2) relating short-term diachronies such as discursive shifts to long-term diachrony, conceptually as well as empirically, (3) the need to critically question researcher assumptions regarding taboos and norms, (4) selecting fields of social action and specific discourses situated in them to conduct a cross-sectional discourse analysis, (5) accounting for the respective discursive changes and stabilities, whether simultaneous or non-simultaneous, within the institutional norms of the respective fields, (6) the limitations of purely lexical CL analyses with regard to political discourse, which typically involves complex textual patterns like argumentation or legitimation, (7) the indispensable combination of qualitative and quantitative approaches in exploring discursive change in complex patterns of language use, and (8) the potential of relatively simple, static visualizations in illustrating discursive change and relating it to context.

With respect to research design and practice, this case study's discussions indicate that we should

- be willing to experiment with operationalizing theoretical concepts empirically, including quantitative operationalization of concepts that have been mainly associated with qualitative work,
- find ways and take the time to test such operationalizations by using alternative datasets, measures, periodizations, and analytical methods,
- triangulate conclusions about discursive change, or short-term discursive shifts, by conducting parallel analyses for other discourses, levels of discourse, or data from other fields of social action,

- find ways to relate short-term discursive shifts to long-term discursive change and stability,
- define normalization as a pattern of language use not limited to the lexical or semantic level, but instead include relevant patterns on and beyond the sentence level,
- use CL tools where the above considerations require us to analyze large datasets, but ensure that quantitative results are valid by grounding them in a qualitative level of analysis,
- consider different forms of visualization not only as illustrations for publication but as tools in the analytical process, and
- ensure data integrity and transparency when publishing, considering that the best option may well be beyond traditional publishing formats, e.g. an online repository.

References

Achtenhagen, Leona, and Friederike Welter. 2008. "Media Discourse in Entrepreneurship Research." In *Handbook of Qualitative Research Methods in Entrepreneurship*, edited by Helle Neergard and John Parm Ulhoi, 193–215. Cheltenham: Elgar.

Bundesministerium für Digitalisierung und Wirtschaftsstandort. 2019. "Rechtsinformationssystem Des Bundes." www.ris.bka.gv.at.

de Cillia, Rudolf. 2012. "Migration Und Sprache / n. Sprachenpolitik – Sprachförderung – Diskursanalyse." In *Migrations- Und Integrationsforschung – Multidisziplinäre Perspektiven*, edited by Heinz Fassmann and Julia Dahlvik, 2., erweiterte und überarbeitete Auflage, 185–212. Wien: Vienna University Press.

de Cillia, Rudolf, and Ruth Wodak, eds. 2009. *Gedenken Im „Gedankenjahr": Zur Diskursiven Konstruktion Österreichischer Identitäten Im Jubiläumsjahr 2005.* Innsbruck: Studienverlag.

Forchtner, Bernhard, Michał Krzyżanowski, and Ruth Wodak. 2013. "Mediatisation, Right-Wing Populism and Political Campaigning: The Case of the Austrian Freedom Party (FPÖ)." In *Media Talk and Political Elections in Europe and America*, edited by M. Ekström and A. Tolson, 205–28. Basingstoke: Palgrave.

Grimm, Jacob, and Wilhelm Grimm. 1965. *Deutsches Wörterbuch*, vol. 30. Stuttgrt and Leipzig: Hirzel.

Jäger, Siegfried. 2001. "Discourse and Knowledge: Theoretical and Methodological Aspects of a Critical Discourse and Dispositive Analysis." In *Methods of Critical Discourse Analysis*, edited by Ruth Wodak and Michael Meyer, 32–62. London: Sage.

Krzyżanowski, Michał. 2013. "From Anti-Immigration and Nationalist Revisionism to Islamophobia: Continuities and Shifts in Recent Discourses and Patterns of Political Communication of the Freedom Party of Austria (FPÖ)." In *Right-Wing Populism in Europe: Politics and Discourse*, edited by Ruth Wodak, Majid KhosraviNik, and Brigitte Mral, 135–48. London: Bloomsburry.

Landtag Steiermark. 2015. "Resolution [Entschließungsantrag] 3237/6." www.landtag.steiermark.at/cms/dokumente/ltpdf.11411653/na/11411653.pdf.

ORF. 2015. "Klare Worte von Voves Zu Terror in Frankreich." *Orf.At*. August 1, 2015. www.steiermark.orf.at/news/stories/2690421.

Österreichische Bundesregierung. 1998. "Regierungsvorlage Zur Staatsbürgerschaftsgesetznovelle 1998" [Government Draft for the Citizenship Law Amendment 1998], 1283 BlgNR 20.GP.

Perchinig, Bernhard. 2010. "All You Need to Know to Become an Austrian: Naturalisation Policy and Citizenship Testing in Austria." In *A Re-definition of Belonging? Language and Integration Tests in Europe*, edited by Ricky van Oers, Eva Ersbøll, and Theodora Kostakopoulou, 25–50. Leiden, Boston: Martinus Nijhoff Publishers.

Preston, Paschal. 2009. *Making the News: Journalism and News Cultures in Europe*. London and New York: Routledge.

Reddemann, Luise. 2005. "Zwischen Schlaf- Und Wachzuständen: Von Elben, Druiden, Nachtmaren, Kobolden Und Anderen Ungeheuerlichkeiten: Alpträume." Vortrag Presented at the 55. Lindauer Psychotherapiewochen 2005, Lindau. April 21. http://www.lptw.de/archiv/vortrag/2005/reddemann.pdf.

Reisigl, Martin, and Ruth Wodak. 2015. "The Discourse Historical Approach (DHA)." In *Methods of Critical Discourse Studies*, edited by Ruth Wodak and Michael Meyer, 23–61. London: Sage.

Rheindorf, Markus. 2017. "Integration Durch Strafe? Die Normalisierung Paternalistischer Diskursfiguren Zur „Integrationsunwilligkeit"." *Zeitschrift Für Diskursforschung* 2/2017: 182–206.

———. 2018a. "Disciplining the Unwilling. Normalisation of (Demands for) Punitive Measures Against Immigrants in Austrian Populist Discourse." In

Doing Politics: Discursivity, Performativity and Mediation in Political Discourse, edited by Michael Kranert and Geraldine Horan, 179–208. Amsterdam: John Benjamins.

———. 2018b. "Integration Durch Strafe? „Integrationsunwilligkeit" Im Politischen Diskurs. Vom Späten Erfolg Eines Umstrittenen Begriffes." In *Migration Und Integration – Wissenschaftliche Perspektiven Aus Österreich*, edited by Jennifer Carvill Schellenbacher, Julia Dahlvik, Heinz Faßmann, and Christoph Reinprecht, 325–44. Wien: Vandenhoeck & Ruprecht; Vienna University Press.

———. 2019. "Discourse, Rhetorics and Populist Politics." In *The Cambridge Handbook of Discourse Studies*, edited by Anna De Fina and Alexandra Georgakopoulou. Cambridge: Cambridge University Press.

Rheindorf, Markus, and Ruth Wodak. 2017. "Borders, Fences, and Limits—Protecting Austria from Refugees: Metadiscursive Negotiation of Meaning in the Current Refugee Crisis." *Journal of Immigrant & Refugee Studies*. April 1–24. https://doi.org/10.1080/15562948.2017.1302032.

Scheibelhofer, Paul. 2012. "From Health Check to Muslim Test: The Shifting Politics of Governing Migrant Masculinity." *Journal of Intercultural Studies* 33 (3): 319–32. https://doi.org/10.1080/07256868.2012.673474.

Stern, Joachim, and Gerd Valchars. 2013a. *Citizenship Law in Austria. European Union Democracy Observatory on Citizenship*. Florence: European University Institute.

———. 2013b. *Naturalisation Procedures for Immigrants in Austria. European Union Democracy Observatory on Citizenship*. Florence: European University Institute.

Strömbäck, Jesper. 2008. "Four Phases of Mediatization. An Analysis of the Mediatization of Politics." *The International Journal of Press/Politics* 13 (3): 228–46. https://doi.org/10.1177/1940161208319097.

Wodak, Ruth. 2002a. "Aspects of Critical Discourse Analysis." *Zeitschrift Für Angewandte Linguistik* 36: 5–31.

———. 2002b. "Friend or Foe." *Language & Communication* 22 (4): 495–517. https://doi.org/10.1016/S0271-5309(02)00022-8.

———. 2011. *The Discourse of Politics in Action: Politics as Usual*. Pbk. ed. New York: Palgrave Macmillan.

———. 2015. *Politics of Fear: What Right-Wing Populist Discourses Mean*. Los Angeles: Sage.

———. 2018. "Driving on the Right: The Austrian Case." Centre for Analysis of the Radical Right. September 4, 2018. https://www.radicalrightanalysis.com/2018/04/09/driving-on-the-right-the-austrian-case/.

Wodak, Ruth, Rudolf de Cillia, Martin Reisigl, and Karin Liebhart. 2009. *The Discursive Construction of National Identity*. 2nd ed. Critical Discourse Analysis. Edinburgh: Edinburgh University Press.
Wodak, Ruth, Rudolf de Cillia, Martin Reisigl, Karin Liebhart, Klaus Hofstätter, and Maria Kargl. 1998. *Zur Diskursiven Konstruktion Nationaler Identität*. 1. Aufl. Suhrkamp Taschenbuch Wissenschaft 1349. Frankfurt: Suhrkamp.

9

Case Study 3: Media Representations of Refugees, Asylum Seekers, Immigrants, and Migrants

9.1 Introduction: The Original Study

This case study revisits work on the representation of refugees, asylum seekers, immigrants, and migrants during the so-called refugee crisis of 2015/2016. The original study was conducted in the course of an extensive research project on the discursive construction of national identities in Austria and has partly been published as Rheindorf and Wodak (2019). The overall project developed a longitudinal perspective on the changing constructions of national identities. What makes that perspective remarkable is the availability and use of similar datasets across two decades, including similar methods of data collection and analysis within the same theoretical framework (e.g. Wodak et al. 2009). This introduction will briefly outline this research context before presenting the case study in its original form and then give a critical discussion of the original study: highlighting limitations and suggesting changes, revising the study and discussing its results, and finally drawing general conclusions for research design and practice.

© The Author(s) 2019
M. Rheindorf, *Revisiting the Toolbox of Discourse Studies*, Postdisciplinary Studies in Discourse,
https://doi.org/10.1007/978-3-030-19369-0_9

This case study, like the larger project, uses the DHA as its theoretical framework, defining discourses as always historically embedded, mutually constitutive with social contexts, and sites of struggle over power (Reisigl and Wodak 2015). The overall project studied the construction of national identities very broadly—in terms of the construction of (1) a Homo Nationalis, (2) a shared culture, (3) a shared past, (4) a shared political present and future, and (5) a national body (Wodak et al. 2009)—on multiple levels of discourse and across several social fields. The project team collected and analyzed data from the fields of politics (parliamentary politics, election campaigns, state representation), the media (print, television, radio, social media, advertisement) as well as quasi-private discourses (data elicited through group discussions and interviews), and ethnographic observations (at rallies and commemorative events). For an overview of all data collected in that project as well as related publications, see the project's website (Wodak et al. 2019).

Among all that material, the original study discussed here focused on one topical discourse, i.e. the discourse about refugees, asylum seekers, immigrants, and migrants, as realized in one social field, i.e. the media. And while it also took a diachronic approach, this was narrowly defined by the period of data collection: the 14 months from January 1, 2015, until February 28, 2016. Specifically, the original study compiled texts from Austrian print media with national distribution containing at least one of the search terms **flüchtling** (refugee), **asyl** (asylum), **geflüchtete** (fleeing), **schutzsuchend** (seeking protection), **immigrant** (immigrant) or **migrant** (migrant). The resulting total of 5739 texts, running to 8,008,536 tokens, were compiled into a machine-processable corpus and coded for date of publication to facilitate diachronic analyses.

The cutoff points for data collection were chosen to cover the height of the "crisis" based on contextual information: The starting point marked the onset of a gradual increase of refugees arriving in 2015, leading to a strongly mediatized 'crisis' in Austria's most prominent refugee center Traiskirchen, the federal government's failed negotiations with the Austrian states over obligatory quotas for refugees, and numerous 'crisis moments' during the summer and fall of 2015. The 'crisis' waned with the Austrian government's heavily mediatized decision to build a border fence, strictly control immigration, and set a maximum limit on the number of asylum

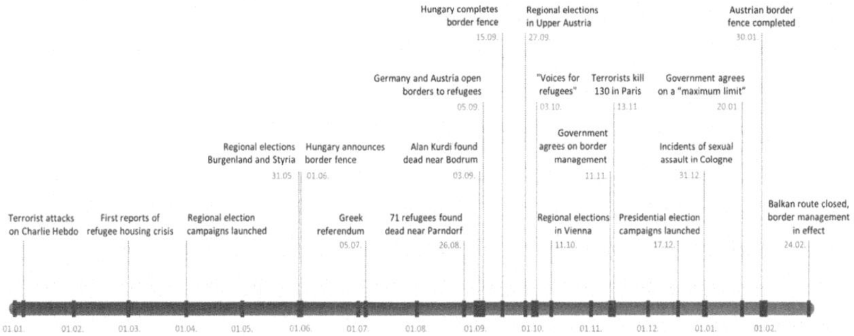

Fig. 9.1 Timeline of the 'refugee crisis' with key events from an Austrian perspective

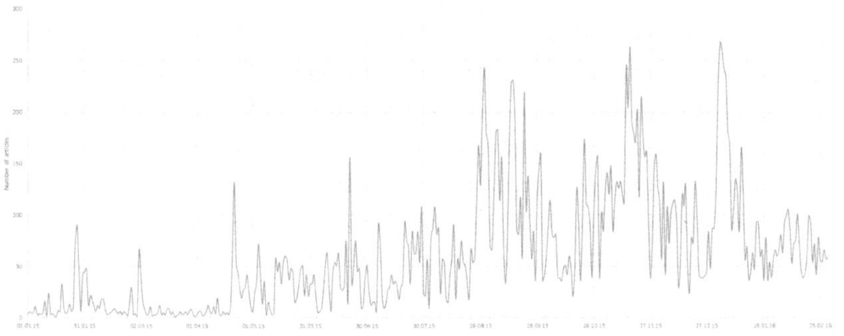

Fig. 9.2 Number of articles on refugees, asylum seekers, and migrants published per day

applications to be accepted per year. In late February 2016, the Austrian government declared the refugee routes closed and the crisis ended (see Fig. 9.1 for a timeline of significant events).

To obtain an overview of the media's strong but context-sensitive coverage during the 14-month period under investigation, the original study used the data's publishing date to calculate the fluctuations in coverage (number of articles/day). In addition to notable peaks in reporting, which correspond roughly to specific events of national or international significance reported as part of the 'crisis', there is an overall increase of media attention on refugees, asylum seekers, and migrants. Figure 9.2 shows the highly fluctuating intensity of news reporting through this period.

Although issues of migration clearly relate to national identity, particularly to constructions of the Homo Nationalis/Homo Externus, a shared past and culture, and the national body, the original study was not part of the larger project's original plan. Neither the so-called refugee crisis nor its intense media coverage had been anticipated by the research team when the project launched on January 1, 2015 (for the project plan, see Wodak et al. 2019). However, the overall research design was open enough to accommodate individual case studies focusing on unanticipated events related to the overall aims.

During the 14 months of data covered by the original study, the Austrian government's stance shifted from a policy of open borders to one of closed borders, recontextualized as a positive contribution to building "Fortress Europe" (Lehner and Rheindorf 2019). While some distinct events, such as the march of thousands of refugees from Hungary to Austria, the gruesome death of 71 refugees at the hands of people smugglers, and the incidents in Cologne during New Year's Eve 2015/2016, can be considered turning points for the extensive debate over how to handle migration; the government's policy reversal was gradual and publicly negotiated (Rheindorf and Wodak 2017).

The original study's approach to media representations of refugees and related, often inadequately distinguished groups, drew on the RASIM project at Lancaster University (e.g. Baker et al. 2008; Gabrielatos and Baker 2008). That research investigated the representation of refugees, asylum seekers, immigrants, and migrants in the UK press (1996–2006) within a CDS framework, using mainly CL methods. It is, to date, one of the largest and most innovative efforts to integrate CL with CDS and therefore a suitable methodological point of reference. Three methodological aspects offered particularly promising points of departure for the original study: First, RASIM integrated the notion of *discourse prosody*, i.e. the persistent relationship between key terms and the recurring, habitual patterns of their usage in context by which a form is "imbued" with a "consistent aura of meaning" on the level of discourse (Gabrielatos and Baker 2008, 10). Second, it pioneered and operationalized the notion of *constant collocates* or *c-collocates* in statistical terms: In order to be classified as consistent, collocates had to be present in at least seven out of ten subcorpora (Gabrielatos and Baker 2008, 11–12). Their consistency over time may indicate their link to persistent topoi and thus represent "the incremental effect of discourse" (Baker 2006, 13). Third, it operationalized the notion of *intercollocation*, i.e. overlap of collocates between key terms such as refugees, asylum seekers and migrants. This method can be used to test the possible conflation of terms, which may be legally distinct, with respect to their usage (Baker and McEnery 2005; Gabrielatos and Baker 2008).

Paralleling this predominantly quantitative approach, the original study started out with the following questions:

1. Which nominations and predications are used to represent refugees, asylum seekers, and migrants in Austrian print media?
2. Which overlaps and differences emerge with respect to the different groups and their varying nominations (e.g. refugees, economic refugees, migrants, and asylum seekers)?
3. Which of the identified patterns of nomination and predication are constant for the period under investigation?

As nomination and predication patterns can be effectively gleaned through CL methods, the original study began with quantitative analyses. First, frequency lists for all likely nominations of the relevant groups were compiled for the entire corpus, then for 14 subsets of the data defined by calendar month.

The individual frequencies of the search term lemmas revealed a strong focus on 'refugees' (**flüchtling**), followed by the less frequent cognates 'asylum applicant' (**asylwerber**), 'asylum seeker' (**asylsuchende**), and nouns denoting 'those seeking protection' (*schutzsuchende**), 'those who have fled' (*geflüchtete**), and 'successful applicants' (*asylberechtigte**). Derogatory terms such as 'bogus asylum seeker' (*scheinasylant**, *asylant**) were rare in the data. However, compounding of *flüchtling** points to more indirect delegitimation as in 'economic refugee' (*wirtschaftsflüchtling**). For migrants, other than the term 'migrant' itself (**migrant**), such derived forms (e.g. *wirtschaftsmigrant**) are much less frequent.

Viewed by month, the frequencies of most nominations broadly correspond to the number of articles published. In absolute numbers, there is thus a clear peak of *flüchtling** in September, which slowly abates in

Table 9.1 Search term lemmas by frequency

	Lemma	Frequency
1.	*flüchtling**	19,164
2.	*asylwerber**	4068
3.	*migrant**	1430
4.	*asylsuchende**	541
5.	*asylbewerber**	512
6.	*wirtschaftsflüchtling**	494
7.	*schutzsuchende**	459
8.	*asylberechtigte**	266
9.	*asylant**	140
10.	*schutzbedürftige**	112
11.	*geflüchtete**	78
12.	*bootsflüchtlinge**	74
13.	*wirtschaftsmigrant**	56
14.	*scheinasylant**	34
15.	*asylantragsteller**	20
16.	*bürgerkriegsflüchtling**	19
17.	*asylanwärter**	2
18.	*asylbetrüger**	2

the course of the following months. However, Table 9.1 also indicates a relative increase of *migrant** and *wirtschaftsflüchtling** towards the end of 2015 and an even stronger relative increase of *migrant** in the early months of 2016. This suggests a *discursive shift* in representation: After the brief surge of solidarity in summer, clearly emphasizing the category 'refugee', the discourse shifts towards 'migrant' even as the political debate focuses on closing the border and restricting the right to asylum; this intensifies further after the incidents of sexual harassment in Cologne (Table 9.2).

The second quantitative perspective focused on the collocations for each of these nominations (5 left, 5 right), first for the entire corpus, then separately for each month (Baker and McEnery 2005, 223), to determine c-collocates. Adapting the original 7:10 ratio, the original study took as "consistent" collocates that were present in 10 of the 14 subcorpora. With respect to the representation of minorities in mediatized politics, c-collocates as a way of viewing discourse prosody have important implications as they help to create and invoke topoi. Such patterns can lead readers from premise to conclusion without explicit argumentation

Table 9.2 Monthly frequency of search term lemma with a total frequency >100

	1.15	2.15	3.15	4.15	5.15	6.15	7.15	8.15	9.15	10.15	11.15	12.15	1.16	2.16
*flüchtling**	250	174	144	125	252	228	471	814	4591	3759	3164	2253	1712	1227
*asylwerber**	53	37	31	26	53	48	101	173	975	798	672	478	363	260
*migrant**	19	13	11	9	19	17	35	61	182	190	196	218	248	212
*asylsuchende**	7	5	4	4	7	6	14	23	130	106	90	64	48	34
*wirtschaftsflüchtling**	2	8	6	4	12	14	21	31	57	74	68	62	73	61
*schutzsuchende**	2	0	3	2	8	12	19	22	24	110	91	76	54	32
*asylant**	2	1	1	1	2	2	4	6	14	28	23	21	18	19
*schutzbedürftige**	2	4	3	2	5	8	11	14	9	13	12	10	9	10

Table 9.3 Number and percentage of collocations by semantic fields

	flüchtling*	asylwerber*	migrant*	asylsuchende*	wirtschaftsflüchtling*
Abuse of system	186; 0.1%	25; 0.06%	77; 0.54%	–	156; 3.16%
Burden	9834; 5.13%	1508; 3.96%	249; 1.74%	279; 5.16%	320; 6.48%
Entry	8689; 4.53%	447; 1.09%	680; 4.76%	126; 2.33%	39; 0.79%
Legality of claim	1899; 1%	510; 1.25%	464; 3.24%	21; 0.39%	196; 3.97%
Number	9462; 4.94%	1936; 4.74%	823; 5.76%	297; 5.49%	24; 0.49
Origin	813; 0.42%	159; 0.39%	47; 0.33%	22; 0.41%	5; 0.1%
Personal trait	1133; 0.59%	474; 1.16%	186; 1.30%	79; 1.46%	181; 3.66%
Plight	2467; 1.29%	56; 0.14%	60; 0.42%	8; 0.15%	4; 0.08%
Positive effect	53; 0.03%	31; 0.08%	14; 0.1%	14; 0.26%	–
Residence	546; 0.29%	794; 1.94%	10; 0.07%	32; 0.59%	28; 0.57%
Threat	2502; 1.31%	487; 1.19%	157; 1.1%	55; 1.02%	13; 0.26%
Welcome	597; 0.31%	134; 0.33%	40; 0.28%	29; 0.54%	57; 1.15%

insofar as readers are more likely to attend to the connotational than the denotational level of specific frequent collocations (Baker et al. 2008).

Moving to a qualitative perspective, the original study then categorized these collocations into semantic fields to gain an overview of the (changing) topical macro-structure of discourse around each key nomination. This technique, also referred to as "key categories" (Baker 2006, 143), uses either a pre-determined set of categories like USAS (e.g. Archer et al. 2002) or inductively develops categories from the material. The original study adapted the categories used in Gabrielatos and Baker (2008), distinguishing between: abuse of system, burden, entry (mode, place, route), legality of claim, number, personal traits, plight, positive effect, residence, threat (crime, terrorism), and welcome. Categorization was done manually and concordance lines were used to disambiguate usage.

Once collocates were aggregated into these categories, the relative frequency of the semantic fields highlight evaluative tendencies in the discourse prosodies of the key nominations. Table 9.3 presents the key categories for the collocations of the five most frequent nominations and gives the percentage of the nominations' occurrences with collocations of that semantic field:

These results reveal striking contrasts between the extent to which *refugees* and *migrants* (but even more so *economic refugees*) are represented as abusing the Austrian asylum and welfare systems. Given the fluidity with which the two terms are used in referring to the same group of people, this suggests that specific nominations are used to (de)legitimize their rights.

This pattern is different regarding *burden*: Although economic refugees are strongly associated with burdens on Austria as a host country, this is also true for representations of refugees and asylum seekers—but less so migrants. Refugees, asylum seekers, and migrants are all commonly aggregated or collectivized in terms of *numbers*. A substantially larger segment of collocates for economic refugees relates to their *personal traits* and their *welcome* than with any other group.

Given these quantitative results, the original study went on to compare in detail which collocates made up the individual key categories for the different nominations. For instance, with *abuse of system* the comparison shows refugees and asylum seekers to be (infrequently) attributed with wrong or false claims, forgery, pretense, and lies, while migrants are (overall much more frequently) associated with abuse, fraud, cheating, and parasite-like behavior. Much of this is also reflected in the different collocates for *burden*: While refugees are strongly represented as being a burden, this happens mostly in terms of expenses (money, costs, budgeting) due to housing, medical treatment, provisions, and education. In contrast, the burden caused by migrants is focused on their unemployment and resulting poverty, their willful dependence on welfare, the number of their children, as well as their alleged unwillingness to integrate.

Particularly salient are the *threats* associated with the different nominations: refugees are linked to a plethora of threats including natural forces (storms, floods, streams, push, pressure), lack of control and order (chaos, uncontrolled, unregistered, unchecked, infiltration), transgressive and violent behavior (assault, aggressive, break through, escalation, violent, beat, sexual harassment, rape, wrangling), armed conflict (tear gas, invasion, fighters, army, soldiers), criminality (damages, delinquent, stealing, police, arrest, fingerprints, suspect, monitor, control, safety risk, punishment), religious extremism and terrorism (Jihadist, extremist, Islamist, terrorist, radicalize). Asylum seekers are associated with many of the same threats, although less frequently. In contrast, migrants are often linked to criminal behavior, chaos, and being a threat to security (see Rheindorf and Wodak 2019, for more details).

This systematic comparison indicates the extent to which the discourse prosodies of the different nominations differ or overlap. These interrelations, also referred to as 'intercollocations', can be used to measure

Table 9.4 Matrix for intercollocations between nominations and cognates

	migrant*	flüchtling*	wirtschaftsflüchtling*	asylwerber*	asylbewerber*	asylant*	asyl-suchende*	schutz-suchende*	geflüchtete*
migrant*	–	45%	28%	32%	29%	26%	34%	30%	32%
flüchtling*	35%	–	34%	65%	62%	42%	62%	60%	72%
wirtschaftsflüchtling*	22%	43%	–	38%	35%	51%	22%	24%	21%
asylwerber*	27%	69%	45%	–	75%	52%	78%	62%	41%
asylbewerber*	24%	64%	41%	79%	–	49%	72%	59%	38%
asylant*	43%	45%	38%	46%	49%	–	51%	24%	28%
asylsuchende*	31%	47%	32%	67%	66%	42%	–	71%	42%
schutzsuchende*	25%	51%	18%	71%	68%	22%	74%	–	42%
geflüchtete*	42%	63%	21%	58%	59%	31%	37%	35%	–

the conflation of terms in their usage. In developing this approach, and Gabrielatos and Baker (2008) concluded that an overlap of 40% was a significant indicator for conflation between distinct terms while cognates (e.g. migrant and immigrant) typically show an overlap of 60% and higher. Table 9.4 presents the overlap rates between collocations for the five most frequent nominations and their cognates. To support the matrix visualization, boxes with values below 33% are in white, with values between 34 and 65% in light grey shading, and with values above 66% in dark grey shading:

The study found the expected strong overlap between cognates such as *asylwerber** and *asylsuchende**, but it also found a strong overlap between the legally separate groups of *flüchtling** and *asylwerber**, where the former denotes the legal status of a recognized refugee and the latter an asylum applicant. Given that various rights, such as access to the labor market, depend on such legal distinctions, the 45% overlap between *migrant** and *flüchtling** may be even more problematic.

9.2 Revisiting the Study

In retrospect, the original study suffered from several limitations. One of these concerns the study's corpus and its relation to *discursive change* or, rather, *permanence*, as operationalized through along the notions of *discourse prosody* and *consistent collocates*. Unlike the RASIM project, the study reported above collected and analyzed data from a relatively short period (14 months as opposed to 10 years); moreover, that period was dominated by an acute crisis, or rather the construction of such a crisis in the media (at least in part constituting mediatized politics), which might invalidate the search for discourse prosodies based on consistent collocates. *An arguably more fruitful approach would be to focus on change instead, reversing the perspective and looking for those collocates that are, as Gabrielatos and Baker* (2008) *phrase it, "seasonal" in the sense that they fluctuate. Such temporary collocates would indicate, in the first instance, not the persistent aura of meaning of a key term but shifts in associations. These shifts would include the appearance of entirely new collocates, the to-be-defined significant increased use of already present collocates, and the decreased use or disappearance of previously present collocates. Clearly, such measures would be highly sensitive to the statistical thresholds and intervals used, much more so than the 7:10 ratio used for c-collocates, and therefore require some testing. In principle, however, they could be used to reveal not only the "seasonal" shifts in reporting, as media respond to context, but also highlight if and when such shifts have lasting effects—after all, changes in collocational patterns may well become permanent over time.*

A further, perhaps more significant limitation of the original study was its focus on lexical patterns, neglecting higher-level textual patterns that might be relevant in the context of media coverage of the so-called refugee crisis. Indeed, inasmuch as the term "refugee crisis" conceals that the crisis was one of European politics, and thus also of Austrian politics, the media discourse represented by the original study's corpus contains much mediatized politics. As even a brief contextualization indicates, the 14-month-period covered by the study saw the complete reversal of the Austrian government's policy on refugees, asylum, and borders; a slightly broader perspective would also reveal that this crisis precipitated the collapse of that government, followed by snap elections for parliament. In these, the Austrian Social-Democrats—who had long defended the human right of asylum and open borders, before reversing course under increasing public and political pressure—suffered a stinging defeat. The conservative People's Party, who had also been part of the coalition government but pursued a restrictive approach to asylum, advocating law and order as well as closed borders, won the elections with 31.5% of the votes. It had campaigned almost exclusively on the so-called refugee crisis and migration problem, adopting many of the positions of the far-right Freedom Party, which won 26% of the votes. This political change is significant insofar is depends on de-legitimizing a long-standing tradition of welcoming refugees, undermining the human right to asylum, and changing policy on a host of issues ranging from closed borders to detention centers and restricting access to welfare for refugees.

Tracing this change through the discourse of mediatized politics requires a conceptual and methodological extension of the original study with respect to legitimation. *Like the original study, the revised study regards discourse as in a dialectical relationship with context, notably institutions and social structures: On the one hand, contexts shape and affect discourses; on the other hand, discourses constitute social reality—broadly speaking through constructing, transforming, maintaining or dismantling strategies. But to focus on legitimation, we cannot simply accept that "media representations" covering a political issue contain statements, claims, proposals or demands made by politicians; we need to add a layer of analysis that focuses on the legitimation strategies that appear in this mediatized political discourse. This perspective also recognizes the stakes of such strategies: Although all social actors act within discourse to constitute and negotiate knowledge, identities, and social relations, the discursive legitimation of policy is one of the most powerful ways to do so.*

9.3 The Revised Study: Results and Discussion

In revising the study, some conceptual and methodological changes are made in order to integrate analyses of (1) short-term discursive change in the form "seasonal collocates" and (2) legitimation as part of mediatized politics. In addition to theoretical and analytical considerations regarding legitimation strategies, this involves developing a quantitative downsampling procedure and qualitative analysis of argumentation. Given these changes, the revised study poses the following new research questions:

- How do the nominations and predications for refugees, asylum seekers, and migrants change over the period under investigation?
- Which argumentative patterns or topoi are used to legitimate new, more restrictive asylum policies, and how do these patterns change across the period covered?
- Do changes in nomination and prediction as well as argumentation reflect events and socio-political changes in the global, European, and national context?

The first extension of the revised study relates to its quantitative dimension. If c-collocates can help identify the persistent "aura" of key terms, i.e. their discourse prosody, then in order to identify short-term changes in these patterns, the opposite was needed: seasonal or temporary collocates. As with c-collocates, these are calculated on the basis of collocate lists for the monthly subcorpora, but using keyness relative to the preceding month (starting with 2.2015 relative to 1.2015, using min. keyness >100 and min. frequency of >2). For the most frequent nomination, i.e. **flüchtling*, this technique reveals the strongest short-term changes in how refugees were presented in the press. Because the resulting tables are massive, an overview is best obtained by categorizing the results into the same semantic fields used in the original study: abuse of system, burden, entry, legality of claim, number, personal traits, plight, positive effect, residence, threat, and welcome. As the categories of *abuse of system*, *threat*, and *burden* prove particularly revealing and interlinked with legitimation strategies, they will serve as illustrative examples here. Results given here include only items with positive keyness, i.e. entirely new or significantly increased collocates. To reduce the number of new but infrequent items, a minimum frequency of 3 in that month was set (see Table 9.5, using translations; for the full table of results, see the companion website REVISITING THE TOOLBOX).

On the most superficial level, the results indicate moments of abrupt shifts in terms of the sheer number of key collocates identified. Significantly, the peaks differ between semantic fields: Thus, peaks can be found

Table 9.5 Key collocates for **flüchtling* for each month relative to the preceding month (keyness of >100, frequency of >2)

	1.2015	2.2015	3.2015	4.2015	5.2015	6.2015	7.2015	8.2015
Abuse of system	–	–	–	–	–	–	–	–
Burden	–	lodging places	money provision	capacity places quarters	tent barracks capacity container housing overcrowded space	distribution jobs unemployed welfare	housing burden costs	courses crisis
Threat	–	police pressure security terrorism threaten	pressure	arrest chaos criminal criminality damage extremists fears fighters harass Islamists police pressure punishment push rape security soldiers storming stealing storm suspected tear gas terrorism terrorists threaten violent	arrest beat up chaos criminal criminality damage delinquent escalate fighters hostile Jihadists police pressure security storm suspected violent	control damage fears Islamists police pressure terrorist threaten wrangling	arrest beat up chaos escalate invasion Jihadists police pressure rape soldiers storm suspected tear gas terrorism violent	army break through criminal soldiers suspected tear gas unchecked

(continued)

Table 9.5 (continued)

	9.2015	10.2015	11.2015	12.2015	1.2016	2.2016
Abuse of system	allege claim	abuse claim pretend	lie wrongly forged	pretend abuse	claim forged	allege fraud
Burden	integration crisis overwhelmed	capacity cost money pay burden	capacity expenses financial increased costs overwhelmed	cost economic cope burden unemployed welfare budget pay	unacceptable money capacity medical care expensive problems	providing housing distribution crisis expenses
Threat	arrest break through chaos control criminality escalate fears police pressure push security sexual soldiers storming tear gas threaten wrangling unchecked	aggressive army beat up damage Islamists pressure soldiers stealing storm violence	arrest assault beat up control criminal criminality damage delinquent escalate extremists fears fighters fingerprints hostile invasion Islamists Jihadists police pressure punishment radicalize security soldiers stealing storm suspected terrorists terrorism threaten violent unchecked unregistered	assault chaos concerns criminal criminality fingerprints fighters Islamists pressure radicalize security risk stealing storm	arrest aggressive army assault fears fears harass monitor molesters police punishment rape security stop suspected terrorist threaten unchecked violent worries unregistered	concerns control criminal extremists fighters fingerprints infiltration Islamists Jihadists problems stealing terror terrorism

for *abuse of system* after 9.2015; for *burden* in 5.2015 and then building up from 9.2015 to 12.2015; and for *threat* at intervals in 4.2015, 7.2015, 9.2015, 11.2015, and 1.2016. The key collocates for each of these peaks point to the shifting focus of media coverage in that month, e.g. make-shift accommodation (tents, barracks, containers) for refugees made necessary by overcrowding of housing capacities in 5.2015 as opposed to the more abstract economic costs, budget considerations, and burden on the welfare state in 12.2015. In the category of *threat*, which provides the lexically most varied of the three fields discussed here, there are clear peaks of terrorist associations in 2.2015, 4.2015, 11.2015, 1.2016, and 2.2016, which can be linked to the terrorist attacks on the editor offices of the satirical magazine Charlie Hebdo and the concert venue Bataclan in Paris. This overwrites the reporting on criminality, except for rioting in the spring of 2015 and sexual assault in 1.2016, which are linked to corresponding incidents at the border and in Cologne, respectively. Taken together rather than individually, the semantic fields show larger patterns, such as a general shift towards refugees' *plight* in 8.2015 and 9.2015, following the death of 71 refugees who had suffocated in an airtight van while being smuggled into Austria. These results can moreover be taken as a rough topical map to the changing public discourse on the so-called refugee crisis, and as such provides a backdrop against which political actors' strategies of legitimation with respect to policy change can be read.

As to strategies of legitimation, the theoretical framework of the original study requires some elaboration. In Western democracies, politicians must seek the approval of the population for policy changes, and such appeals largely depend on the mass media to convince the electorate (hence the importance of mediatized politics, see Strömbäck 2008). Such strategies of legitimation are characteristically used by an elected government that seeks "normative approval for its policies or actions [...] to show that such actions are consistent with the moral order of society" (Rojo and van Dijk 1997, 528). There is, moreover, a specific link between "crises", such as the so-called refugee crisis of 2015–2016, and the legitimation of changes to existing policies. While the events interpreted as crises may not be fabricated, the discursive construction of a crisis, its origins, and threat, are often strategically tied to political agendas. Populists, in particular, are adept at using crises not simply to score electoral wins but also to legitimate their policies. While it was once assumed that populism arose from crises, recent work recognizes that populist actors are actively engaged in discursively constructing, propagating, and maintaining a sense of acute crisis (Moffitt 2016, 113–32). In this strategy, mediatization plays a significant role in dramatizing and amplifying crises (Mazzoleni 2008; Triandafyllidou et al. 2009).

Such crises may be constructed through the "spectacularization of failure", that is, failure by those in power, if the populists are in opposition (Moffitt 2016, 8). In other contexts, populists may blame a minority within the state, possibly "the poor" or "the elite", "the system", or an international enemy such as the EU (Moffitt 2016, 120). In such constructions, "the people" are most threatened by the crisis, while "the elite" are either safe or even benefit; averting the threat requires urgent action to prevent dire and irrevocable consequences (Müller 2017, 43). The so-called refugee crisis of 2015–2016 has provided many European populists with a potent mobilizer to achieve significant electoral wins (Rheindorf and Wodak 2017; Vollmer and Karakayali 2018).

Methodologically, strategies of legitimation can be operationalized as argumentative patterns that include premises on the nature of the proposed action (what must be done) and the phenomena it relates to (the threat to be averted) as well as conclusions that concern said action's social, moral or political acceptability (Rojo and van Dijk 1997, 531–32). Such argumentative schemata or topoi regularly involve not only explicit argumentation but also presupposed knowledge, especially in the specific contexts of national political debates (Zarefsky 2008, 118). As only qualitative analysis can reliably identify such patterns (on the limitations of CL methods regarding higher-level patterns, see Chapter 2), the revised study must find a way to downsample the amount of material to be analyzed. Since the study's focus is on discursive change in relation to policy change, downsampling uses primarily CL methods to select texts that are likely to contain the change of legitimation strategies.

Specifically, the quantitative results on key collocates per month were used for downsampling the corpus for qualitative analysis (for other corpus-based approaches to downsampling, see Baker 2006, 90; 2012, 248), repeated in a cyclical fashion until a saturation point was reached. At the first stage, 70 texts with typical collocational patterns for *flüchtling** were selected, 5 for each month, and analyzed for topoi used in legitimizing either changing or maintaining asylum policies as well as related welfare and border policies. Then, the qualitative sample was expanded by another 5 texts for each month, adding texts that showed the typical changes in collocations for refugees as identified by keyness (see above). These were in turn analyzed, adding any new topoi identified to the preliminary list. This step was repeated at least three times for each month or until the saturation point was reached. This procedure should avoid the known downsampling issue of privileging dominant patterns over infrequent ones (see Chapter 2; see also Freake et al. 2011, 39–43; Baker 2006, 125, for a detailed methodological discussion). The saturation point was reached after different numbers of cycles for the 14 months covered, as shown in Table 9.6. It should be noted that the number of cycles required for saturation seems to roughly correspond to the number of articles published, with more cycles necessary the more texts were in that month's subcorpus. In total, this downsampling process led to 350 texts being analyzed, approximately 6% of the total 5739 in the corpus.

As to the legitimation strategies themselves, the combination of two levels of analysis seems advisable: (1) inductively defining the specific topoi identified in the material as fact-warrant-backing-rebuttal-conclusion patterns and (2) categorization in terms of the broader legitimation strategy. Regarding the first of these levels, the revised study follows the CDS strategy of explicating argumentation in the form of conditional or causal paraphrases that reveal partly implicit argumentation (Reisigl and Wodak 2005, 69–80). In the context of political actors' efforts to legitimate policy, such analyses can reveal flawed logic and manipulative or erroneous conclusions.

The second level of analyzing legitimation addresses the fact that, due to its socio-political embeddedness, legitimation routinely draws on recurring argumentation schemata or topoi to persuade the public of the acceptability or necessity of a specific policy. In doing so, four broad types recur: authorization, moralization, rationalization, and mythopoesis (van Leeuwen 2007; van Leeuwen and Wodak 1999). Legitimation by *authorization* depends on authority (personal, impersonal, expert or role model) or custom (tradition or conformity). Legitimation qua *moralization* is based on abstract moral values (religion, human rights or justice),

Table 9.6 Overview of the downsampling process by number of cycles and texts

	1.15	2.15	3.15	4.15	5.15	6.15	7.15	8.15	9.15	10.15	11.15	12.15	1.16	2.16
Number of cycles	3	3	3	5	5	5	6	5	6	6	7	6	5	5
Number of texts	15	15	15	25	25	25	30	25	30	30	35	30	25	25

direct evaluation (good or bad), or analogy to accepted moral cases. Legitimation through *rationalization* cites either utility, 'common sense' or expert knowledge (economics, biology or technology). Finally, legitimation through *mythopoesis* relies on stories to serve as exemplars or cautionary tales. This broad characterization of legitimation strategies can provide an overview of topoi and shifts in their use, e.g. from rationalization to moralization. Previous work in CDS has identified such patterns in political efforts to legitimate immigration control (Reisigl and Wodak 2005; Reisigl 2007); despite some similarities, however, the patterns emerging during the so-called refugee crisis and their combinations are quite distinct.

For instance, the *topos of burden and responsibility* is often combined with the *topoi of number* and *reality*. In particular, the argument that Austria is bearing an inordinately high burden is based on often hypothetical or projected comparisons to Germany, invoking a sense of unfairness and/or positive self-presentation as generous. The *topos of burden* can be found as early as 4/2015 but grows more dominant in the following months. Here, the overall strategy is *moralization* (the contrast of fairness and unfairness) and the argument is substantiated by the topoi of burden and number.

- Topos of numbers: *If the numbers support a specific claim, a specific action should be taken.*
- Topos of burden: *If a person, an institution or a country is burdened by specific problems, one should act in order to diminish those burdens.*

Example 1 "A German study on the costs of asylum is causing controversy in Austria. 50 billion. [...] Adjusted to Austria, that would be 5 billion in two years. In fact, the government is calculating – even with a maximum limit – 210,000 refugees, about the same number as in ten times larger Germany." (Österreich, February 2016)

The counter-discourse, arguing in defence of human rights and open borders, also employed moralization, supported mainly with the *topos of humanitarianism*. This pattern is present in the corpus through most of 2015 but could not be found after November 2015, i.e. the time of the terrorist attacks on Bataclan. The values, and hence, moralization change as the primary value after the terrorist attacks shifts to the protection of Austria and its people, rather than refugees.

- Topos of humanitarianism: *If people are suffering, it is our duty as fellow human beings to provide humanitarian aid.*

Example 2 "The tragedy of up to 50 dead refugees in Burgenland leaves many politicians in shock. (…) The human rights expert of the Green Party, Alev Korun, said that it was Europe's responsibility to open legal routes for refugees and end the death of war refugees." (Österreich, August 2015)

In total, 26 topoi were identified in the qualitative sample. It must be noted that most of them can be framed differently, e.g. as *moralization* or *rationalization*, without changing the propositional content of the argument (Table 9.7).

The combined results on both levels of analysis confirm but also extend the findings of related work on media reporting on refugees in Austria and elsewhere: The discourse of mediatized politics is a primary site of political legitimation regarding policies on refugees. More specifically, media coverage during the so-called refugee crisis reproduced many of topoi used by political actors. The results, however, do not allow any assessment of the extent to which these were simply reported, affirmed or questioned.

From the longitudinal point of view, several shifts in terms of the topoi and legitimation strategies are indicated by the qualitative sample: While refugees were seen as a *burden* throughout the period, this topos was initially connected to a *humanitarian* obligation and the refugee's *plight*. Already in early 2015, however, a perceived crisis in refugee housing—which also highlighted long-standing tensions between Austria's *federal* government and states—shifted the focus to topoi of *burden*, *threat*, *law and order*, *limited resources*, and *pressure* on Austrian institutions. Mass border crossings in the summer of 2015 were discussed as requiring a *humanitarian* response but also control to ensure *national security*, *sovereignty*, and *citizens' security*. Only at this point did the analysis find a notable presence of topoi of *abuse* and *national solution*. At the end of the year, this is accompanied by a shift towards the topoi of *the real* and *limited resources*. Throughout the period, topoi of *nature* and *culture* became more frequent and prominent as well as more often connected to topoi of *threat*, *criminality*, *citizens' security*, and *fear*, peaking in 2016 after the incidents in Cologne. The topos of *humanitarianism*, in contrast, recedes more and more toward the end of 2015 and has virtually disap-

Table 9.7 Topoi identified in the Austrian media's coverage of the refugee crisis

Topoi	Paraphrase of the argument
Abuse of system	*If a right, help or support is abused, that right should be modified, restricted or withheld*
Burden	*If a person, an institution or a country is burdened by specific problems, one should act in order to diminish those burdens*
Citizens' security	*If something threatens the security of citizens, the state must do whatever is necessary to avert that threat*
Criminality	*If someone breaks the law, for whatever reason, they are criminals and must be treated as such*
Culture	*Since it is the nature of members of a specific culture to be/act/behave in a specific way, specific problems arise in certain situations*
Empathy	*If another human being suffers, we as fellow human beings should feel their suffering*
Fear	*If someone is afraid, that fear must be taken seriously*
Federalism	*If the federal government needs to force individual state governments to fulfil their legal obligations, it should do so*
Historical comparison	*If the present situation is similar to a situation in history, a comparison can help understand or solve the present situation*
Humanitarianism	*If people are suffering, it is our duty as fellow human beings to provide humanitarian aid*
Imported antisemitism	*If the people arriving in Austria come from a region where antisemitism is prevalent, letting them into Austria will import antisemitism*
Law and order	*If current law dictates/forbids a specific action, that action must be taken/foregone*
Limited resources	*If Austria's (natural, financial) resources are limited, the amount of resources used to help refugees must be strictly limited too*
National security	*If national security is threatened by something or someone, the state must act to stop that threat*
National solution	*If the EU fails to solve the problem, any nation has the right to act on its own*
Nature	*Since it is the nature of members of a specific group to be/act/behave in a specific way, specific problems arise in certain situations*

(continued)

Table 9.7 (continued)

Topoi	Paraphrase of the argument
Numbers	*If the numbers prove a specific claim, a specific action should be taken*
Pressure	*If something creates pressure on someone or something, steps should be taken to reduce or relieve that pressure*
Pride	*If we do something without self-interest, we should take pride in our actions*
Reality	*Because reality is as it is, a specific action should be taken*
Refugees' plight	*If refugees suffer or need help, we should act to reduce their suffering or need*
Safety at home	*If we lock our doors at home and do not let in strangers, we should close our borders as well*
Shame	*If we do not help someone in need without self-interest, we should be ashamed*
Slippery slope	*If we let in everyone who is at our borders now, many more will come*
Sovereignty	*To maintain its national sovereignty, any state has the right or obligation to control its borders and/or whoever enters its territory*
Threat	*If there are specific dangers or threats, one should do something to counter them*

peared by early 2016. These shifts are paralleled by an increasing reliance of legitimation on *moralization* and *authorization by personal authority*. Quantification of these trends, however, is not possible on the basis of the limited data sample used to identify strategies of legitimation.

9.4 Research Design and Practice

The case study presented here initially focused on media representations of refugees, asylum seekers, and migrants in the Austrian press during the refugee crisis of 2015–2016, using mainly quantitative methods to identify nominations and predications related to different groups of social actors as well as intercollocation as a measure of terminological conflation. The original study's qualitative analyses provided strong support for the original study's conclusions about short-term discursive shifts, but extended it significantly with respect to mediatized politics. This extension was conceptual as much as it was methodological, highlighting the interdependence of the two aspects in CDS. Here, as in similar research designs, downsampling is crucial to connecting quantitative analyses of lexical patterns in large corpora and close, qualitative analyses of higher-level linguistic phenomena such as argumentation and legitimation.

With respect to research design and practice, this case study indicates that we should

- embrace opportunities to pursue salient and current phenomena within open or exploratory research designs,
- maintain a strong relationship between the theoretical-conceptual level and methodology,
- pursue questions about discursive permanencies as well as change,
- use the strengths of methods to help offset their weaknesses, e.g. use quantitative methods for downsampling so qualitative methods can be used,
- draw on but question and adapt previous work on similar topics, especially their methodology,
- approach large corpora as potentially containing multiple genres, multiple topical discourses, multiple levels of discourse, the voices of multiple social actors, and as potentially cutting across different fields of social action,
- and consider conceptual and methodological paths to approach the same collection of data from different angles, effectively disaggregating it along one or several of the planes listed above.

References

Archer, Dawn, Andrew Wilson, and Paul Rayson. 2002. "Introduction to the USAS Category System." ucrel.lancs.ac.uk/usas/usas_guide.pdf.

Baker, Paul. 2006. *Using Corpora in Discourse Analysis*. Continuum Discourse Series. London and New York: Continuum.
———. 2012. "Acceptable Bias? Using Corpus Linguistics Methods with Critical Discourse Analysis." *Critical Discourse Studies* 9 (3): 247–56. https://doi.org/10.1080/17405904.2012.688297.
Baker, Paul, and Tony McEnery. 2005. "A Corpus-Based Approach to Discourses of Refugees and Asylum Seekers in UN and Newspaper Texts." *Journal of Language and Politics* 4 (2): 197–226. https://doi.org/10.1075/jlp.4.2.04bak.
Baker, Paul, Costas Gabrielatos, Majid KhosraviNik, Mihał Krzyzanowski, Tony McEnery, and Ruth Wodak. 2008. "A Useful Methodological Synergy? Combining Critical Discourse Analysis and Corpus Linguistics to Examine Discourses of Refugees and Asylum Seekers in the UK Press." *Discourse & Society* 19 (3): 273–306. https://doi.org/10.1177/0957926508088962.
Freake, Rachelle, Guillaume Gentil, and Jaffer Sheyholislami. 2011. "A Bilingual Corpus-Assisted Discourse Study of the Construction of Nationhood and Belonging in Quebec." *Discourse & Society* 22 (1): 21–47. https://doi.org/10.1177/0957926510382842.
Gabrielatos, Costas, and Paul Baker. 2008. "Fleeing, Sneaking, Flooding: A Corpus Analysis of Discursive Constructions of Refugees and Asylum Seekers in the UK Press, 1996–2005." *Journal of English Linguistics* 36 (1): 5–38. https://doi.org/10.1177/0075424207311247.
Lehner, Sabine, and Markus Rheindorf. 2019. "'Fortress Europe': Representation and Argumentation in Austrian Media and EU Press Releases on Border Policies." In *Refugee News, Refugee Politics: Journalism, Public Opinion and Policymaking in Europe*, edited by Giovanna Dell'Orto and Irmgard Wetzstein. London: Routledge.
Mazzoleni, Gianpietro. 2008. "Populism and the Media." In *Twenty-First Century Populism*, edited by Daniele Albertazzi and Duncan McDonnell, 49–64. London: Palgrave Macmillan. https://doi.org/10.1057/9780230592100_4.
Moffitt, Benjamin. 2016. *The Global Rise of Populism: Performance, Political Style, and Representation*. Stanford, CA: Stanford University Press.
Müller, Jan-Werner. 2017. *What Is Populism?* London: Penguin Books Ltd.
Reisigl, Martin. 2007. "The Dynamics of Right-Wing Populist Argumentation in Austria." In *Proceedings of the Sixth Conference of the International Society for the Study of Argumentation*, edited by Frans H. van Eemeren, Bart Garssen, J. Anthony Blair, and Charles A. Willard, 1127–34. Amsterdam: International Center for the Study of Argumentation.
Reisigl, Martin, and Ruth Wodak. 2005. *Discourse and Discrimination: Rhetorics of Racism and Antisemitism*. London and New York: Routledge.

———. 2015. "The Discourse-Historical Approach (DHA)." In *Methods of Critical Discourse Studies*, edited by Ruth Wodak and Michael Meyer, 23–61. London: Sage.

Rheindorf, Markus, and Ruth Wodak. 2017. "Borders, Fences, and Limits—Protecting Austria From Refugees: Metadiscursive Negotiation of Meaning in the Current Refugee Crisis." *Journal of Immigrant & Refugee Studies* (April): 1–24. https://doi.org/10.1080/15562948.2017.1302032.

———. 2019. "Building 'Fortress Europe': Legitimizing Exclusion from Basic Human Rights." In *Sociolinguistic Perspectives on Migration Control: Language Policy, Identity, and Belonging*, edited by Markus Rheindorf and Ruth Wodak. Clevedon: Multilingual Matters.

Rojo, Luisa Martín, and Teun A. van Dijk. 1997. "'There Was a Problem, and It Was Solved!': Legitimating the Expulsion of 'Illegal' Migrants in Spanish Parliamentary Discourse." *Discourse & Society* 8 (4): 523–66. https://doi.org/10.1177/0957926597008004005.

Strömbäck, Jesper. 2008. "Four Phases of Mediatization: An Analysis of the Mediatization of Politics." *The International Journal of Press/Politics* 13 (3): 228–46. https://doi.org/10.1177/1940161208319097.

Triandafyllidou, Anna, Ruth Wodak, and Michał Krzyżanowski, eds. 2009. *The European Public Sphere and the Media: Europe in Crisis.* Basingstoke: Palgrave Macmillan.

van Leeuwen, Theo. 2007. "Legitimation in Discourse and Communication." *Discourse & Communication* 1 (1): 91–112. https://doi.org/10.1177/1750481307071986.

van Leeuwen, Theo, and Ruth Wodak. 1999. "Legitimizing Immigration Control: A Discourse-Historical Analysis." *Discourse Studies* 1 (1): 83–118. https://doi.org/10.1177/1461445699001001005.

Vollmer, Bastian, and Serhat Karakayali. 2018. "The Volatility of the Discourse on Refugees in Germany." *Journal of Immigrant & Refugee Studies* 16 (1–2): 118–39. https://doi.org/10.1080/15562948.2017.1288284.

Wodak, Ruth, Rudolf De Cillia, Martin Reisigl, and Karin Liebhart. 2009. *The Discursive Construction of National Identity*. 2nd ed. Critical Discourse Analysis. Edinburgh: Edinburgh University Press.

Wodak, Ruth, Rudolf de Cillia, Markus Rheindorf, and Sabine Lehner. 2019. "Zur Diskursiven Konstruktion Österreichischer Identität/En 2015: Eine Longitudinalstudie." https://nationale-identitaet-2015.univie.ac.at/.

Zarefsky, David. 2008. "Strategic Maneuvering in Political Argumentation." In *Examining Argumentation in Context: Fifteen Studies on Strategic Maneuvering*, edited by Frans H. van Eemeren, 115–30. Amsterdam: John Benjamins.

10

Case Study 4: A Diachronic View of Register and Argumentation in Early Film Theory

10.1 Introduction: The Original Study

This case study revisits work done for my PhD in the 2000s (Rheindorf 2005a, b, 2006, 2007). In the interest of transparency, a brief account of the original work will be given before discussing the research design's limitations and presenting the revised study. The original study analyzed the development of film theory as a multi-lingual, transnational academic discourse in its early decades (from the 1910s until the 1960s). The limits of that timeframe were determined by (a) the earliest publications identified as beginning film theory in the literature of the field (e.g. Elsaesser 2002) and (b) the last significant publications before Christian Metz's exhaustive attempt to (semiotically) settle the question whether film was, indeed, 'a language' or 'like a language' (beginning with Metz 1966). In terms of theoretical framing, the DHA's emphasis on (a) historical context and (b) the mutually constitutive relation between discourse and context allowed me to situate the results of detailed linguistic analyses to the sweeping changes that swept through Europe during those decades as well as the development of film itself (Reisigl 2017; Reisigl and Wodak 2015). More

© The Author(s) 2019

M. Rheindorf, *Revisiting the Toolbox of Discourse Studies*,
Postdisciplinary Studies in Discourse,
https://doi.org/10.1007/978-3-030-19369-0_10

specifically, I used the notion of "articulation" to conceptualize how non-essentially linked concepts and topoi in the discourse became articulated and disarticulated under changing contextual conditions (Grossberg 1992, 1997; Hall 1986).

The data of the original study consisted of 248 film theoretical texts of greatly varying length, published in six languages (English, French, German, Hungarian, Italian, and Russian), amounting to over 965,000 words of running text. Because of the multilingual nature of the corpus, no CL or other quantitative methods were considered in the original study. The 248 texts were chosen for their current status as seminal or canonical texts as indicated by their contemporary reception and retrospectively attributed weight (e.g. reprints, inclusion in readers, introductions, translation into other languages). In terms of genre, the texts selected included reviews originally published in newspapers and magazines, manuals, pamphlets, essays, analyses, research reports, and book-length publications (for a full list, see the companion website REVISITING THE TOOLBOX).

An initial survey of the material indicated two salient aspects: prolific terminological borrowing and terminological innovation, and prevalent argumentation related to descriptive and normative conceptions of film as such. Early film theory, in other words, was looking for terminology to describe its subject matter, film, by borrowing terms from other academic fields (e.g. theatre) as well as inventing new terms; and early film theory was focused on arguing definitions what film really was or should be. The original analysis therefore focused on (1) tracing the development of terminology and (2) identifying prominent topoi related to definitions of film as well as their interrelations—across languages and decades. These two aims were interrelated insofar as the lexical analysis revealed a preponderance of terms related to the notion of 'film language' in descriptive, explicative, and argumentative contexts. These terms constitute a semantic field in the sense that they join 'film' with the feature [+linguistic], i.e. 'film grammar', 'film word', 'film writing', 'film reading', etc. While there were crossovers from other fields as well, i.e. borrowings from the academic fields of literature, theatre, and music, 'film language' proved the most consistent across languages and decades.

Topoi were identified as parts of argumentative *patterns* in the sense of recurring structures that satisfy the minimum structure of data-warrant-

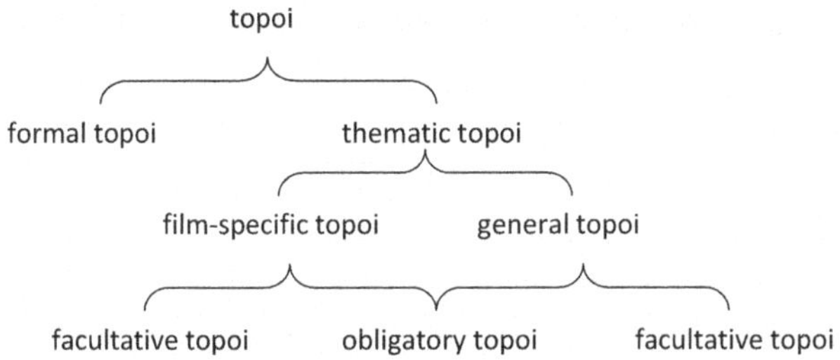

Fig. 10.1 Three-tiered categorization of topoi

conclusion or claim-data-warrant with optional backing and qualifier elements (Toulmin 2003; Kienpointner 1996). As highly conventionalized elements of argumentation, topoi function as formal or content-related warrants or 'conclusion rules' which connect one or several arguments with a claim and/or conclusion in the sense of justifying the transition from an argument (or several arguments) to the conclusion (Kienpointner 1992, 194). As conventional elements of argumentation, topoi are assumed to be recognizable within a particular field of social action, and are thus often not fully explicated, making them difficult to identify (e.g. as allusions) (Wodak et al. 2009, 34–35).

All topoi identified were categorized on three levels of distinction: formal vs. thematic, film-specific vs. general, and obligatory vs. facultative. Purely formal topoi, e.g. *argumentum ad authoritatem*, were not included in the analysis (Kienpointner 1992, 246–50). The thematic topoi found were distinguished by referent: (1) film-specific topoi, i.e. topoi which refer to film specifically and can be paraphrased in the form of 'film as…' conclusion rules; (2) general topoi, i.e. topoi that do not refer directly to film and can thus also be found in other discourses, indicating an overlap between those discourses and that of early film theory. The latter includes topoi such as *modernity as decline*; *language as inauthentic*; *language as inadequate*; *the surface as sincere*; *the masses as inferior*; *the masses as dangerous*; *history as dialectic process*; *art as faithful copy of Nature*; *Nature as unified and whole composition*; and *reality as resisting insight* (Fig. 10.1).

Many of the general topoi identified are facultative rather than obligatory in the sense that they are not integral components of particular definitions of film; however, some general topoi, such as *the human body as expressive*, *language as inauthentic* or *modernity as decline* are key elements in specific conceptualizations of film. Although most film-specific topoi are obligatory, not all of them are. These facultative but film-specific topoi include the following: *film as extension or prosthesis* (specifically the camera as mechanical eye); *film as educator/corruptor of the masses*; *film as folk culture* (made for and by the people); *film as modern successor of fairy tale or myth*; *film as scientific tool*; and *film's affinity with the fair*.

A total of 49 thematic topoi were identified in the original study as occurring more than twice in the data (the only quantitative criterion applied). The following table gives an excerpt of how these results were presented in the original study, specifying the respective topos' status as general/film-specific and obligatory/facultative, paraphrasing the respective conclusion rule, and some additional characteristics.

The original study used source text excerpts to illustrate the topoi and their interrelation, discussing each topos on the pages following a table much like Table 10.1 but listing all topoi. The following example shows a 1923 text arguing the supremacy of (silent) film over language (and the theatre stage) based on the expressiveness of the human body, explicating the topoi of *the superiority of the image* and *the human body as expressive*, while also implicitly drawing on the topoi of *language as inauthentic* and *language as inadequate* (explicated elsewhere in the same source text).

> Kein Wort und kein Satz vermag schlagartig und in organischer Einheit so viel zu sagen wie eine einzelne Geste. Sie hat den Effekt einer vielstimmigen Harmonie und die Nahaufname im Film hat das Lesen physiognomischer Kompositionen ermöglicht wie sie die Bühne nicht bieten kann. (Balázs 1923, 7)
>
> *There is no word and no sentence, which can at once and in organic unity say as much as a single gesture. It has the effect of a many-voiced harmony, and the close-up of film made it possible to read such physiognomic compositions which the stage cannot offer.*

The latter two topoi are explicated, for example, in the following excerpt, also used in the original study:

Table 10.1 Some thematic topoi found in the data (conclusion rules and characteristics)

Topoi	Conclusion rules	Characteristics
Film as national particularity Film-specific, obligatory	If nations and peoples have distinguishing characteristics, and if these are expressed in the respective cultures, then films as cultural products likewise manifest national particularity	Formally a *topos of singularity*, this argumentative pattern is sometimes combined with stereotypical 'national types' (such as dress and gestures) or *genuus locii*. It is commonly realized through genitives, adjectives, predicates or possessive pronouns and linked to *the human body as expressive* and *film as folk culture*
Modernity as decline General, obligatory	If the decline in the quality of life, especially of human contact, communication, and moral values is causally connected to the increasing mechanization and technologization of modern society, Modernity is responsible for the decline of 'civilization'	Identifies a causal relationship between contemporariness and negative properties such as 'alienation', 'distance', and 'abstraction'. These are sometimes connected to Capitalism or, depending on the author's point of view, Liberalism, Socialism, and Communism
The human body as expressive General, obligatory	If the human body is more expressive than other forms of communication, particularly language, film should give primacy to the human body, its physiognomy, movements, and gestures	Often includes reference to particular actors, gestures and physiques. Typically linked to *film as national particularity*, *non-actors as ideal film-actors*, *language as inauthentic*, *language as inadequate*, and *superiority of the image*
Language as inauthentic General, obligatory	If language is a formal and conventional system of signs, the relation of these signs to their referent is inauthentic to the degree that it is arbitrary and mediated by convention	Attributive constructions describe language as 'alien', 'abstract', and 'distanced'. Typically linked to *language as inadequate* and *superiority of the image*

(continued)

Table 10.1 (continued)

Topoi	Conclusion rules	Characteristics
Language as inadequate General, obligatory	If the present state of language has been affected by or is a symptom of modern alienation, it must fail—and already has, as evident in diplomacy's failure to prevent the Great War—in facilitating understanding between the peoples, and is therefore no longer adequate for communication	Often combined with a formal topos of *pars pro toto*, it casts language not only as lacking, but as symptom or cause of *modernity as decline*. This topos is very prominent in the fin de siècle's critique of language or 'Sprachkritik'
Film as specific medium Film-specific, obligatory	If each medium or art has a specific array of expressive possibilities or meaning potentials, film also possesses medial specificity (or may develop it) in contrast to other media or arts	Film is described as medium of the visual and attributed qualities in opposition to 'the word' or language, whether written or spoken. Film is different from other arts or media precisely insofar as it is 'immediate', 'soulful', 'expressive', etc. Typically linked to *film as epigenetic essence* and *film as fulfilling a mission*
Film as epigenetic essence Film-specific, obligatory	If a medium's specificity is derived from its technological or material makeup, film is not only derived or 'descended' from photography, but remains in its essence a visual medium	Biological metaphors of 'evolution' and 'birth' or familial relations describing film as 'child' or photography as 'parent', 'father', or 'mother', are common with this topos. Most of them implicitly cast film as a person or living being. Typically linked to *film as specific medium* and *superiority of the image*
Film as authentic/immediate medium Film-specific, obligatory	If photographic visuals are not mediated by human subjectivity (the way language is), and if such visuals are therefore more 'authentic' of reality, then film is essentially truer to reality than language-dependent forms of art or communication	The reality to which this authenticity appeals is a matter of debate: the soul, Nature, society, or even the unconscious. This argument is valid only under the proviso that film be 'pure' in its visuality, which effects a normative injunction. Typically linked to *film as epigenetic essence* and *the superiority of the image*

(continued)

Table 10.1 (continued)

Topoi	Conclusion rules	Characteristics
Language in film as obstacle Film-specific, obligatory	If film is the medium of the immediate expression (of the soul, etc.), and if visuals are more immediate than language, all use of (spoken and written) language in film is in contradiction to its essence and an obstacle to its purity and mission	Prior to the introduction of sound, the short written texts inserted in silent films or 'intertitles' were already seen as an obstacle in this sense. With sound, however, spoken language, in particular dialogue, came to be perceived as the gravest danger. Typically linked to *language as inauthentic*, *language as inadequate*, *the superiority of the image* and *film as authentic/immediate medium*
Non-actors as ideal film-actors Film-specific, obligatory	If film's specificity and mission depend on its opposition to abstraction (and the difference from other media), the ideal film actor is a non-professional actor	A lay-person or, better still, someone unaware of being filmed and therefore as 'natural' as an inanimate object, is ideal for film. Stage actors and actresses are the anathema to this. Typically linked to *the human body as expressive* and *the surface as sincere*
The surface as sincere General, obligatory	If abstraction distances the object from its referent (and vice versa) and thus also people from reality, the surface as that which does not mean anything but itself is utterly sincere—if only because it makes no claim to obsolete values	In particular unconscious or involuntary 'surfaces', such as gestures or, more generally, popular culture are seen as containing some hidden truth. The lack of language/intellectual argument in the superficial is here rediscovered as its greatest strength. Whether or not this truth is expressed freely in or through the surface depends on the topoi of *reality as resisting insight* and *reality as accomplice to insight*

> Die Sprache ist in einem Zustand der Verlorenheit […] und vermag gewisse Verhaltensmuster nicht einzufangen, die im stummen Film bereits entdeckt und vollkommen dargeboten worden sind. (Kracauer 1931, 186)
>
> *Language today is in a state of disorientation […] and incapable of capturing certain behavioral patterns which have already been discovered and presented in their totality in silent film.*

Other excerpts were used to illustrate the relations between topoi and their use in normatively evaluating concrete films as true to, or failing, film's nature. For example, the following 1928 text lauded Feyder's *Thérèse Raquin* (based on the eponymous novel by Émile Zola) for successfully using 'the language of things' to say what words could not.

> […] verweigert die Darstellung innerer Vorgänge, welche des Wortes bedarf […]. Hier lebt das gesamte Milieu durch die menschliche Handlung mit, und daher sprechen auch die Menschen in der Sprache der Dinge [sodaß] ein jedes Ding die Bedeutung eines Zeugen hat, menschlicher Gehalt ist sichtbar in sie übergegangen und nun reden sie, oft besser noch als es Menschen können. (Kracauer 1928, 136–37)
>
> *[…] refuses the depiction of interior processes which would require words […]. Here, the entire milieu lives vicariously through the human plot, and thus people also speak in the language of things [so that] each and every object has the significance of a witness, human substance has recognizably passed into them and now they talk, often better still than people do.*

The original study's strictly qualitative analysis of topoi and their interrelations also showed that topoi tended to cluster around key notions of what film was or should be and that these notions changed over time. Three distinct versions of 'film as language' emerged from the analysis, each gaining prominence in roughly delineated periods: 'film as Esperanto of the eye' between 1910 and the early 1930s, 'film as the language of the unconscious' in the late 1930s and 1940s, and 'film as the language of things' in the 1950s. Remarkably, each of these was argumentatively tied to socio-political aims that the respective film theorists associated with film: (1) an 'Esperanto' that, as a universal language, should facilitate understanding between the peoples and prevent another great war; (2) a 'symptomatic' language of the 'collective unconscious' that could reveal the spiritual 'diseases' of a nation or people; and (3) a 'pure' language of nature that, being as free from human interference and propaganda as possible, should remain a conduit for the world of things to 'speak for itself'.

Equally remarkably, these notions formed the argumentative center of the respective period's discourse, with numerous topoi used to support them directly or indirectly. Transferring these links to a 'map' of the argumentative field, the original study revealed that, while many of the topoi and smaller clusters persisted throughout many decades, their configuration shifted in support of the changing understanding of 'film language'. For instance, the topos of *the surface as sincere* was found in texts from all three periods. Similarly, the tightly interconnected cluster of topoi concerning the *inauthenticity of language* and consequential *superiority of the image*, jointly supporting the topos of *language in film as an obstacle* to its true calling, persisted once it had formed in response to the first 'talkies', i.e. sound films featuring spoken language.

During this analytical process, I improvised a network of topoi—abbreviated to short handles written on cardboard cards—rearranging them with each topos I added in order to obtain an overview of the respective configuration. This rough map I later reproduced in MS Word, without rearranging the topoi's spatial positioning (see Fig. 10.2), to visualize the extensive description of each configuration including the topoi handles, definition, exemplary excerpts from the corpus, and each topos' links within the respective configuration. Analytically as well as visually, three types of link had to be distinguished: argumentative support in one direction, argumentative support in both directions (indicating circular arguments), and argumentative conflict between topoi. Topoi that newly emerged in the data for a particular period were emphasized (black-background boxes), so as to highlight the impact they had on the configuration. In contrast, topoi that were now rejected (but still reproduced) were deemphasized (white-background boxes).

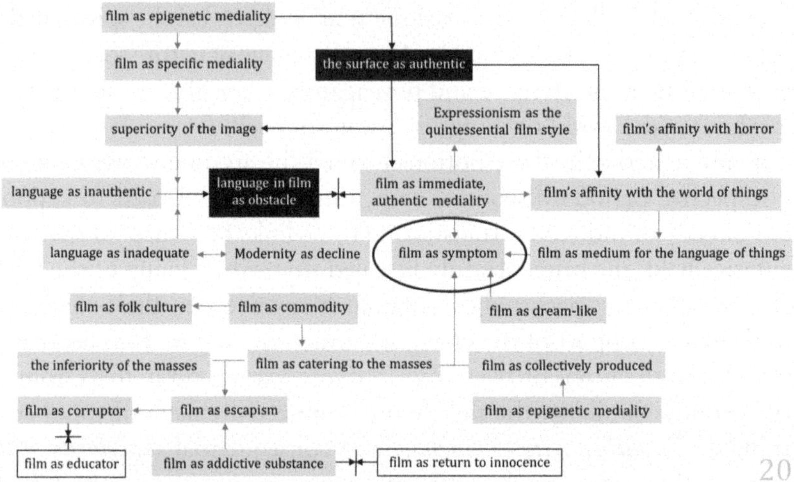

Fig. 10.2 Manually created network graph depicting the argumentative field of early film theory centered on 'film a symptom'

10.2 Revisiting the Study

In retrospect, the original study suffered from some limitations that are easier to address today, given better access to sources as well as advances in CL methodology and interactive visualization technology. In the following, each aspect of the original study design is critically discussed with respect to relevant aspects of the five methodological chapters—the integration of quantitative and qualitative methods in CDS, working with varied data, analyzing different levels of discourse, and visualization—followed by suggestions for revision. The revised study implemented some of these suggestions, and the next section presents and discusses its results with respect to the changed study design.

Discourse and society: The theoretical framework of the study clearly relates to the *diachronic dimension of discourse*, describing *discursive change* as an effect of *social change*, including political, material, and technological aspects of social reality. As this relates to the potential pitfall of reifying discourse-context relations and causality by way of the analytical process, a brief discussion of the sequence seems warranted: The analysis began

(1) as an exploratory survey on the discursive level (textual data), before (2) researching specific contextual information. However, I was obviously aware of the broad social socio-political developments of the period under investigation, so that this sequence did not avoid the pre-existence of some contextual knowledge that would prove relevant to the interpretation of how discursive change related to social change. The next step was (3) the qualitative analysis of terminology across decades and languages, followed by (4) the qualitative identification of topoi, their interrelations and configuration in support of conceptions of 'film language' associated with specific periods. Only then were these changes, i.e. the appearance of new topoi, the resultant rearrangement of the argumentative field, and the prominence of new conceptions of 'film language', related to social change. This was done in two ways: on the generalized level of 'discourse' (aggregated for all text analyzed) and broad social changes (the invention of sound film, World War II, etc.); and through the publications of two prominent theorists (Siegfried Kracauer and Béla Balázs), which span almost the entire period studied, and their respective biographical contexts. In terms of triangulation, this multi-perspectival approach increased the validity of conclusions regarding discursive change, but it also deepened the analysis and provided contrast.

Quantitative methods: As outlined above, discursive change was operationalized in purely qualitative terms on the level of lexis (terminology) and argumentation (topoi and their interrelations). Methodologically, no corpus linguistic methods or tools were used to quantify the findings on the lexical level. Similarly, no quantification of the argumentative topoi themselves or of their interrelations was carried out beyond the criterion that each had to be attested at least twice in the data. The main reason for the former was the multilinguality of the corpus: With six languages present, there would have been six separate results for each sub-corpus, e.g. word frequency. Nor did I have access, at the time, to software that would have been able to automatically carry out part-of-speech tagging for those six languages. *Given a technical solution for these issues, the use of CL methods and tools would provide a more comprehensive, detailed, and robust view on the lexical aspect of discursive change in early film theory. More specifically, word frequency and collocational patterns would confirm* *or modify previous findings. Using subcorpora for each period against the entire corpus as reference corpus, keyword lists might provide additional insights into terminological change. It would also allow testing the effects of the original study's periodization, based as it was on changes in conceptions of 'film language' and related argumentation. Given the scalability of corpus size with relatively little increase in effort, more texts might furthermore be included to expand the empirical basis at least for the lexical analyses. In contrast, using CL tools to identify and quantify argumentative patterns may not be feasible: CL approaches to argumentation remain severely limited (see Chapter 2) in that they ultimately rely on lexical patterns, whose link to topoi is never guaranteed. With that limitation in mind, an attempt might be made to establish the total number of occurrences of each topos already documented, using the qualitatively identified instances to derive lexical patterns to search for. Even so, each occurrence would have to be qualitatively identified. This limitation applies even more so to quantifying the interrelations between topoi, which can be realized both in and outside the text segments containing the topoi proper. Quantifying both topoi and their links within and across periods should provide a more comprehensive and nuanced map of the argumentative field, indicating their varying prevalence and strength.*

Periodization: Apart from the start and end point of the timeframe, which were based on the way current disciplinary historiography constructed early film theory's development, no periodization or assumptions about discursive changes and shifts were made prior to analysis. The work was, however, informed by the contextualist assumption that changing contexts would affect discourse, although the initial (again, strictly qualitative) exploration of the corpus was guided by an interest in the formation of a new academic field through and in its discourse as well as its differentiation from related fields (e.g. drama and literary theory, but also film criticism and practical or instructional texts on film). Information on the establishment of regular film criticism columns in newspapers and magazines, the founding of journals dedicated to various aspects of film, publisher's growing interest in theoretical books on film, and the slow establishment of the field in academia (e.g. positions, lectures) were used to account for that development. *While no direct ethnography is possible to triangulate this context description, it might prove worthwhile to engage analytically with the* *technology of film-making of the respective periods as well as the films most prominently featured in the theoretical texts (see below).*

Corpus size and composition: In terms of text-length (word count, based scanned or digital copies of the texts) and genre, some quantification was possible, indicating the gradual academization of film theory. While almost all texts in the 1910s were short film reviews, pamphlets or essays, by the 1950s most texts were book-length treatises and journal articles—this was easily quantified. Accordingly, audience and register changed as well, although again no corpus linguistic methods were used to quantify this level change. Instead, these findings were demonstrated through description, exemplary analysis, and illustrative source text excerpts. With respect to triangulation, these different genres can be regarded not only as different *types of data* but also as situated on different *levels of discourse* or in different *fields of social action*, i.e. journalism, political activism, film-making, academia, etc. (see Chapter 4 and, e.g., Reisigl 2017; Jäger 2015; Link 2005). As such, they could be taken to indicate a shift from journalism, political activism, and film-making to academia, even as the academic discipline of film theory becomes increasingly differentiated and established as its own *field* (Monteil and Romerio 2017; Kertész 2001; Atkinson 1999). However, there is a serious limitation to the study in this regard: in the original study design, such a conclusion might be regarded as an artefact of the composition of the corpus itself. It simply does not contain any film reviews from the 1940 and 1950s, because none met the criteria of data sampling, i.e. canonical importance for film theory. *To test the assumption of an increasing differentiation of fields and their discourses (at least in terms of terminology and argumentation, perhaps also register), a contrastive analysis with subcorpora or a reference corpus of film reviews would have to be conducted.*

Change and continuity of subject matter: The exploratory survey had quickly made evident that there were strong continuities in terms of authors, some writing throughout all of the decades covered, and—perhaps more surprisingly—also of subject matter in the sense of actual films discussed and used for theorizing. These two continuities may well be connected, but they stand in contrast to the evident change in how the same authors discussed the same films: Here, i.e. on the lexical and argumentative level, appeared the first indicators of changes starker than the gradual academization of film theory: Radical shifts in how individual films, used as exemplars, were written about and assessed in relation to an assumed or explicated, normative definition of 'film'. Among these, films like *The Cabinet of Dr. Caligari* and *Battleship Potemkin* figure heavily across the corpus: Once analyzed as masterpieces in the spirit of true filmmaking, they were later—often by the same authors—identified as symptomatic of subconscious ailments or decried as antithetical to film's true mission. While these discursive dis/continuities were noted, they were not traced systematically through the biographical-textual trajectories of the individual authors, for example as case studies within the larger context of the discourse. *This additional perspective could easily be opened up by means of CL, using adequate search terms and conducting an argumentation analysis of extended concordance lines.*

Visualization: The visualizations used in the original study were, at least initially, an improvised prop to help me map the interrelations between topoi and their connections to changing conceptions of 'film language'. The fact that they were makeshift affairs, using hand-written cards and string on a pin board, meant that they could be rearranged more easily than a drawing. It also manifested, quite physically, the limitations of space and issues of occlusion. Using this visualization technique to communicate my findings to readers later required rebuilding these maps with the limited capabilities of MS Word—of course, alternative software would have been available then, but I lacked both the expertise and awareness of more advanced visualization strategies. *The result seemed adequate at the time, but in retrospect suffers from several limitations: Overall, space was not efficiently used; the design simply reproduced the arrangement on the pin boards, not making use of alternatives offered in a digital environment; the arrows used to indicate relations between topoi sometimes overlapped or merged, not to indicate a specific situation but due to limitations of space or software options; no easily retrieved relation could be established between the topoi in the visualization and their discussion and examples in the text surrounding the figure, sometimes leaving several pages of 'distance' the reader would have to bridge in order to connect the visual map to the description of a particular topos.*

This distance could be bridged in interactive visualizations in a number of forms, e.g. by bringing up definitions and examples upon user actions such as 'mouse click' or 'mouse over', either as text overlay or in a separate window of a dashboard. The visualizations also did not include any quantitative information, since virtually none was available. Given the limitations under which I worked at the time, it would have had to be appended to individual items in numerical form, but more effective visualization might use box size or line strength to indicate (relative) quantities. While the tripartite color coding used in the original study was sufficiently clear and suitable for black-and-white printing, a richer coloring scheme could be used for online publication. Finally, unlike the makeshift maps used during the original study's analysis, the published visualizations were static views, leaving the reader without the ability to rearrange the topoi and thereby obtain a different perspective. Using a javascript distribution like ds3, such interactivity could also be made available to the reader.

10.3 The Revised Study: Results and Discussion

In revising the study, some changes were made on the conceptual, methodological, and representational level. First, the focus was redefined as discursive changes and permanencies as tied to changing social contexts across time and space, i.e. decades and countries, acknowledging *institutional frameworks* (societies and professional organizations, journals, publishers, and academia), *social actors* (authors), *genres*, and *subject matter* (film technology, films, production, and reception). Given the original study's findings on the constitution and establishment of film theory as an academic field, social practice, and discourse with its own register, more emphasis was placed on the concepts of *genre* and *levels of discourse* (as situated in *fields of social action*). While this does not, per se, solve the challenge of modelling the multiple contexts of the strongly transnational discourse of early film theory, it acknowledges the challenge and provides a framework for asking related questions. How are discursive struggles over terminology and the arguments underpinning definitions of film related not only to broad historical changes but to social fields and attendant practices?

In terms of levels of discourse, this differentiation can be seen as both lateral (e.g. film theory to literary theory) and vertical (e.g. newspapers to academia), involving different genres while often covering the same films and written by the same authors.

To operationalize this shift, notable changes were made to the corpus of texts as well as to the methods used to analyze it. The original corpus of canonical film theoretical texts, comprising 248 text or 965,000 words of running text (Film Theory 1, henceforth FT1) was expanded to 359 texts, effectively doubling the number of words to 1,885,000 words (Film Theory 2, henceforth FT2, see the companion website REVISITING THE TOOLBOX for metadata on texts included in both corpora). This was done primarily to balance the presence of different genres across the period covered, but it also gave me the opportunity to include more French- and Russian-language texts in FT2. It must be noted that this change presents a weakening of the data collection principle underlying the original study: while the original corpus FT1 included only key texts according to film theory's own disciplinary history, that criterion was softened for FT2, which includes texts that are less central but still deemed significant enough to have be reprinted and/or translated. The second major change regarding the data is the creation of an English-only corpus (henceforth FT2-E) in which all non-English texts included in FT2 have been substituted by translations. Where no English translation was available (54 texts), I translated the originals myself with the primary aim of maintaining terminological integrity. For these as well as already existing translations included in FT2-E, I created separate annotation files to link the translated, English terminology to its original terminology of the non-English texts (Table 10.2).

Figures 10.3 and 10.4 present the composition of the two corpora in terms of texts/genre for each decade. Out of the 7 genres distinguished, 6 could be given a better balance in FT2—the exception being pamphlets. While the revised study used FT2 for the analysis of topoi and their configurations, the English-only corpus FT2-E was used exclusively for the analysis of terminological differentiation across time and genres, using CL methods.

The texts of FT2-E were compiled in WordSmith Tools to generate word frequency lists and 2-left/2-right collocation frequencies for 'film',

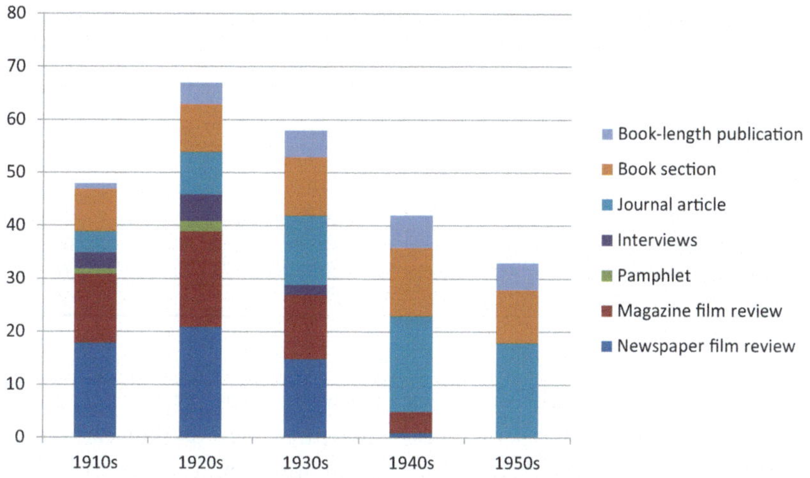

Fig. 10.3 Number of texts included in FT1 by genre and decade

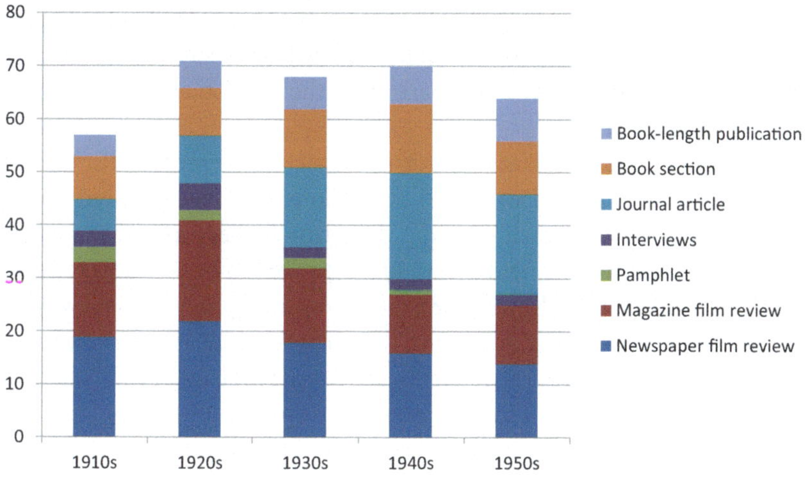

Fig. 10.4 Number of texts included in FT2 by genre and decade

Table 10.2 Distribution of genres in the original and revised studies' corpora

Genres	FT1	FT2/FT2-E
Newspaper film review	55	89
Magazine film review	47	69
Pamphlet	3	8
Interviews	10	14
Journal article	61	81
Book section	51	68
Book-length publication	21	30
Total number of texts	248	359

'filmic', and 'movie' for three settings: (1) for the entire corpus, (2) for each decade separately, and (3) for each of the three periods that can be distinguished by the original study's results on argumentation (1907–1938; 1939–1950; 1951–1960). While step (1) provided an overview, step (2) used an arbitrary, calendar-based periodization to trace terminological change in order to avoid any bias carrying over from the original study. Step (3) used the periods informed by higher-level analysis (i.e. topoi) to provide contrast and allow a comparison of the heuristic values of the two forms of periodization.

The results for FT2-E largely confirmed but complemented the qualitative results of the original study. Of the various semantic fields combined with 'film' through borrowing terminology from other arts, such as music, drama, and painting, the field of 'language' proved to be the most frequent overall. Frequency lists allowed for a more complete and varied view of the range of terms associating 'film' with 'language' as well as their frequency. In FT2-E, the most frequent terms are 'film language' (and 'language of film'), 'film grammar' (and 'grammar of film'), 'film vocabulary' (and 'vocabulary of film'), 'film text', 'film word', and 'film sentence'. To verify this result, each instance of these terms identified in a translated text was checked against and verified in the respective text's original. Significantly, language-related terminology was found in texts from all languages included but was particularly prevalent in German, French, and English texts.

For the diachronic analysis periodized *by decade*, two perspectives were developed: (1) all language-related terms were aggregated into a single frequency by period and then compared, and (2) each of the 6 most frequent terms (see above) was individually compared between periods. In the first perspective, language-related terminology increased by 145% from the 1910s to 1920s; decreased slightly by 18% from the 1920s to 1930s; decreased again by 31% from the 1930s to 1940s; and decreased again by 25% from the 1940s to 1950s. In short, theorizing film by drawing conceptual analogies to 'language' or some of its properties peaked in the 1920s and gradually declined after that—if we aggregate all such terminology. This peak is closely connected to the conception of film as an 'Esperanto of the eye' in the sense of a universal form of communication connecting all of humanity. For individual terms, there are only minor increases and decreases for 'film language' (and 'language of film') across the decades, a gradual decrease for 'film grammar' (and 'grammar of film'), and a rapid decrease for all other language-related terms after the 1930s—to the point where they have almost entirely vanished from film theoretical discourse in the 1950s. This detailed finding complements the original study insofar as it indicates a gradual departure from most specific analogies (such as 'film word') but a retaining of the encompassing 'film language' analogy as well as the montage- or editing-related 'film grammar'.

For the diachronic analysis *by previously established periodization*, the same comparisons were conducted for aggregated and individual terminology. For aggregated terminology relating film to language, the results indicate a steep decrease by 72% from the 'Esperanto' period (1907–1938) to the 'symptomatic language' period (1939–1950), and a smaller decrease of 25% from the former to the 'language of things' period (1951–1960). For individual terminology, the results show a slightly decreasing use of 'film language' and 'film grammar' across the three periods, but the decrease of other terminology is already steep between the first and second period (on average by 80%). These results roughly correspond to the periodization by decade, but they throw into sharp relief the terminological shifts accompanying the conceptual and argumentative changes as well as the concomitant reconfiguration of the field of topoi.

Regarding the academization of film theoretical discourse, the CL perspective suggests a broader focus on register in terms of keywords indicating analysis, theorizing, referencing, and discussing sources. Here, only the periodization by decade was used, since the differentiation of fields of social action cannot be assumed to be related to definitions of film. By decade, the change in register is evident: Already between the 1910s and 1920s, academic keywords (aggregated) increase by 81%, between the 1920s and 1930s by another 62%; the increase continues but appears to slow down to 34% between the 1930s and 1940s, and a 14% increase between the 1940s and 1950s. Academization of early film theory's register thus continued until 1960, but its period of rapid change was between 1910 and 1930. Note that this pattern changes if the same analysis is run not on FT2, which is balanced for genres across decades (see Fig. 10.4), but on FT1, which adheres to a stricter definition of canonical texts in film theory's early history. Here, the increase of academic keywords is even more rapid between the 1910s and 1920s (130%), then slows down to 98% between the 1920s and 1930s; for FT1, too, academization continues in more measured pace between the 1930s and 1940s (54%), and between the 1940s and 1950s (28%). Overall, this contrast shows that the effect of including less-canonical texts is a watering-down of the academization effect on register. In effect, the expansion of the corpus to FT2 translates to the inlusion of more texts of unacademic genres, particularly in the 1930s, 1940s, and 1950s, when academic journals for film theory and film studies as well as academic structures were becoming more common and established.

Using the multilingual FT2 corpus for the revised study, the argumentative analysis proceeded from the same definition and operationalization of topoi as the original study: a qualitative reading of all texts to (1) identify topoi related to the three central conceptions of 'film as language' with the aim of confirming and complementing the original study (finding previously identified and new topoi in the texts added to FT2) and (2) quantify the occurrence of all such topoi and their links in the corpus. Due to the close connection of this approach to the three conceptions of 'film language', this analysis only used the three-point periodization previously established.

Remarkably, the expanded corpus did not contain any previously unidentified topoi linked to any of the three central conceptions of 'film language'. It did contain several additional topoi related to film as such, but these will not enter into the discussion here. It appears that the original study had reached a high saturation point in terms of the field of topoi supporting conceptions of 'film language'. In addition to asking whether the additional texts of the FT2 corpus contained new topoi, however, we should also be asking whether and to which degree they contained already identified topoi. On the one hand, 32 of the 49 thematic topoi documented in FT1 were also found in the additional texts (78% of topoi); on the other hand, of the 111 additional texts only 51 contained three or more of those topoi (46% of texts); 28 contained two (25%); 14 contained only one (13%); and 18 texts contained none of the previously identified topoi (16%). Especially the shorter texts (in genres like the film review) contained few relevant topoi, while the longer texts contained up to 25 (61%).

This spread pattern is difficult to evaluate, however, without a parallel assessment of the texts already included in FT1. Of its 248 texts, 164 contained three or more of the catalogued topoi (66% of texts); 33 texts contained only two relevant topoi (13%); 25 contained only one (10%); and 26 contained none of them (11%). In contrast to the additional texts within FT2, this shows a higher density and consistency of topoi in the more canonical texts of film theory. Even with respect to shorter texts, the pattern is the same: more of them contain higher numbers of relevant topoi, and fewer of them contain no relevant topoi at all. Longer texts in FT1 contain up to 39 of the catalogued topoi (95%). Taken together, these distribution patterns indicate that the argumentative patterns found in core texts of early film theory (as defined by disciplinary history) are indeed present beyond the canon, albeit to a lesser extent and not in every film theoretical text.

In terms of quantifying the thematic topoi's frequencies and spread throughout FT2, a close qualitative analysis of all texts was carried out using the annotation software MAXQDA, using the topoi catalogue as a coding system. The following table gives an overview of the results, presenting topoi with a spread higher than 66% in dark-shaded rows and those with a spread higher than 33% but below 66% in light-shaded rows (Table 10.3).

The quantification of topoi across the entire corpus indicates a wide discrepancy between the least common, facultative topoi such as *film as fairy tale* with a frequency of 28 (3% spread) on the one hand, and the most common topoi such as *film as specific medium* with a frequency of

Table 10.3 Frequency and spread of thematic topoi related to the three central conceptions of 'film language' in FT2

Topoi	Frequency	Spread	Spread in %
Art as faithful copy of Nature	72	52	14
Expressionism as quintessential film style	61	32	9
Film as historical necessity	196	78	22
Film as return to innocence	113	53	15
Film as addictive substance	89	38	11
Film as authentic/immediate medium	572	264	74
Film as catering to the masses	183	89	25
Film as collectively produced	74	39	11
Film as corruptor	62	35	10
Film as deviating from reality	69	41	11
Film as dream work	52	21	6
Film as educator	326	95	26
Film as epigenetic essence	631	237	66
Film as escapism	190	85	24
Film as 'Esperanto' of the eye	938	171	48
Film as fairy tale	28	12	3
Film as faithful to reality	103	38	11
Film as folk culture	41	13	4
Film as fulfilling a mission	617	239	67
Film as grammatical through montage	451	123	34
Film as mass-produced commodity	296	98	27
Film as medium for the 'language of things'	720	103	29
Film medium for social critique	128	48	14
Film as national particularity	257	126	35
Film as negating social differences	42	18	5
Film as pictorial language or pictogram	184	78	22
Film as pure medium	89	63	18
Film as revealing mirror	205	109	30
Film as scientific tool	131	53	15
Film as specific medium	827	249	69
Film as symptomatic language	894	172	48
Film's affinity with the fair	36	23	6
Film's affinity with the world of things	439	181	50
History as dialectic process	33	9	3

(continued)

Table 10.3 (continued)

Language as inadequate	591	255	72
Language as inauthentic	548	262	73
Language in film as obstacle	573	251	71
Modernity as decline	216	84	23
Nature as a unified and whole composition	69	41	11
Reality as accomplice to insight	85	27	8
Reality as resisting insight	61	23	6
Reality as veiled	73	32	9
The human body as expressive	481	216	60
The 'idiota' as naturally wise	37	6	2
The ideal film-actor as non-actor	257	91	25
The masses as inferior	73	38	11
The superiority of the image	349	129	37
The surface as sincere	217	118	33

827 (69% spread) or *film as symptomatic language* with a frequency of 894 (48%). But it also shows that frequency and spread correspond very loosely, with the highest spreads being far from being the most frequent, e.g. *film as authentic* and *language as inauthentic.* Given the diachronic distribution of the corpus, this indicates that some topoi (those with the highest spread) were not confined to one or even two of the conceptual periods deduced in the original study; in contrast topoi with low spread tend to be topoi specific to a single period. This conclusion was tested by way of diachronically tracing the distribution of the topoi with the highest and lowest spread, respectively: While the distribution of the five topoi with the highest spread is far from even, each of them has a spread of at least 20% in each period; the lowest-ranking five, in contrast, were confined to single periods. It should be noted that some general, i.e. non-film-specific topoi like *the masses as inferior,* with only 11% spread, can be found in all three periods. Quantitatively separating topoi by period thus confirms the original study's qualitative finding that the great majority of topoi occurred in all three periods, although their frequency and argumentative configuration changed.

Although the quantification of thematic topoi was a time-intensive process, it presented only moderate challenges in identifying the relevant items; in contrast, quantifying the relationships between them proved much harder. This was due to numerous ambiguities in the source texts, particularly in less academic genres. After an exploratory phase, I adopted the policy of coding only explicit links, i.e. lexically realized relations of *support* or *contradict* in either direction. No doubt, many allusions and implications were thus excluded from the count. Since the relations between topoi are conceptualized here as the network configuration tying together the argumentative field in support of one of the three central conceptions of 'film language', this part of the analysis used the three-point periodization to subdivide the corpus. Results were calculated (a) for each period separately and (b) for the entire corpus.

Given that 49 items with 4 types of relation give a staggering 9.024 possible (if not equally likely) pair combinations—if we accept mutual support and mutual contradiction as possible relations between topoi—a matrix offered the best format to track of relations identified between all thematic topic. Although this form of visualization is highly useful as an analytic tool and contains much more information than the original study's diagrams (e.g. Fig. 10.2), it is highly impractical for publication due to scalability and size considerations (see Fig. 10.5). In direct comparison to the qualitative study, the quantification reveals stark contrasts regarding the strength of argumentative links.

For the separate analysis of links by period, therefore, only those topoi were included in the respective matrixes which linked directly or indirectly to the central conception (with at least one in- or out-going link of a frequency above 9). This removes some minor and infrequently linked topoi, improving visual clarity, resulting in more manageable matrixes. For the period dominated by the conception of film as an 'Esperanto of the eye' (i.e. 1910s–1930s), this procedure yielded 28 interrelated thematic topoi; for the period of 'film as symptomatic language of the collective unconscious' (i.e. 1940s) it showed 25 linked topoi; and for the period dominated by 'film as the language of things' (i.e. 1950s) it yielded 29 interrelated topoi. As can be seen from the example of Fig. 10.6, these matrixes are still visually challenging on a regular page.

Thematic topoi	Art as faithful copy of Nature	Expressionism as the quintessential film style	Film as historical necessity	Film as return to innocence	Film as addictive substance	Film as authentic/immediate medium	Film as catering to the masses	Film as collectively produced	Film as corruptor	Film as deviating from reality	Film as dream work	Film as educator	Film as epigenetic essence	Film as escapism	Film as 'Esperanto' of the eye	Film as fairy tale	Film as faithful to reality	Film as folk culture	Film as fulfilling a mission	Film as grammatical through montage	Film as mass-produced commodity	Film as medium for the 'language of things'	Film as national particularity	Film as negating social differences	Film as pictorial language or pictogram	Film as pure medium	Film as revealing mirror	Film as scientific tool	Film as specific medium	Film as symptomatic language	Film's affinity with the fair	Film's affinity with the world of things	Film as medium for social critique	History as dialectic process	Language as inadequate	Language as inauthentic	Language in film as obstacle	Modernity as decline	Nature as a unified and whole composition	Reality as accomplice to insight	Reality as resisting insight	Reality as veiled	The human body as expressive	The ideal film-actor as non-actor	The 'idiota' as naturally wise	The masses as inferior	The superiority of the image	The surface as sincere
Art as faithful copy of Nature	—	—	—	4	—	—	—	—	—	—	—	—	—	—	—	—	—	—	—	—	—	11	—	—	—	8	7	—	—	—	—	16	—	—	—	—	—	—	—	—	—	—	—	11	—	—	—	—
Expressionism as the quintessential film style	—	—	—	—	—	—	—	—	—	15	—	—	—	—	—	—	—	—	—	—	—	—	—	—	—	—	—	—	—	—	—	—	—	—	—	—	—	—	—	—	—	—	—	—	—	—	—	—
Film as historical necessity	—	—	—	—	—	—	—	—	—	—	—	12	—	—	15	—	—	—	22	—	—	9	—	—	—	—	—	—	—	7	—	—	—	—	—	—	—	—	—	—	5	9	—	—	—	—	—	—
Film as return to innocence	—	—	—	—	52	—	—	—	36	—	11	—	—	19	12	32	—	—	72	—	—	42	—	27	—	39	—	—	—	—	—	28	—	—	—	—	—	—	—	—	—	—	—	—	—	—	—	—
Film as addictive substance	—	—	—	74	—	—	38	—	41	—	—	9	—	52	—	—	—	—	—	—	—	—	—	—	—	14	—	—	—	—	—	—	—	—	—	—	—	—	—	—	—	—	—	—	—	—	—	—
Film as authentic/immediate medium	—	—	—	24	—	—	—	—	—	—	—	16	—	—	118	—	—	—	89	—	—	211	35	—	—	51	48	—	—	216	—	284	—	—	—	—	107	—	—	—	—	—	22	—	—	—	—	—
Film as catering to the masses	—	—	—	—	72	—	—	—	42	21	—	15	—	29	—	—	—	59	16	—	47	24	35	—	—	21	17	—	30	182	—	—	—	—	—	—	—	—	—	—	—	—	—	—	—	—	—	—
Film as collectively produced	—	—	—	—	—	—	—	—	—	—	29	—	—	—	—	—	—	37	—	—	—	—	51	—	—	—	—	—	—	58	—	—	—	—	—	—	—	—	—	—	—	—	—	—	—	—	—	—
Film as corruptor	—	—	—	—	4	—	—	—	—	—	—	29	—	7	—	—	—	—	16	—	—	22	—	—	—	—	19	—	—	—	—	—	—	—	—	—	—	—	—	—	—	—	—	—	—	—	—	—
Film as deviating from reality	—	—	—	—	—	—	—	—	24	—	18	19	—	—	—	—	—	—	12	—	—	—	—	—	—	—	—	—	—	39	—	—	17	—	—	—	—	—	—	—	—	—	—	—	—	—	—	—
Film as dream work	—	42	—	—	—	—	—	—	—	—	—	—	—	—	—	—	—	—	—	—	—	—	—	—	—	—	—	—	—	—	—	—	—	—	—	—	—	—	—	—	—	—	—	—	—	—	—	—
Film as educator	—	—	—	—	—	—	—	—	34	—	—	—	—	—	—	—	—	—	182	—	—	—	—	—	—	—	—	—	—	—	—	—	—	—	—	—	—	—	—	—	—	—	—	—	—	—	—	—
Film as epigenetic essence	14	—	54	—	—	327	—	—	—	—	—	—	—	—	—	—	16	—	—	—	—	189	—	—	—	51	58	48	182	31	—	172	—	—	—	—	—	—	—	—	—	—	—	—	—	—	81	52
Film as escapism	—	83	—	—	73	—	49	—	71	—	—	27	—	—	—	—	—	—	—	—	—	—	—	—	—	—	—	—	—	104	—	—	—	—	—	—	—	—	—	—	—	—	—	—	—	—	—	—
Film as 'Esperanto' of the eye	—	—	—	—	—	—	—	—	—	—	—	—	—	—	—	—	—	—	—	—	—	—	—	—	—	—	—	—	—	—	—	—	—	—	—	—	247	—	—	—	—	—	—	—	—	—	—	—
Film as fairy tale	—	13	—	—	—	—	—	—	—	—	—	—	21	—	—	—	—	18	—	—	—	—	8	—	—	—	—	—	—	—	—	—	—	—	—	—	—	—	—	—	—	—	—	—	—	—	—	—
Film as faithful to reality	—	—	—	—	—	—	—	—	—	29	—	—	—	—	—	—	—	—	—	—	—	56	—	—	—	—	—	—	—	—	—	15	—	—	—	—	—	—	—	—	—	—	—	—	—	—	—	—
Film as folk culture	—	—	—	—	—	—	—	—	—	—	—	—	—	—	—	15	—	—	—	—	—	—	31	—	—	—	—	—	—	—	—	—	—	—	—	—	—	—	—	—	—	—	—	—	—	—	—	—
Film as fulfilling a mission	—	—	35	—	—	—	—	—	—	—	—	11	—	—	—	—	—	—	—	—	—	—	—	—	—	—	21	—	—	—	—	—	—	—	—	—	—	—	—	—	—	—	—	—	—	—	—	—
Film as grammatical through montage	—	—	—	—	—	—	—	—	—	—	—	—	—	—	79	—	—	—	—	—	—	—	—	—	—	—	51	—	—	—	—	—	—	—	—	—	—	—	—	—	—	—	—	—	—	—	—	—
Film as mass-produced commodity	—	—	39	—	—	—	8	—	13	16	—	—	—	—	—	—	—	—	—	—	—	—	71	—	—	—	—	—	—	127	—	—	—	—	—	—	—	—	—	—	—	—	—	—	—	—	—	—
Film as medium for the 'language of things'	—	—	—	—	—	—	—	—	—	—	—	4	—	—	—	—	—	—	58	—	—	—	—	—	—	—	29	—	—	38	—	41	—	—	—	—	—	—	—	—	—	—	—	—	—	—	—	—
Film as medium for social critique	—	—	—	—	—	—	—	—	—	—	—	35	—	—	—	—	—	—	29	—	41	—	—	—	—	—	—	—	—	—	—	31	—	—	—	—	—	—	—	—	—	—	—	—	—	—	—	—
Film as national particularity	—	—	—	—	—	—	—	—	—	—	—	—	—	—	—	—	—	91	—	—	—	—	—	—	—	—	—	—	—	189	—	—	—	—	—	—	—	—	—	—	—	—	—	—	—	—	—	—
Film as negating social differences	—	—	—	—	—	—	—	—	—	—	—	6	—	—	—	—	—	—	2	—	—	—	—	—	—	—	—	—	—	—	—	—	—	—	—	—	—	—	—	—	—	—	—	—	—	—	—	—
Film as pictorial language or pictogram	—	—	—	12	—	9	—	—	—	—	—	—	—	—	—	—	—	—	—	—	—	—	—	—	—	7	—	—	—	—	—	—	—	—	—	—	—	—	—	—	—	—	—	—	—	—	—	—
Film as pure medium	—	—	—	34	—	18	—	—	—	—	—	2	—	7	—	—	—	—	5	—	—	23	—	—	—	—	9	—	—	—	—	—	—	—	—	—	28	—	—	—	—	—	—	28	—	—	—	—
Film as revealing mirror	—	—	—	—	—	—	—	—	—	—	—	67	—	—	—	—	—	—	29	—	—	—	—	—	—	—	—	—	—	—	—	—	14	—	—	—	41	—	—	—	—	—	—	12	—	—	—	—
Film as scientific tool	—	—	—	—	—	—	—	—	—	—	—	39	—	—	—	—	—	—	—	—	—	—	—	—	—	—	—	—	—	—	—	—	27	—	—	—	—	—	—	—	—	—	—	—	—	—	—	—
Film as specific medium	—	—	53	—	—	—	—	—	—	—	—	—	—	—	—	—	—	—	—	12	—	—	—	—	—	34	—	—	—	—	—	—	—	—	—	—	—	—	—	—	—	—	—	—	—	—	—	64
Film as symptomatic language	—	16	—	—	—	—	—	—	—	—	—	—	—	—	—	—	—	—	—	—	—	—	—	—	—	—	—	—	—	—	—	—	—	—	—	—	—	—	—	—	—	—	—	—	—	—	—	—
Film's affinity with the fair	—	—	3	—	—	—	—	—	—	—	—	—	—	—	—	—	—	5	—	—	—	—	—	—	—	—	—	—	—	—	—	—	—	—	—	—	—	—	—	—	—	—	—	—	—	—	—	—
Film's affinity with the world of things	—	—	21	35	—	28	—	—	—	—	18	—	—	—	—	17	—	—	49	—	—	325	—	—	51	—	—	—	—	—	—	—	33	—	—	—	—	—	—	—	—	—	—	25	—	—	—	—
History as dialectic process	—	—	25	—	—	—	—	—	—	—	—	—	—	—	—	—	—	—	—	—	—	—	—	—	—	—	—	—	—	—	—	—	—	—	—	—	—	—	—	—	—	—	—	—	—	—	—	—
Language as inadequate	—	—	41	—	—	—	—	—	—	—	—	—	—	—	—	—	—	—	—	—	—	—	—	—	—	—	—	—	—	—	—	—	—	—	—	—	159	52	—	—	—	9	—	—	—	—	57	—
Language as inauthentic	—	—	19	—	—	—	—	—	—	—	—	—	—	—	—	—	—	—	—	—	—	—	—	—	—	—	—	—	—	—	—	—	—	—	284	—	183	48	—	—	—	5	—	—	—	—	164	—
Language in film as obstacle	—	—	—	—	—	318	—	—	—	—	—	—	—	—	—	—	—	—	—	—	—	—	—	—	—	—	—	—	—	—	—	—	—	—	—	—	—	—	—	—	—	—	—	—	—	—	—	—
Modernity as decline	—	—	26	—	—	—	—	—	—	—	—	—	—	—	—	—	—	—	—	—	—	—	—	—	—	—	—	—	—	—	—	—	—	—	41	33	—	—	—	—	27	41	—	—	8	17	—	—
Nature as a unified and whole composition	16	—	—	—	—	—	—	—	—	—	—	—	—	—	—	—	—	—	—	—	—	—	—	—	2	—	—	—	—	—	—	—	—	—	11	—	20	—	—	7	—	—	—	—	—	—	—	34
Reality as accomplice to insight	—	—	12	—	—	—	—	—	—	—	—	5	—	—	—	—	46	—	14	—	—	9	—	—	—	—	17	—	—	8	—	—	—	—	—	—	—	—	—	—	—	21	—	15	—	—	—	23
Reality as resisting insight	—	—	11	—	—	—	—	—	—	—	—	—	—	—	—	—	—	—	19	—	—	—	—	—	—	—	—	—	—	—	—	—	31	—	—	—	—	—	—	18	—	33	—	—	9	—	—	—
Reality as veiled	—	—	8	—	—	—	—	—	—	—	—	—	—	—	—	—	—	—	—	—	—	—	—	—	—	—	—	—	—	—	—	—	2	—	—	—	—	—	—	—	41	—	—	—	7	—	—	—
The human body as expressive	—	—	—	—	—	—	—	—	—	—	—	—	—	—	28	—	—	—	—	—	—	—	43	—	—	—	—	—	—	—	—	—	—	—	—	—	56	—	—	—	—	—	—	42	—	—	—	38
The ideal film-actor as non-actor	—	—	—	—	—	—	—	—	—	—	—	—	—	—	—	—	—	—	—	—	—	—	—	—	—	—	—	—	—	—	—	—	—	—	—	—	—	—	—	—	—	—	—	—	—	—	—	—
The 'idiota' as naturally wise	—	—	—	—	—	—	—	—	—	—	—	—	—	—	—	—	—	—	—	—	—	—	—	—	—	—	—	—	—	—	—	—	—	—	—	—	—	—	—	—	—	—	—	—	—	—	—	18
The masses as inferior	—	—	—	—	—	—	12	—	8	—	—	—	—	—	—	—	—	—	—	—	—	—	—	—	—	—	—	—	—	14	—	—	—	—	—	—	—	—	—	—	—	—	—	—	—	—	—	—
The superiority of the image	—	—	—	—	—	216	—	—	—	—	—	3	—	—	174	—	25	—	—	—	—	51	—	—	—	15	12	—	28	6	—	—	—	—	8	—	262	—	—	—	—	—	—	—	—	—	—	—
The surface as sincere	—	—	—	16	—	195	—	—	—	—	—	34	—	—	—	—	—	—	—	—	—	—	—	—	—	32	29	—	—	—	—	—	—	—	—	—	—	—	—	47	—	—	45	33	—	—	87	—

Fig. 10.5 Matrix of quantified links between all 49 thematic topoi (*support* links are given in black numbers, *contradict* links in red)

Analytically, the separate matrixes for the three periods broadly confirm the centrality of the three conceptions of 'film language'. Beyond that, they also confirm the pivotal impact of sound film on early film theory, inspiring wide-spread arguments against language in film—that is, in film as a universally understandable language. As could be expected, the matrixes also capture many less frequent argumentative links and characterize some topoi as 'outliers', i.e. only receiving or giving support. In addition to the total number of links a given topos has (supporting or being supported),

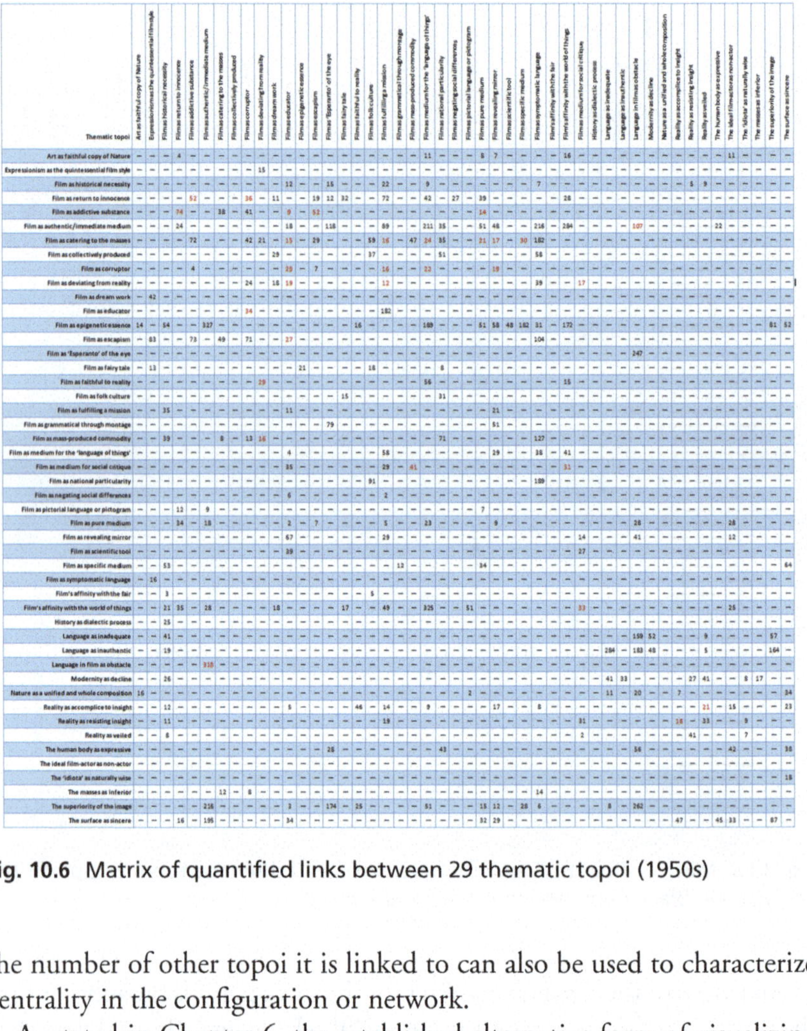

Fig. 10.6 Matrix of quantified links between 29 thematic topoi (1950s)

the number of other topoi it is linked to can also be used to characterize centrality in the configuration or network.

As stated in Chapter 6, the established alternative form of visualizing relationships in networks is a node-link graph, often simply referred to as a network graph. To assess the relative potential of these two forms of visualization in the current case, we may consult the data-user-tasks triangle and its criteria (Miksch and Aigner 2014): In terms of *appropriateness*, networks graphs are likely more readily comprehensible to the target audience of discourse analysists. In terms of *effectiveness*, matrixes excel in cases where there are not only many nodes but most of them are also interlinked, but the current case study features networks with relatively few links, which suggests the use of network graphs; matrixes easily include quantitative information on how often a link occurs, but the inclusion of numbers reduces visual expressiveness and the simultaneous presence of more than one link type between the same nodes is problematic in terms of space available. This can be solved by using color gradients to indicate frequency (low frequencies indicated by light shading of the respective color; high frequencies by dark shading), with each color mapping a particular link type. To accommodate multiple link types, such as *support* and *contradict* in the current case study, the available space can be subdivided into squares or concentric, overlapping rectangles, with each area expressing one type. In contrast, network graphs can offload more relational information into the spatial arrangement of the visualization, exploiting pre-attentive, automatic processing: The configuration of the nodes immediately tells us something about the density of the network, the centrality and marginality of its elements etc. The challenges for expressiveness here lie in expressing quantitative information on links and in expressing multiple link types. The former could be addressed either by appending numbers to the edges connecting nodes, thereby losing an advantage of network graphs over matrixes, or by using the line strength of the edges connecting nodes to express frequency (stronger lines indicating higher frequencies), as color gradients are not reliable on such small areas. The latter can be solved by using a second, differently colored edge for the link type *contradicts* and arrowheads to indicate directionality (A *supports* B vs. B *supports* A). To avoid possible occlusion between the two types of edges (in the rare cases where discourses contain conflicting relations, e.g. A *supports* B, but also A *contradicts* B), the edges have to be slightly curved (Fig. 10.7).

Given these solutions, both visualizations allow similar tasks but at different cognitive costs. Matrixes give easier and more systems access to the quantitative information on links; network graphs take more advantage of pre-attentive processing and spatial pattern recognition. Adding interactivity to both forms of visualization can mitigate these limitations, but it can also heighten their differentiation by enabling certain tasks. For instance, the matrix displaying the field of topoi and its configuration

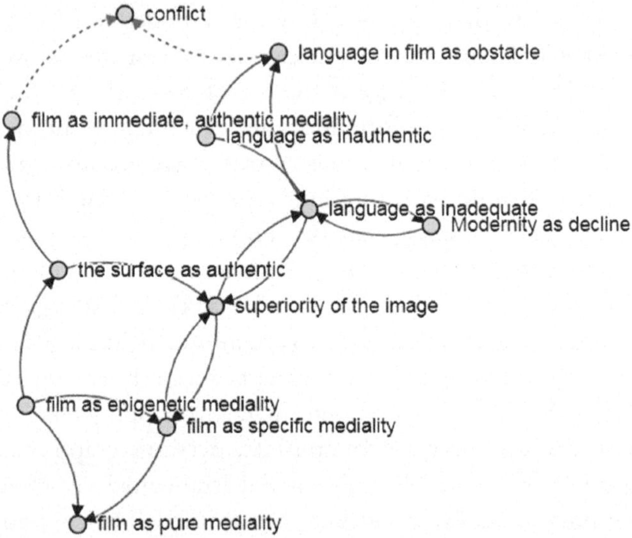

Fig. 10.7 Network graph displaying topoi and their relations

can be embedded in a dashboard-like structure, with additional panels displaying additional information on *mouse-click* or *mouse-over*: the definition of the selected topos, its frequency in the corpus, metadata on texts in which it occurs, text excerpts illustrating its linguistic realization, information on its links to other topoi, including link types and link frequency. The network graph, in addition to similar mouse-click effects in a dashboard structure, can also be given a force-directed 'repulsion' physics that pushes nodes, automatically arranging the network so as to avoid occlusion while effectively using the space available. It can moreover allow the user to drag nodes so as to rearrange the data structure, centering the network on specific topoi or clusters, effectively creating their own map. Both version have been implemented and can be tested on the companion website Revisiting the Toolbox.

While these visualizations make good use of the quantitative information obtained in the revised study and even manage to integrate multiple levels of analysis, including qualitative elements, there are some qualitative aspects of the original study that are lost. (1) In their current form, neither matrix nor network graph capture the more complex relations between topoi in which multiple arguments are joined to support a topos—not separately but only in conjunction. In case of the matrix, this is simply outside its capacities as a two-dimensional map of bidirectional relations (A to B, B to A, but never A + B to C). In case of the network graph, it is of course conceptually possible to include joined edges, but it is a technical challenge to implement them, its feasibility depending on the software tool or programming language selected. (2) The quantification required for both forms of visualization forces the exclusion of all ambiguity or fuzziness: something either is or is not of a certain category or type. In data such as the texts of early film theory, that ambiguity may very well be not an inconvenience but a key characteristic; hence, to filter it out completely because it cannot be quantified might ultimately misrepresent the discourse. In short, the aim of creating visualizations that require quantification should never dictate research procedure entirely, and deliberate inclusion of qualitative aspects may be a necessary safeguard against impoverishing the analytical results.

10.4 Research Design and Practice

The study of gradual academization and argumentative patterns in early film theory highlights several conceptual and methodological issues in contemporary CDS. This chapter has used the revision of previous work to discuss the critical aspects of (1) criteria for data selection, especially with respect to a diachronic corpus, (2) corpus composition and balancing with respect to multiple data types (genres and languages), (3) periodization of data based on either arbitrary/calendar, context- or analysis-based criteria, (4) the consequences of periodization in terms of creating and analyzing subcorpora to trace discursive change, (5) challenges in analyzing multilingual corpora, (6) limitations of qualitative and quantitative methods as well as the potential of integrating them when analyzing argumentation, (7) limitations and benefits of different forms of manual and computer-generated visualizations as tools in the analytical process as well as publishing, and (8) interactive visualizations that use a dashboard-format to provide the user with access to multiple levels of analysis, category systems, metadata, and example texts as well as ways of exploring these and their interrelations on their own.

With respect to research design and practice, the above discussions indicate that we should

- carefully consider a range of options in building corpora, including external criteria that may used for periodization or delimiting the corpus,
- consider the inclusion of varied data, such as multiple genres, not necessarily in terms of balancing them equally but to reflect or test diachronic change,
- consider different strategies for periodization and conduct at least preliminary tests on how they affect diachronic results,
- be mindful that any of the above decisions are not simply of a practical nature but must be related to our underlying conception of discursive change, its relation to social change, and the role of social actors/agency within contexts,
- depending on research aims and level of analysis, consider multi-lingual data for highly international discourses or comparative studies,
- consider triangulating our analyses by combining qualitative and quantitative methods in approaching high-level linguistic phenomena such as argumentation or topoi, particularly if regarded on the level of discourse rather than individual texts,
- plan and test visualization strategies as part of the research process, not simply as an after-thought in setting up a publication or presentation,
- acknowledge that different forms of visualization may well be needed for analysis and publication,
- research adequate forms of visualization and technological options, both static and interactive, keeping in mind the data-user-tasks triangle,
- acquire relevant technical competence or collaborate with visualization specialists, and
- ensure data integrity and transparency, considering that the best option may well be beyond traditional publishing formats, e.g. an online repository.

References

Atkinson, Dwight. 1999. *Scientific Discourse in Sociohistorical Context: The Philosophical Transactions of the Royal Society of London, 1675–1975*. Rhetoric, Knowledge, and Society. Mahwah, NJ: L. Erlbaum Associates.

Balázs, Béla. 1923. "Alles Für Geld." *Der Tag*, November 14, 1923.

Elsaesser, Thomas. 2002. *Filmgeschichte Und Frühes Kino: Archäologie Eines Medienwandels*. München: Edition text + kritik.

Grossberg, Lawrence. 1992. *We Gotta Get Out of This Place: Popular Conservatism and Postmodern Culture*. New York: Routledge.

———. 1997. *Bringing It All Back Home: Essays on Cultural Studies*. Durham, NC: Duke University Press.

Hall, Stuart. 1986. "On Postmodernism and Articulation: An Interview." *Journal of Communication Inquiry* 10: 45–60.

Jäger, Siegfried. 2015. *Kritische Diskursanalyse: eine Einführung*. 7, vollständig überarbeitete Auflage. Edition DISS, Bd. 3. Münster: Unrast.

Kertész, András, ed. 2001. *Approaches to the Pragmatics of Scientific Discourse*. Metalinguistica 9. Frankfurt am Main: Lang.

Kienpointner, Manfred. 1992. *Alltagslogik: Struktur Und Funktion von Argumentationsmustern*. Problemata 126. Stuttgart-Bad Cannstatt: Frommann-Holzboog.

———. 1996. *Vernünftig argumentieren: Regeln und Techniken der Diskussion*. Reinbek bei Hamburg: Rowohlt-Taschenbuch-Verl.

Kracauer, Siegfried. 1928. "Thérèse Raquin". Reprinted in. *Kino: Essays, Studien, Glossen zum Film*, edited by Karsten Witte, 136–138. Frankfurt am Main: Suhrkamp, 1974.

———. 1931. "Free and Easy". Reprinted in. *Kino: Essays, Studien, Glossen zum Film*, edited by Karsten Witte, 184–186. Frankfurt am Main: Suhrkamp, 1974.

Link, Jürgen. 2005. "Warum Diskurse Nicht von Personalen Subjekten „ausgehandelt" Werden. Von Der Diskurs- Zur Interdiskurstheorie." In *Die Diskursive Konstruktion von Wirklichkeit: Zum Verhältnis von Wissenssoziologie Und Diskursforschung*, edited by Reiner Keller, Andreas Hirseland, Werner Schneider, and Willy Viehöfer, 77–100. Konstanz: UVK Verlagsgesellschaft.

Metz, Christian. 1966. "La Grande Syntagmatique Du Film Narratif." *Communications* 8: 126–30.

Miksch, Silvia, and Wolfgang Aigner. 2014. "A Matter of Time: Applying a Data–Users–Tasks Design Triangle to Visual Analytics of Time-Oriented Data." *Computers & Graphics* 38 (February): 286–90. https://doi.org/10.1016/j.cag.2013.11.002.

Monteil, Lucas, and Alice Romerio. 2017. "From Disciplines to 'Studies': Knowledge, Trajectories, Policies." *Revue d'anthropologie des connaissances* 11 (3): a. https://doi.org/10.3917/rac.036.a.

Reisigl, Martin. 2017. "The Discourse-Historical Approach." In *The Routledge Handbook of Critical Discourse Studies*, edited by John Flowerdew and John E. Richardson, 44–59. London: Routledge.

Reisigl, Martin, and Ruth Wodak. 2015. "The Discourse-Historical Approach (DHA)." In *Methods of Critical Discourse Studies*, edited by Ruth Wodak and Michael Meyer, 23–61. London: Sage.

Rheindorf, Markus. 2005a. "Die Ausdruckskraft Der Körper: Natürlichkeit Und Physiognomie in Der Filmtheorie Der Zwischenkriegszeit." In *Leibhaftige Moderne: Körper in Kunst Und Massenmedien 1918 Bis 1938*, edited by Michael Cowan and Kai M. Sicks, 217–30. Bielefeld: transcript.

———. 2005b. "Film as Language: The Politics of Early Film Theory (1920–1960)." *Journal of Language and Politics* 4 (1): 143–59.

———. 2006. "The Languages That Films Speak. Discourse-Historical Perspectives on Film Theory: Dis/continuities and Contexts." PhD thesis, University of Vienna, Vienna.

———. 2007. "Die Sprachen, Die Filme Sprechen: Die Geschichte Der Deutschsprachigen Filmtheorie Als Diskursgeschichte." *Zeitschrift Für Kulturwissenschaften. Themenheft Filmwissenschaft Als Kulturwissenschaft* 2: 11–24.

Toulmin, Stephen. 2003. *The Uses of Argument.* Updated Edition. Cambridge, UK and New York: Cambridge University Press.

Wodak, Ruth, Rudolf de Cillia, Martin Reisigl, and Karin Liebhart. 2009. *The Discursive Construction of National Identity.* 2nd ed. Critical Discourse Analysis. Edinburgh: Edinburgh University Press.

11

Concluding Remarks

In concluding this book, I want to return to the toolbox analogy for methods in Critical Discourse Studies. In the course of years, the contents of some toolboxes change very little, while those of others change substantially. Whether they do or not, one may argue, will depend on the number and variety of tasks such toolboxes are used for and adapted to. Of course, it will also depend on the individual(s) using that toolbox, which tasks they seek out, and which they pass by as well as their skills, competences, and inclination to take up challenges. The resulting change may be a gradual expansion of tools, a slow replacement of old tools, or the development of new multi-tools that resemble a Swiss Army knife. Ultimately, one may end up with a toolbox whose contents have changed so much that the seemingly philosophical question 'But is it still the same toolbox?' becomes a very practical issue: Reaching into the box, one might find instead of a hammer, screwdriver, and wrench—a pocket calculator, stencil cutter, and caliper.

In Critical Discourse Studies, the choice of tools we use depends, first, on our research interests and the kinds of questions we ask; second, on our own academic training and socialization; third, on the availability of resources, including of the tools themselves; and, fourth, on the socio-

© The Author(s) 2019

M. Rheindorf, *Revisiting the Toolbox of Discourse Studies*,
Postdisciplinary Studies in Discourse,
https://doi.org/10.1007/978-3-030-19369-0_11

political development of the world we would research. While the first two of these dimensions are highly individual, the third has seen a rapid expansion of highly technologized methods, producing tools that offer a better grasp of more data than ever before. The fourth dimension, too, has been affected by rapid change: In today's short-lived media environment, we are dealing with ever new types of texts and images, new genres that seemingly spread across the globe in a few days, to be joined or replaced by new forms soon thereafter. In some cases, this may make once-established tools increasingly marginal as they are outperformed by innovative tools; in other cases, old tools are refined and adapted to the new tasks.

Without a doubt, the toolbox analogy has its limitations. Are we to think of it as one, communally shared toolbox that is gradually transformed by every member of the 'discourse studies community' who adds to it? Can anyone actually *remove* tools from it, or does the lack of use of a particular tool simply indicate its outdatedness? Are we looking at an almost sedimentary process of accretion, with new tools added on top of established ones? Imagine the clutter in that toolbox. Or should we think of it as a virtually shared, distributed network of toolboxes, with each researcher gradually establishing their own version of its contents and sometimes sharing a new tool, although rarely with perfect transparency, through publication? For me, a key takeaway of writing this book is the emphasis on sharing and openness, as ideas but also in the actual exchange with colleagues while working on each chapter. In this sense, then, Open Science offers a well-suited challenge to the toolbox of discourse studies: sharing data and/or metadata, but even more so explicating and sharing methodologies, research designs, and conceptual frames facilitates discussion, experimentation, revision, and development.

There is enormous potential for creativity in such exchanges, even if they are at times uneasy, well outside the usual comfort zone of academia. Especially in Critical Discourse Studies, however, we should not fear and preempt criticism of our own work. All analysis, all research is fluid and temporary, or should be: This is what work on the case studies of Chapters 7–10 has shown me. Traditional publication formats and conventions have, sometimes to the detriment of academic exchange, reified the research process into a fixed, one-version act, subject to the aim of being perfect and unassailable, simply because it is singular and fixed. Critical discussion and revision of my own previous work has served to decenter the research process, as an experience but also conceptually.

Decentering the research process throws into relief both the contingencies and decisions that inform discourse analytical research. Since the term 'research design', which I have used throughout this book, emphasizes deliberate planning, this conclusion seeks to acknowledge the contingency and temporary state of research. It is my hope that the strategy of offering revisions and alternative versions of research, as the case studies of Chapters 7–10 have done, proves to be productive beyond this book. Other approaches with similar effects include story-telling techniques, narrativizing research, or dialogic formats. Indeed, a growing number of journals invites contribution formats that break the mold of the research paper, such as the formats '...is thinking about...' or 'Dialogue' in the applied linguistics journal *10plus1*, the formats 'forum' or 'commentary' in the *German Political Science Quarterly* or the 'reply' or 'response' formats printed in journals such as *Discourse & Society*. Thus thrown off-balance, our accounts of research can become prisms that reveal the consequences of conceptual and methodological decisions. All this, of course, comes at a price measured not only in time and resources but possibly also traditional respectability, which is informed by the idea of closure.

In retrospect, each of the five chapters in Part I of this book can be seen as contributing to this decentering, even as they can be seen as supporting triangulation. While arguments for triangulation often draw on the idea of closure—making results more robust, eliminating ambiguity, dispelling doubts, rooting out contradiction—the reality of using multiple methodologies, varied data sets, diachronically dispersed data or interactive visualization often raises more questions than it answers, reveals new complexities or un-fixes meaning. For instance, using qualitative analysis to identify topoi in the case study on media representations of refugees (Chapter 9) after quantitative downsampling of a large corpus does not only provide new insights into the diachronic shift of legitimation, it also makes painfully obvious that these shifts cannot be quantified in the same confident manner as lexical shifts in the representation of refugees. Similarly, using translations to transform a multilingual selection of texts into a monolingual corpus that can be analyzed using CL methods, as in the case study on early film theory (Chapter 10), reveals the limitations of any lexis-based results thus obtained as well as the monolingual frame of virtually all corpus-based discourse studies.

With these important qualifications in mind, I now want to revisit the potential benefits of triangulation as set out in the introduction. These were, in brief, the effects of

- corroboration or confirmation of results,
- diversity of views (e.g. different levels of analysis, but also levels of discourse),
- offset or contrast,
- complementing (e.g., quantitative methods for patterns, qualitative methods for strategies),
- enhancement (expanding, detailing or deepening analysis),
- explanation or clarification (usually of quantitative results by qualitative analysis),
- exploration/initiation,
- instrument development,
- sampling/downsampling,
- contextualization (e.g. through attendant social practices or adding a historical dimension),
- illustration, and
- increased credibility (based on Bryman 2006, 105–7).

Each chapter in Part I relates to several of these effects, as different methodologies and their combinations open up potentials. In the case studies of Part II, however, we see that the specific research interests we pursue, the questions we ask, lead to more specific potentials of triangulation:

(1) The use of (largely) quantitative methods established in Corpus Linguistics within discourse studies can *corroborate* or *confirm* in large datasets the results previously obtained by qualitative analysis of smaller datasets—provided we can establish a sufficiently robust link between the qualitative phenomena studied and the lexical focus of CL methods. In doing so, quantitative analysis can at the same time enhance the results by *expansion. For instance, the case study on Holocaust narratives (Chapter 7) used frequency analysis to confirm the lack of specific temporal references*

in narratives situated between 1938 and 1945, which helped to characterize the chronotope shared between these stories.

More or less free-roaming frequency- or keyness-based analyses can serve to *explore* or *initiate* research (similar to the corpus-driven approach), to be then followed up with further quantitative or qualitative methods. *Thus, the case study on normalization of the term "unwillingness to integrate" (Chapter 8) explored the semantic macrostructure of its media corpus through frequency analysis before manually aggregating the results into semantic fields.* Qualitative analyses, in turn, often serve to illustrate, detail or deepen the broad, lexis-based perspectives of quantitative analyses. *For instance, the case study on media representations of refugees (Chapter 9) followed a wide range of qualitative analyses with a detailed analysis of topoi and legitimation strategies in a subset of the same data.*

In diachronic corpora tagged for date, frequency analysis can indicate both broad and minute trends or shifts in discourse, depending on periodization. This can point to socio-political changes and thus link to *contextualization* through qualitative methods. *The case study on normalization of the term "unwillingness to integrate" (Chapter 8) was not simply inspired by such a change, it also identified several discursive events and long-term trends through frequency analyses. Using more complex approaches to shifting collocation patterns, the case study on media representations of refugees (Chapter 9) found several shifts in reporting on refugees that were linked to specific events or contextual changes.*

Especially in diachronic studies, using time-tagged data, quantitative methods provide ways to characterize temporally segmented subcorpora so as to facilitate downsampling, helping qualitative analysis to 'pick the right cherries'. *The case study on media representations of refugees (Chapter 9) demonstrated the potential of such quantitative downsampling in conjunction with multiple cycles of qualitative analyses and saturation criteria.*

(2) Working with different kinds of data may be the most obvious way to diversify views on the same topical discourse or social practice. This characteristically entails the use of different methods of analysis as well as data collection (e.g. interviews, group discussions, and ethnography in addition to text collection), with each distinct type of data requiring adequate methodological choices. The many interrelated approaches to multimodal discourse analysis that have been developed over the last two

decades provide a rich choice of tools for such research. Depending on the data chosen, such research can achieve stark *contrast* (e.g. between a predominantly text-based social practice like commemorative speeches and the predominantly non-linguistic practices of monuments or memorials) or *explanation* (e.g. of a subculture's codes through ethnography). Triangulation through different types of data can also facilitate *exploration, instrument development,* and *contextualization,* when the methodological combination is sequenced to these ends. By definition, such triangulation also *expands* the empirical scope of research, be it across media, modes or genres. *For instance, the case study on the normalization of the term "unwillingness to integrate" (Chapter 8) combined the analysis of news reports, parliamentary debates, legal texts, and jurisprudence, partly corroborating and offsetting results, and in so doing greatly expanded the scope of research. The case study on argumentation in early film theory (Chapter 10) analyzed multiple genres that served film critics, directors, art theorists, and others in developing their thinking on film since the early twentieth century. Pamphlets and manifestos, film reviews, essays, manuals, research reports, and monographs not only document the increasing academization of the field but also demonstrate the wide-spread use of argumentation patterns across genres.*

(3) Combining analyses of different levels of discourse, when taken to mean discourses at different levels of hierarchy, public-ness, or in different fields of social action, can serve to *diversify views* or *complement* results, especially if the levels or fields ares interrelated (e.g. legislation and jurisprudence, political debate and policy). In such cases, *explanation* and *contextualization* can also be facilitated. *Contrast* is likely, in form as well as substance, particularly if the levels or fields included are dissimilar (e.g. different institutions, following distinct social conventions, or formal and informal discourses). If a topical discourse or interconnected social practice is thereby traced through different fields of social action, or layers of hierarchy, this form of triangulation will also *enhance* the insights gained (e.g. in the study of discourses across fields, or across the backstage and frontstage of political discourse). *The case study on normalization of the term "unwillingness to integrate" (Chapter 8) analyzed data from the fields of politics, legislation, and jurisprudence to expand and in so doing correct the initial focus on media reporting.*

Combining analyses of different levels discourse, when taken to mean different levels of linguistic realization, e.g. lexical frequency, collocation patterns, and higher-level textual phenomena like argumentation, will *enhance* and *deepen* the analysis. In so doing, it may *complement* or *contrast* results as, e.g., lexical patterns confirm or counteract the legitimation strategies evidenced in argumentative patterns. In some cases, the deepened analysis will serve to *explain* initial findings. Such triangulation will almost always involve different methods, models or even theories (e.g. discourse prosody and legitimation), necessitating a careful discussion on the conceptual level. *The case study on media representations of refugees (Chapter 9) expanded the analysis from lexis-based perspectives (frequency, keyness, collocations) to high-level patterns of legitimation and argumentation. Taking a further step, the case study on argumentation in early film theory (Chapter 10) approached argumentation not on the level of individual texts but on the level of discourse to trace the shifting configuration of argumentative fields supporting key conceptualizations of film as language.*

(4) Taking a diachronic perspective on discourse may *confirm* and *contrast* results from a purely synchronic perspective, revealing both change and stability in discourse. Analyzing the historical development of a discourse may help to *explain* the current state of that discourse. Given that an interest in discursive change is closely related to an interest in social change—and the interdependency between the two—diachronic studies will likely strive for *explanations* of change and/or stability as well *contextualization. For instance, the case study on normalization of the term "unwillingness to integrate" (Chapter 8) indicated changes in both legislation and the organization of courts as impactful. It also indicated, however, that political discourse itself is an arena of contestation where normalization can be stemmed.* More specifically, different strategies of periodization may serve to *detail* the analysis, provide *contrast*, or help with *downsampling* for further analysis. *The case study on media representations of refugees (Chapter 9) divided its corpus into 14 calendar-month periods in order to localize shifts. In contrast, the case study on early film theory (Chapter 10) periodized its data according to contextual events –from the first canonical writings in film theory until World War II, during the war, and from the end of the war until Christian Metz's thorough critique of the 'film as language' analogy that had been so productive until then.*

(5) The visualization of discourse-related data (e.g. lexical frequencies) or meta-data (e.g. number and date of news reports on a given topic) is well-suited to gain and/or give an overview of frequencies, distributions or change over time. The visualization of results, especially when it entails and connects *multiple analytical steps and perspectives*, can efficiently convey the *corroboration* or *contrast* of results and the *detailing* or *deepening* of the analysis. Indeed, visualization has potential as a tool in the analytical process as well as in publishing research. In the latter case, interactive visualization in particular can also serve to open up the research process to the public to some extent, facilitating *exploration* and encouraging *diversity of views. For instance, the case study on argumentation in early film theory (Chapter 10) used interactive visualization techniques to give the reader a manipulable overview of results that can be explored across several levels of abstraction: at the highest level, a force-directed network graph of argumentative patterns that can be rearranged spatially, visually expresses argumentative support and contradiction as well as the strength of these links; at the lower levels, Toulmin-scheme analyses of each pattern as highlighted by the reader as well as exemplary text extracts from the corpus, and a list of sources.*

Triangulation, in all these instances, always contains the potential of decentering the research process. But it is a question of selective presentation, of narrative or reification, whether this decentering becomes visible in publication. In this sense, then, the methods by which we tell our research belong into the toolbox of Discourse Studies as much as our methods of collecting, analyzing, and visualizing data or the models that help conceptualize the hierarchical and diachronic structuredness of discourse. Although these are clearly 'tools' of different orders, they are all available, exchangeable, combinable, and adaptable—but most importantly our use of them defines what we do when we conduct discourse studies.

Reference

Bryman, Alan. 2006. "Integrating Quantitative and Qualitative Research: How Is It Done?" *Qualitative Research* 6 (1): 97–113. https://doi.org/10.1177/1468794106058877.

Reference

Index

© The Editor(s) (if applicable) and The Author(s) 2019
M. Rheindorf, *Revisiting the Toolbox of Discourse Studies*, Postdisciplinary Studies in Discourse
https://doi.org/10.1007/978-3-030-19369-0

I

K

L

M

The manufacturer's authorised representative in the EU is Springer Nature Customer Service Centre GmbH, Europaplatz 3, 69115 Heidelberg, Germany. If you have any concerns regarding our products, please contact ProductSafety@springernature.com

Printed and bound by CPI Group (UK) Ltd, Croydon, CR0 4YY
05/10/2026
02228123-0006